ResponsAbility

ResponsAbility challenges conventional thinking about our governance and legal frameworks. The cross-currents of persisting, established worldviews, knowledge systems, institutions, law and forms of governance are now at odds with future-facing innovations designed to help societies transition to both low-carbon economies and social equity. This book explores the ways in which we can move to new governance and legal structures that more effectively reflect our changed relationship with the earth in the Anthropocene.

The book is written by a group of eminent scholars and leading experts from a diverse range of backgrounds, all of whom bring new knowledge and analysis from across oceanic and continental regions. Many are from the discipline of law, whilst others bring expertise on indigenous knowledge, climate, water, governance and philosophy to engage with law. Contributors include His Highness Tui Atua Tupua Tamasese Ta'isi Efi, Head of State of Samoa, Sir Eddie Durie, Dame Anne Salmond, Pierre Calame and Adrian Macy. A number of scenarios are presented throughout the book for the realignment of global and local law to institutionalise responsibility for social, environmental and earth-centred equity.

Betsan Martin is a founding member and Executive Chair of the International Alliance for Responsible and Sustainable Societies, an inspirational think tank and resource centre working with responsibility as a framework for 21st-century issues. Betsan had a leading role in establishing the UNU Centre of Expertise in Education for Sustainable Development at the University of Waikato. She is active with the global network of UNU Centres of Expertise. Betsan's academic research in philosophy of education specialized in an ethics of responsibility, which informs themes in her work in integrating social, environmental and economic areas. Publications include focus on water governance, responsibility and ethics, education for sustainability, and responsibility in law.

Linda Te Aho is of Waikato-Tainui descent and serves on the tribal executive committee, Te Arataura, and as a director of the commercial entity Tainui Group Holdings Ltd. An Associate Professor in Law, Linda's research focuses on contemporary issues in Law and Governance, with a particular interest in Indigenous Peoples' rights and responsibilities in relation to land and freshwater issues. Linda was the founding director of the Māori and Indigenous Governance Centre at the University of Waikato and provides legal and strategic advice to both Māori and the Crown in relation to negotiated Treaty Settlements and law reform. Linda served as a guardian under the Waikato River Settlement and is currently the editor of the *Waikato Law Review*.

Maria Humphries-Kil has academic and research interests in Management Education. She is a co-author of the text-book published by Sage: *Understanding Management Critically* (2014). Informing this publication are over 50 academic papers and many conference contributions.

Observing that social movements often play an important role as fore-runners for commonly accepted principles of justice, this boundary breaking book asks the difficult question of how to engender responsibility in society and in law to live sustainably and well on our shared planet.

Drawing on legal jurisprudence and philosophy from indigenous and western traditions, the book explores new concepts such as instilling legal rights and personality to rivers or other entities of nature. The book recognizes the imperative role that the private sector holds as the primary generator of economic activity, thus driving jobs, poverty reduction and government income streams, but notes that given its heavy environmental footprint, a "duty of care" emerges for the private sector. The book explores how to reconcile and combine the health of our economies with societal and planetary health.

As a species, humans have reached the point where our actions are impacting the very sustainability of the planet – our one and only home. IUCN has long championed the concept of the rights of nature. This book explores this notion and further expands that with such rights comes a human responsibility of caring for the earth. The book concludes that by challenging the existing set of social practices and the rules that those practices reflect, social movements, almost by definition are engaged in a form of law making. For the sustainability of the planet as we know it, informed social engagement is therefore critical.

Inger Anderson, *Director General, International Union for Conservation of Nature, Switzerland*

As the state of the Earth gets more dire, many are grappling for new ideas and approaches in the quest for fresh solutions. This volume is one trove of such alternatives. Take "responsAbility" for example. If you try and google it you will most probably get no hit. Or at best an error message directing you to "responsibility." That briefly sums up how refreshing this volume is, written by various experts and practitioners on the subject from the western, eastern and indigenous perspectives. It throws light on the issues of law and governance. More so in the context for living well with Mother Earth aligned to the Paris Agreement of 2015 and the Sustainable Development Goals 2016–2030.

It brings the discussion to the next level on trusteeship and legal personhood for nature. And raises new challenges "to find law which recognizes and supports interdependencies, with the relationships between the different parts of society, and between human and non-human forms of life" – it includes the need for eco-centric law. New challenges include redefining existing relationship and paradigms to give greater meaning and relevance in the search for a sustainable future. There is no doubt that this timely volume is a tour de force meant for those are serious in translating the "future that we want" into reality.

ResponsAbility: Law and Governance for Living Well with the Earth is addressed to law and governance and it goes beyond the confines of state interests and opens the horizon of law in the interests of the planet.

Prof. Dzulkifli Abdul Razak, *Immediate Past President, International Association of Universities*

ResponsAbility

Law and Governance for Living Well with the Earth

Edited by
Betsan Martin, Linda Te Aho and Maria Humphries-Kil

Routledge
Taylor & Francis Group
LONDON AND NEW YORK

First published 2019
by Routledge
2 Park Square, Milton Park, Abingdon, Oxon OX14 4RN

and by Routledge
711 Third Avenue, New York, NY 10017

Routledge is an imprint of the Taylor & Francis Group, an informa business

British Library Cataloguing-in-Publication Data
A catalogue record for this book is available from the British Library

Library of Congress Cataloging-in-Publication Data
Names: Martin, Betsan, editor. | Te Aho, Linda, editor. | Humphries-Kil, Maria, editor.
Title: ResponsAbility : law and governance for living well with the earth / edited by Betsan Martin, Linda Te Aho, and Maria Humphries-Kil.
Description: Abingdon, Oxon [UK] ; New York, NY : Routledge, 2018. | Includes index.
Identifiers: LCCN 2018009970 | ISBN 9781138606494
Subjects: LCSH: Liability (Law) | Responsibility.
Classification: LCC K579.L5 R49 2018 | DDC 340/.112—dc23
LC record available at https://lccn.loc.gov/2018009970

ISBN: 978-1-138-60649-4 (hbk)
ISBN: 978-0-429-46762-2 (ebk)

Typeset in Times New Roman
by Apex CoVantage, LLC

Contents

About the authors

Klaus Bosselmann is Professor of Law and Founding Director of the New Zealand Centre for Environmental Law at the University of Auckland. He is Chair of the IUCN World Commission on Environmental Law Ethics Specialist Group, Chair of the Ecological Law and Governance Association (ELGA) and Co-Chair of the Global Ecological Integrity Group (GEIG).

Pierre Calame's early professional life was as senior civil servant then CEO of the international Fondation pour le Progrès de l'Homme, in Paris. His major quest has been to identify the emergence of a global community to face global interdependencies, with universal responsibilities and revolutions in governance. Pierre's significant publication "Essay on Oeconomy" is a formalization of an economy of accountability in the use of resources.

Sir Edward Durie (Ngāti Kauwhata, Ngāti Raukawa, Rangitāne) is a leading Māori scholar. Sir Edward is a former High Court Judge, Chief Judge of the Māori Land Court and Chairperson of the Waitangi Tribunal. He is currently the Chair of the New Zealand Māori Council and its spokesperson on freshwater issues.

His Highness Tui Atua Tupua Tamasese Ta'isi Efi is former Head of State of Samoa (also known as "*O le Ao o le Malo*") from 2007 to 2017. He is an experienced former politician, a writer, an academic historian and a cultural expert. He is the Tama-a-Aiga and holds the paramount chiefly titles of Tui Atua Tupua Tamasese Ta'isi. Tamasese is one of the leading custodians of Samoa's indigenous knowledge.

Mark Hickford is currently Pro Vice-Chancellor and Dean of Law at Victoria University of Wellington. He served as the Prime Minister's advisor (legal and justice) from 2010 until 2015. Mark has been a Crown counsel specialising in the Treaty of Waitangi and natural resources law, and is the director of legal services at the Ministry for Primary Industries.

Adrian Macey is Adjunct Professor at the New Zealand Climate Change Research Institute and a Senior Associate of the Institute for Governance and Policy Studies, Victoria University of Wellington. He was previously New Zealand's Chief

Trade Negotiator and Ambassador to France and the OECD, and was New Zealand's first climate change ambassador. In 2011 he chaired the UNFCCC Kyoto Protocol negotiations.

Catherine Iorns Magallanes is a Reader in the School of Law at Victoria University of Wellington. Catherine is the Academic Adviser to the NZ Council of Legal Education, a national board member of Amnesty International Aotearoa New Zealand, a member of the International Law Association Committee on the Implementation of the Rights of Indigenous Peoples, and a member of the IUCN World Commission on Environmental Law.

Betsan Martin is Director of RESPONSE, an organisation working to develop an ethics of responsibility and engage in research and initiatives to support integrated environmental governance. RESPONSE works in partnership with Māori. RESPONSE has programmes in the Pacific region and is associated with an international Alliance for Responsible and Interdependent Societies, of which Betsan has been the Executive Chair since 2015.

Gay Morgan is Senior Lecturer, Te Piringa Faculty of Law, University of Waikato. Gay is a member of the New Zealand Human Rights Foundation and the Australia and New Zealand Law and History Society. She has worked on public infrastructure and community self-development projects in Africa and for the United States Court of Appeal. These experiences are central to her research interests in public law and in jurisprudence.

Dame Anne Salmond is a Distinguished Professor in Māori Studies and Anthropology at the University of Auckland, with a long-standing interest in cross-cultural encounters, Māori and Pacific philosophies and human-environment relations. She is a Corresponding Fellow of the British Academy and a Foreign Associate of the US National Academy of Sciences.

Neetu Sharma (PhD) is a development researcher with training in human rights. She has been exploring the role, significance and limitations of law towards ensuring the common good. Her areas of interest include food security, rights of vulnerable groups and climate justice. She is associated with the National Law School of India University, Bangalore, India.

Kapua Sproat joined the University of Hawai'i William Richardson School of Law in 2007, with the Ka Huli Ao Center for Excellence in Native Hawaiian Law and the Environmental Law Program. She teaches courses in Native Hawaiian and Environmental Law, and Legal Research and Writing. Her areas of scholarship and interest include Native Hawaiian law, Indigenous rights, and natural resource protection and management. Previously Kapua spent nine years as an attorney in the Hawai'i office of Earthjustice and worked on litigation in the *Waiahole* case and Nā Wai 'Ehā, Maui.

Alain Supiot was a professor at the University of Poitiers and Nantes and member of the Institut Universitaire de France (2001–2012), before his election in

2012 to the Collège de France, where he held the Chair. From 1998 to 2000, he chaired the Conseil national du développement des sciences humaines et sociales and is from 2013 onwards member of the French Conseil Stratégique de la Recherche.

Linda Te Aho (Ngāti Koroki Kahukura, Ngāti Mahuta) is a tribal leader of Waikato-Tainui, a large iwi in Aotearoa New Zealand. Linda helped develop the long-term vision for the holistic restoration of the Waikato River ecosystem. Linda is also Associate Professor in Law at Te Piringa – Faculty of Law, University of Waikato, Hamilton, New Zealand.

Gerald Torres is the Jane Foster Professor of Law, Cornell University, USA. He is a leader in critical race theory, environmental law and federal Indian Law. He previously served as the Bryant Smith Chair in Law at the University of Texas School of Law and taught at The University of Minnesota Law School, where he served as Associate Dean.

Mahina Tuteur, raised on the windward side of O'ahu, is a Post-Juris Doctor Research and Teaching Fellow at the Ka Huli Ao Center for Excellence in Native Hawaiian Law. She specializes in Environmental and Native Hawaiian Law, and currently serves on the State of Hawai'i Environmental Council.

Foreword

ResponsAbility: Law and Governance for Living Well with the Earth is addressed to law and governance and yet it ventures into the domain of going beyond the confines of state interests to the need of the environmental rule of law for the planet.

While *rights* have gained a high profile as a means to providing legal standing for Nature, *responsibility* has been given weight only recently – in particular through the 2015 Paris Climate Agreement and the Sustainable Development Goals – SDGs. As well as carrying the prospect of legal liability for damage, responsibility highlights a prospective and intergenerational orientation based on prevention and precaution.

This book brings a finer-grained exploration of philosophy, law, and matters of governance to give life to the respons*ability* dimension of law and governance.

The coinage of *responsability* has the effect of drawing attention to the power and duty to act with regard to the community of life. It emphasizes that we shape the future together not just through rights, but also through obligations – many of them of intergenerational character. At the same time, contributing authors of the book do not shirk from criticizing the pervasive forces of inertia and the continuing influences of outmoded economic paradigms.

"Respons*ability*" captures the impetus for public engagement with contributions and accountabilities of non-state actors as touchstones for environmental justice and the environmental rule of law.

From the Pacific region, indigenous influence on law and its future directions is a strong feature of the book. Indigenous authors themselves speak to a future orientation of knowledge traditions steeped in understanding humans and other sentient forms of life as being trustees and guardians with a duty to hold the many dimensions of Earth's systems in harmony. Such a comprehensive view of the world encompasses the spiritual and sacred realms, the known and unknowable, and the physical and spiritual domains as inseparable. The basic proposition of the book is one that rejects a *shallow environmental law paradigm* and instead focuses on a perspective of the discipline that emphasizes its importance to the whole community of life and to the protection of ecological processes.

Of course, indigenous influences are – and should be – vital for new thinking in governance and law. The advances in trusteeship and the innovation of legal personality provided by the contributors are derived from efforts for restitution for indigenous peoples that respond to the harm of colonial histories. Specifically, we hear from Māori, Samoan, and Hawai'ian authors. Indigenous references permeate the thinking of several of the non-indigenous authors seeking to recognize traditions and systems of law and governance beyond Western worldviews, thought, and social order. It is a true global formulation and understanding of environmental law. The authors do so with awareness of injustice and from a commitment to wellbeing anchored in the ontologies of both.

The worldwide scope of the contributors offers an eclectic lens on matters of responsibility. Generated in southern Oceania, we see the capacity of small states to influence global affairs. The attribution of corporate personality to a New Zealand river sparked the imagination and flowed rapidly to much larger jurisdictions such as India, Bolivia, and Colombia – to be implemented as a new form of proactive responsibility that does not rely on citizen or state initiatives to activate rights. Environmental law, in general, and standing to sue, in particular, will be profoundly transformed by these new approaches to Nature and its position in the legal system.

This book may be read as a companion to *The Global Pact for the Environment*, launched in Paris in 2017 with the support and contribution of the IUCN World Commission on Environmental Law. The Pact is still a draft proposal that is beginning its diplomatic journey within the United Nations, with the hope that it will become an international agreement in the near future.

The *Pact* endeavors to bring momentum and a clear legal mandate to advance the sustainability agenda of states. It sets out a balance of rights and duties, reflecting historic initiatives such as the 2016 IUCN World Declaration on the Environmental Rule of Law, the Earth Charter, the 1982 World Charter for Nature, the Declaration of Interdependence, and the Declaration of Responsibility in an Interdependent World – documents also referenced in this book.

As with the intent of this book as a whole, the theme of duty and responsibility runs through the *Pact*, strengthening the mandate for Earth's community to "participate in an international, effective and appropriate action according to their common but differentiated responsibilities and respective capabilities in the light of their different national circumstances" (Global Pact for the Environment (draft project). Launched at La Sorbonne, Paris, 2017. Chaired by Laurent Fabius with support of Le Club des Jurists, France. Preamble, p. 1. paragraph 8).

While the aim of the *Pact* is to advance the ambition of state responsibility, the scope of this book pushes beyond state boundaries and jurisdictions to the premises of living well with the earth: more than the traditional dignity of life goal, it advocates *dignity of life with and within Nature*. This reaches from personal and local to global and intergenerational domains. Benefiting from historical reflection and indigenous traditions, we can better propose advances in law for Earth's common goods, going beyond the present *status* of irresponsibility in local and globalized legal systems towards the community of life and its existential ecological processes.

The view of trusteeship and legal personhood for Nature that the book formulates is not without its own controversies. But historically ethical and theoretical disputes are at the basis of the evolution of law and legal institutions. Therefore, both the academic debate and the concrete experiences of indigenous peoples can enrich our present legislative and judicial horizons for regeneration, or perhaps (re)foundation, respons*ability* as a pre-eminent ethical, but also legal, orientation for the age of ecological interdependence.

by Justice Antonio Herman Benjamin
January 2018

Introduction

Betsan Martin

In this book the theme of responsibility underscores the urgent need for the strengthening of law and governance for public good. It is oriented to safeguarding the global community of all of life.

The authors write in the context of a turbulent world. The cross-currents of persisting, established worldviews, knowledge systems, institutions, law and forms of governance are often at odds with future-facing innovations designed to help societies transition to low-carbon economies underpinned by social equity.

This book is a contribution to law to support transitions for stabilising the climate, safeguarding water and making equity a principle of sustainability.

With a vision of living well with the earth, the book has contributions from Western, indigenous and Indian authors; and the scope of the book includes legal history, global initiatives for governance such as the Paris Agreement, and studies in different jurisdictions on water, governance and climate change. These examples present and at times problematise innovations in law; they explore tradition as well as new horizons for law in conditions of the interdependence of life on earth. Law to regulate human conduct in accordance with these standards for affirmative action also needs to provide sanctions for breaches. Liability for irresponsible use of resources and serious environmental destruction is the most prevalent orientation of law for responsibility. France's Duty of Vigilance Law[1] and the proposed law of ecocide are examples. Some authors face the crisis of irresponsibility from the perspective of the drive for economic advantage where these are driven by state and corporate actors. Others face the social and environmental impacts of colonisation and seek environmental and cultural restitution.

Law has to be expanded to address the accountabilities, liabilities and potential of globalised forces that are often beyond the jurisdiction of sovereign states, and provide a means for humans to live well with the earth.

We are now in a time when the law must not deal solely with humans as "subjects of law". In several jurisdictions, rivers have become subjects of law by being vested as legal persons. One of the great challenges is to find law which recognises and supports interdependencies and the relationships between the different parts of society and between human and non-human forms of life. Often this is referred to ecocentric law.

In reality, we see that the capacity of law to guide and re-orient society is moderated by opposing views and the cross-currents of contested priorities, both positive and perverse. The law may even bend to serve vested interests to the extent of over-riding current law and constitutional provisions for economic expediency.

A relational paradigm in law for living well with the earth

Interdependence calls for a relational paradigm with an ability to respect the difference of the other. In this regard it has an ethical quality, captured in the notion of responsibility in both its accountable and relational dimensions. To emphasise the paradigm shift intended by responsibility, the coinage of "respons*ability*" is used for the title, and variously in the Introduction and also by author Betsan Martin in Chapter 1.

The authors in Respons*ability: Law and Governance for Living Well with the Earth* are as diversely positioned as the evening stars, bringing knowledge, analysis and prospects from oceanic and continental regions. Some address the global drivers of what Professor Alain Supiot and others refer to as the juggernaut of the globalised market economy.[2] The potential of technology to build a global community is also recognised, along with appreciating that it is often businesses which are leading transitions to an economy of sustainability, or oeconomy.[3]

Some authors take their specific jurisdictions (Hawai'i and Aotearoa New Zealand) as their starting point. Others work from historic and global standpoints and also bring expertise in indigenous knowledge, climate, water, governance and philosophy to engage with law. All bring scenarios for realignment of global and local law to institutionalise respons*ability* in regulation. These interests are informed from the Pacific region and also from France, New Zealand, India and the United States. From these vastly different points on the compass, there is a common interest in a relational paradigm.

Prospective responsibility and public good innovations

An ethics of respons*ability* is oriented to prospective and intergenerational equity. Alain Supiot introduces the question of guardianship for the future by asking, "who are the guardians of tomorrow?" What safeguards are needed, and what legal provisions are necessary to sanction failure to provide environmental protection? Interestingly, guardianship is provided for in the legislation vesting certain rivers as legal persons. In another sense, social movements often have a guardianship role as forerunners for justice. We see a strong thread of social movements influencing law in the various chapters. Gerald Torres focuses on the power of citizens to mobilise and shape public awareness as well as constitutions.

We have within these chapters, broadly, two discrete traditions or ontologies, as proposed by Mark Hickford, each developed with significantly different principles and references: indigenous law and Western-derived law with the tension in colonial contexts that Western law has been exercised as a form of mastery over indigenous people. We see here the outcomes of strenuous and effective endeavours by indigenous litigants through courts and tribunals that have brought new interpretation of law, such as in the public trust doctrine, and the innovation of attributing legal personhood to nature.

Legal personality is a corporate concept which has been given innovative application to a national park and a water body in New Zealand as part of the settlements of Te Urewera and the Whanganui River through Waitangi Tribunal claims.[4] The vesting of Te Urewera and the Whanganui River as legal persons gives standing in law to these entities in their own right, via statute. This legal concept has also been taken up in India, Ecuador and Colombia. The granting of legal personality to rivers and other entities is resetting governance for the relationship between people and nature, in a way that is more in tune with indigenous law.

Another focus of interest is public trust, a doctrine that has been amplified through common law cases in Hawai'i discussed by Kapua Sproat and Mahina Tuteur. The Hawai'ian State constitutional provision of water as a public trust has been given renewed stature through indigenous-initiated legal proceedings in which Kapua Sproat had a leading role.

Klaus Bosselmann presents the case for public trusteeship of the global commons, such as the atmosphere, oceans and polar regions as a framework in law for earth governance. Earth governance would have a global reach beyond the territorial boundaries of nation states. States are constrained by national interests and fall short in their responsibility for the global commons. Bosselmann states: "The public trust doctrine says that natural commons should be held in trust as assets serve the public good."

Generally a trust is a property administered by trustees, whereas a legal person is vested with its own rights and duties.[5] Usually human guardians are appointed to represent the interests of a legal person, which in this case is a river or other entity of nature. Significantly, a legal person such as a river or forest becomes a *subject* of law. Both legal personhood and public trusteeship have the advantage of possessing a status beyond an exploitable resource, and therefore avoid the commodification often associated with the value of a resource, as if its value were solely the economic benefits that could be extracted from it.

Overall, one can readily observe the incremental and evolutionary processes of the law. While matters of governance and legal development are urgent, such as for climate change and transitions to low-carbon economies, the pace is set by public opinion and sometimes by political leadership, with all the attendant fluctuations and inertia.

Similarly, colonial injustice and the social and environmental legacy of harm need swift and effective remedies such as through redress and restitution. Several authors point to the slow and incremental process for recognition of a grievance and for the evolution of remedial justice. These depend on the perseverance and resources of the litigants. Perceptively, Catherine Iorns Magallanes (Chapter 4, this volume) observes that just cause and entitlements depend on activation of legal means to gain recognition and enforcement.

Authors consider the need for more proactive frameworks in law, such as through trusteeship and legal personality which are less reliant on litigation and more oriented to active respons*ability*.

Restorative justice is an approach that is usually applied as a remedy for criminal justice on the basis that an offence is not just an individual breach – it is also a matter of social harm and needs to be remedied at that level. Given the social *and* environmental harm of environmental damage in need of remedy, restorative justice is not developed by authors here, but is a field for further inquiry that may well sit alongside negotiations for common and differentiated responsibilities, in accordance with capability.

Genesis of the book

The year 2014 was propitious for the quest for law and governance with a responsibility framing. A Symposium on Governance, Law and Responsibility at Hopuhopu, New Zealand, was held in 2014 and was the basis for this book.

Also in 2014, an initiative on Responsibility and Law was begun with the Collège de France, led by Professor Mireille Delmas-Marty, Professor Alain Supiot and researcher Dr Luca d'Ambrosio in collaboration with Pierre Calame, an author in this book and Emeritus President of the Fondation pour le Progrés de l'Homme.[6]

We have the privilege of eminent contributions from Western and indigenous views in face-to-face encounter with shared dedication to a joint endeavour for living well with the earth.

Structure of the book

The introduction reflects the structure of the book. The first part of this introduction headed 'Respons*ability*' sets out premises for developing law for respons*ability*. This section addresses the big picture and makes a case for respons*ability* with a philosophical reference and with governance in the global aspect. It includes a portrayal of "illimited irresponsibility" and the case for law that strengthens liability for climate (ir)responsibility. An historical analysis by Gay Morgan shows the interests of capitalism served by sidelining responsibility during the period of the Enlightenment and the rise of liberalism.

The second part of the introduction brings specific contexts and studies in different jurisdictions. Here the concepts of public trust and legal personality show ways in which rivers and other natural entities are being brought under more effective forms of protection. Many of these chapters are on indigenous legal initiatives derived from worldviews centred on obligation and the capacity to integrate the different dimensions of physical and metaphysical elements, including economy, society and environment.

Respons*ability*

Respons*ability* is the beginning of living well with the other. Betsan Martin takes the premise that respons*ability* is the source of community. She begins with a philosophical introduction to respons*ability* arising from face-to-face encounter as a source of relation ethics, and then transposes this to the public domain of law. Human rights and environmental rights are recognised as complementary to respons*ability* and also scrutinised for their limitations to meet the complexity of the inter-related dynamics of humans and the earth.

With an interest in law and governance to cross the boundaries of discrete fields such as water, forests and atmosphere and to account for the interacting dynamics of humans and nature, Martin provides indicative guidelines for respons*ability* in law. In the light of these markers of respons*ability*, she reviews examples of trusteeship and corporate personality to evaluate the capacity of these legal frameworks to support accountability and beneficial interdependence.

Klaus Bosselmann works with trusteeship of the global commons as a framework to remedy the lack of governance for the earth's global commons. Bosselmann makes a compelling case for trusteeship as the basis of a system for earth governance with capacity beyond the boundaries of nation states and national jurisdictions and interests. In the trust doctrine, assets are held in the service of common good and trustees have a responsibility to protect them from harm. Earth governance envisages legal responsibility for the global commons with state, citizen and stakeholder parties – thus strengthening the democratic power of citizens to use trusteeship as a mechanism for action, such as advocating for costs and liability for damage.

Bosselmann considers the tensions within the model of state sovereignty for earth governance and explores a co-operation model. The Paris Agreement offers a sophisticated rapprochement between sovereignty and co-operation, and Adrian Macey's insightful historical interpretation leaves no doubt that despite urgency, change is evolutionary. Seeking to address similar questions, in preparation for the Paris Agreement, Collège de France Professor Mireille Delmas-Marty ventured the notion of "solidarity-sovereignty" to underpin inter-state cooperation.[7]

With a comprehensive account of globalised irresponsibility, Alain Supiot turns towards the endeavours for respons*ability* with the observation that "we fight for what we lack". With globalisation he observes the rise of inequality, unemployment, ecological risk, economic migration and violence as shaking the institutional edifice of social protection in Western industrialised countries. In this case, globalisation has brought the world into the grip of market-driven preoccupation with financial profit that failed to account for the full systemic effects of industrialisation. The consequences of this are destabilising the climate system. Seeing the dynamics at work where the state can no longer be the guarantor of responsibility, Supiot mentions the emergence of the duty of care by businesses for their employees and thus marks a shift towards business responsibility.

In the same logic of lack and agonism, the momentous environmental movements resound with the message of failure to protect forests, oceans, waterways and the atmosphere. In very broad terms, we have the complex realities of institutions with a global reach, such as environmental non-state organisations, able to expose damage and insist on corrective measures, amidst a prevailing economic system governed by a market logic and measured with the limited criteria of gross domestic product. There are mounting demands for alternative economic frameworks with measures of economic activity that incorporate wellbeing and the integration of environmental and human health.

Pierre Calame analyses the failure to ensure accountability for resource depletion and environmental damage and attributes the failure to weak regulation with laws in which the freedom to exploit are embedded without responsibility to protect. The notion of "unlimited irresponsibility" in Calame's chapter derives from the law of limited liability, originating in the East India Company in 1600. In a recent paper, Calame, citing Collège de France researcher Luca d'Ambrosio, sees the law as furthering the crisis of the climate:[8]

> the law has made the anthropocene possible by radically distinguishing between the all-powerful subject and its environment, hence the challenge or rethinking law that has become hostile to the human race itself.

The source of this hostility can be attributed historically to the laws of limited liability, and Gay Morgan's chapter draws this conclusion via an historical review of Western and Asian traditions. Morgan traces the genealogy of the emergence of "irresponsibility" in the Western liberal tradition; she asks, "how did we get into the situation of destroying the integrity of the planet's ecosystems, and what was the role of law?" Her research brings into focus the universality of responsibility with protections of the commons and public welfare across all great traditions – Hindu, Greek, Buddhism, Islam, Christianity and Roman thought. Modern renditions of public interests emphasise rights as a form of protection from state tyranny, as seen in the French Declaration of the Inalienable and Sacred Rights of Man, the United States Constitution and the Universal Declaration of Human Rights. In the German Constitution, the emphasis on individualised human rights is balanced by a collective responsibility of the State to ensure provisions for human dignity for fellow citizens. In this provision the person is seen as having dependence on and commitment to the community.

Morgan appreciates that the rise of rights in liberal political history is to ensure that governments are restrained from exercising oppressive power. However, her historical lens enables her to speak of the divorce between rights and responsibilities beginning with the limited liability provisions for the East India Company, in 1600. This was a company with "mercantile interests" with a purpose of "extracting value from colonial peoples to increase government reserves and provide significant colonial administration"[9]. Limited liability was explicitly introduced to encourage investment in the colonies – India specifically at that time – by limiting the risk to investors. As limited liability was applied further throughout the 17th and 18th centuries, corporates were distanced from responsibility for the impacts of their ventures on society, which reached critical levels of impact in the phenomenon of corporate capitalism.

Neetu Sharma begins with duties as an assumed premise of modern societies and which serve to mitigate conflict. Based on Gandhian philosophy, Sharma proposes that rights arise from duties and that duties have dimensions of spirituality and trusteeship to energize and enhance egalitarian values. She reviews the fundamental duties in the Indian Constitution and reflects on the ascendance of rights through the Universal Declaration of Human Rights. The effect has been that civil, political and economic rights became the domain of civil society and responsibility became limited to states – a dualistic attribution of rights and responsibilities. Sharma says:[10]

> In the post-war period, and especially in newly independent nations, constitutions began reflecting a strong dislike of tyrannical regimes and hence fundamental rights became the nucleus for constitutional development.

Sharma shifts the ground by reviewing the potential for citizen movements to take up some of the accountabilities of responsibility, or better still, proportionate responsibility and share in developing their own solutions to issues facing them. Transformative law gains its power when it reflects the needs of a social milieu, or arises from social movements to address injustice, such as the mal-distribution of wealth that produces poverty and inequality.

In the face of corporate drivers of irresponsibility, the Global Compact and the soft law notion of corporate social responsibility (CSR) has been taken to a level of hard law in India, with the Companies Act 2013, which requires companies to set aside at least 2 per cent of their average profit in the last three years for CSR activities for the promotion of education, gender equity and women's empowerment, combating HIV/AIDS, malaria and other diseases, or the eradication of extreme poverty. Strenuous avoidance of the CSR requirements has been exacerbated by poor implementation.

This claim echoes Supiot's idea that we fight for what we lack. In this case the strengthening of bottom lines for human life, dignity and wellbeing was given greater legal recognition against the atrocities against human life. Despite laws for rights, Sharma notes that vulnerabilities, aggravated by globalisation, continue to exist as "there is not an environment conducive to the enjoyment of these entitlements." Yet, Sharma claims, law can be transformative – perhaps nowhere better seen than in the Paris Agreement, which represents a remarkable global consensus for a process for progressing the common destiny of nations.

Global and local realities

The second part of this book starts with the global dimension of climate change governance. Adrian Macey provides an exposé of the ways in which common and differentiated responsibilities have been contentious and then brought to a universally accepted framework in the Paris Agreement. Reviewing the years leading to this agreement, Macey appreciates the ways in which the United Nations Framework Convention on Climate Change parties moved from a binary approach structured on developing and developed categories to a sophisticated universal agreement to reduce carbon emissions. Arguments for the rights to development are moderated by equity considerations.

We see here a gradual re-orientation from retrospective responsibility to prospective responsibility, a shift that Macey aligns with a move from an imposed regime, as envisaged by Kyoto, to a framework for voluntary commitments. While historical accountability is retained through the system of financial transfers to developing nations and the idea of burden sharing, the move to a future orientation has brought a cohesive force to the transitions to zero-carbon economies, involving states, the private sector, cities and financial institutions.

The following chapters introduce indigenous traditions of responsibility face-to-face with climate change and water interests. Tui Atua Tamasese shows how global corporate values and the pressures for development intersect with forms of governance in Samoa. Samoa is a case study of the global drivers bringing commodified interests, mediated by central government, into engagement with traditions of highly accountable and localised forms of authority and governance. This could be understood as active subsidiarity – one of the centrepieces of sustainable development, which is in effect being undermined by economically driven development imperatives.

Taihākurei Durie explains Māori interests in water, while he also touches lightly on a wider context by referring to Malaysian law. This comes from the invitation to present the Tun Suffian memorial lecture in Malaysia in 2017 as a specific opportunity to share common interests in indigenous thought. The plurality of legal traditions in Malaysia lends itself to a breadth of jurisprudence and interest in indigenous law as part of the endeavour to resist the imposition of external dehumanising values driven by the globalised market.

Durie's chapter draws on a range of his writing on indigenous law and worldviews for which genealogy and spirituality are touchstones. Precepts of spirituality include that the world is occupied with the living and the departed. Waters, land and wildlife are related as primordial ancestors to whom there are ongoing obligations. Durie takes the view that ownership interests emanate from these relationships, although he articulates ownership interest as a different order from that of private property; it encompasses both private and public good interests.[11] This multidimensional concept of property is the signature aspect to the Durie paper on governance of water presented at the Hopuhopu Symposium in 2014.[12] Here, Durie set out a framework for the governance of water that encompasses Māori property interests in water and restitution of Māori interests and also provides for wider public good interests. With the health of waterways as a paramount responsibility, revenue for commercial use is proposed alongside provisions for commercial interests in water.

Linda Te Aho similarly grounds her study in the context of Aotearoa New Zealand while drawing on larger references, such as the United Nations Declaration on the Rights of Indigenous Peoples, the Rio+20 Declaration and the provisions for Rights of Nature in the Ecuadorian Constitution. She begins with referring to Durie's 2014 paper on the governance of water, which serves as a springboard into the complex world of state–Māori relations. These span attempts to have provisions for Māori interests incorporated into law, pre-eminently in the Resource Management Act 1991. The Treaty of Waitangi Settlement process has been the arena for even stronger provisions to protect Māori rights and interests. After sustained endeavours for rights-based justice, Te Aho asks whether responsibility offers a more promising means for living well with the earth.

Mark Hickford and Dame Anne Salmond scrutinise the potential of law to redress indigenous peoples' grievances. They see pathways for respectful relations between Māori and the Crown that incorporate intergenerational justice.

Hickford opens his chapter with the matter of different ontologies and innovative law in New Zealand. Vesting the Whanganui River with legal personality makes the river an ontological subject as opposed to an object. He pursues the theme of ontological difference in treaty settlements from the viewpoint of the Crown engaging with Māori tribes in the Waitangi Tribunal process.[13] He observes how progress of the law here is slow, incremental and evolutionary in nature, as it is for climate change, despite the urgent cause.

Salmond draws on the concept of two worlds and elaborates a particular Whanganui tribal interest in their river and the iconic provisions, enacted in 2017, for attributing legal personality to the Whanganui River. This is a new use of a corporate legal concept for recognising the river as an ancestor. She is careful to address the matter of ownership and property in water, being averse to any system that entrenches the commodification of water. As an example, she moves away from the idea of land as property to speak of land as a beloved woman, as used by the Māori King Tawhiao. Salmond suggests public trusteeship as a solution to the essentially economic conflicts around ownership of water.

Kapua Sproat and Mahina Tuteur show how the constitutional provision of water as a public trust has been significantly developed in Hawai'i, as a legal framework which promotes living well with the earth. The concept has been highlighted through the *Waiahole* case[14] in Hawai'i to address the massive engineering diversion of water for the sugar industry that destroyed the natural flows and quality of water. Water is protected as a public trust in the State Constitution, a provision that allowed campaigners to seek redress in law. The legal case also derives from Hawaiian custodial traditions which regard water as a physical manifestation of the deity Akua Kāne, who also carries the authority of trusteeship over water for communal benefit. The reinstatement of the constitutional public trust in water is iconic in establishing a legal precedent for prioritising the ecosystem health of water, providing for indigenous interests to be met. Commercial interests are subject to environmental and indigenous priorities.

Catherine Iorns Magallanes tackles the dissonance between the Rights of Nature and legal personhood head on. The Rights of Nature is a framework for environmental protection emanating from Christopher Stone's argument to achieve legal standing for nature.[15]

Iorns Magallanes gives due regard to the Rights of Nature movement particularly for its significance in the United States and the prospect it allows for litigation in defence of nature's interests. Alongside this, she explores the significance of legal personality as lending itself to collective responsibility, or duties, and marking a paradigm shift in favour of collaboration and sustainability. Legal personhood of natural entities such as the Whanganui River arises through *parens patriae*. This principle describes the state's duty to step in to protect a child who is being abused or neglected. It has been successfully applied to the environment in the United States.[16] With that in mind, she furthers her inquiry into legal personality beyond New Zealand to India, Colombia and Ecuador where the Yamuna and Ganges rivers (India), the Atrato River in Colombia and the Vilcabamba River in Ecuador have become legal persons.

The development of legal personality has come from the failure of the state to exercise guardianship of the rivers even though there are provisions for duties of environmental care in their respective constitutions. These have received much less attention than rights. Iorns Magallanes offers the insight that rights rely on being activated and enforced, whereas duty, or responsibility, arises through the appointment of guardians of the legal person of the river, for example, on page 233:

> Ensure[s] that all activities affecting the river are monitored, and at all stages the interests of the river are upheld by a body appointed to do just that.

A guardian is appointed to exercise their duty at all times. Such legal provision opens the prospect of duties as a key to reordered relationships between humans and nature.

Professor Gerald Torres writes the final chapter on the transformative power of social movements – and how they influence law and constitutions. His considerations of democracy turn on the vital role of contention to restrain unbridled power (page 241).

> Democracy is supposed to protect the plurality of the good and politics is the forum where that struggle over the good is supposed to take place . . . [C]orrectly understood, contentious politics are a means through which the actions of the formal players are constrained.

With the idea that "the law laces us together", Torres refers to the constituting of the people of the United States as a political community rather than in an ethnonationalistic identity. Such a liberal democracy is therefore a contentious space open to the making and remaking of social life and where law can be evolutionary and transformative.

Torres introduces us to "demosprudence", an invention by him and Lani Guinier for a study of lawmaking by the people. Despite the seeming failures of social activism and the prospect of the seeming futility of initiatives such as the Occupy Movement, Torres ends on a note of affirmation. The Occupy Movement put the issues of inequality on the national agenda. Furthermore, it raised the flag of inequality globally.

Conclusion

These contributions demonstrate that effective law needs to be able to cope with changes that new situations and new technologies will bring. It can be strengthened by guardians, those empowered to safeguard ecosystems of nature and impose accountabilities for the use of nature's resources.

These considerations may hasten law to strengthen liability for environmental damage and provide for prospective responsibility as has emerged with the Paris Agreement. Whereas there is a prevalence of reporting on corporate transgressions with regard to the environment and social exploitation, business is indeed central to solutions. Responsibility to prevent irreversible damage is enduring and cannot be excused. Therefore, the tasks at hand rely on both business co-operation and a new level of consciousness in a collective sense, of collective respons*ability*. Most likely further development of such law will be borne out of accepting mutual commitments as citizens of the planet.

Notes

1 Duty of Vigilance 2017 <www.csrandthelaw.com/2017/08/03/the-french-duty-of-vigilance-law-what-you-need-to-know/>.
2 See Alain Supiot "Confronting the Insupportable: Resources of the Law of Responsibility" in Chapter 5 of this book; D.S. Steingad and D.E. Fitzgibbons "Challenging the Juggernaut of Globalisation: A Manifest for Academic Praxis" (1995) 8(4) *Journal of Organisational Change Management* 30; J.E. Lane *Globalization: The Juggernaut of the 21st Century* (Routledge, Oxford, 2013).
3 Pierre Calame *L'Essai sur l'Oecomomie* (Editions Charles Leopold Mayer, Paris, 2009) (translated: Michale C. Behrent (translator), P. Calame *Essay on Oeconomy*).
4 Waitangi Tribunal settlements provide recognition of Crown breaches of the Treaty of Waitangi and generally provide some compensation by way of funds, assets, land and agreements for Māori participation in environmental governance.
5 Anthony H. Angelo "Personality and Legal Culture" (1996) 26 *VUWLR* 395.
6 Mireille Delmas-Marty and others "Climate Change: A Challenge for Humanity. Twelve Legal Proposals for the Paris Climate Conference" (Collège de France, FPH, October 2015).
7 Ibid.
8 Pierre Calame "The Age of the Anthropocene that We Have Now Entered Requires the Revisiting of the Fundamental Categories and the Essential Nature of Law, as Part of the Governance Revolution" (2017) <www.alliance-respons.net>.
9 Gay Morgan "Public Responsibility" Chapter 4 (p. 65) of this volume.
10 Neetu Sharma "Responsibility and the Transformative Role of Law" Chapter 6 (p. 104) of this volume.
11 Taihākurei Durie and others Robert Joseph, Andrew Erueti, Valmain Toki "Ngā Wai o te Māori. Na Tikanga me Ngā Ture Roia: The Waters of the Māori: Māori Law and State Law" (paper prepared for the New Zealand Māori Council, 2017).
12 Taihākurei Durie "Law, Responsibility and Māori Proprietary Interests in Water" <www.response.org.nz/wp-content/uploads/2013/02/Durie-Full-Law-Water-Responsibility-ed-2014.pdf>.
13 The Waitangi Tribunal was established in 1975 to hear claims in respect of Crown breaches of the Treaty of Waitangi, and to make recommendations for restitution and compensation, via settlements.
14 In re *Waiāhole Combined Contested Case* [Waiāhole] 94 Hawai'i 97, 9 P 3d 409.
15 Christopher Stone "Should Trees Have Standing? Towards Legal Rights for Natural Objects" (1972) 45 *Southern California Law Review* 450.
16 Guardianship has some negative associations in New Zealand and Australia, where the state has demonstrably failed in its guardianship duties to Māori, by the removal of Māori and aboriginal children from families into abusive state care – a situation which should be the subject of an Independent Inquiry; see Human Rights Commission <www.hrc.co.nz/news/>.

1 Ngā Pou Rāhui[1]

Respons*able* laws for water and climate

Betsan Martin

Introduction

Respons*ability* creates community because it is about "my" respectful response to another and to others.[2] It comes from our relational life and our bonds with others and may be expressed as love, as a response to need, as remedial action. Respon*sability* is for beneficial purpose; it is precautionary and intended to avert harm. Respons*ability* builds the interconnecting dynamics of life. At the large scale of a globalised world, we are bound to a common destiny, and respons*ability* is an orientation for recovering the stability of life on earth.

Respons*ability* is a relational ethic. The conventional notion of responsibility can be burdened with a sense of onerous duty and legal liability. This chapter begins with the relational underpinnings of respons*able* justice. I introduce "respons*ability*"[3] to emphasise both the accountable *and* relational aspects of respons*ability*, and to denote a proactive and prospective orientation, denoted by this spelling. The conventional spelling is used as appropriate.

After outlining the premises of respons*ability* as an ethic, I transpose this as a reference for the social sphere and for the public good aspects of law and governance. Duty is fundamental to all traditions of law[4] and includes citizen duties, public trust, corporate responsibility and the common heritage of humankind. Nevertheless, climate change signifies the loss of orientation to duty and public good in favour of industrialised economic development which has not included adequate precautionary law or accountability for environmental (or social) harm. Respons*ability* is a framework to catalyse law and governance for accountability and to serve as a reference for action on climate change and the governance of water.

Part A introduces respons*ability* in its accountability and relational dimensions, proposing these as a counterpoint to established norms of individual self-interest and the norms of liberal societies. In many ways, respons*ability* runs against the grain of such norms that allow and enable exploitation. This section touches on private property rights and individual freedoms – cornerstones of liberalism that also harbour interests which may be perverse to foundations of respons*ability* for a more eco-centric world.[5]

The relational situation of our "self with others", with other humans and all forms of life, informs social relations and shapes the ways in which we order society. Some of the attributes of respons*ability* are explored through the motif of the face-to-face encounter and considered for the public domain, including law.

It is fitting in the context of Aotearoa New Zealand to draw on Māori indigenous law; this is law that is constituted on a relational paradigm and is significant for a world where interdependence is intensified. The use of *Nga Pou Rahui* in the title to this chapter is an example of such law; it refers to a Māori system of regulation to protect land, waters, ocean areas or species which are at risk or under threat, by the imposition of a restriction on access to the environment or prohibition on use of such resources. A rahui may be imposed for a limited period of time or for the longer term, subject to assessing remediation of damage or threat, and is thus is a law for respons*able* proprietorship. Māori indigenous law is gaining greater recognition through common law litigation and through the Treaty of Waitangi settlement process.[6] The Waitangi Tribunal addresses grievances arising from the imposition of British law and the severance of Māori from their land, language and taonga, or treasured possessions.[7]

It is important to consider rights for their complementarity with respons*ability*, and because a rights framework is increasingly being applied to environmental law. While responsibility, or duty, and rights need to go hand in hand to ensure their implementation, I will question whether rights are sufficient in themselves to serve as transitions to sustainable, culturally respectful societies. A reference to some of the premises of rights will sit alongside the discussion on responsibility.

We have the crucial situation of state law being out of step with ecosystems and the great dynamics of the planet. In general, governance of the earth's common goods is being developed out of systems designed for industrial economies which externalise impacts on nature. We therefore map a system of laws designed for industrial development onto the dynamic, multidimensional systems for which they are not designed.

In this section, I propose guidelines for law for "living well with the earth" as a prelude to introducing law with attributes of respons*able* governance. These guidelines are used to evaluate whether law of public trusteeship and for legal personhood of a river contain these attributes and measure up to standards of respons*ability*.

The condition of interdependence is a key issue to be addressed in law. In the dynamics of a globalised world, no activity can be isolated from its wider effects. The Paris Agreement has attributes of law with capacity for integrating multiple domains; its provisions include being responsive to local conditions along with reference to the wider global situation.[8] Only time will test its capacity to deliver effective accountabilities for the mitigation of greenhouse gases and for climate finance while retaining the collaborative attributes of interdependence.

Part A: respons*ability* as a future orientation

The discussion of respons*ability* takes us to studies in philosophy, ethics, indigenous knowledge and a surprising further source for thinking on respons*ability* – quantum physics.

Safeguarding the conditions of life for future generations was the concern of Hans Jonas and Emmanuel Levinas, Jewish philosophers who saw in responsibility a hope to ensure that humanity would never again succumb to the depravity of the Holocaust. Hans Jonas saw that technology extended humanity's capacity for altering the natural order with unforeseeable consequences. He extended the concept of responsibility beyond a means of accountability for past actions, such as reparation for environmental damage, to take account of the *future* of life on earth. We are challenged to act in ways "compatible with the permanence of genuine human life on earth".[9]

Respons*ability* for the future requires our recognition that we cannot know all the unintended and unforeseen consequences of technological innovation and interventions, and therefore need precautionary decision-making. Initiatives such as the Universal Declaration of Responsibility for an Interdependent World, the World Declaration on the Environmental Rule of Law,[10] the Earth Charter and the Global Pact for the Environment articulate the search for agreements to safeguard life on the planet:[11]

> Our shared responsibility is to preserve planet earth and the integrity of her ecosystems by preventing destruction from ecological and social disasters that will affect all the peoples of the Earth . . .
>
> Effective transitions to responsible societies means operationalizing rights, as well as developing social and legal frameworks of responsibility to restore the relationship of humanity with the planet, to develop environmentally and socially accountable economies, and create effective solidarity with those put at risk by the distortions of profit and power at the expense of sustainability and public good.

High-level agreements give momentum to the need to re-orient present systems. They call for solidarity with conscious action to restore relations of people with the planet, and this means every dimension of life – working, shopping, eating, travelling, learning; use of land and water become matters of responsible action. Respons*ability* is proposed for generating a change in the system towards earth-inclusive law, and here I conceptualise some of its key attributes.

This orientation brings the prospect of revising liberal concepts of the individual, freedom, rights and property. An ethics of respons*ability* is informative for showing the limits of liberal constructs and for re-centring law to address the relational conditions of life. Reference to the ethics of Emmanuel Levinas in this chapter may be seen as problematic for re-orienting law because of the humanist orientation of his work. In my view, expressed elsewhere, these ethics and relational values continue to speak within and beyond the humanist tradition.[12]

Premises of irresponsibility

Liberalism and its traditions embrace a wide and complex range of thought, the central tenets of which have been widely documented and researched. It is important to touch on the premises of this system which poorly recognises relationship and respons*ability*.

The anchor points within the wide-ranging tenets of liberalism include the rights and interests of the individual, freedom, competition with systems of private property rights to support the individual and corporate wealth creation.[13] While questioning the premises of freedom in the following analysis, it is also essential to recognise the importance of freedom which protects the dignity of persons and which enables the realisation of human potential and aspirations as articulated by Amartya Sen.[14]

Prue Taylor identifies the foundational premises of property rights in law. She says, "the function of property rights in law is continuing to facilitate and incentivise forms of economic activity that cause widespread ecological harm."[15] Taylor identifies the principle of wealth creation in the context of an economic model of growth that externalises and does not measure impacts on ecological systems. As an example, the environmental priorities of New Zealand's Resource Management Act 1991 have been seen by those with more aggressive development interests as an impediment to property development, and revisions to the legislation freed up the process of consents for development. The effects of this can be seen when, in 2016 a Chinese-owned company, Ngongfu Spring, applied to draw 580 million litres of water per year from the pristine Otakiri Springs, near Whakatane, to bottle and ship overseas.[16] This is enough to give every person in New Zealand a 330-ml bottle of water every day for a year. The consent was granted based on economic interests. Similarly, in the same year, the Ashburton District Council gave a resource consent to SpringFresh to bottle 1.4 billion litres of water.[17] These consents would formerly have come under greater scrutiny in favour of environmental resource protections through notifications and Environment Court proceedings.

Property rights go hand in hand with the other cornerstone of liberal tradition, the freedom of the individual with protection of individual rights, which come from classical economic theory derived from John Locke.[18] Individual interests, in many aspects, are underpinned by freedom from responsibility. This is a freedom from obligation that supports work and enterprise, property rights and the accumulation of wealth.

A Hobbesian view of responsibility argues that humans are sovereign individuals who enter society and agree to assume some responsibilities in order better to pursue self-interest.[19] Underlying the arguments for the views expressed by Locke and Hobbes was a prior strong assumption of public duty, and this was the background against which individual interests were forged.[20] In the context of the Industrial Revolution, duty and responsibilities became redefined and were tolerated only insofar as they furnished the conditions for autonomy, private interest and freedom. Far from being ethically questionable, the pursuit of self-interest was regarded as the central tenet of the liberal life. In this order, human rights became the social justice dimension and serve to provide the means of legal protection against harm and undue exercise of coercive power.[21]

These foundational concepts were developed alongside Enlightenment ideas which granted man a position of mastery over the earth and its species.[22] Francis

Bacon advocated science as a new experimental philosophy able to "lead men to nature with all her children, to bind her to your service and make her your slave . . . to conquer and subdue her, to shake her to her foundations".[23] Such views opened the way to forms of scientific inquiry that objectified nature and to knowledge formation and technological development that has removed human accountability to nature.

These tenets are the enduring foundations of contemporary political and economic systems, often identified as Western, which have an increasingly global reach. Today these ideas manifest in the intensification of globalised markets, the removal of regulation, privatisation and the replacement of concepts of public good with individualised responsibility. It is grossly simplistic to suggest that these are the only forces at work, in particular in view of initiatives such as the Global Compact and leading initiatives through corporate social and environmental responsibility, such as for climate change transitions. The foundational precepts are set out here to show the contesting forces and to underline the embedded system against which change has to be wrought.

Respons*ability* – a bridge from an individual to a relational ontology

Levinas offers an alternative to the autonomous ontological subject, with refreshed insights into relationship as pre-eminent for human life, and as the source of respons*ability*. Whereas the references to different ontologies by authors Dame Anne Salmond and Mark Hickford in this book refer to different cultural traditions, Levinas proposes an ontology of a relational person as a correction to the Western ontology of the individual; he does so through an ontology constituted on the relation between two; a one-to-one, or face-to-face, relationship which becomes the genesis and the reference for the social order.

Respons*ability* arises from our bonds with others, physical, emotional, conscious and unconscious bonds which antecede the development of agency and the exercise of free will. We are connected to one another through sight and touch, in a caress, in the sharing of food, not only with humans but also with animals. Our senses connect us to water, to place and culture. Very simply, our sensuous life can be thought of as the source of relational ethics because of these primary bonds.

Our interrelatedness evokes qualities of a different order from rationality; love, kindness and respect are responses of care with sensual and spiritual aspects entwined with a response of respons*ability*.

The call to respons*ability* is as ancient as Cain's answer to God when asked about his brother Abel. Drawing to Jewish traditions and Talmudic law, Levinas asks in a new time and setting, "Am I my brother's keeper?"[24] This question resonates with the enduring expectation to be both responsive and accountable in our inescapable human condition of respons*ability*.

Levinas's work is part of the body of Western philosophical thought, originating with Descartes, that is concerned with the power dynamics of the system constituted on mastery. This dualistic system is variously referred to as the subject-object binary, the same-other or self-other in the master-slave dialectic. In this schema the other is the other of myself and positioned as subordinate to the self.

Violence is central to this structure, because identity and recognition are achieved at the expense of the other – by objectifying the other. Objectifying the other can take many forms – reducing their value, assimilating them, not recognising their "difference"; it does not provide for two (or more) ontologies. The capacity to understand and honour difference is central to relational ethics in Levinas[25] and also to philosopher Luce Irigaray, who develops a thesis for respectful, regenerative relationships constituted through the dynamics of sexual difference.[26]

It is important to reference human violence; it is endemic in inter-human relations and in human relations with nature, and it underlies many endeavours in ethics and in so many other spheres to correct violence and protect relationships. Restorative justice is one example being used in criminal justice to move from punishment to the healing of harm, under the understanding that crime is a social harm rather than an individual transgression. For the restorative process, victim and perpetrator can meet, and in this face-to-face process acknowledge harm and decide on appropriate remedial action. The restorative process will take account of safety and protection and work towards reintegration of the offender into a community that will support their goals for reform.

Levinas, like Hans Jonas, Hanna Arendt and so many others, sought to address the question of how humanity, especially "civilised" humanity, could fall into the depravity of National Socialism. Their philosophical inquiries led them to propose that violence could be averted through an ethic of responsibility. The legacy of their far-reaching inquiries into Cartesian metaphysics is a source of thought that deserves attention in a world that is facing different challenges yet persisting in destructiveness. For Levinas, responsibility arises from the ethical response to the other, the neighbour, the stranger, the one in need. Responsibility here is justice, and the call of the other can thus be understood as the foundation of ethics because it changes the response of mastery, to welcome of the other. To turn away from the violence of assimilation Levinas asks:[27]

> Can the Same welcome the Other, not by giving itself to the Other as a theme, (that is to say as being) but by putting itself in question?

Freedom, as mentioned, is often understood as the condition for autonomy and thus stands in the way of responsibility:[28]

> The more I divest myself of my freedom as a constituted willful, imperialist subject, the more I discover myself to be responsible; the more just I am.

Taken even further, freedom harbours injustice because it protects self-interest; a notion expressed succinctly as:[29]

> Responsibility grows in importance as the life of freedom discovers itself to be unjust.

The presence of the stranger and the neighbour has an effect on us, regardless of how we respond. Thus, we can say that when faced with the need of another we experience a certain call to respond, even if we choose to evade the call. In this sense, when faced with the need of another, our freedom and our self-interest is interrupted. By the same token, the need of another brings the opportunity to set aside self-interest to meet their need. And, where we respond, we create the conditions for community.

Clearly the metaphors of neighbour and stranger evoke Judaic traditions of justice, and the imperative to respond to the vulnerable and bring justice to those in marginal situations. It is a call to inclusiveness and to respond to those in need with practical assistance – a call which is rendered more imperative if we ask, "to whom am I a neighbour?"[30]

If respons*ability* is given a pre-eminent value, and expressed metaphorically and practically in welcome and hospitality, the other does not limit our freedom, but expands the opportunity to act with justice:[31]

> Freedom is unmasked as injustice and summoned to change the exercise of violence into goodness and hospitality.

In thinking more laterally about welcome and hospitality, we can readily see that humans are intertwined with nature. Food and water are at the interface of humans with nature. Similarly, the face is the interface with air – in breath, speech, language and communication – and our connection with light and sound are concentrated in the face.

The face-to-face relation is most of all where we encounter the need or the destitution of another and where the opportunity to respond presents itself. Indeed, it may not be a human face – it may be an animal, a body of degraded water or damaged earth.

Respons*ability* is a form of answerability to the need of another. It is rooted in our relational condition and forms a different basis for sociality than the concept of an autonomous individual who is guided by self-interest. It is completely at odds with the conventions of selfhood or agency with a value on freedom that disregards the interwoven web of wellbeing.

The possibility that respons*ability* is part of the living dynamics of all matter is argued for by quantum physicist Karen Barad. Barad shows that the interactive process in quantum physics is fundamental to the dynamics of all forms of life or phenomena.[32]

Barad refers to Danish quantum physicist Niels Bohr's observation that particles can behave like particles or waves depending on how they are measured.[33] Experiments with waves and particles show that the characteristics of phenomena may be determined from their interactions with the measuring apparatus. This implies there is no pre-existing identity but that entities, or phenomena, arise from intra-actions; and while a phenomenon or species may appear distinct, it is also "entangled"; it is indivisible from the histories from which it emerged. A phenomenon that has identifiable properties is an expression of diffraction – of histories of interaction, disturbance, dispersion.

Encounters between all forms of matter produce infinite new expressions of matter; while life is reproduced and forms become differentiated, it also remains connected, entangled, intertwined, never fully differentiated from its source. While seemingly distinct identities and entities emerge, and express themselves in ways that are characteristic of their form, or phenomena, all forms of life are always part of others.

Wonderfully, Barad breaks with the idea that only humans have language, consciousness and intelligence. She observes:[34]

> Nature is not mute and culture the articulate one. Nature writes, scribbles, experiments, calculates, thinks, breathes and laughs.

The idea of nature having consciousness and intelligence disrupts the assumption that only humans have consciousness. It throws into question the nature-culture split at the heart of the Cartesian worldview and the hierarchical order of things. This understanding nature as articulate, as expressing intelligence, raises a question of whether non-humans are subjects? And, importantly for the theme of law in the following section, are they subjects in law? Furthermore is nature relational with capacity for respons*ability?*[35]

Considering nature as intelligent and conscious has taken legal form in Aotearoa New Zealand where the Whanganui River is recognized as an ancestor and vested as a legal person. A legal person, in this case, is an acknowledgement of the river as a living ancestor with all the rights, duties and liabilities of a legal person. The river includes tributaries and all the physical and metaphysical attributes of the river. The scope for interpretation of legal personhood derives from the river itself being vested with legal standing.

Importantly, legal personality is a framework that places the river, or other entity, beyond the confines of human interests, in that it has standing itself.[36] This recent move of applying the corporate concept of legal personality to natural entities is a means to give legal standing to nature, and is elaborated further in Part B.

Justice arising from ethics

The groundwork of this relational ethics is needed in order to develop thinking on law, justice and governance. Respons*ability* arises from an inter-personal ethic, in face-to-face relations, and expands to communal ties thus providing a fundamental reference for public life.

This proposal for society based on and enlivened by relationships of respons*ability* prepares the ground for justice. This prospect is vastly different from the premise that sociality is founded on a war of all against all, with institutions that are designed to protect self-interest, autonomy and freedom. The thesis is that a relational social order could have greater commitment to stewardship of people and nature. This is not the same ontology that privileges freedom and self-interest; it now embodies principles which are more oriented to common good.

Respons*ability* in this order may be introduced into law, but can never be confined to legalistic definition or expression. It has legal and non-legal dimensions. Respons*ability* urges us beyond what can and should be codified in legislation and policy. Although respons*ability* will require codification, with specific accountabilities, codes do not *exhaust* the ethical demand of respons*ability*. Ethical respons*ability* transcends or exceeds what is possible to legislate.[37] The realm beyond what can be codified is the arena of transcendent values of the human spirit which reach beyond legal duty to the dimensions which extend from joy to sacrifice.

Transcendent qualities are a touchstone for judgment and discernment in public life, and in particular, a touchstone for the voice of the marginalised, for advocacy against injustice in the public arena.

Respons*ability* and indigenous law

Relational metaphysics is foundational in indigenous cultures and in other traditional societies. In contrast to the Western philosophical tradition where identity is anchored in the Cartesian dualistic system and achieved through the self-other relation, indigenous identity arises from land and ancestral genealogical relations.

Indigenous thought is informed by a complex web of ancestral connections and forms a worldview that is firmly anchored in the living dynamics of nature.[38]

> Māori for example see themselves as part of a familial web in which humans are junior siblings to other species beings and forms of life. People therefore don't understand themselves as exercising knowledge over the natural world but as existing always already *inside* or *as* relationships (italics in original).

Sir Taihākurei Durie places the law of relationship as the first recognised law for Māori with protocols for keeping peace in the spiritual and earthly realms.[39]

> All things come from the spiritual realm, all things are tapu [sacred], existing under the protection of atua [divine entities] and from this flows laws of restrictions for the use and recognition of different places, things, and activities. Land, waters, environment, all inhabitants of the natural world including people now and of time before and to come are intertwined.
>
> The land and waterways are shared between those who have passed on to te arai (the spirit world), the living and those yet to be born. Ancestors, whether remote or recent, occupy a spiritual world that is as real to Māori as the physical world. Accordingly, forebears are not spoken of but are spoken to, and creation stories are not myths but beliefs, beliefs which are the foundation of Māori law.

All these realms are alive and present and can be recognised in the protocols of hospitality – a foremost expression of respect for guests and duty of care for the land.[40]

Durie boldly refers to respons*ability* as a higher form of ethics and order because it requires an account of effects on others and benefit to the community as a whole, and carries obligations to ancestors:[41]

> Embedded in Tikanga Māori is a concept which transcends right use. It is the responsibility to so use as to maintain to the fullest practicable extent, pure, freshwater regimes. It is a concept which requires a balancing of the benefits of ownership with the responsibilities of ownership. It is a responsibility which is owed to one's forebears and one's descendants.

This notion of multidimensional ownership and "responsibility" can be linked with an understanding of trusteeship in which common goods such as water are assured of ecological viability and used for beneficial purposes within a framework of safeguards for future generations. There is a groundswell for wider applications of trusteeship law to protect common goods, which comes from its effective implementation in some jurisdictions, in particular Hawai'i where there is a confluence of indigenous tradition and constitutional provisions for water as a public trust. This is elaborated further in Part B.

Human rights – can they deliver justice for nature?

It has been suggested that responsibility is the hidden face of human rights, although respons*ability* is poorly developed as a partner concept to rights. Some issues concerning rights are raised, noting that rights on their own present an aporia that can only be filled by a corresponding system for implementation – an enactment of respons*ability* to meet the rights entitlement.

Ensuring human rights for those who are vulnerable requires an effective regime of responsibility – respons*ability* as accountability for implementing rights. Many innovations aimed at providing safeguards for planetary ecosystems and environmental stewardship are being shaped through human rights – such as the declaration of the Rights of Mother Earth. No doubt this is because of the established basis for rights in law. Rights without a corresponding regime of respons*ability* is insufficient to achieve the protections intended by rights alone. Giving effect to rights requires an adequate development of respons*ability*.

The eloquence of the cases made for eco-centric law and earth jurisprudence in *Exploring Wild Law* is limited by the direction taken via the path of rights.[42] While many authors, including Thomas Berry and Jules Cashford, express reservations about using the rights framework to advance the cause of legal accountability for the use of resources and for the protection of ecological integrity, the theme of rights prevails as a means to build a case for eco-centric law.

There is evidence that when the attempts to achieve justice are framed in terms of rights there emerges the need to balance competing claims to rights; the ensuing conflicts are then managed through litigation.[43]

The strong move for the "rights of nature" in law comes from an influential paper published in 1972 titled "Should Trees Have Standing?" by Harvard

Professor of Law Christopher Stone. Stone refers to the historical expansion of the notion of rights to children, prisoners, women and Indigenous Peoples to argue for extending rights to nature. The more recent development of earth jurisprudence[44] began with reference to the great laws of nature, and then moved towards rights as established body of law that provides a source of legal development to achieve standing for nature.

A difficulty I see with the argument for giving legal standing to nature through the rights approach is that rights are drawn from the conceptual frameworks of the liberal legal tradition and may be insufficient to meet the complexities and richness of interdependencies at every scale in the globalized world. A more extended discussion on this has been developed elsewhere.[45]

Rights are a product of liberal history. Peter Burdon elaborates the rapprochement of rights in the post-war settlement as an accommodation of the need for a way to take account of human suffering within liberal economic interests. Rights do not challenge private property and economic interests, and thus re-inscribe the system that we now understand is perpetrating environmental destruction:[46]

> As Moyn illustrates the contemporary discourse of human rights is marked by the conditions of its historical emergence – it provides a liberal democratic form of utopianism that is predicated upon the abandonment of alternative political formations and the vision of human emancipation that they contained. It also involved the acceptance of the fundamental co-ordinates of the political and economic system of liberal democratic capitalism. The utopia they provide is not a substantive vision of the good, but a negative or minimalist utopia of rights which seeks to mitigate suffering within the co-ordinates of the current system.

It is possible that respons*ability* can be understood as the basis of rights, in that rights arise from a failure of respons*ability* and can be remedied through more affirmative and proactive forms of law and governance. Public policy needs institutions and citizens' organisations actively watching, researching and speaking out with mandates for injustice to be met with corrective measures. Catherine Iorns Magallanes[47] perceptively writes of one of the difficulties of rights as needing to be active by an aggrieved respondent. Where law is designed to activate respons*ability*, such as in the Whanganui River provisions for guardianship, it mandates proactive work for wellbeing and prevention of harm.

Tensions of rights for earth jurisprudence and sustainability

Rights are produced from liberal foundations and are being grafted onto systems and institutions that were not designed for integration, collaboration and respons*ability*. The orientation of safeguarding earth's common goods for future generations is central to the purpose of sustainability, yet the need for long-term accountabilities is recent. Sustainability is a challenge to the separated systems within liberalism, but the systems of its production are often not scrutinised in the effort to design and implement a new paradigm for law and governance.

Part B: respons*able* law and interdependence Different laws – how can they co-exist?

The quest for law for the governance of earth's common goods is catalysed by climate change unravelling the fabric of life as we know it and destabilising the planet's ecosystems and human patterns of social and economic life.

Indigenous systems of governance offer insights for including humans and nature, economy and environment, society and spirituality, and obligation to future generations as touchstones in law. New law needs an attunement to the systems of the planet, similar to the aspirations of earth jurisprudence. The innovation of "earth jurisprudence" to achieve an eco-centric reference in law, through alignment with law of the cosmos, is elaborated by contributors to *Exploring Wild Law*.[48] In her "Dedication to Thomas Berry" Jules Cashford writes:[49]

> As with all other forms of human culture, the anthropocentrism of human law for human beings had to become integral to the primary lawgiver, the universe. This is what Thomas called the 'Great Jurisprudence', the inherent order and lawfulness of the cosmos which structures and sustains all life within it.

Earth jurisprudence has largely morphed into the rights of nature movement – a pragmatic move in the face of the destruction of nature but with limited long-term benefit. The remedy in rights has to solve competing rights. The new scale of interdependencies in a globalised world requires integrative and responsive frameworks in law and public policy, as stated in the Universal Declaration of Responsibility for an Interdependent World:[50]

> The scope and irreversibility of the interdependences that have been generated among human beings, among societies, and between humankind and the biosphere constitute a radically new situation in the history of humankind, changing it irrevocably into a community of destiny.

In reviewing state law, indigenous law and the need to evolve law for the planet, I see three key references for law:

- The Great Law, or Law of Nature, which is the source of inspiration for Thomas Berry and the principal reference for Peter Burdon's work on earth jurisprudence.
- Indigenous Law – established long before European settlement and emerging into greater public view via case law, such as through cases taken by Māori in respect of rivers: *Huakina Development Trust*[51] and *Paki v. Attorney General*.[52] These represent the growing articulation and recognition of indigenous law.[53]
- Public or State Law – the law of England, its development in New Zealand, North America and countries such as Malaysia, which have been influenced by British colonial administration.

These different forms of law do not sit easily together and Durie states the need for plurality in law with recognition of both Western and indigenous law, where resolutions for public policy are generated through full regard for the respective interests of parties and for common good:[54]

> I have constantly in mind that the laws of the state or of a people are culturally laden. They do not purport to give vent to universal truths but to express the mores of a society; that is they reflect the people's history, institutions, values and beliefs. It follows that the relevant law in this case is not just the standard law of New Zealand (based on that of England).
>
> The relevant law is also the distinctive Māori law that was here long before. The result is that when two are in conflict, it is not principled to talk in terms of one legal dogma alone. It is necessary to consider both legal theories and then find a sound framework in which the conflicts can be debated.

The context for these comments comes from contested views about ownership and interests in water in New Zealand and differences between Māori and English law.

The key issue for addressing environmental harm is to internalise the use of environmental resources and the effects on ecosystems and habitats into economic transactions, referred to as 'oeconomy' by Pierre Calame.[55] Legal development may be through "Hard law"[56] or soft law which can encompass policy, guidelines and codes of practice which are not legally binding, as with corporate social responsibility. Sometimes hard law and soft law are combined, such as in the Paris Agreement, the *Waiahole* public trust law in Hawai'i, and legal personhood of the Whanganui River, *Te Awa Tupua* in Aotearoa New Zealand.

New forms of corporates are emerging which demonstrate changing finance and business law with a shift towards mission, public good and integrated accountability as well as profit. For example, the directors of Benefit Corporations have a fiduciary duty to non-financial stakeholders as well as to the financial interests of investor shareholders. They are required to publish their environmental and social performance with evaluations of governance and the web of relationships between suppliers, customers, employees, and the environment.[57]

As our planetary consciousness grows new conceptual frameworks are being used for policy development; these include the Sustainble Development Goals, IPCC reports,[58] the Intergovernmental Science-Policy Platform on Biodiversity and Ecosystem Services,[59] and Planetary Boundaries for biophysical systems[60] which include acidification of oceans, land use change, climate change and nitrogen and phosphorous loading. These do not demonstrate the dynamic interations between the biophysical processes, nor address human operating systems required for resilience and social inclusion. Facing planetary boundaries in policy requires going beyond conceptual boundaries with more capacity for synthesis and integration for equity and intergenerational governance. The following guidelines venture towards principles of respons*ability* in the human interface with ecological systems.[61]

Nga Pou: guidelines for living well with the earth

In reality the aspiration for cohesion and integration are sought in contested situations with contradictions and power dynamics. Respons*ability* is tempered with mistakes and misjudgements in the complex arena of interdependence and accountability.

Consideration of immediate and deferred effects of decisions and actions requires an assessment of risks of unforeseen consequences, both beneficial and harmful. Such assement requires multiple resources of knowledge for contextual decison-making; these encompass biophysical science, analysis of economic and business transactions, supply chains and renewable energy, food and agricultural futures, land use, freshwater, fisheries and oceans. Water and environmental policy, and law, need to be developed in dialogue with forestry and agriculture and with policy for family and community wellbeing.

Law, regulation and decision-making with an explicit ethics for public good, social equity, integrated economy with safeguards for ecosystems is therefore procedural and will be inclusive of stakeholders with vested interests and short term priorities along with those with wider concerns and long-term interests. The participation of Indigenous Peoples and those with traditional local knowledge is not only to ensure inclusion, it will safeguard practice-based experiential wisdom and foresight. Inclusion means the involvement of those with legacies of exclusion and marginalization from slavery, forced migration, and colonization – and may well open up restorative justice and the need to address restitution from harms from colonisation and war.

Different cultural knowledge traditions are instrinsic to a principle of diversity for "living well with the earth". Respons*able* proceedures ensure cultural diversity and male and female participation. Masculine and feminine attributes are a source of regeneration and need to be assured in decision-making, law and governance, bearing in mind the particular role of women in giving birth to the future.[62]

Integrative work is the deepest challenge for law and the transactional systems of the economy. It will mean curtailing limitations on liability and removing subsidies for extractive non-renewable resources, and counteracting externalized environmental and social factors with integrated assessments.[63] Procedures to assist integration will be multisectoral, multidisciplinary and cross borders of interests, geography and politics.

Finance and investment need to be coherent with environmental, economic and social policy. The pressing issues of the global community and global common goods, in particular climate change, need the contributions of companies to address transitions to low carbon economies. Regulation alone will not be sufficient.

Asymmetries of power are always present. Ideally, those in positions of power legitimate their respons*ability* through accountability for the wellbeing of people and for common goods. Deterrents and sanctions against exploitation are necessary. France's Duty of Vigilance legislation, for example, requires corporates to prevent human rights violations and report on environmental impacts of their operations, including in supply chains.[64]

The global scale of transformation needed for interdependent and sustainable societies needs to be matched with local, contextual engagement; thus the imperative for men and women, students, young people and the elderly to unite with others. In acting with co-respons*ability*, information can be produced and shared to build solidarity, plan action, expose harm and contribute to creating cultures of living well with peoples, oceans, earth and the atmosphere.

Dynamics of contestation

The expectation is that good law will include common good benefits for the long term and intergenerational justice with multisector engagement. However, these ideals become tempered with awareness that the power of remarkable law can be muted by vigorous advocacy for development rights, by poor implementation and by a broader environment of governance and policy that is unsupportive or hostile to the intention of the law.

At the global level, an example of the interplay between power dynamics and interdependence is seen in the pathway to the Paris Agreement. The negotiations were plagued with contestation over common and differentiated responsibilities according to capability.[65] Finally, the Intended Nationally Determined Contributions (INDCs) under the Paris Agreement hold both promise and tension for achieving a global consensus on a goal of two degrees atmospheric warming. Once agreed to, INDCs will provide legally binding pathways for mitigating carbon emissions. This does not venture into cross-border law with systems of surveillance in deference to the sovereign authority of states; this is done elsewhere, in respect of oceans through the United Nations Law of the Sea.

The Resource Management Act 1991 (RMA) in New Zealand provides a local example of contested interests. The Act has the purpose of supporting sustainable development and with provisions for stewardship, landscape values and relationship of Māori to the environment, and thus meets many of the criteria and the guidelines for respons*ability*. Yet the years since 1991 have seen the dramatic decline in freshwater quality, largely due to agricultural policy to convert land to intensified dairy production. While degraded waterways are now recognised as a policy failure, the causes are multiple. Research attributes failure of implementation of the RMA to be at the Regional Council level and based on vested interests and the many drivers for economic development at the local level.[66]

David Grinlinton and Prue Taylor discern the underlying forces that pull interpretation of the law towards economic interests:[67]

> Recognition and enforcement of critical ecological constraints is left to be imposed externally, via the state (as the protector of the common good) through policy and remedial regulation, or through the limited reconciliation of conflicting private rights and duties via traditional legal processes (e.g., through the modern law of torts, contract law, and property law). Although

> not without benefits, the body of environmental law does not adequately challenge the status quo, or "business as usual" because it "generally harbors the same core presumption that economic activity provides a net social benefit.
>
> Thus, economic interests, rather than ecological interests in support of human well-being, remain the explicit or implicit priority. For this reason, property laws and environmental laws, as currently formed and interpreted, are at odds with the concept of sustainability.

Not only are the economic drivers undermining of the effectiveness of environmental law, but also the anthropocentric orientation of law is considered to be a foundational flaw from the point of view of an eco-centric jurisprudence, thus the move to expand the horizons of law to accommodate the dynamics of living ecosystems.

Public trust for water in Hawai'i

There has been an increase in cases on public trusteeship in the courts in the face of failure of governments to legislate and implement environmental protections.[68] Hawai'i is important for showing how common law cases create an evolution in interpretation of common law. The *Waiahole* case in Hawai'i[69] was taken with legal expert Kapua Sproat to litigate for the recovery of water as a public trust as embodied in the Hawai'ian State Constitution and also in Hawai'ian traditions of spiritual association with water as a public trust resource to be managed for future generations.[70]

Hawai'i's constitution was amended in 1978 and a new framework for water management was shaped. Article XI provides that all public resources be held in trust by the state for the benefit of its present and future generations.[71] The public trust imposes "a dual mandate of 1) protection and 2) maximum reasonable and beneficial use" with specific provision "to protect, control, and regulate the use of Hawai'ian water resources for the benefit of its people". Despite these provisions, the diversion of waterways for the sugar industry was allowed. This destroyed the natural flows and quality of water and traditional agriculture was decimated by the industrial water regime.

The doctrine of public trust provides for continuity that goes beyond the lifespan of persons and assists in overcoming the limitations of short-term policy inherent in electoral cycles of government. Public trust, and the law of a legal person discussed below, aligns with many of guidelines for respons*ability* including meeting the criteria of a long-term framework to entrench public good over the encroachment of private property interests.

Key principles of the public trust are that resources cannot be alienated by government, or be transferred or controlled for private purposes only; a public purpose is required along with a corresponding requirement that users cannot materially impair the quality of the resource or its availability to the public. Citizen duties correspond with that of governments in that governments are required to account for its actions or approvals of a use, thus curbing adverse power dynamics and providing adequate ways to removing self-interest. Findings on the effects of a proposed use must be recorded to assure that there is no unlawful alienation or transfer for private purpose, and that there is no material impairment of public trust resources or uses.[72] These public good benefits have added requirements of transparency.

Public trust requires public information to be provided, with public participation to encourage the greater democratisation of decision-making. Indeed, the doctrine equips the public with the standing to challenge government and private proposals that threaten the trust's environmental and public access purposes; and courts are strengthened in their ability to balance proposed development against longstanding public uses grounded on reasonable public expectations. Public engagement needs finer-grained analysis of who is able to represent the interests of the trust entity and who is excluded. I would ask about the protocols of respectful engagement to ensure indigenous participation and how conflict is managed between groups with contested interests.

Furthermore, the matter of different cultures requires respect for different knowledge systems, and these can be a requirement for deliberations. The process of negotiation means sitting at the table with industry, scientists, traditional knowledge experts, law experts, custodians of the resource and local government.

This greater democratisation through trusteeship increases public scrutiny of consents and licenses and the giveaways of environmental resources to private interests. Although water is not acknowledged as a public trust in New Zealand, we see the process of public scrutiny in the exposure of local government providing consents for free water for bottling to private for-profit companies. The law as it stands could not prevent free water being made available to commercial companies.

There are tensions in the State role as public trustee with the responsibilities of being a representative body. The State can exercise its trusteeship role to act as a brake on claims to resources that might not be in the wider or long-term public interests. Alongside this, the State can be in a compromised position by supporting economic growth interests which undermine its public trust responsibilities.

We can see many of the key principles of the guidelines for respons*ability* in the public trust doctrine and the example of *Waiahole*. A priority on long-term ecological integrity goes together with the requirement to meet indigenous interests. The Water Code reinforces Hawai'i's constitutional requirement that "traditional and customary rights of ahupua'a tenants who are descendants of native Hawaiians since 1778 shall not be abridged or denied by this chapter."[73]

In addition to the protections prescribed through the *Waiāhole* case, the public trust prescribes a higher level of scrutiny for private commercial uses. State and county boards and commissions must, therefore, closely examine requests to use public resources for private gain to ensure that the public's interest in the resource is fully protected.

Matters of representation and power dynamics in the working of the Water Code are under ongoing scrutiny and are, no doubt, a contested space. At best, divergent interests are answerable to the clear provisions of the Code, which can be upheld through any legal proceedings. On the matter of gender representation, the *Waiahole* case was driven by Kapua Sproat with colleagues, and guardianship of the law and ancestral interest continues to be overseen by both women and men.

A river is an ancestor and a legal person

In Aotearoa New Zealand, Te Awa Tupua Act 2017 recognises the Whanganui River as an ancestor and vests the river as a legal person. Soon after, legal personhood was taken up for rivers in India, Ecuador and Colombia. It has opened a new horizon in law and environmental governance.

In the Waitangi Tribunal process of redress for breaches of the Treaty of Waitangi, the claim on behalf of the Whanganui River led to settlement legislation in favour of the river.

The claim itself is set against the background of a polluted river, diversions for the Tongariro Power Scheme and the general historic statutory fragmentation of riverbeds, riverbanks, minerals beneath the riverbed, air above the water and the water column. This regime has been of great distress to Māori and those who understand rivers as a living whole.

By statute, riverbeds were vested in the Crown for purposes of navigation and mining.[74] Historically these purposes were to protect navigation and travel, the allocation of water and, to a lesser extent, fishing, and still less, recreation and public gatherings.[75] The effect was to divide up rivers into the bed, the water column and the air above the water for purposes of legal administration, with the added view that "no one owns water". This regime is completely contrary to Māori views of the river as a living whole under the authority of the tribal lands through which it flows. The concept that no-one owns water is a position taken by the Crown, which is well recognized as being anomalous in that the purchase of consents for water allocation are tantamount to property and ownership.

In the Te Awa Tupua Act 2017, the Whanganui River has been given recognition as an ancestor and as an integrated living whole which flows from mountains to sea, with all interests in the river to have regard to its wellbeing. This framing recognises the systemic nature of the river ecosystem, with an added significant change of vesting the riverbed (subsoil), the plants and the air above the water.[76]

In this sense, the provisions for Te Awa Tupua meet long term interests for ecological integrity, for interdependencies and inclusion of multiple interests. Guardians, Te Pou Tupua, are appointed for the river from the Whanganui people and the Crown, and therefore hold the prospect of managing the power dynamics between Māori, the Crown and the multiple parties with interests in the river. Guardianship introduces a principle of active custodial respons*abilities*.

A management strategy provides for the engagement of all stakeholders in collaborative management process to advance "environmental, social, cultural, and economic health and wellbeing of Te Awa Tupua," with elaborate process of governance and management spelled out in the Act. This offers inclusion of all environmental, economic and human intersecting interests in the river. The law provides for a procedural process of engagement in conflicting and converging interests in the river with a mandate to restore the health of the river in its geographical scope. The influence of the river being vested as a legal person reaches beyond borders.

Soon after the Te Awa Tupua Act, part of the Ganges and Yamuna rivers were given the status of legal persons. Legal proceedings followed in the Ganges and Yamuna case, *Mohammed Salim v. State of Uttarakhand*, in which the Court declared that the Himalayan mountain glaciers and "rivers, streams, rivulets, lakes, air, meadows, dales, jungles, forests, wetlands, grasslands, springs and waterfalls" were all legal entities or persons, "with all corresponding rights, duties and liabilities of a living person, in order to preserve and conserve them."[77] However, legal challenges have ensued on "border" interest, which is not to say they cannot be resolved.

Te Awa Tupua Act has strong dimensions of pubic good interests with intergenerational responsibility embedded within it. Above all, the result is a major shift from human interest to the relational and integrated attributes of the river and all associated with her.

Conclusion

The understanding of ethics as respons*ability* for another, or as "being-for-the-other", is a departure from principles underpinning the liberal tradition and its various formations in current social institutions.

As an alternative to self-interest, respons*ability* could be the groundwork for social order which is more eco-centric and unsettles the paradigm of exploitative growth.

The indicative guidelines outlined here provide markers for a systematic framework for the evolution of laws and governance for public good with an account of interdependence. While this suggests codification, guidelines are to support governance and institutional innovation that is contextual and also global in reference. Indigenous law was traditionally exercised by communities which belong to the land; these systems of governance, which are drawn from an inter-related "woven universe", are being increasingly articulated and are thus available for wider engagement.

Public trust, amongst benefits of public good, long-term interests and environmental safeguards, also equips the public with the standing to challenge government and private proposals that threaten the trust's environmental and public access purposes; and courts are strengthened in their ability to balance proposed development against longstanding public uses grounded on reasonable public expectations.

Public trusts, such as national parks and other protected areas, establish a preferential legal status for specific ecosystems or attributes of ecosystems, normally for the beneficial use of humans, not necessarily for the intrinsic worth or direct and primary benefit of the ecosystem or its elements.

A key element of legal personhood is that the resource itself has rights, duties and liabilities. The case of the Whanganui River is a reference for this framework of vesting of nature's entities as legal persons with a regime of guardianship; however, it is too recent to evaluate. It can be noted that the city of Pittsburgh in Pennsylvania declared that nature is a legal person and banned fracking through this law.[78]

Respons*ability*, understood in its relational and accountability dimensions, offers a way for giving effect to human interdependence with nature in law. Yet the law is not the limit of respons*ability*. The law is but one dimension, the regulatory dimension of a greater impulse for harmonising humanity with the planet.

Notes

1 Ngā Pou Rāhui, markers of protection.

2 Revisionary comment by Professor Feleterika Nokise October 2017.

3 The spelling "respons*ability*" is used to denote the relational quality of responsibility. The conventional spelling "responsibility" is not altered when it refers to standard use or the use of other authors, such as Levinas.

4 Gay Morgan "Public Responsibility." Chapter 4 (p. 66 ff) of this book.

5 Prue Taylor "Ecological Integrity, Responsibilities and Rights: Insights From *The Imperative of Responsibility* by Hans Jonas" (paper delivered at the Ecological Integrity Conference, La Rochelle, France, June 2012).

6 The Waitangi Tribunal was established in 1975 to hear claims in respect of Crown breaches of the Treaty of Waitangi and to make recommendations for restitution and compensation, via settlements.

7 Carwyn Jones *New Treaty, New Tradition: Reconciling New Zealand and Māori Law* (University of British Columbia Press, Vancouver, 2016).

8 In 2015 many countries "adopted a set of goals to end poverty, protect the planet, and ensure prosperity for all as part of a new sustainable development agenda" <www.un.org/sustainabledevelopment/sustainable-development-goals/>.

9 Hans Jonas *The Imperative of Responsibility: In Search of Ethics for the Technological Age* (University of Chicago Press, Chicago, 1985) at 11.

10 International Union for the Conservation of Nature "IUCN Experts Provide Input Into Draft Treaty Recognising Fundamental Environmental Rights" (20 July 2017) <www.iucn.org/news/secretariat/201707/iucn-experts-provide-input-draft-treaty-recognising-fundamental-environmental-rights>.

11 Declaration of Responsibility in an Interdependent World (preamble) <http://base.alliance-respons.net/docs/_eng_udir_decl_interdependence_responsibility17.pdf>.

12 Betsan Martin "Taking Responsibility into All Matter: Engaging Levinas in Matters of the 21st Century" (2016) 48 *Educational Philosophy and Theory* 418.

13 Stuart Hall "Variants of Liberalism" in J. Donald and S. Hall (eds) *Politics and Ideology* (Open University Press, Philadelphia, 1986); G.J. Oddie and R.W. Perrett (eds) *Justice, Ethics and New Zealand Society* (Oxford University Press, Auckland, 1992).

14 Amartya Sen *Development as Freedom* (Oxford University Press, Oxford, 1999).

15 Prue Taylor "Notes on Responsibility and Law" *Personal Communication* (October 2014); P. Taylor, above n 5.

16 Matt Shand "Chinese company seeks consent to draw 580 million litres of pristine spring water" <www.stuff.co.nz/business/industries/95670283/Chinese-company-seeks-consent-to-draw-580-million-litres-of-pristine-spring-water>..
17 Charlie Mitchel "The bottled-water giants who are taking our water" <www.stuff.co.nz/business/78652406/the-bottledwater-giants-who-are-taking-our-water>.
18 John Locke *Two Treatises on Government* (Hollis ed, A. Millar, London, 1764).
19 Thomas Hobbes *Leviathan* (Macpherson ed, Penguin, London, 1988).
20 Gay Morgan. Chapter 4 of this book.
21 See Stuart Hall "Variants of Liberalism" in J. Donald and S. Hall (eds) *Politics and Ideology* (Open University Press, Philadelphia, 1986); David Grinlinton and Prue Taylor (eds) *Property Rights and Sustainability* (Brill, Leiden, 2011).
22 Linda Jean Shepherd *Lifting Veil: The Feminine Face of Science* (Shambhala, Boston, 1993).
23 Cited in Shepherd, above n 22.
24 Emmanuel Levinas *Otherwise than Being or Beyond Essence* (translated ed: Alphonso Lingis (translator), Dusquesne University Press, Pittsburgh, PA, 2009) at 117.
25 Emmanuel Levinas *Totality and Infinity* (translated ed: Alphonso Lingis (translator), Dusquesne University Press, Pittsburgh, PA, 1969); E. Levinas *Collected Philosophical Papers* (translated ed: Alphonso Lingis (translator), Dusquesne University Press, Pittsburgh, PA, 1987); E. Levinas "Transcendence and Height" in A.T. Peperzak, S. Critchey and R. Bernasconi (eds) *Emanuel Levinas: Basic Philosophical Writings* (Indiana University Press, Bloomington, IA, 1996).
26 Luce Irigaray "The Fecundity of the Caress" in *An Ethics of Sexual Difference* (translated ed: C. Burke and C.G. Gill (translators), Athlone, London, 1993) at 116.
27 Emmanuel Levinas "Transcendence and Height" in A.T. Peperzak, S. Critchey and R. Bernasconi (eds) *Emanuel Levinas: Basic Philosophical Writings*, above n 25, at 16.
28 Emmanuel Levinas *Otherwise than Being or Beyond Essence*, above n 24, at 112 (abbreviated).
29 Emmanuel Levinas *Collected Philosophical Papers*, above n 25, at 58. This paper follows Levinas's line of thought in order to develop this relational understanding of responsibility. Other work on freedom as justice, such as that of Amartya Sen *Development as Freedom*, is not included here.
30 This phrase is attributed to Professor Feleterika Nokise. Informal conversation, August 2017.
31 Theodore de Boer "An Ethical Transcendental Philosophy" in Richard Cohen (ed) *Face to Face With Levinas* (State University of New York Press, Albany, 1986) at 83.
32 Karen Barad "Posthumanist Performativity: Towards an Understanding of How Matter Comes to Matter" (2003) 28 *Signs* 801; Karen Barad *Meeting the Universe Halfway: Quantum Physics and the Entanglement of Matter and Meaning* (Duke University Press, Durham, NC, 2007).
33 Karen Barad "Quantum Entanglements and Hauntological Relations of Inheritance: Dis/Continuities, SpaceTime Enfoldings and Justice-to-Come" (2010) *Derrida Today* 240.
34 Ibid. at 268.
35 Betsan Martin "Taking Responsibility into All Matter" (2015) *Educational Philosophy and Theory* 418.
36 Dinah Shelton "Nature as a Legal Person" *VertigO-la revie électronique en sciences de l'environment*. Hors-série 22, September 2015.
37 Te Kawehau Hoskins, Betsan Martin and Maria Humphries "The Power of Relational Responsibility" (2011) 16(2) *EJBO* 22.
38 Ibid.
39 See Waitangi Tribunal *Muriwhenua Land Report* 1997 at 21–23 and especially the evidence cited of Dame Anne Salmond – "Māori were operating in a world governed

by *whakapapa* . . . Ancestors intervened in everyday affairs, *mana* was understood as proceeding from the ancestor-gods and *tapu* was the sign of their presence in the human world. Life was kept in balance by the principle of *utu* (reciprocal exchanges) which operated in relations between individuals, groups and ancestors." See also E.T. Durie and others "Ngā Wai o te Māori. Na Tikanga me Ngā Ture Roia: The Waters of the Māori: Māori Law and State Law" (paper prepared for the New Zealand Māori Council, 2017) at 33.

40 Ibid. at 32.
41 Ibid. at 119.
42 Peter Burdon (ed) *Exploring Wild Law* (Wakefield Press, Adelaide, SA, 2011).
43 Prue Taylor "Ecological Integrity, Responsibilities and Rights: Insights from *The Imperative of Responsibility* by Hans Jonas" in Laura Westra and Klaus Bosselmann (eds) *Reconciling Human Existence with Ecological Integrity* (Earthscan, London, 2008); Christopher Stone "Should Trees Have Standing? Towards Legal Rights for Natural Objects" (1972) 45 *Southern California Law Review* 450.
44 Peter Burdon, above n 43.
45 Catherine Iorns Magallanes "From Rights to Responsibilities Using Legal Personhood and Guardianship for Rivers." Chapter 14 (pp. 233–234) of this book.
46 Peter Burdon "A Constructive Critique of Environment Human Rights" (Paper presented to Environmental Human Rights Conference, Costa Rica, 2013).
47 Catherine Iorns Magallanes "From Rights to Responsibilities Using Legal Personhood and Guardianship for Rivers." Chapter 14 (pp. 233–234) of this book.
48 Peter Burdon, above n 43.
49 Jules Cashford "Dedication to Thomas Berry" in P. Burdon, above n 49, at 7.
50 Ibid. at 268.
51 *Huakina Development Trust v. Waikato Valley Authority* [1987] 2 NZLR 188 (HC).
52 *Paki v. Attorney General* [2012] NZSC 50, [2012] 3 NZLR 277.
53 Edward Taihākurei Durie "Indigenous Law and Responsible Water Governance" (Tun Suffian Memorial Lecture, Kuala Lumpur, 26 September 2017); E.T. Durie and others "Ngā Wai o te Māori. Na Tikanga me Ngā Ture: The Waters of the Māori: Māori Law and State Law" (paper prepared for the New Zealand Māori Council, 2017).
54 Edward Taihākurei Durie "Ka Te Rangikaheke Raua ko Pirihira" in Gary Williams and Betsan Martin (eds) *Responsible Governance of Watersheds* (RESPONSE Trust, Waikato, 2010) at 33.
55 Pierre Calame. *Essay on Oeconomy*. Published by Editions Charles Léopold Mayer, Paris, 2009. Translated from French by Michael C. Behrent, except for the table of contents, translated by Ethan Rundell.
56 Joseph Sax "The Public Trust Doctrine in Natural Resource Law: Effective Judicial Intervention" (1970) 68 *Michigan Law Review* 471.
57 Jeroen Veldman and Filip Gregor and Page Morrow. 'The Purposeful Corporation Project.' Corporate Governance for a Changing World, Report of a Global Roundtable Series. Cass Business School, University of London. 2016.
58 United Nations Intergovernmental Panel on Climate Change. Fifth Assessment Report 2014.
59 Intergovernmental Science-Policy Ptatform on Biodiversity and Ecosystem Services. www.ipbes.net
60 Johan Rockstrõm et al. 'A Safe Operating Space for Humanity', *Nature* 461, pp. 472–475. 2009.

Will Steffan et al. 'Planetary Boundaries: Guiding Human Development on a Changing Planet'. *Science* 13. February 2015: Vol 347. No 6223.

61 Reference also to the Universal Declaration of Responsibility for an Interdependent World, prepared by the Alliance for Responsible and Sustainable Societies originally in 2014, edited in 2017. http://base.alliance-respons.net/docs/_eng_udir_decl_interdependence_responsibility17.pdf

62 Rakato Te Rangiita Oral communication. August 2017.
63 Jorge Vinuales “In Our Hands. The legal organization of the Anthropocene.” Presentation at ‘Right Use of the Earth’ Conference, École Normale Superiéure, Paris, France May 2018.
64 National Assembly of France. Assemblée Nationale. Constitution du 4 Octobre 1958. Session Ordinaire de 2016-2017, 21 Février 2017. Proposition de loi relative au devoir de vigilance des sociétés mères et des entreprises donneuses d’ordre. http://www.assemblee-nationale.fr/14/pdf/ta/ta0924.pdf.
English reference: <https://business-humanrights.org/en/french-duty-of-vigilance-law>.
65 Adrian Macey. Chapter 7 (p. 119 ff) of this book.
66 Marie Brown *Last Line of Defence* (Environmental Defence Society, New Zealand, 2016).
67 David Grinlinton and Prue Taylor (eds) *Property Rights and Sustainability* (Brill, Leiden, 2011) at 4.
68 Clair Browning “Why the ‘Public Trust’ Should Be at the Heart of an Overhaul of NZ Environmental Rules” *The Spinoff* (May 22, 2017).
69 *Ola kai Wai: A Legal Primer for Water Use and Management, Hawai‘i* (Ka Huli Ao Center for Excellence in Native Hawaiian Law, Hawai‘i, 2009) at 4.
70 Kapua Sproat and Mahina Tuteur. Chapter 13 (pp. 193, 194, 196) of this book.
71 Hawai‘i Revised Statutes (HRS) §174C–101(c). Retrieved from <http://lrbhawaii.org/con/conart11.html>. See also Sproat and Tuteur, Chapter 13, Endnote 22.
72 Joseph Sax “The Public Trust Doctrine in Natural Resource Law: Effective Judicial Intervention”, n 56.
73 Hawai‘i Revised Statutes (HRS) § 174C–101(c).
74 Coal-mines Act Amendment Act 1903, 3 Edw VII.
75 C.M. Rose “Joseph Sax and the Idea of the Public Trust” <http://digitalcommons.law.yale.edu/fss_papers/1805>.
76 *Te Awa Tapua* (Whanganui River Claims Settlement) Act 2017, s 7.
77 This is discussed more fully by Catherine Iorns Magallanes in Chapter 14 of this book.
78 Dinah Shelton “Nature as a Legal Person” *VertigO la revue électronique en sciences de l’environnement*. Horssérie 22, Septembre 2015, La représentation de la nature devant le juge: approaches comparative et prospective at 28.

2 Reclaiming the global commons

Towards earth trusteeship

Klaus Bosselmann

Introduction

This chapter offers some ideas about the global commons – the polar regions, the oceans, the atmosphere and outer space – and how they can be reclaimed under a system of governance based on trusteeship. States, driven by their national interests, have been largely resistant to accepting responsibility for the global commons and the earth system.[1] Essentially, the political focus needs to shift from nation-states (and their often competing interests) to the earth as a whole, describing a system of governance that can be termed "Earth governance".[2]

Earth governance proclaims a shift from state-centred governance to multi-actors governance. This still involves states, but not exclusively. The new approach emphasises the role of the citizen rather than the nation-state as the source of governance. In a democracy, governance is rooted in citizenship; hence, consensus building ultimately resides with citizens, not with governments. It is appropriate, therefore, to perceive of governments as trustees acting for, and on behalf of, citizens as beneficiaries.[3] In the Anthropocene, citizenship has ecological and global dimensions,[4] which calls for transnational processes of forming the collective will. In this way, we can perceive earth, not states, as the common reference point and develop a strong sense of stewardship or guardianship for the global commons.

The chapter makes the case that states can – and must – accept fiduciary duties for the global commons.

Reclaiming earth: the global commons

One prominent example of the global commons is the atmosphere. Intuitively, the atmosphere belongs to all living things, including humans, as our well-being and existence depends on a relatively stable climate system. The problem here is that, currently, the atmosphere is being treated as an open access resource without any legal status; it is widely regarded as *ius nullius*, that is, a legal nullity or vacuum. This has worked to the advantage of property owners who have filled the vacuum by exercising their property rights over it. Property rights may not include a right to pollute, but the absence of someone who could claim violation of own rights means that actual pollution goes without any sanction. In fact, it is free of any restriction. Any person or, indeed, the entire fossil fuel industry can freely emit greenhouse gases into the atmosphere simply because nobody's property rights are affected. This is the status quo. It will only be qualified if and as far as the law sets rights-limiting emissions standards. To date, engaging the law in this way has been an uphill battle, which has not been made any easier merely by having the Paris Agreement[5] (which still requires further negotiation refinement).

However, the battle may still be won and the solution is quite simple. If civil society asserts common ownership of the atmosphere, the institutions of law will start to work in society's favour. As legal owners, members of society can charge for damage of the common property, provide rewards to those who protect it (for example, producers and users of renewable energy) and in this way eliminate greenhouse gases. All that is required is a concerted insistence on the protection of public common goods from the fossil fuel industry and their supporters (states, banks, corporations). Positively speaking, private property rights or state sovereignty continues to exist, but only to the point where common property begins.

This is a very simple mechanism and could, for example, be supported by the well-established public trust doctrine. The public trust doctrine says that natural commons should be held in trust as assets to serve the public good. It is the responsibility of the government, as trustee, to protect these assets from harm and ensure their use for the public and future generations. So, nationally, the government would act as an environmental trustee; internationally, states would act jointly as trustees for the global commons, such as the atmosphere. Considering that only about 90 companies are responsible for two-thirds of the carbon emitted into the atmosphere, a global trusteeship institution could quickly fix the problem of climate change.[6]

The idea of global nature's trusts has been promoted by environmental lawyers Mary Wood[7] and Peter Sand[8] and economist Peter Barnes.[9] More recently, the global petition "Claim the Sky" was started by Robert Costanza[10] with support from the Club of Rome and many other institutions and individuals. And, in April 2017, the "Planetary Integrity Project"[11] announced a proposal for "Earth Trusteeship" at a meeting of the United Nations General Assembly to be presented to the United Nations (UN).[12] Trusteeship governance is also advocated by the rich literature on the global commons.[13] The "Reclaiming the Commons" movement has gained traction in recent times.

A strong case can be made to suggest that international law and the UN are not only in need of, but practically ready to develop, institutions of trusteeship governance. There is, for example, a tradition of UN institutions with a trusteeship mandate including the (now defunct) UN Trusteeship Council, the World Health Organisation (WHO) with respect to public health and, ironically, also the World Trade Organisation (WTO) with respect to free trade.[14] A number of other UN or UN-related institutions with weaker trusteeship functions also exist.[15] Quite obviously, states have been capable, expressly or implicitly, of creating international trusteeship institutions. These developments – and in particular the existence of supranational organisations such as the European Union – demonstrate that sovereignty of states can be transferred to international levels. The underpinning motives are not particularly of a legal nature, but rather more driven by politics. And politics are driven by moralities that presently favour exploitation. But, moralities can change. By insisting on the common good, civil society can reclaim lost ground and rebuild democracy.

A combination of ethically motivated activism and new political alliances, for example between particularly motivated progressive states, can make a crucial difference. Chances are that this combination will become very powerful as our global ecological, financial, political and democratic systems continue to disintegrate.

One major stumbling block in the way of trusteeship for the global commons lies in the states themselves. Will they be ready and able to act as trustees? Trusteeship governance is not something that should be initiated from the "top", that is by the UN and its member states, but rather engendered by forces outside the system, in particular global civil society. The groundwork laid down by many years of activism and proposals for institutional change provide the starting point. Nor should states be in sole charge of administering, managing and controlling global trusteeship institutions such as a World Environment Organisation or a Global Atmospheric Trust. Rather, trusteeship governance should be seen as a joint effort of the UN, states and civil society organisations with an equal say in decision-making.

Sovereignty and trusteeship

There is, at present, an unholy alliance between politics ("sovereignty") and private interests ("property") severely undermining democratic processes and the public concern for safeguarding the global commons. Furthermore, as Barnes points out, "[n]ot even seated at democracy's table – not organized, not propertied, and not enfranchised – are future generations, ecosystems, and nonhuman species."[16]

The practice of state governance in times of economic neoliberalism has affected how environmental policies and laws are conceived, largely, as entirely discretionary and located somewhere between resource exploitation and environmental protection. Mary Wood calls this a "discretionary frame",[17] which means that governments see themselves as perfectly entitled to give priority to short-term resource exploitation over long-term resource conservation.[18] Environmental commons are perceived as "government-owned" but without any concern for future generations, nonhuman species or even ordinary citizens.[19] In fact, over the last few decades, commons such as forests, water and energy have been privatised and commercialised in most countries.

It is obvious that "governance" today is about a quid pro quo, symbiotic relationship between political institutions and corporations.[20] The rewards include property rights, friendly regulators, subsidies, tax breaks, and free or cheap use of the commons. This leaves very little for the "common" good. In the words of Peter Barnes:[21]

> we face a disheartening quandary here. Profit-maximizing corporations dominate our economy. Their programming makes them enclose and diminish common wealth. The only obvious counterweight is government, yet government is dominated by these same corporations.

Fundamentally, the legitimacy of the state rests on its function to act for, and on behalf of, its citizens. This requires consent of the governed.[22] Governmental duties can therefore be understood as fiduciary obligations towards citizens.[23] Such fiduciary obligations are recognised typically in public law,[24] exist in common law and civil law (although in varying forms and degrees)[25] and are also known in international law.[26] The fiduciary function of the state can also be described as a trusteeship function.[27]

The following section examines how state sovereignty can be reconciled with trusteeship. At first glance, both seem to have different purposes; however, they are, in fact, part of the same basic function of the state, to serve the citizens on which it depends and to whom it is accountable.

The environmental crisis and the state of the global commons give rise to the need for revisiting the relationship between sovereignty and trusteeship.[28] Trusteeship must be pursued at both the international level and the domestic "internal" level. As Eyal Benvenisti notes, the private, self-contained concept of sovereignty is less compelling than it was in the past because of the "glaring misfit between the scope of the sovereign's authority and the sphere of the affected stakeholders".[29] This "glaring misfit" engenders inefficient, undemocratic and unjust outcomes for under- or unrepresented affected stakeholders.[30] Non-citizens, future generations and the natural environment all fall into the category of "affected stakeholders".

Trusteeship for sustainability needs to be a ubiquitous principle at all levels of governance down to even the family unit, in the same way that other fundamental ethical principles, such as fairness, are implicit in all social lives. There are two challenges to advancing the idea of trusteeship and both are reducible to sovereignty. On the one hand, to propose a system of international trusteeship is directly to challenge the principle of non-interference in states' domestic affairs. On the other hand, to propose that states become trustees themselves, in addition to an international system of trusteeship, is again, an intrusion into states' sovereign right to determine their own approach to environmental regulation. However, without the latter we will not achieve the former. Regardless of what one thinks about the legitimacy of sovereignty and the entire makeup of international relations, the reality is that states are in the position of power and control. In the absence of a radical reorganisation of global politics, the state-centric context is the only available option.

The trusteeship model is a viable option for what would otherwise be seen as unprecedented intrusion into sovereign state affairs. Trustees are not states; a trust council might not even be an intergovernmental institution if its membership were comprised of individuals rather than drawn exclusively from states. Arguably, this represents a less threatening intrusion into sovereignty. After all, this is a type of intervention that was not envisaged in the UN Charter, but may be seen as desirable and legitimate.[31] As Catherine Redgwell explains:[32]

> trust arrangements do not challenge sovereignty directly, for one of the advantages of trusteeship arrangements is the absence of sovereignty in the exercise of trusteeship functions – there is no transfer of sovereignty to the trust authority.

But, what if trust arrangements were perceived as a significant intrusion into sovereignty? The many proposals of trusteeship arrangements at the level of the UN have been, more often than not, greeted with hostility. States seem too attached to the principle of non-interference to appreciate cooperation of this kind. Yet, the very origins of the concept of state sovereignty are closely linked with humanitarian concerns. The Peace of Westphalia, as the foundation of state sovereignty, was a key instrument for upholding humanitarian precepts relating to freedom of conscience and religion.[33] The treaty resolved a crisis of freedom of conscience and equality before the law; state sovereignty was thus justified even though many pre-existing institutions lost their legitimacy and ultimately collapsed. But it should also be remembered that humanitarian concerns were at the root of the crisis that the new order resolved. Where new crises emerge, can the principle of non-interference really be justified?

Similarly, the notion of the state itself as environmental trustee for those over whom it governs implies that a democratically elected government does owe its citizens a duty to govern their natural wealth and resources in a sustainable way.[34] The first step, then, is for civil society to recognise it is the owner of and repository for environmental rights and responsibilities despite the state acting as its representative. The second step entails convincing the consumer society of what these rights and responsibilities entail. This is no small feat.

Although there is a dedicated green movement, and ever more "lite" green sentiment, convincing people to alter their engrained, even unconscious neoliberal proclivities in favour of an ethic of stewardship and trusteeship is a very trying task, especially with the economic wind blowing in their faces. Without a mobilised civil society – a *demos* – that is willing to hold governments to account and demand that they represent their ecological interests internationally, states will continue to behave in the way they always have – reacting to the global environmental crisis according to the familiar conflict model of international law.

Fiduciary duties of the state

The only way to turn things around and move international law from the Westphalian conflict model to a 21st-century cooperation model is to re-define states as trusteeship organisations. Sovereignty and trusteeship must be seen as complementary, not mutually exclusive. The argument in favour of states as trustees proceeds as outlined below.

The state gains its legitimacy exclusively from the people who created it. While the legality of a state depends on recognition by other states, once in existence a state can only ever legitimise its continued existence through ongoing trust by its people. The core idea of the modern democratic state is that it acts through its people, by its people and for its people. This implies a fiduciary relationship between people and state and is arguably the only legitimate basis for political authority as demonstrated in the English civil war, the American Revolution, and then again confirmed in the French Revolution.[35] It is echoed in constitutional documents such as the 1776 Pennsylvania Declaration of Rights: "[A]ll power being . . . derived from the people; therefore all officers of government, whether legislative or executive, are their trustees and servants, and at all times accountable to them."[36] John Locke famously asserted that legislative power is "only a fiduciary power to act for certain ends" and that "there remains still in the people a supreme power to remove or alter the legislative, when they find the legislative act contrary to the trust reposed in them."

Likewise, Immanuel Kant drew the moral basis of fiduciary obligations from the duty-bound relationship between parents and children.[37] Kant claimed that children have an innate and legal right to their parents' care. In a similar sense, he believed that state legitimacy was the result of a contract that is necessarily created between people to form a Rousseauian "general will." Through this process, Kant claimed, we jointly authorise the state to announce and enforce law.

The notion that state sovereignty is fundamentally a trust relationship cannot be dismissed as a Western ideal; trusts and the implicit fiduciary relationship may be traced back to Middle Eastern origins and Roman and Germanic law as well as being inherent in religious teachings. The idea is perhaps even more prevalent in non-Western societies than present-day Western societies because the former emphasise collective identities (for example, family, clan, nation, religion) over individual freedom and dignity, imbuing implied fiduciary obligations into the structure of public and private legal institutions.[38]

Article 21(3) of the Universal Declaration of Human Rights states, "the will of the people shall be the basis of the authority of government."[39] But as Ron Engel points out, "democracy" can have differing interpretations. There is the "thin" interpretation which includes procedural democracy, liberal democracy, representative democracy, or simply put, the democratic process.[40] He explains:[41]

> In this view, the democratic ideal is a way of bringing free and equal but competitive individuals and groups (or "interests") into cooperative and stable relationships by such devices as constitutionally protected civil and political rights, limited government, basic fairness in the distribution of social goods, and opportunities for citizen participation in the formation of public policy through membership in the voluntary associations of civil society and voting in electoral politics.

Engel contends that the problem with this approach is that "its principle and narrative, while essential components of the democratic inheritance, are not a complete account of the moral and spiritual requirements of human self-governance."[42] The role of government is to act as conscientious trustee of the citizens' resources.[43] In contemporary market-based societies, governments fail in both the interpretation and application of what this means – a systematic failure of neoliberalism.[44]

So, although many states are democratic in nature, both governments and their people seem to have lost sight of the duties states owe to those they govern. At its most simplistic, the state's legitimacy to govern is based on its ability to serve the common interest. Aristotle saw the purpose of the State as for the "common good". John Locke also hinted at such a purpose. But, of course, who defines common good and what does it include? According to Locke's definition, the common good was what arose from there being surplus produce that could be sold in the marketplace. As Sheila Collins explains, Locke's

> definition of the common good is a quantifiable one, not a moral one. From this concept of quantity would flow the modern measure of the common good – the Gross Domestic Product – a poor measure of any society's real quality of life.[45]

But because "common interests" are socially conceived, they are not static and can be contested. The logical argument may then be made that new functions and responsibilities ought to become a part of a state's mandate to govern.

While the definition of the common good is an important issue, so too is the normative nature of the relationship between government and the governed. In current times a typical government perceives its role largely as a facilitator of economic growth, seen as analogous with "prosperity", and thus the protector of private property;[46] that is, the government subscribes to the belief that allowing individuals to pursue their own interests will result in the best possible social organisation. Few governments could argue that they do not owe a fiduciary duty to their constituents. Indeed, now more than ever, governments are scrambling to reduce deficits in order to fulfil their obligation to the public not to overspend. The problem is that states have neglected the ecological aspects of their fiduciary duty. And, the voting public have let them.

Benvenisti conceives of three other normative bases according to which we should ascribe a trusteeship function to states' mandates to govern. The first two grounds lend themselves most easily to the development of rights and obligations under a concept of state trusteeship limited to intra-generational concerns. A normative approach which grounds itself in global resource distribution may be more conducive to the realisation of state trusteeship according to principles of inter-generational equity.[47]

First, sovereignty should be viewed as a vehicle for the exercise of personal and collective self-determination.[48] Collective self-determination embodies the freedom of a group to pursue its interests, further its political status and "freely dispose of [its] natural wealth and resources."[49] An outdated concept of sovereignty which equates the voting constituency with only affected stakeholders can undermine communities' ability to exercise their rights to self-determination.

Second, Benvenisti refers to an understanding of sovereign states as agents of humanity as a whole.[50] He bases this conception largely on the equal moral worth of all human beings[51] and the corresponding foundation of international law in universal human rights. He argues that it is humanity at large that assigns to certain groups of citizens the power to form national governments.[52] Accordingly, states can and should be viewed as agents of a global system that allocates competences and responsibilities for the promotion of the rights of all human beings and their interest in the sustainable utilisation of global resources.[53] As such, the corollary of states' authority to manage public affairs within their domestic jurisdictions is an obligation to take account of external interests and balance internal against external interests.[54]

Similarly, it could be argued that the privilege of territorial sovereignty can be legitimised only as far as universal interests of humanity as a whole are not severely affected. This argument is based on ecological realities defying national state boundaries, but also on the observation that boundaries of states do not necessarily coincide with boundaries of nationalities, or more generally, with the boundaries of the groups whose members commonly share a distinct interest or conception of the good.[55]

Third, Benvenisti also refers to a conception of sovereignty as the power to exclude portions of global resources.[56] He notes that both ownership and sovereignty are claims for the intervention in the state of nature by carving out valuable space for exclusive use.[57] Such a perception of states as power-wielding property owners provides a solid normative foundation for the imposition of a positive obligation on states to take other-regarding considerations into account when managing the resources assigned to them.[58] Property law theory can thus provide a framework within which these moral grounds may be translated into legal obligations.[59] Accordingly, ownership of global resources can and should be conceptualised as originating from a collective regulatory decision at the global level, rather than as an entitlement of sovereign states.[60]

Despite agreement that a government has fiduciary duties, there is seemingly little readiness to establish a precedent of state *environmental* trusteeship.[61] What is generally unknown or overlooked is that the Magna Carta of 1215, the armistice in civil war between commoners and King John, "contained largely unappreciated calls against the exploitation of the forests as ordained by the king at that time." In a scenario potently familiar to many current governments, "the king wanted to degrade the forests to a source of lumber, convert the lumber into money, and invest it in those who promised him their loyalty."[62] The accompanying "Forest Charter" comprises landmark statements of commoners' rights. It included a statement of common rights of the forest (chapters 47 and 48), and the common right of the piscary, or fishing rights (chapter 33).[63] Yet in the 1870s, the champions of Anglo-American capitalism recast the Magna Carta to justify their imperial ambitions and racist politics. Certain portions of the Magna Carta have been celebrated and enshrined while other portions – especially those dealing with commoners' rights to the fruits of the commons[64] – have been portrayed as feudal relics and local "particularities". This gives rise to the question, if environmental trusteeship was a seemingly ingrained part of life around the world, why did this aspect of social organisation not get translated into state governance? The short answer is that emerging capitalism dramatically changed the fundamental viewpoints. It replaced nature, as the basis of everything, with money. In the course of unfolding the social order, the now unfettered capitalist governments and businesses lost interest in safeguarding natural cycles and ecological integrity. Only a blunt move to environmental trusteeship can change that.

Conclusion

Global commons governance reverses the traditional rule that international law and governance ends where national borders begin. The dichotomy between national law and international law defies ecological reality. States need to exempt transnational ecological aspects from the concept of exclusive territorial sovereignty, making way for global commons governance. Through environmental trusteeship at the state level, territorial sovereignty is conceptually restricted at the global level, leading to a paradigm shift in international environmental law. Instead of state sovereignty setting limits to environmental protection, environmental protection would set the limits to state sovereignty. Indeed, "limiting the self-interest of states by taking into account global concerns of humanity has become a fundamental aspect of international law."[65]

In political praxis, states are in a paradoxical situation. They cannot shake off the capitalistic logic of profits at all costs, even at social and environmental costs of detrimental dimensions. States may well want to avoid collective suicide, but they are as yet unable to resist the forces of global markets. These forces have heavily eroded state sovereignty – the same state sovereignty that is needed to resist complete dominance of global markets. The paradox of states surrendering sovereignty to free trade and market forces, on the one hand, and on the other hand insisting on sovereignty when they are expected to protect the commons, has been described as the "sovereignty paradox".[66]

The solution to the sovereignty paradox is differentiation; more sovereignty where possible, less sovereignty where necessary. In a globalised world this means protecting citizens and the environment from global economic forces (more sovereignty) and protecting the global commons through international rules controlling financial and economic markets (less sovereignty). The perspective of differentiated sovereignty, also referred to as "responsible" or "smart" sovereignty,[67] inevitably calls for reforming and strengthening global institutions. Nothing could be more urgent than matching political institutions to the global challenges that we face.

The drivers for responsible and smart sovereignty are not states themselves, of course, but real people: citizens, activists, advocates and decision-makers in a bottom-up approach called democracy. But this requires an idea of citizenship that operates at all levels, locally, nationally and globally.

This is also the only way to reclaim the global commons that is so rapidly being lost. Arguably, the concern for the global commons is a unifying feature of humanity. If civil society views itself as stewards of the earth and states as trustees of the common good, then this is a crucial step towards earth governance, perhaps then more appropriately called earth democracy.[68]

Notes

1 For an overview, see <www.iucn.org/global-commons>.
2 Klaus Bosselmann *Earth Governance: Trusteeship of the Global Commons* (Edward Elgar, Cheltenham, UK, 2015).
3 Ibid. at 155–197.
4 Ibid. at 42–45.
5 UNFCCC/CP/2015/L.9/Rev.1 12 December 2015 <https://unfccc.int/resource/docs/2015/cop21/eng/l09r01.pdf>.
6 Robert Costanza "Claim the Sky!" (2015) 6 *Solutions* 21.
7 Mary C. Wood "Nature's Trust: A Legal, Political and Moral Frame for Global Warming" (2007) 34 *Environmental Affairs* 577; Mary C. Wood *Nature's Trust: Environmental Law for a New Ecological Age* (Carolina University Press, Durham, NC, 2013).
8 Peter Sand "Sovereignty Bounded: Public Trusteeship for Common Pool Resources" (2004) 4 *Global Environmental Politics* 47; Peter Sand "The Rise of Public Trusteeship in International Law" (Global Trust Working Paper Series 04/2013) 21; Peter Sand "The Concept of Public Trusteeship in the Transboundary Governance of Biodiversity" in Louis J. Kotzé and Thilo Marauhn (eds) *Transboundary Governance of Biodiversity* (Brill, Leiden, 2014).
9 Peter Barnes *Who Owns the Sky? Our Common Assets and the Future of Capitalism* (Island Press, Washington DC, 2001); Peter Barnes *Capitalism 3.0: A Guide to Reclaiming the Commons* (Berret-Koehler Publisher, Oakland, CA, 2006).
10 Aavaz.org <https://secure.avaaz.org/en/petition/Claim_the_Sky/?pv=58>.
11 The Planetary Integrity Project (PIP) is an interdisciplinary collaboration between several universities, research centres and non-governmental organisations <http://planetaryboundariesinitiative.org/>.
12 Klaus Bosselmann "The Next Step: Earth Trusteeship" (Address to the United Nations General Assembly, 21 April 2017) <http://harmonywithnatureun.org/>.
13 See for example, David Bollier *Think Like a Commoner: A Short Introduction to the Life of the Commons* (New Society Publishers, British Columbia, 2014); David Bollier and Burns Weston *Green Governance: Ecological Survival, Human Rights and the Law of the Commons* (Cambridge University Press, Cambridge, 2013); Silke Helfrich and Jörg Haas (eds) *The Commons: A New Narrative for Our Time* (Heinrich Böll Stiftung, Berlin, 2009).
14 Bosselmann, above n 2, at 198–232.
15 Ibid. at 206.
16 Barnes, *Capitalism 3.0*, above n 9, at 38.
17 Wood, "Nature's Trust", above n 7.
18 Ibid. at 592.
19 Barnes, aboven 9, at 43.
20 Ibid. at 37.
21 Ibid. at 45.
22 John Locke wrote: "[G]overnment Is Not Legitimate Unless It Is Carried on With the Consent of the Governed" in R. Ashcraft (ed) *John Locke: Critical Assessments* (Routledge, Oxford, 1991) at 524.
23 Evan Fox-Decent *Sovereignty's Promise: The State as a Fiduciary* (Oxford University Press, Oxford, 2012); Tamar Frankel "Fiduciary Law" (1983) 71 *California Law Review* 795.

24 Including constitutional law, administrative law, tax law, criminal law and environmental law.
25 For example, the United States, Canada, Australia and New Zealand recognise them with respect to indigenous peoples and ratepayers and (with the exception of New Zealand) in the form of public trusts, whereas continental European countries more fundamentally rely on public law to assume fiduciary relationships between individuals and governments.
26 Michael Blumm and Rachel Guthrie "Internationalizing the Public Trust Doctrine" (2012) 45 *UC Davis Law Review* 741; Henry Perritt "Structures and Standards for Political Trusteeships" (2004) 8 *UCLA Journal of International Law and Foreign Affairs* 391; Edith Brown Weiss "The Planetary Trust: Conservation and Intergenerational Equity" (1984) 11 *Ecology Law Quaterly* 495.
27 Paul Finn "The Forgotten 'Trust': The People and the State" in Malcolm Cope (ed) *Equity: Issues and Trends* (Federation Press, Sydney, 1995) at 131–151.
28 Stephen Stec "Humanitarian Limits to Sovereignty: Common Concern and Common Heritage Approaches to Natural Resources and Environment" (2010) 12 *International Community Law Review* 361 at 384–385 and 378–380.
29 Eyal Benvenisti "Sovereigns as Trustees of Humanity: On the Accountability of States to Foreign Stakeholders" (2013) 107 *American Journal of International Law* 295 at 301.
30 Ibid.
31 Ilias Bantekas *Trust Funds Under International Law: Trustee Obligations of the United Nations and International Development Banks* (TMC Asser Press, Den Haag, 2009) at 19.
32 Catherine Redgwell "Reforming the UN Trusteeship Council" in W. Bradnee Chambers and Jessica F. Green (eds) *Reforming International Environmental Governance: From Institutional Limits to Innovative* (United Nations University Press, Tokyo, 2005) at 179.
33 Stec, above n 28, at 378–380.
34 See for example "Declaration on Permanent Sovereignty Over Natural Resources" (1962) *GA Res* 1803, XVII.
35 W. Michael Reisman "Sovereignty and Human Rights in Contemporary International Law" (1990) 84 *American Journal of International Law* 886 at 867.
36 Evan Criddle and Evan Fox-Decent "A Fiduciary Theory of Jus Cogens" (2009) 34 *Yale Journal of International Law* 331; Pennsylvania Constitution of 1776, article IV.
37 Ibid. at 352.
38 Ibid. at 378–379.
39 "Universal Declaration of Human Rights" *GA Res* 217 A(III) (adopted 10 December 1948).
40 Ron Engel "Contesting Democracy" in Ron Engel, Laura Westra and Klaus Bosselmann (eds) *Democracy, Ecological Integrity and International Law* (Cambridge Scholars Publishing, Newcastle Upon Tyne, 2010) at 28.
41 Above n 28.
42 Ibid. at 31.
43 David Bollier "The Commons: A Neglected Sector of Wealth Creation" in Silke Heinrich (ed) *Genes, Bytes and Emissions: To Whom Does the World Belong?* (Heinrich Böll Stiftung, Berlin, 2008); Peter Barnes, Jonathan Rowe and David Bollier *The State of the Commons 2003/04: A Report to Owners* (Tomales Bay Institute, Point Reyes Station, 2004).
44 Bollier "The Commons", above n 43.
45 Sheila Collins "Interrogating and Reconceptualizing Natural Law to Protect the Integrity of the Earth" in L. Westra, K. Bosselmann and R. Westra (eds) *Reconciling Human Existence With Ecological Integrity* (Earthscan, London, 2008) at 455.
46 Ibid.
47 As initially expounded by Edith Brown-White, see Edith Brown White "The Planetary Trust: Conservation and Intergenerational Equity" (1984) 11 *Ecology Law Q* 495.

48 Benvenisti, above n 29, at 301.
49 "International Covenant on Civil and Political Rights" 999 *UNTS* 171 (adopted 16 December 1966, entered into force 23 March 1976), article 1.
50 Benvenisti, above n 29, at 305.
51 Ibid. at 305, referring to John Stewart Mill *Considerations on Representative Government* (1861).
52 Benevisti, above n 29, at 306.
53 Ibid. at 308, paraphrasing Huber in *Island of Palmas (Netherlands v. United States)* 1928 2 RIAA 829 at 869.
54 Ibid. at 308, paraphrasing Huber in *British Claims in the Spanish Zone of Morocco (Spain v. United Kingdom)* (1925) 2 RIAA 615 at 641.
55 Chaim Gans *The Limits of Nationalism* (Cambridge University Press, Cambridge, 2003).
56 Benvenisti, above n 29, at 308.
57 Ibid. at 308.
58 Ibid. at 309 and 310. Also when making rival claims on transboundary and public resources.
59 Klaus Bosselmann "Property Rights and Sustainability: Can They Be Reconciled?" in David Grinlinton and Prue Taylor (eds) *Property Rights and Sustainability: The Evolution of Property Rights to Meet Ecological Challenges* (Martinus Nijhoff, Leiden, 2011) at 23–42.
60 Benvenisiti, above n 29, at 309.
61 See generally Bosselmann, *Earth Governance*, above n 2, at 155–197. and KlausBosselmann *The Principle of Sustainability: Transforming Law and Governance* (2nd ed, Routledge, Oxford, 2016) at 145–174.
62 Silke Helfrich "Commons: The Network of Life and Creativity" in Heinrich (ed) *Genes, Bytes and Emissions*, above n 42, at 1.
63 Ibid. at 1.
64 Nicholas Robinson "The Charter of the Forest: Evolving Human Rights in Nature" (2014) Pace Law Faculty Publications <http://digitalcommons.pace.edu/cgi/viewcontent.cgi?article=1988&context=lawfaculty>.
65 See above n 28, at 364.
66 Inge Kaul "Meeting Global Challenges: Assessing Governance Readiness" in Hertie School of Governance (ed) *Governance Report 2013* (Oxford University Press, Oxford, 2013) at 33–34.
67 Ibid. at 34–58.
68 Klaus Bosselmann "Earth Democracy: Institutionalizing Ecological Integrity and Sustainability" in Ron Engel, Laura Westra and Klaus Bosselmann (eds) *Democracy, Ecological Integrity and International Law*, above n 40, at 319–330.

3 Responsibility, state and international law

Pierre Calame

Responsibility, law and governance

In 2014, the Collège de France launched a dialogue with prominent international jurists from the United States, Brazil, China and France in a programme called "Taking Responsibility Seriously".[1] This programme was designed to develop legal recommendations for the 21st Conference of Parties (COP21) negotiation on climate change based on three premises: first, international law and legal systems have not kept pace with the reality of the challenges facing society as epitomised by climate change; second, international and national legal systems need to undergo a transformative process to be able to respond to global societal challenges; and third, "responsibility" is a lynchpin in transformative change and even though it has been at the core of legal systems for centuries, it has not received the acknowledgment it deserves.

This chapter further considers these aspects under the following four headings: (1) An historical perspective of the discovery of the decisive role the responsibility principle is likely to play in forthcoming international regulation; (2) Deficiencies in current international law and the need to take a broader vision of the international regulation in order to fill the gaps; (3) Recent developments in law and governance which align with the responsibility principle. The ongoing process of constitutionalisation of laws and the relevance of the responsibility approach in accordance with this constitutionalisation, illustrated by cases for the protection of children and food security; and (4) Commentary on the draft of a Universal Declaration of Human Responsibilities.

An historical perspective: responsibility and international regulations

Traditionally, there has been a tendency to reduce international regulation to international law and inter-state relations. This cannot be the case anymore. Other major global players have emerged: transnational corporates, large financial institutions, and international non-governmental organisations, some of which are more powerful than states themselves. There are also many other forms of regulation than international conventions. Consequently, international law should be regarded as one integral part of a more comprehensive global governance paradigm. In an interdependent planet with transnational actors, international law should deal with all stakeholders whose impact extends beyond national borders.[2]

Some 20 years ago, humanity's difficulty in facing present and coming challenges was first recognised. It has now become patently clear that, during the next decades, humanity will have to undertake a significant systemic transition towards sustainable societies. Global regulation is but one part of this challenge; extensive change is required, from individual behaviours and modes of life to a new vision of economy and governance and new ethics. But, the creation of new international regulation will be a very important component of this global transition.

What form should international regulation take? Over the last 40 years the world order has actually faced a contradictory situation. There has been dramatic growth of global interdependencies, among societies with the globalisation of trade, economy and finance, and between humanity and biosphere. To balance this, there needed to be a corresponding increase in the strength, scope and efficiency of global governance. However, this has not happened to any significant degree, despite the signing of a number of international agreements. One view is that the consensus which presently prevails within the United Nations (UN) upholds the exclusive sovereignty of states, except for European Union member states, and that it is this very consensus that has been a major obstacle to any substantive progress. But the fact that there is resistance to the development of stronger global governance indicates that present governance is generally deemed neither legitimate, nor democratic, nor efficient. As long as this contradiction remains unresolved, future development will be difficult.

Four components are required to build the necessary level of global governance. First, global regulation has to be recognised as a response to the need to manage the common good, which is of importance to all humanity and which cannot be managed separately by different nations. Climate, and more broadly stewardship of the planet, health, science and technology, among other things, are examples of common goods. The mutual recognition that the survival of the common good demands cooperative management outweighs the resultant diminution of states' sovereignty and autonomy.

Second, despite our increasingly globalised world with flows of goods, services, information and money across the continents, there is little real sense of a unified community (information, goods and services are traded and shared but only at a superficial level). While some talk about a "global village", the famous sociologist Edgar Morin at the opening ceremony of the World Citizens Assembly, in December 2001 –says that it is a village without rules, justice and reciprocity. The sense of belonging to one greater community is an anthropological leap forward from a regime of opposing nations, which can only arise from a social process. Such a process was started in the 1990s, with the establishment of the Alliance for a United and Responsible World, which involved people from the different regions and religions of the world and from different social and professional backgrounds. The resultant dialogue demonstrated that what unites people is stronger than what separates them. However, the current trend in international affairs is focused on so-called national interests of nation states.

The third component is the agreement of common values inspired by the different cultural, religious and philosophical traditions which are fit for the coming challenges, that is, through sharing common values which are integral to the feeling of belonging to the same community.

Finally, there must be agreed mechanisms which enhance unity while recognising the importance of allowing diversity. This dimension of international regulation is often underestimated. Regulations which mandate uniform rules and behaviour, without acknowledging diversity of global contexts, ultimately prove to be unfit for all contexts and therefore lack legitimacy. One of the important consequences of a generalised globalisation is that there is no clear distinction) between what is considered domestic affairs and what is considered international ones. On the contrary, the new situation is better described by the concept of "glocalisation", encompassing both local and global. Actually, this is the reason why every serious global issue requires being addressed simultaneously at different levels, which means that coordination between those different levels becomes paramount. This is what is widely known as multi-level governance for which there must be dialogue between the different levels of stakeholders. European integration is a good example of multi-level governance: issues directly relating to the European Union and issues which are of a more national or subnational concern are dealt with at their respective levels without disrupting the system. In a way, it is the same with the World Trade Organisation (WTO); where China's entry has given rise to many domestic reforms.

Currently, the only common value agreed upon by the international community is human rights, which was adopted just after World War II by what was then the "international community" comprising mainly Western countries. The draft and endorsement of the Universal Declaration of Human Rights (UDHR) was initiated, in part, by a French jurist, René Cassin, and by Eleanor Roosevelt, the wife of a former president of the United States, and was undoubtedly inspired by the historical experience of similar declarations relating to the independence of United States and the French Revolution. Of course, the adoption of the UDHR by all the countries has assisted in significant progress being made in the recognition of human rights; however, not even the Declaration's staunchest supporters could deny that the concept of human rights is grounded in Western culture and is not fully universal.

It is often assumed that human rights could become the one overarching value, as it is said to be "universal." Unfortunately this is not so. As early as 1972 at the First International Conference on the Environment, it was acknowledged that UDHR could not deal with the relationships between humanity and the biosphere, and more broadly would not properly address the issue of global interdependencies.[3] As stated by the Belgian jurist François Ost, "responsibility is the hidden face of human rights" ("la responsabilité, face cachée des droits de l'homme"). Furthermore, in a multipolar world, Western countries cannot pretend to decide alone, as they did when drafting the UDHR in 1948. At the moment of the drafting of the Universal Declaration of Human Rights, in particular by René Cassin, the outcome was that Western countries would still, in effect, rule the world in terms of what is universal and what is not. These are the reasons why a truly interfaith and intercultural dialogue is required to discover what these universal values could be, allowing for the possibility that agreement may be impossible. Such a dialogue was initiated by the Alliance for a United and Responsible world during the nineties and this showed that such a dialogue can successfully identify the characteristics of such universal values. These may be broadly stated as follows:

- to be truly universal, the values should be found in different cultural traditions;
- they should help address issues of global interdependencies, among societies as well as between humanity and the planet;
- they have to be integral to human freedom and to orient individual choices, as well as underpin the exercise of power and the implementation of knowledge which regulates humanity's potential impact on the rest of the world;
- they must fit with what is generally called the new Anthropocene; an era when the impact of human activities on biosphere had become so great as to be an integral part of biosphere regulation, as is illustrated by climate change, atmospheric change, loss of biodiversity, acidification of oceans, and so on; and
- they must complement human rights.

Previous dialogue and research has found that there was one unique value compatible with these five criteria and it is responsibility.

Is responsibility found in any cultural tradition? The answer is affirmative because responsibility is an integral component of any community. Responsibility reflects reciprocity: broadly speaking, my impact on the other members of the community concerns me. Ultimately, responsibility is the conscience of the community as is reflected in legal systems: the impact of a person's actions outside of that community is not taken in account. One illustration is the cultural difference between communities which make a clear distinction between man and nature, the latter being not part of the community, and the cultures, often called "indigenous" or "traditional", for which the relationships between human beings and the rest of the living realm are "familial relationships" with the corresponding feeling of responsibility towards nature. The corollary of globalisation and the anthropocenic era is that the conscience of responsibility is now expanding to the whole of humanity and the whole biosphere. Thus, the search for common values satisfies the need to build the feeling of being part of one community. In that respect, what was considered traditional or outdated during the "modern age" might well prove to be valid in the Anthropocene. The famous jurist, Mireille Delmas Marty, convened an interdisciplinary seminar in February 2017 devoted to the law at the time of Anthropocene.[4] This seminar led one to wonder whether the present structure of law with its dramatic split between human beings as the "subjects" of the law and the "objects" of law including animals, plants and the living community, is not one of the reasons why humanity is losing control of its own destiny. The same principle may be applied to the word "economy", which until the mid-18th century used to be spelled "oeconomy". The latter spelling gave expression to the meaning of wise rule (*nomoï*) of our common home (*oïkos*). Over the years, humanity has forgotten this meaning and has acted as if economics were comparable to a natural science. The time has come to revert to oeconomy.

The role and scope of values in a society operate at three levels: at the level of individual behaviour, values orient and guide the resolution of ethical dilemmas; at the collective level, they guide the aggregated norms of different stakeholders and are the basis for the social contract which connects each stakeholder with the rest of society; and at the societal level, they are the ultimate reference for normative regulation and the legal system. In complex societies, human activities are interwoven. This means that individuals cannot be held to account for the subsequent impact of such activities and this is the reason why the responsibility principle, as it is now called, requires rules of co-responsibility.

The foregoing has dealt with the origin of the responsibility principle in relation with two of the four components of international regulations: a sense of belonging to one community and common values; now, it is appropriate to consider whether it is consonant with the two other components: dealing with common challenges and reconciling unity and diversity.

The management of global common goods not only calls for new rules defining the normative way of ensuring individual accountability for negative impacts on the common good but also calls for strong rules for the exercise of co-responsibility. To do this, both the responsibility principle and the exercise of co-responsibility must entail a normative value. This is the rationale for having a Universal Declaration of Human Responsibility which is endorsed by the international community as a third pillar of human values, which then aligns with the two existing pillars of international regulation: the United Nations Charter and the Universal Declaration of Human Rights.

The strength of the responsibility principle is that it meets perfectly the last requirement for international regulation: the reconciliation of unity and diversity. The dichotomy of unity and diversity is the main difference between duties and responsibilities. Duty implies compliance with precise rules; there is no room for diversity. On the other hand, the responsibility principle translates the unity requirements into general, common guidelines and the exercise of responsibility, at any level, will require the translation of these guidelines into specific conduct, as well as into public policies grounded in each specific context. For example, from the general principles of responsibility, as stated in the Universal Declaration of Human Responsibilities, it is comparatively easy to draw out more specific principles which fit to individual stakeholders, such as scientists, universities, shareholders, chief executives, inhabitants, and so on.

This ability of the responsibility principle to meet the four requirements of international regulation explains why it should be the pivotal principle underpinning the transition towards responsible societies.

Deficiencies in the present international legal system

A. The concept of the sovereignty of states does not align with global challenges

Far from being the way to solve global problems and manage the global common good, the concept of the sovereignty of states, the fundamental principle of the United Nations, has become a major obstacle to solutions. This is aptly illustrated by the international negotiations on climate change. The countries' Ministers of Foreign Affairs and their diplomats are leading the negotiations. This means that a country's climate, which impacts all the society and as such is altogether a global and (essentially) a domestic matter, is dealt with as if it were a foreign affair. And, the very nature of the negotiations is closer to traditional international negotiations, when diplomats had to confront and conciliate opposed "national interests" rather than seek consensus on the management of common goods. Climate issues are glocal that is, they are both local and global and they must be addressed coherently; they cannot be dealt with as a confrontation of conflicting national interests. National interests exist only because nations and states exist! If climate negotiations were structured in a different way, for example through dialogue rather than negotiation among the different stakeholders at a global level, then a completely different set of interests might emerge and the outcome would probably reach completely different results. The occurrence and content of such an international dialogue is not inconceivable. It is highly probable that the stakeholders would soon become aware that the gravity of global climate change issues requires far more vigorous measures than mere inter-state negotiations.

The Paris Agreement at the COP 21 witnessed a small breakthrough; for the first time all countries agreed to share co-responsibility in fighting climate change, thereby substantiating, for the first time, the "common but differentiated responsibilities principle" since the Rio Declaration in 1992. However, even the Paris Agreement had to water this down to a voluntary commitment from each individual state.

B. The deficiencies of current civil and penal laws

The second gap between the international legal system and reality of global challenges lies between the law itself and its implementation. This is especially apparent when considering international agreements relating to the environment and their actual implementation.

On one hand, there are no dispute settlement regimes comparable to those for the WTO, or to those that exist for the delimitation of maritime exclusive economic zones. And, states are generally not yet ready to sue one another for an environmental wrong, unless it has direct impact on their own territory, as illustrated by the litigation between Canada and the United States over the former's inability to control acid rain. In practical terms, no state can be, or dare pretend to be, the defender of humanitarian causes. When the Netherlands and Pakistan were (morally) condemned by their own national courts for their inertia in dealing with climate change, the actions were brought by civil society organisations, not other states. On the other hand, an examination of civil and penal laws' capacity to impose deterrent sanctions on wrongdoers reveals only ineffective systems.

Civil law may be deemed ineffective for three reasons. First, it requires identification of the specific interests which have been damaged by others' actions, and this does not allow for global harm caused by the same actions. Second, civil law is concerned with identifying damage caused and awarding compensation, but how could compensation for the destruction of the living conditions be quantified? Third, for some wrongdoers, such as major corporations or states, the payment of compensation is rarely viewed as a deterrent. In fact, if the wrongdoing is of a repetitive nature the probable quantum of compensation is likely simply to be incorporated into balance sheets.

The penal law requires proof "beyond reasonable doubt" and a causality link between an action and its impact. This standard of proof is not feasible in complex societies where actions are interwoven and not separable. A striking example of this occurred after the global financial crisis (GFC) of 2007, which resulted from irresponsible behaviours, largely driven by greed for profit by major financial institutions. None of the CEO's of climate inducing corporates have been held responsible for the crisis and been imprisoned. Similarly, few people responsible for the Global Financial Crisis (GFC) have been convicted and imprisoned, and these failures to attribute liability are partly attributable to the difficulty of proving the impact of individual behaviours on the global crisis.

The GFC illustrated that, in a new globalised world, irresponsibility has become the rule and not the exception. In the 19th century, the concept of the limited liability company was invented as a method of fostering entrepreneurship and as a means of separating the capital invested in a company from personal and family capital. It proved highly effective, but it has given rise to a culture of irresponsibility.

C. States are not the only actors requiring international regulation

The third weakness of current international regulation is that it defines the relationships between states as if they were the only actors in the global arena. However, over the last 40 years states have been challenged by the emergence of new, powerful actors on the world stage. These new actors include major corporations, financial institutions, territories, such as the autonomous development of the main megacities, and international non-governmental organisations (NGOs). These non-state actors are able to compete globally with states, sometimes to detrimental effect, especially in the financial sphere. NGOs, too, are much more likely to sue states which have failed to meet their international obligations.

D. The two existing pillars of international regulation are in jeopardy

The two pillars of international regulation upholding the international community are now in jeopardy, as they are incapable of addressing the major issues of the relationships between humanity and biosphere.

The first example is the role of the international community for keeping peace and security. The writers of the UN Charter had in mind war between states and dispute settlements between states. But most present conflicts are principally civil wars, even if each party to the conflict is supported by external states or organisations. Furthermore, the threats to peace and security come largely from non-state actors such as Islamist terrorists or drug cartels. This redefined conflict arena leaves the UN system unable to adapt its mission to deal with these new threats to peace and security.

Occurrences in Libya and Mali offer good examples of this point. A coalition of United States, English and French troops, under a vague mandate from the UN in terms of its "obligation to protect" principle, brought about the end of Gaddafi's regime in Libya. This mission could be counted as a success, but it resulted in two major consequences: first, it left catastrophic destruction in Libya, thereby contributing to the insecurity of the vast Sahara zone and the neighbouring countries; second, the intervention of Western troops allowed Gaddafi's African mercenaries to escape with armaments and munitions, contributing to the spread of insecurity and instability in different sub-Saharan African states. However, in international law, no accountability for these resultant tragedies can be sheeted home to the international community nor the leaders of the Western countries. In 2012, the crisis in Mali was a direct result of the earlier events in Libya. The deal between the personal guard of Khadafi, formed of sub-Saharan soldiers and the French President Sarkozy was: you let Khadafi in our hands and you are free to leave the country with arms and vehicles: they formed the core armed force of the Malian rebels The rebels, first Tuareg autonomists but, in short order followed by Islamic terrorists, were on the verge of taking control of an airport near Mopti, which would have opened the way to Bamako. The peace and security principles contained in the UN Charter were impotent in this situation. It was only the timely intervention of French troops which saved Mali from becoming an Islamic fundamentalist caliphate. The UN mission which was sent some months later and which was supposed to ensure the security of Mali was totally ineffective in the face of intermittent terrorist attacks.

The second pillar of the International Declaration on Human Rights is also in jeopardy. Over the years, the Declaration has spawned a number of international conventions expanding the original political and human rights to economic, housing and environmental rights. This is a good first step, but difficulty arises with enforcement. Political rights relate to political regimes, but the enforcement of economic or environmental rights calls for enforcement actors, in particular, at state or public authority level. In 1994, the President of the European Commission, Jacques Delors, launched a pan-European reflexion and I was in charge of the coordination of the theme on the extension of social rights in Europe. It became clear that claiming new rights was meaningless if there was no authority responsible for their enforcement. However, in most cases, this responsibility to make rights effective does not exist, thereby rendering the multiplication of "rights" mere lip service.

E. Non-state actors are unable to sue states

Another limitation of the present international legal system relates to the ability of non-state organisations to call the states to account via legal proceedings. However, such a process is possible within the European system; non-state actors may go directly to the European Court and this provides a powerful incentive for the member states to respect their obligations. The creation of the International Criminal Court was the result of joint action by NGOs and states. In 2016, a coalition of NGO's from Pakistan and Netherlands were able to have their respective governments condemned by a national court for their inertia in front of global warming. These court decisions mean that things have started to move in the right direction. In this way, comparative jurisprudence from regional and national courts may contribute to the development of international law, notwithstanding resistance from some states. It is part of the metamorphosis of international law, albeit that the change is slow.

The above five limitations can be viewed in the context of climate issues, as follows.

The case for climate change: an illimited irresponsibility

First, can anyone be held responsible of the rise of in sea levels, which is a direct consequence of climate change and which threatens, among others, the Pacific islands or a large state like Bangladesh with ecocide? The answer is, undoubtedly, no-one. There is neither a court in which to lodge an action nor a legal system within which the major emitters of greenhouse gases may be held accountable.

Similarly, the present climate change commitments of the international community have no legal consequences. In Cancun, at the 16th Conference of Parties, states agreed to limit the temperature rise to 2 degrees Celsius before the end of the 21st century. Five years later, it is obvious that measures taken by the different states to curb greenhouse gas emissions would still fall very short of this goal, even though the 2-degree limit was acknowledged as essential to preserve humanity from major climate catastrophes. Unsurprisingly, there are no legal repercussions arising from these failures to meet agreed deadlines.

In similar vein, the climate enjoys no legal status and there is no designated body responsible for this indispensable common good. Unlike the sea, in legal terms, the climate remains res nullius which impact can be caused by anyone without any legal consequence. Air and climate are different issues. Even though "space" is considered a common good, it is not the case for air. The only accepted disputes over pollution of air are among states with common border as was the case between US and Canada.[5] In 1991, Canada and the United States signed The Canada–United States Accord on transboundary air quality and pollution of the atmosphere and acid rain.

A fairly recent discovery has been the vital importance of ocean carbon sinks in arresting the increase in the average temperature of the planet. However, there are no readily identifiable legal owners and beneficiaries of these carbon sinks.

At best, perhaps the major emitters of greenhouse gases are the de facto exclusive beneficiaries of these sinks.

Recent developments in international law and governance which align with the responsibility principle

The foregoing picture drawn of the present international legal system provides a dispiriting summation of the status quo. However, even though the global legal system is evolving far too slowly compared with the reality of our interdependencies, it would be unjust not to acknowledge the positive developments that have occurred over the last decades. The implication of this is that even if the international community is resisting endorsing a Universal Declaration of Human Responsibilities on sovereignty grounds, the need to build this vital third pillar will remain a major goal for the formation of a truly global legal system, but it is not necessarily a prerequisite for the creation of such a system. It is now appropriate to examine the positive transformative processes currently underway.

A. Porosity between soft and hard law has steadily increased

The first development is the emergence of soft law and the connections created between soft law and hard law. Not so long ago, many jurists would have argued that soft law was not law at all, as law is mandatory and cannot be confused with the voluntary commitments which characterise soft law. But, this situation has changed over time. Control of laws for "private" interests are, in some countries through voluntary regulations such as for organic food or sustainable fisheries, whereas regulation under the control of ISO (International Standardisation Organisation) norms can often be stricter than mandatory laws. Under mandatory laws, control is often exercised by administrations that are under-resourced and more open to arguments based on economic interests and norms which have a negative impact on employment. It is the convention that such administrators should respect public norms of economic priorities, even to the extent of colluding in corruption. The endeavour to achieve accountability for social and environmental impacts of business through corporate social responsibility (CSR) commitments of corporations might once have been mere lip service and public relations-driven; however, as it becomes a part of the "contract" between a corporation and its clients, publication of non-compliance with these commitments may have serious reputational consequences. Knowledge of this may operate more as an incentive for compliance than any court-ordered penalty. Globally, soft law and hard law are finding some middle ground: the increased influence of soft law and a greater porosity between soft law and hard law – soft becoming hard and hard becoming soft.

B. The constitutionalisation of the laws

A second, interesting development is what some jurists call the "constitutionalisation" of the law. Until recently, written constitutions were generally considered to be instruments which confined themselves exclusively to the balance and devolution of powers of government. The preambles of those constitutions describe the major common values upholding those societies and are largely aspirational, as they are phrased in general terms. But things have changed in two ways. First, as stated in international seminar of jurists which took place in France in 2015, the role and influence of the courts with jurisdiction to deal with constitutional matters are more often using the preamble of the constitution as an aid to its interpretation, meaning that the preamble has become a major legal reference. Second, there are now opportunities for non-state actors, organisations or even individuals to seek relief from legislation that is seen as unconstitutional. This broadened view of the jurisdiction of the courts is perceived by some to be a threat to the sovereignty of the people. According to this view the sovereignty of the people is enshrined by law enacted by parliament, and is not under the jurisdiction of the courts.

The implications of these two developments should not be underestimated. They may be used to regulate either acts of commission or omission: regulating an act of commission may be the censuring of laws which do not conform to constitutional principles, and an act of omission permits the censuring of governments which do not act in conformity with constitutional principles. In other words, a government may be held responsible either for what it does or for what it fails to do. There is a clear juxtaposition between this and the responsibility principle.

C. A growing attention paid to "commons"

A third very pertinent development has taken place within the economics discipline. The Nobel economics prize was awarded to Elinor Ostrom for her pioneering work on the commons, which has brought increased global attention to this concept. A "common" is a good or service which benefits a community and which needs collective governance by that community. It falls within the Latin juridical concept of *res communis omnium*, which is broader than a "public good" capable of being administered by public authorities. The "commons" covers a very large spectrum of goods and services, from soil or water to knowledge and experience. It highlights the importance of cooperative behaviour, multi-stakeholder governance and elaboration of specific rules of governance to ensure a fair balance between contributions made to the maintenance of the common good and the benefits that may be acquired from its use. It is not difficult to imagine that the concept of public trust could open new avenues for the management of the climate or other public goods of this nature. Rather than international laws imposing obligations on the states, this approach allows for new kinds of regulation through the creation of autonomous governance of certain global common goods.

D. The co-production of public good

This new interest in the commons has also aided the development of the concept of governance. The notion of a common good lies between the interests of the market and the public good, the evolving concept of governance now allows that the common good can only be produced by the cooperation of different actors. This is what is called the co-production of the public good. In this environment, states and private interests cooperate to provide for the public good – another example which is aligned to the co-responsibility principle.

E. The growing trans-national regulation of trans-national corporations

The transforming regulation of transnational corporations also demonstrates elements of responsibility. Traditionally, companies or corporations would use their "juridical veil" to protect directors and stakeholders from liability to their foreign subsidiaries, contractors or subcontractors. This meant that those in charge of the corporation escaped personal responsibility for wrongdoing within the jurisdiction of their registered office. But things are changing quite quickly. Regrettably, though, this generally occurs because of some major catastrophe, such as coastal oil pollution caused by the *MV Erika* or the building collapse of the Rana Plaza in Bangladesh. Such disasters have given life to the concepts of "sphere of influence" and "due diligence". There is increasing recognition of co-responsibility along a supply chain. For example, the 2017 French law on corporate duty of vigilance (*devoir de vigilance*) requires companies to assess and address human rights infringements along their supply chains. This is another of the increasing porosity between soft and hard law, mentioned above. Via global campaigns to boycott goods and services, the general public has become aware of integrated supply chains and of the ultimate responsibility of the major corporations heading them. Both the wrecking of the *MV Erika* and the destruction of Rana Plaza gave birth to new jurisprudence, which has historical parallels with the development of welfare laws more than one century ago. The law of the duty of vigilance could become a more general European rule in the coming years, thereby enshrining a mandatory obligation for large corporations.

Another example is the Principles for Responsible Investments (PRIs), promoted by the United Nations Environment Programme since 2006 and the Organisation for Economic Cooperation and Development (OECD), which have dramatically grown in importance since the GFC. The PRIs have been endorsed by diverse asset managers with control over not less than 45,000 billion dollars. Presently, as in the case of CSR, this endorsement of principles, starting as mere aspirational lip service, is developing a new momentum for the responsibility of economic and financial actors. Using a clearinghouse approach, asset managers are increasingly conducting in-depth research on the companies and their supply chains in which they have shares. The creation of national focal points within states allows civil society organisations to present statements about corporations' non-compliance with the PRIs, and these place a moral and/or economic imperative on the corporation to respond. For any corporation, a loss of public confidence in its products or services can be more harmful than a fine imposed by a court. Consequently, corporations will often prefer to engage in conciliation processes rather than litigation. Furthermore, a company or asset manager who falsely claims compliance with the PRIs may be held liable for breach of contract and/or false advertising. The PRI guidelines are not normative detailed obligations; rather they are by nature closer to the responsibility principle. In endorsing these guidelines, corporations become responsible for creating their own processes for compliance.

Commentary on the eight principles of the Universal Declaration of Human Responsibilities

A critique often made about responsibility is that it is such a general principle that everybody can pretend to be responsible and that many governments call for responsible citizenship without showing comparable responsibility towards their citizens.

Over the years, the Alliance for Responsible and Sustainable Societies has worked to give depth and substance to the responsibility principle, largely through numerous inter-cultural and inter-professional dialogues. The Alliance has distilled the principle into eight detailed sub-principles. These will now be considered, particularly in relation to the search for international legal regulation of the climate.

1 The exercise of one's responsibilities is the expression of one's freedom and dignity as a citizen of the world community.

This first principle associates responsibility with membership of a world community. Linking responsibility with freedom and dignity clearly distinguishes it from the concept of duties. For example, many constitutions refer to the duties of citizens. This notion of duties is much more in tune with an authoritarian regime, where citizens are subjects of the state, than of a democracy where citizens are invited to exercise his or her responsibility as part of freedom and dignity. This is not to suggest that in a democratic state citizens have responsibilities rather than duties. Obviously, there will always be duties, such as sending children to school, complying with the law, and paying the taxes, but, generally, the more democratic a state is, the more freedom will be given to its citizens and the larger the scope of citizens' responsibilities.

2 All human beings have a shared responsibility to others, in close and distant communities, and to the planet, each proportionately to his/her assets, power and knowledge.

For many proponents of human rights, rights are on the side of the poor, and responsibilities are on the side of the powerful and the rich. This is disputed by many vulnerable groups who claim their own responsibilities, especially towards their own local communities, as these responsibilities are viewed as the expression of their dignity and citizenship. But, rights and responsibilities are complementary concepts; they are the two sides of the same coin. The scope of responsibility correlates to the amount of power, knowledge, and the potential impact on local and distant communities. In a democracy, governments are responsible to their electorates, and corporations are responsible to their shareholders. But, it is the gap which exists between the extent of the impacts and the consequences of the political and economic institutions which make our societies irresponsible.

3 *Responsibility involves taking into account and mitigating the immediate or diverse effects of all acts, whether or not they were voluntary and whether or not they affect subjects of the law. It applies to all fields of human activity and all scales of time and space.*

This chapter has already discussed the ability of the civil and penal laws to deal with damage caused to the climate. The damage-compensation approach is inappropriate for climate wrongs: everyone must share responsibility to avoid deleterious effects of climate change and not to just rely on the justice system to award compensation for damage caused to specific countries or human groups. The penal law concept of intent does not apply to the responsibility principle. Additionally, responsibility extends to all acts which affect a common good, which by their nature are recognised as legal subjects by domestic law. This extended understanding of responsibility is, in the author's opinion, better than assigning "rights" to non-human entities, as has occurred in some countries; for example, New Zealand has legislated legal personhood to a river.

4 *Responsibility is not subject to time limitation.*

Unlike some criminal offences, liability for responsibility is not subject to a limitation period. This is the case for what is usually called the "ecological debt", that is the impact of the industrialised societies, mainly Western societies, on the biosphere since the beginning of the Industrial Revolution. But, it is unjust to hold that societies have negatively or positively impacted the biosphere since the Industrial Revolution. Deforestation, loss of soil fertility, desertification or loss of biodiversity have been realities in many societies and even the cause of their ultimate ruin. But this sub-principle calls for the greatest attention to be paid to actions which may provoke irreversible effects. It is actually the situation with climate change. The precautionary principle is increasingly referred to and tends to be part of the common law. In the case of France, it is being incorporated into the Constitution. The precautionary principle calls for caution with respect to decision-making and to technological innovations whose potential effects have not yet been clearly evaluated. This principle is close to the responsibility principle as both address risk. But the same may be said about inertia: failure to act is as detrimental, especially for climate protection, as poorly evaluated innovations.

5 *The responsibility of institutions, public and private, does not exonerate their leaders of responsibility for wrongdoing.*

Current civil and penal laws target neither individuals nor institutions, but both of them. In the GFC, the distinction between the institutions and individuals was ineffective. Financial institutions, their executives and traders were enabled by moral hazard; that is, impunity for irresponsible and reckless behaviours. There is a recent apposite precedent, the case of BNP Paribas, the largest French bank. It has been fined USD 8.9 billion by a United States District Court for violating American embargoes against Sudan, Cuba and Iran: the actions giving rise to the conviction did not take place on American territory nor is PNB Paribas, an American company. This case is an example of truly extra-territorial application of the American law. If BNP Paribas refused to pay the fine, it would be banned from conducting business in the American market. The other interesting aspect of the judgment is that the court required that the executive officers responsible for the non-compliance be removed from their positions with the bank. The application of this fifth sub-principle of responsibility is likely to have considerable impact. It potentially means that the inability of some governments to take measures to curb greenhouse gas emissions could see responsibility sheeted home to those states and, more particularly, the heads of state.

6 *The possession or enjoyment of a natural resource entails responsibility to manage it to the best of the common good.*

According to international rules, the states have full sovereignty on the use of their own natural resources and can be only sued if this use has a direct negative impact on a neighbouring state. The responsibility principle involved here is the stewardship of the planet. This notion is aptly expressed in the well-known saying, "We borrow the planet from the future generations". This is what is also sometimes referred to as "functional ownership"; the biosphere in general, as well as specific natural resources, must be considered as part of a global common good and the owners of them as custodians for the sake of the whole humanity. This mindset represents a breakthrough when compared to the traditional idea of sovereignty, which acquiesces in the uses and abuses of natural resources by their owner.

7 *A state's exercise of power is legitimate only if it is accountable for its acts to those over whom that power is exercised and if it comes within the rules of responsibility.*

In democracies, legitimacy and legality are often confused. Generally, the phrase the "legitimate exercise of power" is referred to as soon as power is devolved in accordance with the constitution or other legislation. But, this is not the real meaning of legitimacy. Legitimacy of power carries with it the notion that this power is used in conformity with the common good. Even in authoritarian regimes, such as the former Chinese imperial regime, the emperor would lose his legitimacy, thereby justifying popular uprisings, if he had not been able to prevent his people from starvation. In our present day, power is only legitimate when it has been used properly in the service of the common good. This holds true even for governments which have been freely elected.

A similar scenario applies to the concept of justice. In 2017, a network of international jurists from the United States, France, Brazil and China and legal historians met to discuss the possible emergence of global principles of law. This meant confronting the different juridical traditions: Romano-canonic, common law, Chinese and Islamic. The convergence between these difference traditions is striking. In every tradition there is a clear separation between the "spirit of the law", which reflects core values, and the "law itself" which has to adapt to various situations. And, although precise formulations differ from one tradition to another (a feature of the responsibility principle), convergences are readily apparent. This finding signifies that the emergence of an international "spirit of the law" in a multi-polar and multi-cultural world is not out of reach. It is unlikely that the initiation of such a development will come from national governments, but it will evolve slowly. Thus, the link between legitimacy and compliance with the spirit of the law will become obvious.

8 No-one is exempt from responsibility either on the grounds of powerlessness, if no effort of cooperating with others is made, or for reasons of ignorance, if there is no effort made to be informed.

This last principle is of utmost importance in the 21st century. A useful example of irresponsibility may be found in the European rules for allowing new genetically modified organisms (GMOs) to be put on the market. The rules provide that a company should not be held responsible for any negative impact of this new organism if, at the moment when it had been put on the market, the company was ignorant of scientific findings about possible negative impacts. This is illustrated by the famous Séralini controversy [6] over Monsanto's GMOs, where Monsanto had restricted its studies on the impact of GMO consumption to short-term studies. This ploy of restricting the time span of research enabled the company to hold the view that three-months of testing was sufficient, even though was known that the most dangerous impacts of GMOs are the long-term ones. The same controversy continues to rage presently in Europe about the endocrine disrupters.[7] Furthermore, this limitation on the time frame of the research was exposed as enabling Monsanto to avoid the production of further scientific knowledge.

It is the same with the argument of powerlessness. No one state, organisation or person is able alone to deal with the climate change issue alone. This powerlessness argument would seem logically to imply that no-one then has responsibility for climate change or that it is enough to make a lone contribution. Responsibility is about building cooperation and looking for allies. After the Paris Agreement, there has been a concerted development by non-state actors, who meet annually to discuss climate change. The annual Conference of Parties is an example of the efforts being made by parties to assume co-responsibilities by joining together and gathering cooperative strength. The decision of some

American states, such as California, to not follow the Trump decision to withdraw from the Paris Agreement is another illustration of the new conscience of power and responsibility.

Constitutionalisation of responsibility

Globally, there is a move towards the constitutionalisation of the law, which is linked to the responsibility principle. Governments may be held accountable for the way they translate into practice the dutiful intentions included in the preamble of the constitution. However, a very important step forward should be to include the responsibility principle in the constitution, which would mean to endorse at the state or even sub-national level the Universal Declaration of Human Responsibilities or the eight sub-principles presented by the Declaration. It would be an original contribution to a complete renewal of governance. As described previously, responsibility means looking at the best ways to reach an objective, through multi-level governance and co-responsibility of the different actors in the producing of the public good, in consideration of the means at hand.

Who will be able to push forwards the Universal declaration of Human Responsibilities at the table of the General Assembly of the UN in order for it to be endorsed as the third pillar of the international community? Members of the Alliance for a Responsible and Sustainable World attended RIO+20 in 2012, and tried to use the opportunity to make a significant step in that direction. Unfortunately the Rio+20 summit took place in Brazil at a moment when the President Dilma Rousseff was much more concerned with the exploitation of huge offshore fuel reserves and was not giving her attention to the survival of the planet. The triumphalist conclusion of Rio+20 that "we succeeded in not going backwards" reflects the lack of ambition of the Summit. And, more generally speaking, there is one single motto on which all governments agree: sovereignty! And the Paris Treaty in 2015 has not been an exception. Therefore we cannot dream that all at a sudden governments will be "touched by the grace" and decide to acknowledge their responsibilité towards humanity. Nor does it mean that we are powerless. I do think that the trend towards a Declaration of Human Responsibility is irreversible and will follow many different processes. I can see many evolutions that go in that direction. A major one will be the endorsement of Charters of societal responsibilities by different stakeholders; just to take an example, the adoption of such Charter by the major pension funds could have a decisive effect. But we also need to have a significant group of countries take the lead. Leadership might come from a refounded European Union. The present crisis of the European Union has also a great advantage: it shows that the EU cannot keep doing business as usual and will need to redefine itself. Jerome Vignon, who was once the head of the prospective mission of the EU, was asked by a Chinese audience: "although there are huge differences of social organization between say Anglo-Saxon and Latin countries in Europe, do you think one can speak of a "European social model"? Vignon answered: "yes, finally there is something common: the idea of a social contract". And in many ways a social contract refers to co-responsibility.

As I documented all along this chapter, there are many ways through which we can go ahead, but with the condition of having a clear view of where we want to go. As the Roman philosopher Seneque would remind us, "there is no propitious wind for a sailor who does not know where he wants to go".

Notes

1 Mireille Delmas-Marty and Alain Supiot. Prenons la responsabilité au sérieux, PUF, novembre 2015.
2 Editeur : Presses Universitaires de France – P.U.F. Collège de France working group on international law.
3 Hugues Dumont, François Ost, Bruyant, 2005.
4 Collège de France, Paris. ISBN : 978-2-13-073259-4.
5 Wikipedia "U.S.–Canada Air Quality Agreement" <https://en.wikipedia.org/wiki/U.S.%E2%80%93Canada_Air_Quality_Agreement>. Accessed 20 April 2018. 430 pages – Parution : November, 2015.
6 Giles-Éric Séralini "Hidden Poisons. GMO's and pesticides" (2015) <www.criigen.org>; R. Mesnage, B. Bernayc, G.-E. Séralini (2013) "Ethoxylated adjuvants of glyphosate-based herbicides are active principles of human cell toxicity" (2013) *Toxicology* 313, 122–128.
7 "Farm Groups Threaten Legal Action if EU Fails To Decide On Glyphosate Renewal" *Farminguk* (October 20, 2017) <https://www.farminguk.com/news/Farm-groups-threaten-legal-action-if-EU-fails-to-decide-on glyphosate-renewal_47707.html>.

4 Public responsibility

A fundamental concept reflected throughout the ages; where did we lose the plot?

Gay Morgan

Introduction

The purpose of this chapter is to show that throughout most of humanity's recorded history around the globe, there has been a widely shared fundamental understanding of people's (and their governors') public responsibility to work for the common good, in conjunction with and sometimes to the exclusion of pursuing their own particular ends. It explores the development of these ideas in different historical settings around the globe, working its way to the modern era, as defined by the emergence of liberalism and liberal inspired thought. It then argues that liberalism, properly understood, also embraced the concept of citizens and communities' public responsibility to pursue the common good, rather than the more purely individualistic paradigm which is often attributed to it. It argues that this misuse or deformation of the actual liberal ideals occurred as of result of an accident of timing, as liberalism was emerging at the same time as colonisation and the corporate capitalism was being developed and used by colonising states, and particularly Britain, to encourage efficient extraction of value from their colonies. The divorce of investors' full personal responsibility to the community for the acts of corporate 'persons' led, by example, to eventual public acceptance that people had no positive duties and responsibilities vis-à-vis communal interests, but rather that person's responsibilities were to maximise their personal self-interest (neoliberalism). The nascent liberal philosophy was in essence hijacked by corporate capitalism to validate 'selfish' corporate and corporate owners' interests, promoting individualism (of the corporate person) as the point of living in community, rather than public responsibility as the core prerequisite for living in community. The chapter concludes with some recommendations and proposals to counteract corporate capitalism's negative impact on public responsibility as a fundamental shared social paradigm.

Conceptions of 'public responsibility' reflected in antiquity

When surveying the evidence available to us as to the common norms shared across societies in ancient times, one finds various natural law conceptions of human solidarity. These tend to reflect that a sense of shared responsibility for each other and for the common good were normative fundamentals. As will be discussed, this seems to be a shared narrative, threaded through much of ancient morality. One might think that such narratives could have been a result of communities facing more challenging survival conditions in those times, but a number of things militate against that explanation. One is that many such narratives arise from complex civilisations, where basic survival needs were not in daily question. A second is that those narratives tend to extend not just to the community, but, importantly, to all humanity. Sometimes those narratives also included elements of humanity's shared responsibility to protect the physical environment and other forms of life being considered as a natural duty. A very common theme was a focus on the responsibility of those in governance roles to assure the well-being of the common people, with the understanding that the well-being of the community and the safety and security of the society depended on that. In the current context of environmental degradation leading to climate and other disruption, which will inevitably have the most detrimental impact on the people with the least ability to 'buy' their way out, the ancient moralities would insist that those more advantaged and those charged with governance have a non-defeasible responsibility or duty to remediate the causes of such degradation.[1]

Some of the evidence for an ancient morality of state or sovereign responsibility to assure the well-being of the people and the environment can be found in Hammurabi's Code, a Babylonian code from ancient Mesopotamia, dating from about the mid-1700s B.C.E. That code required, among its more famous 'eye for an eye' edicts, that labourers be paid fair wages, and on time; it protected the ill and the weak from abuse and exploitation and set out restrictions on how land could be worked or used, reflecting a concern for both the well-being of the present common people and for the sustained sustenance of those of future generations. The Code also invited the oppressed to migrate to a realm that would treat them with concern and fairness.[2]

Another example is found in the Arthashastra, a treatise from ancient India on the science of politics, dated around 300 B.C.E. This text explained that there was a universal family of humanity and universal responsibilities not only to refrain from oppressing but also to take positive action to relieve suffering, such as providing public works projects and tax relief to help the people through hard times and protecting employees from abuse or exploitation by their employers. The text also sets out deep normative rules against harming any living thing, with those rules extending to the natural environment, with a flourishing natural environment being a prerequisite on which the well-being of all living beings depended.

The Arthashastra had explicit advice about the responsibilities of employers to pay a fair wage on time, as well as assigning to the labouring class or employees a responsibility to work. The responsibility to work was relieved if sickness, tragedy, etcetera intervened, and the responsibility to work did not extend beyond the contract period or to work on a project other than that which had been agreed. There was no responsibility to work without an actual, not just promised, wage, or beyond agreed periods. Interestingly, while the death penalty was to be used sparingly, one of the offenses for which the death penalty was advised was for fault-based harm to the water infrastructure (on which welfare and lives of entire community depended). For our purposes, it is even more interesting that the fault basis did not require any specific intent to harm the community's water infrastructure; rather, it seems to have been negligence or responsibility based, i.e., acting in a way that failed to take care to fulfil responsibility not to harm water infrastructure, and if such damage resulted as a side effect of 'a scuffle or dispute',[3] the penalty was still to be imposed. This commentary reflects an understanding that responsibility flowed in all directions, members of the community towards the community at large, from the governors to the governed, and from all of society towards the well-being of the biosphere.

A further example of an ethic of responsibility as a fundamental norm of ancient morality can be found in the Hebrew Bible. The norms of ancient Judaism as reflected in that Bible (written over quite a period of time, from perhaps the 700s B.C.E. through to very early in the C.E.)[4] reflect a deep belief in a universal family of humanity, i.e., that all people, the poor, the disabled, the foreigner,[5] are God's children whom he loves. Hence, it was everyone's responsibility to actively engage with all, Jewish or non-Jewish, as one would wish to be engaged with, and one can fairly presume that most people would wish to be treated with fairness and respect, not to be oppressed or for themselves, their children or their children's children to be left to live in poor conditions or in a ruined environment.

These writings also imposed a responsibility to feed and to provide water and succour to wounded or captured enemies, along with a responsibility not to steal enemies' property, nor to lay waste to their land. Whether this was because of a direct concern for the integrity of the land itself, as part of God's creation, or more likely because of a concern for the consequences of laying waste to land for the present and future generations, is unclear. The Hebrew Bible also allowed for sparing the lives and property of cities and citizens who surrendered to it, reflecting a notion of responsibility for the well-being of all humanity, even those with whom one had been at war.

Among other things, in regards to social justice, the Hebrew Bible imposed a restriction on farmers which reflects a sense of responsibility for the less fortunate as well as towards other inhabitants of our biosphere, and that was that farmers must harvest their fields only once. They were to leave the gleanings, what was left in the field from that one harvest operation, for the poor and the wild beasts. In a similar vein was the requirement that farmers must leave the land to rest every seventh year, a reflection of a sense of humanity's duty to be responsible stewards of the environment, not exhausting its resources but rather husbanding them for the future benefit of the whole community.

The general gist has been understood as setting out that the Jewish, as the chosen people, were as a people chosen for service to humanity, not for elevation above God's other children. Likewise, whoever was chosen as their ruler was responsible to promote the good of the whole people, by fair and just treatment, with duties not to oppress, not to kill, not to steal and so forth. So in this ancient morality, one sees positive duties to share what the earth produces with all inhabitants of the biosphere and to respect the earth itself by refraining from exhausting its resources, thus imposing a responsibility to future generations, as well as negative duties not to harm either the persons or the environment of other human communities.

Other evidence of ancient norms of public responsibility is provided by philosophers from ancient Greece. While the morality of the ancient Greeks varied in detail, there seems to have been shared themes. From the total devotion to (their own) community responsibilities required of Spartans to Athenian norms around the civic responsibility of citizens, one can see a shared fundamental idea that one was responsible to contribute to the well-being of the whole community (although just who counted as that community did differ concerning responsibility).

Dating from about the mid-4th century B.C.E., Plato's *Republic* and other writings reflect an ethic complete with communal responsibility. He proposes that there is (or should be) a reciprocal community responsible to make sure people are provided with roles that suit their talents, while the people of the community are responsible to fulfil their roles. Plato argued that the State had a responsibility to act temperately towards all humanity, as it was not to oppress or mistreat fellow Greeks and to treat all humans, barbarians included, as if they were Greeks. This thinking of Plato's of universal duties to all peoples is later echoed by Zeno of Citium's arguments of a universal humanity.

Plato's student Aristotle also wrote on what ancient Greek morality required in regards to communal life. According to Aristotle, justice required that those governing rule for the common good (whether or not in a democracy) and that any burdens imposed on the populace for such good should not be disproportionate, put proportionately shared by all. Aristotle was also very concerned that the ruler not rule or create law for self-benefit or for the benefit of the few, but for the benefit of all (citizens). He was also concerned, as mentioned, that the burdens to promote the common good not be imposed disproportionately, and that those burdens should not be imposed on those least able to bear them.[6] He too imposed a reciprocal responsibility on citizens, that their exercises of rights ought to be to the benefit of the whole state and in the interests of the city, not merely in self-interest.

Mentioned above, Zeno of Citium,[7] one of the two famous Greek Zenos, was born shortly after Plato died. Zeno of Citium, founder the Stoic school of thought, argued for the unity of humanity. He reasoned that there is but one shared human family and only one universal life; that we are all humans together and therefore we are responsible for each other.[8]

Returning to the East, at about the same period of time (slightly earlier, around mid-500s to mid-400s B.C.E.), Confucianism as well as other ancient Chinese thought considered it as the responsibility of the ruler to serve and to follow the mandate of heaven, which meant to promote the well-being of the people and not to engage in oppression. This thought held that a tyrannical or selfish ruler lost the mandate of heaven and was rightly opposed. Echoing the thought of the Hebrew Bible discussed above, Confucianism reasoned that as we all have similar desires, so we should treat each other as we would be treated.

While the ruler was not to oppress, but to rule benevolently, the responsibility of the people was to fulfil their roles faithfully and to develop their characters and abilities, as it was only the developed person who could truly well serve the community. As in Plato's thought, Confucianism requires a reciprocal balance of responsibility and self-development, along with respectful treatment of all people. Unlike many of the other paradigms discussed, the responsibilities to serve were to the community, not to humanity at large, although it advised that while a ruler has a responsibility to enlarge the realm, a wise one does this by running a well-ordered, thriving and just culture such that people will be attracted to it, thus attracting other communities to join voluntarily.

Nagarjuna's (Mahayana) Buddhism is another ancient morality from a slightly later period of antiquity (from 150–250 C.E.). This Buddhism reflected a deep commitment to the idea of a universal human family or even of a universal family of living beings, with all persons having the responsibility to pursue good actions and to relieve suffering of others. This is combined with a duty to refrain from harming any living thing or that on which it may depend for its flourishing and survival. This would translate directly to a responsibility on all to protect the natural environment and to remediate any damage done thereto.

According to Nagarjuna's Buddhism, the path to Nirvana was not (as a competing sect taught) a complete withdrawal from world affairs, but rather a middle way of sustained and detached (or, in other words, not self-interested) labouring dedicated to relieve the suffering of humanity. According to this conception of public responsibility, rulers as well as the unselfish individual on the path to Nirvana must work to alleviate suffering. To further this goal, it imposes on rulers an explicit responsibility to tax the wealthy to relieve the suffering of the poor and to provide the people of the realm with health care, wells, beds, ponds, water and parks; shelter for the disadvantaged (beggars and cripples); as well as hostels, food, grass, and firewood for travellers. All this must be achieved peaceably and without harming other living things or the environment.

Returning to the West, just before this time, in the 1st century B.C.E, in then contemporary Roman thought, Cicero promoted the Greek Stoic philosophy of universal natural law, Zeno's idea of a universal human family, and that the world was but one great, interconnected city. That everyone had the responsibility to treat all fairly, to oppress no one, and to not despoil the lands of the defeated (this may have been influenced by the utter destruction of the ancient and venerable city of Carthage about 50 years prior to Cicero's birth). Cicero lost his life opposing tyranny and argued not only for the republic, but for the responsibility of the rulers to promote and protect the common good, rather than to use their power for self-enrichment and self-interest. He also argued that each person had an obligation to attend to all things pertaining to world affairs and peace. Not long after this, early Christianity similarly advocated universal compassion toward the suffering, i.e., humanity's responsibility to care for all members of, at least, the human family, which included requirements to distribute wealth to those in need. Beyond this, it insisted upon the moral equality of all souls. In this view, early Christianity practiced and preached an ethic of communal responsibility.

Lastly, and although technically in the Middle Ages, Islamic texts and teachings also promoted the universality of the human family, the common origins of all beings and the universal responsibilities of all to feed, to house, to care for and to protect those in need. These likewise imposed a duty not to oppress nonbelievers, but did allow for violence if needed to protect Islam or Muslims from those who would harm either.

Thus one can see that narratives of responsibility of the state's responsibility to provide for the well-being of its residents and citizens, and their responsibilities to work to promote the common good of present and future generations, were not seen as oppressive or freedom infringing. Rather, they were seen as essential, and the right and proper way for humanity, or communities of humans, to organise and be governed.

Through the Middle Ages to the Enlightenment

The narrative of responsibility continued as the widely shared understanding and fundamental norm guiding systems of and thought about proper governance. The feudal systems of medieval Europe were explicitly based on reciprocal and interlocking responsibilities, to those governing to protect and provide, to those governed to serve and produce, responsibilities to and of the church and to future descendants. The worst fate, perhaps even worse than death, was to become an outcast, to be cast out of the system of reciprocal community responsibility, to be the responsibility of and responsible to no one; something often now portrayed as an idyllic situation was seen as a dreaded fate.

In the 1200s C.E., Thomas Aquinas, heavily influenced by Aristotle and Augustine, articulated what became Thomist thought and the prevailing Western doctrine on the appropriate responsibilities and duties of those living in community. As argued by both Aristotle and Augustine, it was deemed to be clear that citizens had no responsibility to respect unjust (or ungodly) laws. Augustine had opined that, nonetheless, they had a duty to accept their punishment for disobedience to those human laws contrary to God's (eternal and natural) law, as suffering poor governance was part of humanity's ongoing punishment for the fall of Adam, while Aristotle had argued those who made unjust laws deserved to be overthrown.

Aquinas accepted Aristotle's view that unjust laws included those which did not promote the common good, but rather promoted only special interests, or those laws that actually did promote the common good, but did so through disproportionate means. He specified that the disproportionality could arise through the over-burdening of those already burdened or through using means unacceptable to the conscience; he also wrote of the right, even the responsibility, to resist tyranny through whatever public means or authority were available, although he also cautioned that resorting to the murder of a tyrant went against Christian teaching. Aquinas was also a natural law advocate, that what is right or just is an objective fact existing outside the person, and that humanity, both citizen and ruler, had a responsibility to pursue right actions in alignment with natural law, while using Aristotle's teaching to provide much of the content of what natural law might require. Aquinas also taught that good governance included a responsibility to maintain a healthy and flourishing physical environment for the community's common good, both for reasons of assuring abundance and wise husbandry of resources.[9]

During roughly the same period (about 100 years earlier), the great Jewish philosopher Maimonides was teaching that our fundamental responsibility was to serve humankind, not merely ourselves.[10] During the same epoch, Islam and Buddhism continued to assert humanity's shared responsibility for the well-being of the community, as did Hinduism, although this was becoming undermined by the rigidifying of the caste system. The ethic of public responsibility seems to have been widely accepted and shared from antiquity through the Middle Ages, with the feudal system reflecting a system of interlocking responsibilities and the worst fate being 'cast out' or becoming an outcast, not only being outside of the law, but outside of the system on mutual responsibility. This commonality of enterprise and rights to shared resources (the commons) persisted in Britain until the enclosure period of the late 1700s and early 1800s, where concentrations of wealth and power were used to legally create a landless class as a ready labour force for the emerging industrialisation of production. As will be discussed, this is also the period when Enlightenment thinkers were becoming very concerned about the growing use of the corporate form to pursue nothing more than commercial gain as a force that would undermine civic virtue and public responsibility.

Western Reformation and Enlightenment

The Reformation period was one of turmoil around deeply established understandings and the perceived straying of Rome from the fundamental tenets of Christian beliefs. Series of wars were fought essentially about the right to some sort of freedom of conscience. The first treaty aimed at ending this period of bloodshed, the 1555 Treaty of Augsburg, failed to preserve the peace, as it assigned that freedom only to the head of state. The fundamental conflict was finally resolved by the 1648 Treaty of Westphalia, which although allowing the head of state to choose one of three 'approved' Christian sects as the official religion, extended to citizens a freedom of choice as far as practicing their religion.

During this period, theories of inherent personal rights as underpinning justice and the social contract were formalised. This period of articulation of personal rights and freedoms is often claimed as a turning point in the retreat of the universal responsibility narrative which had persisted from antiquity. It is often portrayed as representing a shift from an understanding that personal rights arise from membership within a community (state), to an understanding that the community (state) arises to vindicate pre-political inherent personal rights. For example, although the Magna Carta of 1215 was very much a rights-based document, the text also incorporates explicit mention of citizens' duties to contribute to the public good, from rendering 'aid' and paying agreed taxes to contributing labour and building public infrastructure.[11]

The development of social contract theory and its underlying presumption of inherent individual rights was driven by the unravelling of the prevailing ontological consensus and the resulting mayhem of Reformation. It can be seen as an attempt to replace the formerly accepted papally based mandate emanating from Rome, such as that lost by Henry the VIII, with some form of presumed reasoned consent as a broadly acceptable ontological basis of governmental authority. I argue that these Enlightenment thinkers continued the narrative of responsibility rather than undermining it. The reason I focus on this period of Western thought is because it is (and I believe wrongly so) not only assigned responsibility for the retreat of the narrative of responsibility, at least in the West, but also because it both precedes and coincides with the rise of the Western device of the for-profit corporation, which many of those thinkers warned would undermine the accepted narrative of individual responsibilities to the community and for the common good, locally and globally.

Thinking rationally about governance: social contract and Enlightenment thought[12]

At first glance, one might think the period around the Enlightenment was purely individualistic. For example, Hugo Grotius[13] argued that rights are subjective, personal powers to act without the permission of the state, but also could also be traded away for safety or for whatever purpose. That doesn't seem to reflect much narrative of responsibility for others, more of a bargaining quid pro quo. He also declared that humans have rationality, a drive to survive and a need for society, again reflecting more self-interest in community than responsibility towards community.[14]

Similarly, Thomas Hobbes asserted that if authority to govern does not come from the divine (problem to be solved throughout Reformation), it comes from necessary consent or from a presumed 'social contract'. In his *Leviathan*, Hobbes maintained that we are born free with natural rights to survive and that we institute government to keep us from the brutish survival wars of all against all. It is to government that we cede all our rights in return for safety and protection, with the caveat that if that government fails to protect us, it loses its legitimacy and our consent, thus returning our rights to us to war until we establish a new government. That again does not seem to resonate with any sense or narrative of responsibility of other than to ourselves.

John Locke, following Hobbes, modified the idea of the social contract as a more limited cession of rights. According to Locke's *Two Treatises on Government*, people, by virtue of their humanity, have inherent natural rights, which include the right to ownership of their bodies and labour, i.e., Locke was arguing that people ought not to be serfs or slaves. In his view, we institute governments to keep us safe from evil doers, but we do not cede to governments all our rights for this purpose. We retain our rights to liberty and to property in order that government may not become oppressive and abuse us, as those evil doers did who inspired the need for government in the first place. And finally, we gain property by mixing our labour with it, and it is that property that enables us to survive independently of any oppressive feudal overlord or government. This too seems to support the idea that the Enlightenment thinkers were abandoning any sense of responsibility to the community and replacing it with the notion of the community as somehow a tool for our own self-interest.

Likewise, Jean-Jacques Rousseau's thought can seem to be at best ambiguous, as he is most well-known for the proposition that people are inherently free and equal and ought to have an equal voice in governance. That proposition is at most somewhat neutral towards any proposition of people's responsibilities toward community.

However, both Grotius and Hobbes not only allowed rights to be exchanged for sake of rational sociability and social security, but also both explicitly saw a healthy society as essential to human survival. Neither saw rights as inalienable or as inconsistent with responsibility, rather it was presumed as understood.

Locke also explicitly embedded into his contract a universal responsibility for human well-being; his focus on rights was a response against tyrannical excesses of the upheavals in 1600s, of both monarchs and of Oliver Cromwell. Locke considered inherent rights as a tool to protect against injustice, and because they were universally shared, as imposing a responsibility on the community on the whole. This is reflected in his requirement for a 'restart', if there were not enough unclaimed property for all to work to own, as for Locke, the point of property was to assure a life free of oppression for each member of society.[15] In Locke's view, if such a situation came about, there was a responsibility to divest holdings and to redistribute so that everyone could have 'enough'. It seems that he believed the right to property ought to translate to a universal holding of 'enough' property, and in order to achieve that Locke was not hostile to limiting rights for the common good, in fact it seems he required it. That does echo an embracing of the narrative of responsibility.

Rousseau's requirements for responsibility were quite explicit, with almost authoritarian overtones. At the very least Rousseau had a strong communitarian voice, as the right to equal voice and participation meant to uncover the general will of the community as to the common good. As well, once uncovered, Rousseau insisted that dissenters must comply for the greater good, i.e., be 'forced to be free', or, more gently, that all had a responsibility to participate and to cooperate with the community once a decision is made.

Later thinkers continued quite explicitly with the narrative of responsibility to the community rather than unfettered individualism. For example, Jeremy Bentham's utilitarianism asserted that everyone has equal right to happiness, but their rights count only as one, so that anyone's personal preferences can be outvoted. This follows on from Rousseau's thought, with Bentham's utilitarianism arguing that government's duty is to provide for the greatest good for the greatest number. While Bentham quite believed people's rights ought to be secure, that was because he believed secure rights would enhance the overall happiness of society. Thus for Bentham, it was in reality an empirical question, and where the general disutility from insecurity of rights outweighs benefit to overall happiness, society's interests trump.

Bentham's disciple, John Stuart Mill, agreed with Bentham's utilitarianism and with decisions being based on the collective good, but added the caveat that society would never be justified to interfere with someone's liberty or rights simply for their own good. People may not be required to refrain from conduct or to do conduct, unless such conduct interferes with the rights of others. This caveat did not interfere with public responsibilities, however, as people were not released from their civic responsibilities nor were they allowed to make a nuisance of themselves.

Finally, the thought of 1700s deontologist Immanuel Kant may seem focused on individualism, in that Kant insisted that we should be and are independent free moral agents and that we must at least perceive ourselves to be free in order to think rationally. However, Kant also insisted on the categorical imperative, which imparts a responsibility or duty to act in the way that we would wish would be the universal conduct rule, that is, we must act as we would wish all people to act. Also, in Kant's thought, we are never justified in treating other people as only means to an end, but must always also consider them as ends in themselves. The categorical imperative is completely consistent with universal human responsibility, and, as will be discussed, many in the Enlightenment period reasoned that the for-profit corporate form would guarantee that people would indeed be treated as mere means to profit, rather than ends in themselves.

The narrative of responsibility as foundational to post-Enlightenment governance

Just as Enlightenment thinkers did not abandon the narrative of reciprocal responsibilities as essential just governance and communal life, neither do those iconic foundational documents reflecting at least Western basic norms and expectations of living in community. These documents span across the Middle, Enlightenment and Modern Ages and still guide modern norms of governance. Their texts reflect an uninterrupted continuation of the narrative of responsibility, with a focus on the common good of the communities in question. Rights are articulated as means to prevent governors from becoming tyrannical, in the Thomist sense of pursuing self-interest or using unjust means to pursue appropriate goals, rather than fulfilling their responsibility to promote the flourishing of the whole community.

As previously mentioned, the Magna Carta is an early example of the compatibility of public responsibility and individual rights narratives. It asserted rights as protections against tyrannical self-interested government, and also community specific rights, those of the Welsh community, of the Marsh community (Scotland) and of the English community. Primary rights asserted are those not to be oppressed by King John, i.e., that he act according to community norms. Magna Carta in fact requires King John to fulfil his governing responsibilities non-oppressively, as per Thomist philosophy, or face the consequences of being dismissed by the barons. That authority is specifically retained by the barons, in the text, even setting out the procedure by which such dismissal would be decided.[16] The document also contained a number of sections specifying ongoing individual responsibilities and duties for the common good.[17]

England's 1629 Right of Petition again is about the ruler's responsibilities towards the ruled and enforces the king's duty not to oppress those who petition him for redress of wrongs committed against them. Likewise, the 1688 Bill of Rights enforces the king's duty to act under the law, rather than in a self-interested or oppressive manner. It affirms the narrative of responsibility and asserts the superiority of the common good through section 1's assertion of parliamentary sovereignty. It attempts to guarantee that that good will indeed be determined and pursued through Parliament, by protecting Parliament's unimpeded ability to determine that good through its guarantee against the government punishing Parliamentarians on the basis of thought, critical speech in the House, or on the basis of conscience.

The 1776 American Declaration of Independence, in essence, boils down to an elegant (I think) assertion that the people inherently have that same authority that the barons reserved to themselves as the people's representatives[18] in the 1215 Magna Carta, that is to depose a sovereign who has become a tyrant, abandoning the pursuit of the good of that people, thus integrating ideas from both Enlightenment-era social contract theory as to the appropriate limitations on the sovereign's power and Thomist thought that a people should pursue authorised pathways to oppose tyranny.

The 1789 French Declaration of the Rights of Man also maintains a narrative of responsibility and duty of all to promote the common good. For example, its Preamble avers that the declaration is to forever remind all members of the social body of their rights and of their duties . . . so that the principles can go towards maintaining the general welfare. Section 2 sets out individual rights, in that 'the purpose of all political association is the preservation of the natural and imprescriptible rights of man. These rights are liberty, property, security, and resistance to oppression.' Section 2 can be seen as reminding governments of their responsibility to govern for all rather than degenerating into self-interested tyrannies using improper means, against which medieval Thomas warns.

Other articles limit individual rights and import responsibilities for the common good, as well as assert that the entirety of the people together as the nation are sovereign. For example, section 4 allows liberty to be limited by law to protect others' liberty; section 6 allows the law to be as expressed by the general will of the people (the community); section 12 explicitly grants public powers to be used for the benefit of all, not special interests; and section13 grants progressive taxation powers. That authorisation can be seen as reflecting both Aristotle's and Thomist ideas about the responsibility to distribute the burdens of living in community equitably (and the responsibility of citizens to accept that equitable distribution of burden when it falls upon them).

Of the same moment, the US Constitution also reflects more than a concern that individuals pursue selfish interests. Voting was the original right, as well as a protection against the privileges and immunities of US citizenship being abridged by state governments. Both these devices can be seen as aimed at promoting the unity, health and viability of the newly created federated community against any attempts by its members to minimise the input or allegiance of their respective citizens.

The United States Bill of Rights, adopted 2 years later, was to appease those who were fearful that limiting the powers of the federal government to only those powers enumerated in the US Constitution., together with guaranteeing each colony's equal representation in the Senate would be inadequate devices to protect against the development of federal tyranny. Their concern was to protect the autonomy of the thirteen states, and their ability to direct their own affairs. At the time of adoption and well after, the individual states retained their full sovereignty, with their constitutions often permitting those state governments to act in strongly communitarian ways, which were later interpreted to be denied to the federal government (such as official churches, supported by taxpayer funds). This is further evidence of the strength accorded to community interests and individual responsibility towards the community (and vice versa).

Rights, rather than being the fundamental point, were seen explicitly as expedient prophylactic devices, which along with voting, separation of powers and differentially allocated bicameralism were hoped to constrain against tyranny of rulers, or as a hedge against rulers failing in their responsibility to govern in the general interest and oppressing the people. Protection of rights was not presented as the point of government; rather the preamble states the purpose was:

> to form a more perfect Union, establish Justice, insure domestic Tranquillity, provide for the common defence, promote the general Welfare, and secure the Blessings of Liberty (from tyranny) to ourselves and our Posterity.

That preamble is an unambiguous acknowledgement of the idea that the people of the present have responsibility to the future and must erect structures and makes plans in the present to meet that responsibility. Far from indicating that their writers were trying to design a minimal laissez faire 'nightwatchman', these documents are rather structures to assure that governments and citizens meet their respective responsibilities to promote the common good of the present and the future.

More recent universal 'rights' documents, upon examination, are also trying to use 'rights' as devices to assure responsibilities are met. For example, the 1948 United Nations Declaration of Human Rights includes many 'rights' that protect against a State acting tyrannically (in the Aristotelian or Thomist sense of tyranny, rulers pursuing self-interest rather fulfilling their responsibility to promote the common good or pursuing their ends through unacceptable means). The Declaration also takes time, in Article 29, to explicitly recognise individual responsibilities to the community:

(1) Everyone has duties to the community in which alone the free and full development of his personality is possible
(2) In the exercise of his rights and freedoms, everyone shall be subject only to such limitations as are determined by law, solely for the purpose of securing due recognition and respect for the rights and freedoms of others and of meeting the just requirements of morality, public order, and the general welfare of society

(3) These rights and freedoms may in no case be exercised contrary to the purposes and principles of the UN [which are Peace, Friendship, Good Neighbourliness, International Economic and Social Advancement, Promoting Social Progress and Better Standards of Living]

The International Covenant on Civil and Political Rights 1966 (ICCPR) was adopted, with some reservations,[19] by both New Zealand (1978) and Australia (1980), and while the title seems focused on individual rights, again those rights are being used as prophylactic protections against tyrannical governments failing in their responsibilities, either in purpose or through pursuing unacceptable means. In fact, the preamble of ICCPR explicitly sets the rights affirmed as being an embedded pre-existing paradigm of responsibility. To wit:

> Realizing that the individual, having duties to other individuals and to the community to which he belongs, is under a responsibility to strive for the promotion and observation of rights recognised in the present.

Further, Article 83(c) of the Covenant makes clear that the individual's responsibilities to their community remain intact, by exempting (ii) National Service (iii) Community Aid in Emergency and (iv) Service work as part of Normal Civil Obligations from all restrictions on 'forced labour'. This exemption would not be possible if the ICCPR reflected heavily individualistic philosophies espoused by neoliberals of today, and often (mis)attributed to Enlightenment founders of liberal thought on which those espousing radical individualism would depend.[20]

Of the modern documents serving as authoritative statements of fundamental norms, Germany's post-war constitution ranks as one of the most rights-based documents, including absolutely entrenched rights, meaning that as long as that constitution is still authoritative, those rights may not be modified even by constitutional amendment[21] (Section 3, Article 79).

Those absolutely entrenched elements of the Basic Law stating what are seen to be that society's fundamental values and asserting a panoply of rights (Section 1, Articles 1–20), including those to freedom of conscience, equality, freedom of occupation, free expression, freedom of assembly, freedom of association, privacy, etcetera show that the underlying conception of human dignity, which the Basic Law is to protect, is strongly individually rights based and rights protective. For example, the German Constitutional Court (final and binding), in this most 'rights aware' jurisdiction, has held that persons must never be considered as mere tools of the state, but as valuable ends (Kant). It holds that the highest value is the free human person and his dignity, as a spiritual-moral being endowed with freedom to develop himself (*The Life Imprisonment Case*, 45 BVerfGE, 227–28 (1977)). However that same Court goes on to qualify that these rights are embedded in an ethic of responsibility:

> The image of man in the Basic Law is not that of an isolated, sovereign individual; rather, the Basic Law has decided in favour of a relationship between

> individual and community in the sense of a person's dependence on and commitment to the community, without infringing upon a person's individual value *Investment Aid Case*, 4 BVerfBE 15–16 (1954) and . . .
>
> This freedom within the meaning of the Basic Law is not that of an isolated and self-regarding individual but rather [that] of a person related to and bound by the community. In the light of this community-boundedness it cannot be 'in principle unlimited.' The individual must allow those limits on his freedom of action that the legislature deems necessary in the interest of the community's social life; . . . [yet people must be regarded as of equal worth, not be mere means of the State and their ability to exercise moral autonomy be respected (Kant)]; and . . .
>
> The responsibility of the State to not just protect the rights, but to promote the welfare of the citizens and the responsibility of the citizens to the community are in evidence in this most rights protective Constitution.

The Basic Law also imposes a collective responsibility, 'a duty', on members of the community, qua state, to assure a basic minimal provision for fellow citizens which is consistent with human dignity (Article 1(1))[22] requiring an activist interventionist state. And in 2002, new Article 20(a) expanded the state's duty towards future generations.

> Mindful also of its responsibility toward future generations, the state shall protect the natural foundations of life and animals by legislation and, in accordance with law and justice, by executive and judicial action, all within the framework of the constitutional order.

Also, Article 18 allows for forfeiture of certain civil and political rights, should they be used for the purpose of imperilling that democracy and constitutional order, imposing a responsibility on citizens not to work against the common good.

Other notable contemporary and seemingly rights-based texts also reveal an underlying ethic of reciprocal responsibility. The Canadian charter specifically provides for limitations of rights for other community values as well as for legislatures to legislate against charter rights, as long as they do so specifically and renew that specificity regularly (section 1, reasonable limits; section 6, provinces can favour long term or disadvantaged (violating equality, but promoting the continuity of the community); and section 33, which allows provinces and the federal government to legislate against charter rights not intrinsic to free elections, so long as the legislation declares that it is violating a charter right; to remain effective, it must be renewed every 5 years. When New Zealand was beginning its moves towards some more formalised statement of its unwritten constitution, the draft proposed in 1961 was criticised as pointless because for every right, a limitation for the public interest was permitted, but as has been discussed that is typical, as the responsibility norm is the fundamental norm over which rights have been laid, not to undo responsibility, but to prevent tyranny. In 1990 New Zealand was one of the latest Western jurisdictions to formally enact rights protecting legislation.

However, *but* while that legislation encourages courts to interpret legislation consistently with those acts, the legislation explicitly forbids courts to use those acts to invalidate other Parliamentary legislation,[23] thus reflecting the notion that the state's and the people's responsibility towards promoting the common good is the greater value. New Zealand relies on frequent elections and a proportional system of voting as its brake against Parliamentary tyranny, and leaves rights to confine any excesses of the executive or subordinate bodies.

Responsibility narrative silenced, but why and how?

Why is the responsibility narrative so silenced when clearly present and in operation? The undermining of the responsibility narrative has not been due to the rise of the rights-based narrative either pre- or post-Enlightenment. As discussed, rights texts across the span of (at least Western) history have been aimed at holding governments to their responsibility to act for the common good, and not to act in tyrannical self-interested ways or to use improper means. This is consistent with the responsibility-based thought of medieval Aquinas and of those writing in antiquity. These post-Enlightenment texts make explicit space for governments and citizens responsibilities to promote the general welfare, through authorisation of taxes for such things as education, health care and support of those in need, through public or civil service obligations, through limitations on individual rights to promote the public interest, and through duties to act reasonably. After all, Enlightenment thought developed to solve a pressing communal problem flowing from the Reformation and a period of near continual strife and upheaval. That problem was how to get people to reembrace the responsibility narrative handed down from antiquity, how to enable those in community to live together constructively and responsibly, rather than ripping themselves apart through ideological or ontological strife (lessons humanity seems to need to learn over and over again, as that problem seems as pressing today across the globe as it did during that period of near universal strife).

If not liberalism

But there is no doubt that the responsibility narrative has been undermined, and from roughly the period of the Enlightenment. If the Enlightenment didn't divorce responsibility from rights, then what did? I believe, as do others, that the divorce was effected by a parallel process which was reaching fruition concurrently with the Enlightenment. And that process was the decision to modify the restrictions on the corporate form, in order to encourage and facilitate the economic exploitation of Europe's and particularly Britain's overseas colonies, and to promote the development of America. This explicit divorce of responsibility from right, developed to encourage 'risk free' investment in corporate colonisers, an early form of the State using private sector funds to fund public sector works.

The original corporations where created by Parliament (or other governments) for specific public purposes, universities and church originally, such that the organisation would succeed the death of its members, or guilds, which granted monopoly rights in exchange for quality training and policing of their members, concerning assurance of competency and public safety. Also, where capital was needed, limited charters were granted, but always with a public service aspect in exchange for the privilege, such as to build roadways and bridges when the exchequer did not have adequate funds in the coffers. Those sorts of corporations were authorised to raise a fixed amount of capital, for a particular project, to recoup their investment by the ability to charge tolls for a fixed period of time, and were required to wind down and distribute the profits, if any, after usually a period of no more than 50 years.

Charter corporations were not based on limited liability; rather, the charter could permit members to be levied upon for corporate debts, thus becoming personally liable for the actions of the corporations in effect.[24] Until the epoch of colonisation, charter corporations were not common and incorporation was a privilege, usually accompanied by a monopoly, to provide some public service for the people and or the state.[25]

During the colonising era, the colonising countries utilised 'Trading Companies', chartered incorporations to conduct trade with the colonies, and in the case of the British East Indies Company, to administer and govern the colony. The Dutch had a similarly or even more successful chartered trading company, which had a device the British admired as efficient but did not adopt for 50 years. That was not limited liability, but it was that once money was invested in a shipping undertaking, the investor could not withdraw their funds and walk away mid-enterprise.[26] This stability of finance gave the Dutch an efficiency advantage. It helped with continuity rather than having to gather new investors for every trading voyage, and the Dutch Charter outperformed the British. These charter corporations gave contributions to the exchequer, which in the day were considered more bribes than taxes, as if to curry favour to retain their charter, but such was the birth of corporate taxation.

Charter corporations were controversial, with suspicions of unfair privilege (monopoly) and greasing palms. Adam Smith was quite suspicious of the corporate form over the personal form, and argued they should only be allowed for purposes of public benefit (roads etc.), where they created or maintained a public service that required a high capital investment that it might not be convenient for the government to make on its own. He suspected that the corporate form would otherwise be wasteful of other people's money and would focus on enriching its managers more than growing investors' profit or being wise stewards of capital.[27]

Thus, even before the devices of limited liability was embedded into company law, that Enlightenment thinker was worried the such forms would almost intrinsically undermine the sense of responsibility of those involved, unless specifically limited to public service goals, and even then was unsure that it was enough to give people a sense of responsibility for how their actions impacted on the interests of others, as they wouldn't really be 'their' actions, but the corporation's, and they wouldn't be managing their own funds, but those of the subscribers, hence they wouldn't have as much at stake.

As industrialisation proceeded, many in Parliament, worried that liberalisation of the corporate form would eventually lead to corporations vying with the State in power, as artificial persons with unlimited lifetimes, unlimited ability to accumulate capital and no restriction on their purpose other than to make a profit through some legal enterprise. It was also at this moment of liberalisation, in the 1820s, that limited liability became a standard feature, limiting an investor's liability to the amount invested. Thus Smith's fears were fulfilled, as now not only did managers have no real incentive to act in a responsible fashion, i.e., for the public good, neither did investors have any incentive to do so, as there was no need to convince Parliament that the investment proposed would be to such public benefit, that it ought to grant a charter. Rather, the only incentive would be private gain, to make a profit, regardless of any positive or negative impact on the public good, and the only restraint to stay within the bounds of legality and efficiency, which set in motion a different conception of just what the public interest and public good was. It is from this moment that the idea of self-interest and economic profitability became a narrative that would overwhelm the responsibility narrative, and ironically even Adam Smith was not a proponent of unfettered free market, because while he thought it would be efficient, he was quite uncertain that that efficiency would lead to anything positive for the public good unless consumption was promoted, and that consumption ought to be in 'plentiful support of one's children, generosity to kinsmen and indigent men of worth and by compassion to the poor'.

He was especially sceptical of the corporate form, viewing it as an underminer of responsible action on a number of different grounds.

> The directors of such companies, however, being the managers rather of other people's money than their own, it cannot well be expected that they should watch over it with the same anxious vigilance with which the partners in a private co-partnery frequently watch over their own.
>
> Adam Smith, Wealth of Nations (Random House, NY, 1994 edition of 1776 original) 800 (BkV, Ch.1, PT.III)

He thus thought management would likely be self-interested and not good stewards for both the reason that their own funds were not at stake, and similarly, that the investors did not have enough incentive to make sure those managers did act responsibly, as the investors did not have enough at stake. In other words, investors who stood to lose everything if things went pear-shaped tended to make better decisions than those who merely pocketed their regular dividends and stood to lose only the amount they invested in their shares.

Smith, writing during the Scottish Enlightenment period, worried that the corporate form also undermined any sense of responsibility to the State or the people it governed. He used the depredations of the British East India Company as an example of the dangers of the corporate enterprise, as essentially unaccountable and prone to promoting irresponsible behaviour damaging to the public good. He also advised that real power was not in wealth alone, but in the control of others' labour.[28] We see today Adam Smith's fear and misgivings about corporations being used solely for profit rather than being restricted to providing public goods, infrastructure or services, from which both the corporation and the public profited.[29] Smith could see no public good, rather an abdication of both government and corporate responsibility for such good from the devolved colonising authority of the British East Indies Company (a chartered corporation) and its disruption of local productive economies solely for profit. Many also criticised the self-interested behaviour of municipal corporations, where landowners and freemen (tradesmen) were able to impose costs on the general population for their own special benefit.[30]

Similarly in the United States, the corporation was viewed as a tool for development which must be controlled and treated with caution because of its likely propensity to detract from its members' sense of public responsibility. It was also viewed as a potential rival of the State, but without the democratic accountability to the general public that constrained the State to act in the public interest. Likewise, it was feared that members of corporations (or stockholders) would put the interests and affairs of the corporation and their own self-interest ahead of their civic mindedness and public duties, with corporations becoming little mini states, with their own internal governance, focused on only the corporate interest to the detriment of the community at large. Fears were voiced that corporations could corrupt legislatures, using their collective power to push lawmakers to pass legislation favourable to the corporation but not to the public at large. As one writer put it

> the State, instead of being a community of free citizens pursuing the public interest, may become a community of corporations, influenced by partial views, and perhaps in a little time, (under the direction of artful men) composing an aristocracy destructive to the constitution and independency of the State.[31]

Thus, the argument that the corporate form was inherently a danger to public responsibility was voiced on the American side of the Atlantic as well. In 1786 legislative debates around whether to revoke a bank's corporate charter, William Findley argued that the evidence available had shown that people will act with public responsibly with their own property, as they are held personally responsible for those actions, while the corporate 'veil' not only invites but guarantees that the soulless corporation, with a sole purpose of making money and no one person being responsible for its actions, will not act in a principled way.[32] Findley and other legislators argued that it was simply 'the nature of the institution' that would make corporate directors act against the public interest, as it was almost their duty to do so. In their opinion, the relatively novel, at that time, profit-only focused corporation had (unsurprisingly) been shown to be a dehumanised 'engine of power' that promoted greed and undermined civic responsibility.[33] Findley also observed that

> We are too unequal in wealth to render a perfect democracy suitable to our circumstances, yet we are so equal in wealth [and] power . . . that we have no

> counterpoise sufficient to check or control an institution of such vast influence and magnitude [as the bank].[34]

Likewise, James Madison (one of the American 'founding fathers' as well as the fourth US president) was concerned that corporations would have a corrupting influence on legislators and public policy as he observed had happened in Europe. Madison deemed that a corporation amounted to a "powerful machine . . . [operating] in a great measure independent of the People".[35]

And, arguably, the cautions of the Enlightenment-era liberal worrywarts could not stem the tide of the increasing legislative grants of corporate charters, with ever fewer restrictions on corporate purpose and shareholder responsibility. Limited liability became the norm and the 'race to the bottom' – to attract corporate income as a revenue source for state tax coffers, as well as, one might argue, the political influence of those profiting from the corporate form, including the corporations themselves, about which the Enlightenment-era writers were concerned – won the day. Incorporation moved from a careful and special legislative concern, with the corporate purpose examined for public good, to a standardised form restricting corporations from having illegal purposes. The development of corporate law has long been argued to reflect a natural economic evolution due to jurisdictional competition.[36] However, it can also be argued that the law tolerating and even facilitating the corporate form's drain on the ethos of individuals' responsibilities to promote the public good is the result of the political process behind law making,[37] a political process that Enlightenment thinkers warned would become overly influenced by corporate money and power and one for which law makers could and should take responsibility, rather than hiding behind the myth of economic necessity and inevitability.[38]

Earlier responses to the negative influences of corporate capitalism, as they materialised almost precisely as the Enlightenment worriers imagined, have been, sequentially, Marxism, anarchism, fascism, anti-colonialism and the late welfare state. With the demise of Marxism as a credible alternative to corporate capitalism in the late 1980s, the resistance to the State overtly embracing the responsibility narrative, i.e., neoliberal ideology, has increased. That ideology, founded by Hayek in response to the excesses of some of the aforementioned 'solidarity' ideologies, does advocate the excision of the responsibility narrative from rights. One would suspect that corporations are not displeased.

Corporate political power: the dangers of forgetting the purpose of a legal fiction

In the 20th century, the corporation became a normal, nearly universal, form for doing business. Corporate legal persons now abound. What corporate political influence has achieved is the 'humanisation' of that form, which results in even further dilution of the ethic of public responsibility and concomitant dehumanisation of the citizen. I will explain. As discussed above, during the Enlightenment period, individual rights were proposed as natural and necessary for human freedom from oppression, but not as an abdication of public responsibility. Those rights, as illustrated both in the Enlightenment philosophies and in the classic older and modern rights-affirming documents, were intended to be for the benefit of human individuals and the human community, such that people would live better lives in healthy communities.

The 'for profit' corporate form evolved from equitable trusts, with such trusts being given the independent right to make contracts for convenience's sake. That way the trustees could obligate the trust to a contract, without the necessity of consent from every beneficiary of the trust. Likewise, limited liability was often granted to equitable trusts, on the condition that the other party to any contract was aware that only the assets of the trust, and not those of the beneficiaries, were available to satisfy any debt. Hence the common 'Ltd.' designation. The 'for profit' corporation was granted 'personality' in the sense of that of the equitable trust, such that it could make contracts without the necessity of involving all the stockholders. Limited liability followed. Facilitating the ease of groups of people who had pooled their capital was the purpose of the grant of legal 'personhood', as in contract law, a contract required that there be 'a meeting of the minds' for a contract to be considered binding, i.e., an actual agreement between two people. The fiction of corporate personhood flowed from the requirements of English common law that developed before there were 'for profit' corporations.[39]

As Enlightenment-era thinkers had worried, corporations did become politically influential and did seek more rights and favourable treatment. This is reflected in the extension to corporate persons the rights intended to protect human persons from oppression. In the United States, first corporations were unilaterally deemed to qualify as 'persons' guaranteed 'equal protection under the law' by that constitution's 14th amendment in an 1886 report of a Supreme Court case, *Santa Clara County v. Southern Pacific Rail Road*,[40] although as far back as 1819 the Court had held that legislative interference with the articles of incorporation, after the fact, would be interference with a contract and violate the federal constitution.[41]

The US legislated against corporate political contributions to federal campaigns in 1907, in response to corporate bribery scandals. The Enlightenment worriers would have approved. However, starting from 1978, a sharply divided Court started extending First Amendment freedom of speech rights to corporations, in the context of ballot initiatives.[42] In 2010, that same Court overturned long-standing state and federal practice of limiting independent corporate spending on political speech, allowing unlimited corporate spending to advocate for or against candidates (as opposed to directly contributing to those campaigns).[43] The Court's reasoning was that corporations are really groups of people; hence, they ignored the legal fiction for one purpose, but reified it for another, and in both cases to extend to corporate interests the protections intended to assure individual persons freedoms.

This is not a US-limited phenomenon; for example, the New Zealand Bill of Rights 1990 covers political and human rights, from the life and security of the person, democratic and civil rights, non-discrimination rights through to search, arrest, trial and punishment rights. That Bill of Rights, in the last sentence of the last section, explicitly extends Bill of Rights protections to corporate persons, to the extent possible,[44] with the text clearly excepting the right to vote and to enter New Zealand, which are limited to citizens.

Similarly, Germany's Basic Law, discussed above, specifically extends those fundamental and unamendable rights[45] protections of sections 1 through 19 to corporate persons.[46] However, that extension of protection is limited to domestic corporations, which would be of some, but not much, comfort to those Enlightenment thinkers worried about the impact of the spread of the corporate form on civic virtue and the narrative of responsibility.

This extension of the civil, political and criminal justice rights deemed necessary to protect human freedom and self-governance of a community to non-human legal business devices may be argued to reflect a forgetting by legal system of the fact that the corporate 'person', with a separate will and being, is a legal fiction, designed to satisfy the requirements of contract law and to serve a certain purpose of efficiency. Lon Fuller's seminal work *Legal Fictions*[47] explains the utility of 'legal fictions' to law, as a form of shorthand or as a way to elide injustice as reality outstrips legal development. He warns that such fictions only become dangerous when those who employ them begin to believe that they are true, and in such cases, the fiction becomes a dangerous lie. If the extensions of fundamental political and civil rights and freedoms to corporate 'persons' has occurred on the basis of concern to prevent oppression and ill treatment of those persons, one must wonder whether a corporation can 'suffer' oppression or ill treatment, and whether such extension is dangerous. The Enlightenment worriers would certainly think so, with their insights as to the derogation from public responsibility and civic virtue inherently encouraged or made inevitable by the corporate form, both by members and employees of corporations, as well as by the ordinary citizen who witnesses the elevation of a purely profit-seeking enterprise to equal standing as themselves. Further, unless the 'participation' paradigm of responsibility, where one is held responsible for the harmful consequences of those acts in which one has participated, is imposed on those participating and benefiting from corporate activities, at least to the level of their profit from the same, the actual legal fiction is not the corporation as a person with an independent will with which to engage in contracts, but that legal system imposes 'responsibility' for those who facilitate or engage harmful actions.

If, on the other hand, that extension has not been done by any 'forgetting', but has been done as a result of corporate lobbying and corporate influence on the political processes, then Thomist and Enlightenment ideas that government ought to be done for the common good of the people and not for special interests would seem to be violated. Aquinas was particularly concerned that government not spread the burdens of society, the public responsibility, disproportionately. That would seem to point to a requirement that government demand more from large accumulations of capital, in terms of contribution and burden bearing, rather than work to extend to such accumulations those protections designed for the benefit of the vulnerable. That the opposite has happened would seem to vindicate Enlightenment concerns that corporations would pursue only self-interest to the exclusion of the public good. And that is why I argue that the main impediment to the overt embracing of the narrative of responsibility in contrast to that of rights is not attributable to Enlightenment individualism, but rather to corporate power and self-interest.

Notes

1 See David Slebourne *The Principle of Duty* (Notre Dame Press, Notre Dame, IN, 2001), ch 9 for an explanation of such civic duties to the citizens and an argument that those were transferred from ancient sovereigns to modern democratic orders. Selbourne too mentions the corruption of liberal thought as one of the problems impeding the democratic order's acceptance of such responsibility, assigning that corruption to the rise of the idea of the night watchman state, rather than the more parentalistic state envisaged even by J.S. Mill.

2 Michelene R. Ishay *The History of Human Rights: From Ancient Times to the Globalisation Era* (University of California Press, Berkley, CA and London, 2004) at 19, 28–29, 35–37 and 47. For the translated text, see <http://avalon.law.yale.edu/ancient/hamframe.asp>.

3 Ibid. at 29, 36–37 and 41.

4 Although see <www.livescience.com/8008-bible-possibly-written-centuries-earlier-text-suggests.html>.

5 See Leviticus 19:18; Deuteronomy I:16–17; Proverbs14:31–35; Exodus 22:20 and Leviticus 19:14–15 in Ishay, n2 at 28.

6 This deeply influenced the Thomist (Aquinas) school of justice (discussed below), which thought about the legal responsibilities of rulers and ruled predominant in the West pre-Enlightenment.

7 This not the Zeno of the mathematical paradoxes, Zeno of Elea, who lived about 100 years prior to Plato.

8 The discussion of Plato, Aristotle and Zeno of Citium's thought is drawn from the *Republic*, from Freeman on Jurisprudence, from Ishay n 2 above, and from Douglas Hodgson, *Individual Duty Within a Human Rights Discourse* (London, Ashgate, 2003), ch 2.

9 De regno ad regem Cypri, *On Kingship to the King of Cyprus*, by Thomas Aquinas (Books 1 & 2), translated by Gerald B. Phelan, revised by I. Th. Eschmann, O.P. (Toronto: The Pontifical Institute of Mediaeval Studies, 1949) Re-edited and chapter numbers aligned with Latin, by Joseph Kenny, O.P. <http://dhspriory.org/thomas/DeRegno.htm>.

10 William Street (ed) *Philosophical Theory and the Universal Declaration of Human Rights* (University of Ottawa Press, 2003) ch 12, 184.

11 Magna Carta 1215, sections 12, 14, 15, 16 and 23, for example.

12 This is a period celebrating reason as the basis for ordering human affairs and understanding the world, as reflected by Descartes's famous 'I think therefore I am'. Social contract thinkers laid the foundations for much Enlightenment thought. The thinkers discussed here cover a period in the West from the early 1600s through the mid-1800s.

13 Who might be considered as pre-Enlightenment (most of his work is from early 1600s), but who was nonetheless a rationalist.

14 Micheline R. Ishay *The History of Human Rights: From Ancient Times to the Globalisation Era* (University of California Press, Berkeley, CA, 2003) at 100.

15 Although, unfortunately, he subsumed women into their husbands, as the law did in his time, and did not recognise the property rights of those with non-European ways of being on the land.

16 Thus the Magna Carta complied with Thomist philosophy, even though it was created 10 years before Thomas Aquinas's birth.

17 Above, n. 13.

18 In the feudal system, the lord of the manor was seen as protecting and representing the interests of all those attached to the manor and in his service.

19 New Zealand had reservations in the areas of detained children's rights, compensation for miscarriages of justice, regulation of hate speech and organised labour's rights <www.justice.govt.nz/justice-sector-policy/constitutional-issues-and-human-rights/human-rights/international-human-rights/international-covenant-on-civil-and-political-rights/>.

20 See Robert Nozick *Anarchy, State and Utopia* (Basic Books, New York, 1974) for an exposition on what, in a quintessentially neoliberal view of justice, the State may or may not do. Nozick essentially reduces any responsibility of the State towards the citizen to protection against external aggression, protection against crimes against the person and property, enforcement of contract (how odd) and the protection of private property. Individual legal responsibility is limited to refraining from aggression and crime, and contributing to the funding of the 'night-watchman state'.

21 Basic Law for the Federal Republic of Germany, Section VII, Article 79(3): 'Amendments to this Basic Law affecting the division of the Federation into Länder, their participation on principle in the legislative process, or the principles laid down in Articles 1 and 20 shall be inadmissible. Section I articles 1 through 20 list fundamental rights, including a provision that, while regulable by ordinary generally applicable law article 19(2) provides that "In no case may the essence of a basic right be affected", "the essence" of a fundamental right.' Article 18 tellingly provides that if listed civil and political rights are used to imperil Germany's democratic order, that may by declared forfeited by the Constitutional Court, which also reflects a responsibility paradigm, contrasting with the seeming absolutism of Article 19.

22 'Human dignity shall be inviolable. To respect and protect it shall be the duty of all state authority.'

23 New Zealand Bill of Rights Act 1990, section 4: 'Other enactments not affected No court shall, in relation to any enactment (whether passed or made before or after the commencement of this Bill of Rights), – (a) hold any provision of the enactment to be impliedly repealed or revoked, or to be in any way invalid or ineffective; or (b) decline to apply any provision of the enactment – by reason only that the provision is inconsistent with any provision of this Bill of Rights.'

24 Frederick B. Kempin Jr. "Limited Liability in Historical Perspective" (1960) 4(1) *American Business Law Association Bulletin*, discussing two cases from the 1400s saying liability limited to corp assets, with another allowing levies on members.

25 Christopher Stone, *Where the Law Ends: The Social Control of Corporate Behavior* (Waveland Press, IL, 1991 reissue of Harper Collins, NY, 1975); Kempin n. 26 above.

26 Giuseppe Dari-Mattiacci, Oscar Gelderblom, Joost Jonker and Enrico Perotti "The Emergence of the Corporate Form" (2017) 33(2) *The Journal of Law, Economics, & Organization* 193–236.

27 Adam Smith, *Wealth of Nations* (Random House, NY, 1994 edition of 1776 original).

28 Smith also argued that non-local corporations were destined to be exploitative of those in the other countries in which they functioned; i.e., he foresaw that distant global corporations would inherently tend to irresponsible exploitative behaviour in local communities.

> "The directors actually would have little interest in the actual prosperity of India (and even of the company itself) but would, instead, desire to buy their way onto the board in order to arrange for 'friends' to be appointed to jobs in India where they could engage in the kind of individualized plunder that the *supposed* 'owners' back home in Britain were powerless to prevent. Once such an individual had succeeded in placing friends in such potentially lucrative jobs, '. . . he frequently cares little about the dividend; or even upon the value of the stock . . . About the prosperity of the great empire, in the government of which that vote gives him a share, he seldom cares at all. No other sovereigns ever were, or, from the nature

of things, ever could be, so perfectly indifferent upon the happiness or misery of their subjects . . .' Smith, (II: 276). It is clear from these passages, that Smith saw the kind of world embraced by the neo-liberal analysis as not at all conducive to the 'wealth of nations'."

Michael Meeropol "Another Distortion of Adam Smith: The Case of the 'Invisible Hand'" (Working Paper Series No. 79, Political Economy Research Institute, University of Massachusetts, Amherst, 2004).

29 Corporations were often granted rights of eminent domain, in order to build infrastructure, with employees sometimes exempted from normal public duties.

30 Ian Speir, "Corporations, the Original Understanding, and the Problem of Power" (2012) 10 *Georgetown J of Law & Public Policy* 115.

31 Alfred Billings Street *The Council of Revision of the State of New York* (William Gould, Albany, 1859) 261–264, at 262 as quoted in Speir above.

32 Debates and Proceedings of the General Assembly of Pennsylvania *On the Memorials Praying a Repeal or Suspension of the Law Annulling the Charter of the Bank* (Matthew Carey ed., Seddon & Pritchard, Philadelphia, PA, 1786) 66, at 129 in Speir above.

33 Ibid., 129–130.

34 Ibid.

35 *Legislative and Documentary History of the Bank of the United States* 82 (M. St. Claire Clark and D. A. Hall eds, Gales & Seaton, Washington, DC, 1832) at 130 in Speir above.

36 Daniel J.H. Greenwood "Democracy and Delaware: The Mysterious Race to the Bottom/Top" (2005) 23(2) *Yale Law & Policy Review* 381.

37 Ibid.

38 Ibid.

39 See Speir, above.

40 118 U.S. 394 (1886).

41 *Trustees of Dartmouth College v. Woodward*, 17 US 518 (1819).

42 *First National Bank of Boston v. Bellotti*, 435 U.S. 765 (1978).

43 *Citizens United v. Federal Election Commission*, 558 U.S. 310 (2010).

44 N.Z. Bill of Rights, section 29: 'Application to legal persons: Except where the provisions of this Bill of Rights otherwise provide, the provisions of this Bill of Rights apply, so far as practicable, for the benefit of all legal person as well as for the benefit of all natural persons.'

45 Although Article 18 provides that if certain political and property rights are used to combat the democratic order, they are forfeited.

46 Basic Law, Article 19(3): 'The basic rights shall also apply to domestic artificial persons to the extent that the nature of the right permits.'

47 (Stanford University Press, 1967).

5 Confronting the insupportable

Resources of the law of responsibility[1]

Alain Supiot

"Everyone fights for what he lacks" Surcouf[2] is said to have replied to an English captain who was boasting about fighting for honour and not for money. The indiscriminate invocation of republican or democratic values is a sign of their weakness; there should be no need for such proclamations if these principles were part of everyday experience. The same goes for 'social responsibility', so often bandied about by big business or political leaders. Its omnipresence in political and economic circles is a symptom of the juridical crisis that responsibility is going through. It expresses a general feeling that the breaking down of trade borders and the weakening of the pursuit of the public good are leading to widespread irresponsibility.

Over a century ago, the welfare state was born of a crisis of this sort. The proliferation of industrial accidents for which nobody accepted responsibility sparked a major legal revolution. Under civil law, responsibility was essentially individual and derived from the concept of fault. The responsible person appeared as the one who, adult and of sound mind, had to repair the harmful consequences of their guilty actions, negligence or carelessness. It was only by exception that an individual's responsibility could be directly invoked without fault on their part because of certain things 'placed in their care' (their ruined buildings or their animals) or because of people they were in charge of (children, pupils or representatives). These were a finite list of exceptions to the rule of irresponsibility that applied to both things and other people.

To be able to repair harm for which no-one was judged to be responsible – notably a reduced or lost capacity to earn a living – people had to rely largely on their own resources, i.e. their prudential arrangements, or failing that on the older of younger generations of their own family or on charity. This was notably the type of charity that was known as 'paternalism'. It is making a come-back today in the guise of 'corporate social responsibility' (CSR). As is implied by the notion of *patronat*,[3] which has since been rejected by business leaders, some employers motivated by faith or morality felt that they had responsibilities towards their workers comparable to those of a father towards his children. They thus looked after their workers like children, watching over their conduct and providing them help and assistance as needed. This social responsibility was voluntary, and God was its only guarantor.

These limits to civil responsibility did not survive the shock of the Industrial Revolution and the large increase in harm caused by machines. The shock brought about the broadening of responsibility for things that one has under one's care. The starting point for this broadening in all industrialised countries was the introduction at the end of the nineteenth and the beginning of the twentieth centuries of a specific regime of reparation for workplace accidents. This legal turning point led not only to a broadening of responsibility for things, but also to a corresponding expansion of risk insurance mechanisms. Initially voluntary, the responsibility for things became obligatory for the most serious risks to which the working class were exposed: accidents but also illness, old age and unemployment. The combination of broader responsibility and compulsory insurance was the mortar of the first pillar of the welfare state, i.e. a state guarantor of solidarity in the face of risks. This legal revolution brought about the decline of paternalism: so long as they acquitted themselves of their insurance obligations by paying the relevant dues, businesses no longer had to be concerned about misfortunes affecting their employees. Family solidarity underwent a similar evolution. The rise of pension schemes freed those active in the workforce from having to provide financially for the needs of their ageing parents. Thus an impersonal duty of solidarity requiring the payment of taxes and levies took over in large measure from the personal duties of help and assistance which ensured the cohesion of traditional societies. The expansion of capitalism was thus facilitated by the transfer of responsibility for risks affecting employees to social insurance mechanisms. Employers were able, legitimately, to no longer concern themselves with the lives of their employees – their education, health, financial security, education, health and family costs – and thus to treat work as an economic resource available on a market determined solely by the calculation of utility. More generally this transfer of responsibilities has nurtured in the population as a whole the illusion of neither being responsible nor needing to rely on anyone else, in other words the illusion of a subject capable of independently determining their life.

The whole of this institutional edifice is being shaken today in the context of what is called globalisation, which is the establishment of a total market on a planetary scale. Free circulation of capital and goods thrusts all states into a global competition where each one must, according to the liberal doctrine of David Ricardo, pursue its 'comparative advantage'. This comparative advantage may lie in natural or 'human' resources which states are thereby encouraged to over-exploit to maintain their global competitiveness. They all find themselves engaged, willy-nilly, in what the British prime minister recently called a 'global race', that's to say a mortal race whose guiding principle is reduction of labour costs, which has become the be-all and end-all of the economic policies followed by all governing parties in Europe. By resorting to outsourcing, international subcontracting or expatriate staff, a company can operate in a market while largely escaping taxes and social levies. The establishment of this total market brings with it an increase in systemic risks. These risks includes financial risk, with the abandonment in 1971 of fixed exchange rates in favour of floating currencies, considered as commodities like others and whose value no longer has any internationally recognised guarantee; as well as ecological risk, of which climate change is but one of its multiple aspects with the over-exploitation of natural resources, which continue to be treated as commodities whereas they are a vital means for the survival of our societies. These new risks add to the resurgence of social risks that the welfare state had succeeded in curbing. The lesson from the two world wars according to which "universal and lasting peace can be established only if it is based on social justice"[4] is forgotten and the abandonment of any social justice objective at the international level is accompanied unsurprisingly by a huge rise in inequality, unemployment and economic migrants, and a return of religious, nationalist, and identity extremism and more broadly of violence.

The rise of these dangers is accompanied by the weakening of the capacity of states to remain the guarantors of the principle of responsibility, i.e. of their capacity to make those who hold economic power answerable for the consequences of their decisions. This dissociation of the place of power from the place where responsibility lies imposes risks on those least able to protect themselves. From a legal point of view, the question is thus how to reconnect power and responsibility so as to avoid the transfer of risks to the weakest. To achieve this it is necessary to 'take responsibility seriously'.[5] This question leads one to extend the principle of responsibility in a broader sense such as the obligation to prevent or repair the harmful consequences of one's actions without prejudice to whether the responsibility is civil, penal or contractual or fault- or risk-based.

Our collective thinking focuses on responsibilities for what Karl Polanyi has termed 'fictitious commodities' – nature, labour and currency. They are fictitious because capitalism causes them to be treated as commodities despite the fact that they are not the products of economic activity. They are in fact preconditions for any market activity. What is in play here are legal fictions, i.e. non-material means whose function is to make a certain mental representation of the world liveable. To fulfil this function, legal fictions must – unlike literary fiction – take into account the principle of reality. Property law for example gives legal form and force to humanity as 'master and possessor of nature'. But for this representation to be sustainable over the long term, it is necessary to take full account of reality, which is also that of man's dependence with respect to nature. So it is necessary to regulate the use of property law in order to avoid the destruction of our rural milieu. That is precisely the purpose of environmental law. By means of legal provisions guaranteeing the protection of nature, one can act *as if the* earth were a commodity. Similarly, through labour law ensuring long-term training and replenishment of the workforce, one can act *as if* labour were a commodity and thus institute a labour *market*. And through those institutions that guarantee the value of currency, one can act as if currency were a commodity like any other, able to be traded on financial *markets*.

The danger of these constructs is that they encourage the treatment of fictions as real and the forgetting of the legal foundation on which capitalism rests. As it is no longer supported in this way, capitalism becomes 'insupportable' – neither sustainable nor tolerable. This omission is widespread because of the economic orthodoxy which serves as a credo of globalisation and thrusts all states into a race to deregulate the use of nature, labour and currency. Treating nature, work and currency as realities and not as fictions clearly runs the risk of a brutal return of the principle of reality. For example, it was foreseeable that financial markets, which were the most thoroughly deregulated, would be where this principle would return first. But the implosion of financial markets in 2008 was not enough to shake the world, or rather the world's leaders, out of their doctrinal sleep. Instead of working to re-regulate failing financial markets, all governmental parties in Europe made deregulation of labour markets their overriding political priority. The disappearance of trade borders having replaced the rule of law by 'law shopping' on a global level, each state tries to acquire or maintain its comparative advantage embodied in more and more lax and thus more 'attractive' regulation for investors. Such a system undermines the financial foundations of the welfare state just where it was the most fully developed. It also slows its development in the emerging economies who are always threatened with losing their comparative advantage if they take it upon themselves to raise labour costs, increase taxes or protect the environment. It also makes businesses themselves more vulnerable. Their networked organisation exposes them to new risks insofar as they now only have indirect control over the production chain of their products. And they find themselves subject to higher and higher demands for short-term profitability, notwithstanding their financial security and long-term investment needs.

Given their crucial importance for the common future of humanity, fictitious commodities are at the same time those for which irresponsible behaviours are the most dangerous and where it is the most difficult to apply the principle of responsibility. That is why we have centred our work on responsibilities with regard to ecological, social and financial risks. Each of these risks raises specific questions, which should not be ignored, but they are also interdependent, so one must also take account of what links them. There are many examples of these links. The financial crisis of 2008 gave us an idea of the social disasters that that could be brought about through the collapse of deregulated financial markets. More broadly, a system that encourages sourcing from distant suppliers rather than those closer to home for purely financial reasons based on comparative advantage and lower labour and environmental constraints engenders irresponsibility in all these areas at the same time. For example, the recent dismantling of customs barriers which protected agriculture or small farmers in African countries to increase the profits of European agri-food companies is a decision with severe consequences for labour (unemployment and mass emigration in Africa, proletarianisation of farm labour in Europe) and the environment (pollution and the many other harmful effects of industrial farming). So the risks attached to fictitious commodities are not only systemic, they are also inter-systemic.

These themes are reflected in the organisation of our work.[6] Following a method that reflects a perspective of *mondialisation*,[7] the first part aims to examine the notion of responsibility through the lens of the diversity of civilisations. Our legal concepts are neither intemporal nor universal. They have a history and are not necessarily identical everywhere they occur. It was thus useful to explore this historical depth and adopt for a moment outside perspectives on what we call 'responsibility'. We can learn a great deal from this exploration. It shows both the distinctiveness and the diversity of the different branches of our own legal tradition and how it was appropriated by other civilisations in the form of neologisms each with its own shade of meaning. It shows too that these civilisations share an idea that is masked in our case by the crushing weight of the concept of property: the idea that all human societies, if they are to last, need guardians of their *oecumene*, the guarantors of the ties between people and their milieu in which they live. [. . .] This is an important lesson which invites us to see responsibility in terms of duty to take charge, conduct to follow and balances to preserve and not only as the duty to respond to harm that may be caused after the event. This lesson also raises a major question that has had no response: who are the guardians of the earth in the age of globalisation?

In the second section,[8] the responsibility for fictitious commodities is dealt with by themes, through the study of questions relating to ecological, social and financial responsibility. [. . .] From this panorama a contrasting picture emerges: where the shadows unsurprisingly dominate over the highlights. The Ebola crisis revealed the deadly effects of structural adjustment policies imposed by the International Monetary Fund (IMF) as well as the serious shortcomings of the World Health Organization (WHO). Where it is not simply misleading advertising, corporate social responsibility appears as neo-paternalism, admirable no doubt, but without any significant legal weight.

Lacking meaningful reforms, financial markets are now latching on to the ecological crisis as a new gaming table, from which they can take profits without providing in compensation the least protection against the ensuing risks. There are some encouraging signs, however, which can guide future reforms. This is notably the case of ecological responsibility, which is appearing in both civil and criminal contexts. This legal progress is happening in tandem with greater political awareness as is shown by regulatory initiatives in the United States designed to mitigate climate change. Finally, there are increasing signs that corporate social responsibility is acquiring a degree of legal force as is shown in France by legislation on the duty of care by multinational companies and the recent reforms of commercial law in China.

The third part[9] considers responsibility for fictitious commodities from a horizontal point of view, starting from three unavoidable questions for anyone who takes responsibility seriously: who are those responsible? Who can initiate recourse relating to responsibility? Who is the judge of responsibility? The first question is especially important when it comes to invoking the responsibility of businesses. Recourse to moral personality, in other words legal masks, gives economic decision-makers the ability to appear masked on the stage where transactions take place. Thus the responsibility of their actions falls on other people whom they are in control of or for whom they establish a legal presence. The limitation of responsibility was since the beginnings both one of the most powerful levers and one of the greatest dangers of recourse to two important tools of capitalism, the trust and the limited company. Nowadays, the internationalisation and the networked organisation of companies enables them to be made the tools of what

Pierre Calame has called an 'unlimited irresponsibility company'. Lacking legal means to remove these masks, it is always in the end states that find themselves having to be the response of last resort to ecological, social or financial disasters brought about by this irresponsibility. That is a reason to impose on large companies a social and environmental responsibility worthy of the name, with legal force and applicable to the management level. There has been some progress in this direction as is seen by the legal status given to corporate social responsibility in India, and US laws establishing the personal responsibility of business leaders for accounting and finance. But the competition of standards that characterises globalisation pushes states towards complacency or even complicity with the irresponsible behaviour of 'their' major companies. This leads to the growing issue of the protection of whistleblowers who expose this behaviour and more generally of action by civil society or unions.

The third challenge in order for responsibility for fictitious commodities to be taken seriously is establishing the competent authority to judge it. The judge is the cornerstone of any legal system. Our work has shown that there are ways of bringing those responsible for ecological, social or financial disasters to justice either nationally or internationally. If they are little used, it is often because of timidity or the collusion of states with the perpetrators. The contrast between Europe and the United States here is striking. In order to bring to heel multinationals guilty of corruption, the US Department of Justice has acquired extraterritorial powers to apply US law abroad so sweeping that they have become matters of concern. In Europe, however, it seems no-one dares to point out the responsibility of Goldman Sachs bank in the bankruptcy of Greece by assisting with the false accounting that allowed Greece's entry into the Eurozone. And this was despite the fact that the market power available to the EU to investigate such questions of responsibility would be equivalent to that of the US.

We are at a turning point in the law of responsibility comparable to the one that gave rise to the welfare state. In some respects this turning point might seem like a U-turn. States can no longer assume their role of guarantors of an objective responsibility in the face of risks stemming from the dynamic of capitalism. The mechanisms advocated by liberalism of old resurface: savings, corporate paternalism and private or public charity. But this resurgence is not simply a repeat, for these mechanisms have taken on a new character when employed at a global level. Today, savings take the form of pension funds and banking insurance, promising financial security that has no need for a guarantor of the value of the currency. Paternalism has taken the form of corporate social and environmental responsibility, promising self-regulation which by virtue of procedure-based compliance systems provides freedom from any heteronomous responsibility. Public charity has taken the form of *workfare* or the *active welfare state*, promising to make poor people more responsible, and to control public expenditure, while universal social security is changed by stealth into a minimum foundation of social rights. Private charity has taken on the form of non-governmental organisations and foundations whose growth corresponds to the withdrawal of the state. In all but extreme cases, the state hands over to private entities a large share of its social, environmental and financial powers. This should logically be accompanied by a greater responsibility on the part of these entities, first and foremost transnational corporations whose choices contribute to determining the fate of people and nature and the value of the currency. But it must be said that this transfer of power has not been accompanied by a corresponding transfer of responsibilities, i.e. by a re-articulation of public and private responsibilities which reflects the new distribution of power.

If such a re-articulation appears difficult to conceive, it is because we continue to think within a paradigm of a legal order ruled by the law. Under such an order, which corresponded to a society of sovereign states, the latter were responsible for preserving the long-term viability of people, nature and the currency. This responsibility does not arise from an economic assessment; it is the necessary condition for making such an assessment. As long as these unquantifiable values are the responsibility of states, businesses have no responsibility towards them beyond obeying the laws by which states undertake their protection. As long as they pay their taxes and social levies and respect labour and environmental law, they are free to concentrate solely on the calculation of their utilities. In this context, the famous statement by Milton Friedman according to which "the only social responsibility of businesses is to make a profit"[10] reflected a very primitive conception of the company, but was not at all shocking at the time.

The situation is different in a legal universe where the free circulation of goods and capital allows companies to escape from oversight by states through law shopping. At this global level there is no independent external body which can assume social, environmental or monetary responsibilities, which consequently fall on the businesses themselves. For financial risks, they have had recourse to derivatives whose enormous growth over the past 30 years is well-known. The amount tied up in derivatives held off-balance sheet by so-called systemically important banks reached the extraordinary amount of 720,324 billion dollars in 2012, fifteen times their balance sheets and ten times global GDP. The 2008 financial collapse nonetheless showed that these horizontal guarantees, far from militating against the absence of an international guarantor of the value of currency, were leading instead to an uncontrollable dissemination of risks in this area, reinforcing irresponsibility rather than responsibility.

For natural and human resources, environmental and social responsibility (ESR) like the former paternalism has a purely voluntary basis and businesses that adopt it seek as far as possible to keep it out of legal frameworks. Taking responsibility seriously implies on the contrary giving legal force and coherence to these undertakings. This can occur in specific cases through a legislator, a national judge or a collective international negotiation. But more broadly, the question of the re-articulation of corporate or state responsibility for social or environmental matters cannot be understood independently of the profound changes affecting legal relationships in the post-industrial world.

The thinking embodied in 'government by numbers' which accompanies the digital revolution and the plan to establish a total market has the dual effect of overturning the rule of law and creating a resurgence of ties of allegiance as a paradigm of a legal relationship. This new paradigm makes one subject subordinate to the objectives of another which at the same time oversees it and cedes a degree of autonomy to it or accords it a degree of protection. It takes account of new form of individual labour relationships (salaried or non-salaried) as well as new forms of organisation of businesses (in production chains and networks) and new forms of dependency of some states through their voluntary adherence to unequal treaties or structural adjustment programmes which take away part of their sovereignty. Instead of being occupied by subjects acting feely under the auspices of a common law through which all responsibilities are determined, the legal stage is now occupied by subjects engaged in multiple ties of allegiance.

This retreat of the law in favour of allegiances throws light on the present impasses of social, environmental and financial responsibility. The tie of allegiance allows the dominant party (the lord) to impose on the dominated party (the vassal) responsibility for decisions that the latter is obliged to take in the management of its affairs. The Guinean or Greek state will thus be held responsible for the deterioration of the health situation among their population even though this deterioration results from conditions imposed by the IMF or the Troïka. The sub-contracting business, the farmer who is a part of the agri-food industry or the subsidiary of a multinational will be judged solely responsible for the pollution or work accidents which stem from the economic conditions which are imposed on them by those they are contracted to. But the structure of the tie of allegiance also provides an insight into the means of avoiding these perverse effects. The power of control they give to the dominant party is both a right of oversight and a duty to protect the long-term interests of the dependent party. That is where the German notion of *Sorgenpflicht* is reappearing, a duty of care which includes oversight and protection, control and support. It has been rediscovered in modern law as the 'duty of care'. The evolution of the employment contract is as always a good indicator of this resurgence. The 'flexibility' now demanded of the employee calls for a corresponding duty on the employer's part to ensure the maintenance of the employee's professional skills and an obligation to provide security of earnings. The logic of a more or less long-term personal relationship thus goes beyond that of a simple exchange of services.

This evolution is not confined to employment contracts. It is seen also in networks of companies and more generally what are called relational contracts. It leads to a distribution of responsibilities through networks of dependence which rest not on obedience but rather on the workings of the entities that they link. This carries the risk of allowing those who create and profit from these networks to get rid of their responsibilities by handing them over to subordinates. To confront this risk various legal instruments have arisen, which however so far lack a sound theoretical base or a coherent framework. In France the Catala bill (2005) to reform the law of obligations proposed giving this type of responsibility a broad application, envisaging that "a person who manages or organises a work activity of another person and gains economic advantage from it is responsible for the harm caused by the latter in the exercise of this activity."[11]

Many of these arrangements seek to 'lift the veil' of moral personality to expose the person actually responsible for the harm. They are found within the laws pertaining to competition, undeclared work, dismissals, workplace safety, expatriation of employees and the environment. In France, a similar rule was envisaged for the person "who controls the economic or capital activities of a professional in a situation of dependence even if acting independently, when the victim can establish that the harm caused is related to the exercise of control".[12] The adoption of this far-reaching proposal would have given a legal foundation to the phrase *ubi emolumentum ibi onus* (the onus should lie where the profit is) by linking the harmful consequences of an economic activity to the person who controls it or profits from it. This could potentially have been able to make French companies accountable in the Rana Plaza[13] disaster. Parliament held back at the time because of the threat of production moving abroad, but the idea resurfaces from time to time, most recently in the form of a bill on the duty of care of parent companies.

At the end of the nineteenth century, it was the judge who, confronted with the inaction of the legislator, first discovered the founding principles of the responsibility for things. And today still, the judge could find responses to the new questions raised by the ties of allegiance in the law of responsibility. Following the model of 'tenure-service', these ties combine real and personal elements. A dominant party cedes to a subservient party the use of a good (the real element) accompanied by the obligation to achieve objectives stipulated by the dominant party (the personal element). Allegiance thus combines techniques of concession with subservience of persons. The refinement of the notion of guardian in respect of civil liability should allow a fair distribution of responsibilities in the case of concessions of things while the general principle of responsibility for others should allow the same in the case of the subservience of persons.

The responsibility for things creates as yet under-utilised possibilities for lifting the veil of moral responsibility in case of transfer of guardianship. The Court of Cassation concluded for the first time in 1993 that the owner of the thing, even though it had been entrusted to a third party, does not cease to be responsible for it unless it is established that the party has itself been given the means of prevention for the harm it could cause. The case concerned pollution of water caused by barley waste which was dumped by the business entrusted with the demolition and removal of an industrial building belonging to the company La Malterie de Moselle. The Court of Cassation found the latter responsible, holding that the company:

> could not be unaware in its professional quality, of the risk presented by barley, a substance which may undergo a dangerous fermentation and had not drawn this to the attention of the company [tasked with its removal] to the risk that could not reasonably have been assumed to exist, from which it followed that La Malterie de Moselle had retained guardianship of the thing, which had caused the harm.[14]

This general rule enables the seeking out of the responsibility of the person who has the knowledge and the power to prevent the harm. It involves all forms of allegiance where a subservient party is granted some authority along with the guardianship of dangerous things. It could also notably be applicable to intellectual property, where the distinction in medieval property law between an eminent domain which retains the intellectual property and a domain of utility devolved to the owner of the thing could apply. The result is to create between the two parties a bond of allegiance, since the possessor can only make use of their good under conditions and limits that have been ceded to it and which accompany the thing no matter in whose hands it is. The appropriately named operating systems of computers provide us with the everyday experience of dependence of this type with respect to the IT giants which have given us the use of them. Another example with broad implications is that of genetically modified organisms (GMOs) sold by their manufacturers to farmers who then are placed into a long-term relationship of allegiance towards them. In these various circumstances, one should consider that the owners of the intellectual property remain the guardians and thus the responsible entities for the products that they bring to market. Such an objective possibility should be incurred, each time that the intellectual property goes hand in hand with the technological know-how of the object that is marketed. The responsibility for defective goods as it is today regulated by European law[15] is a particular case of this general principle of the objective responsibility of the guardian. Thus the principle should be applicable in cases where, as in the 1993 judgment by the Court of Cassation, the conditions for its effective application of the directive are not met.

Thus many tools exist for the establishment of responsibility of those who put dangerous goods into circulation, for example the creators of financial products, especially so-called structured products, whose explosive dimension was revealed in 2008. The idea of applying responsibility for defective products to them was put forward by Jean-Francois Gayraud, a police superintendent specialised in financial crime. It is particularly interesting because there is no reason that this type of product should escape the reach of the European directive, according to which "A product is defective when it does not offer the degree of safety that one could legitimately expect".[16] It could however be argued (and the financial institutions concerned would not hesitate to do so) that the directive only covers bodily harm, or harm caused by something other than the product itself, which would risk excluding purely financial harm. Assuming that they were outside the coverage of the directive, another possibility would be to make use of responsibility of the originators of financial products under the principle of 'guardianship of the structure', which unlike guardianship of behaviour is not necessarily transferred with the ownership of the good. The notion of 'guardian of the structure' also has the advantage of putting into practice an active conception of responsibility as an obligation to act in a responsible manner, and not solely an obligation to repair harm once it has occurred.

Secondly, *responsibility for actions of others* [vicarious liability] offers the means of a fair division of responsibilities within a relationship of allegiance.

As it did a century earlier for responsibility for things, the Court of Cassation upheld in 1991 in paragraph 1 of article 1384 of the Civil Code a general principle of responsibility for actions of others. It is also a strict liability, from which an entity cannot be exonerated by proving that it has committed no fault. The reach of this general principle has not yet been fully established by case law. Originally, it was limited to institutions in charge of organising and controlling on a *permanent basis* the *living conditions* of others (in practice minors and the disabled). But these references to the permanence of living conditions have disappeared from subsequent jurisprudence which has laid this responsibility on associations – mostly sporting – who on a professional basis take on the organisation, direction and control of the activities of their members.

The power of organisation, direction and control is thus the source of vicarious liability for actions of others which goes beyond special cases already recognised by the law (i.e. the responsibility for actions by one's agents, children or pupils). As has been pointed out earlier, the emergence of this general principle responds to the necessity of repairing harm that results from the degree of freedom granted to those persons through whom authority is exercised. This consideration could be applied fully to the ties of allegiance that are woven in the economic sphere. They imply the exercise of control by a dominant entity, a degree of autonomy granted to the subordinate entities and a distribution of risks. The holding or ownership of the material means of production is conferred on subsidiaries, suppliers or subcontractors. That means managers operating with degrees of autonomy within an organisation that they do not control, but rather which controls them. The way of understanding these ties and organising them in networks is central to the new forms of organisation of major companies whose value is less dependent on the material ownership of the means of production than on the conception and oversight over the information systems that determine the structure of these networks. A source of value for the business, this articulation of networks of allegiance also gives rise to new types of risks – *organisational risks* stemming from the dilution of responsibilities down through the value chain.

In this way, the potential of the general principle of vicarious liability can be better understood. Responsibility for the actions of agents reflects integrated and hierarchical systems whose members must obey the orders that they receive. In such systems, typical of the Fordist industrial world, the responsibility fell to managers and led to the civil immunity of their agents in the exercising of their functions. Unlike the latter, ties of allegiance introduce a degree of freedom of operators. This freedom is codified and monitored but it is still freedom, which thus takes away a necessary share of responsibility from each operator bound up in the network of allegiance. When harm has been determined to be imputable exclusively to one or the other, there is no need to mobilise vicarious liability. But it is different when the harm has wholly or partly been attributable to the overall conception and coordination of the supply, manufacturing or distribution system as a whole. In such circumstances, which applied in the Rana Plaza case, the manifest fault of one of the members of the production system (the Bangladeshi garment manufacturer) does not absolve from their responsibilities the major companies which organised the system (i.e. the leading US and European brands).

The case may also arise that no individual responsibility can be attributed because the harm results from an inherent risk in the organisation of the activity. It was a case of this type that led to the widening the perimeter of the general principle of vicarious liability – the case of a rugby match that led to the death of one of the players not being attributable to one identified player; the responsibility of the club was found to be involved. There is no need to refer to game theory or sporting metaphors in vogue in management speak to understand that a multinational company which has organised a value chain to win market share is in a similar situation. It should be judged responsible for harm caused by the organisation when it cannot be exclusively imputable to any one link in the chain. In other words, the general principle of vicarious liability is an appropriate response to the specific risks engendered by these new forms of allegiance-based organisations. When the existence of these risks cannot be imputable to the sole fault of the subsidiary, supplier or sub-contractor of a dominant enterprise, the latter thus should in principle be fully or jointly liable. And it should be the same in the case where a country's economic policy has become subject to control by international institutions such as the IMF or the Troïka.

[. . .] It is thus possible to affirm that there is no lack of legal instruments for 'taking responsibility seriously'. The true difficulties lie elsewhere: in the crushing weight of the economic ideology that leads judges and legislators to think that any far-reaching initiative would risk harming their country's comparative advantage on a global stage dominated by law shopping. Or, in the strength of the illusions maintained by the ideology of the total market which taking the earth, work and currency as commodities like any others is fated sooner or later to come up against its catastrophic limit. As Paul Valéry pointed out:

> Society lives by illusions. Every society is a sort of collective dream. These illusions become dangerous when they no longer create illusion. The awakening from this kind of dream is a nightmare.[17]

To avoid the illusions of globalisation and the total market turning into a nightmare, we need to break away from what Karl Polyani called the 'economic solipsism'. This would require of law the regulation of financial markets and making the free circulation of capital and goods subject to social and economic conditions. As the century-long experience of the International Labour Organization shows, it is a vain hope that all states in the world might agree on ambitious international rules respected by all. But it is realistic to think that some states, determined to respect within their territory strict labour and environmental laws, would make access to their markets conditional on respecting a similar level, thereby encouraging a movement of positive emulation. There are resources in the law which would enable the replacement of the globalisation juggernaut by a *mondialisation* which respects the diversity of people and of the conditions under which they live out their lives.

Notes

1 This introduction originally appeared in *Prendre la responsabilité au sérieux*, Alain Supiot, Mireille Delmas-Marty (eds) Presses Universitaires de France 2015. It is translated and reproduced here by kind permission of the author Alain Supiot.
2 Robert Surcouf (1773–1827).
3 The notion of *patronat* comes from Roman law, where it designated the obligations that tied a freed slave to his former master, the one who had given him a place in civil life and whose name he now carried.
4 Preamble to the ILO Constitution (1919), reaffirmed by the Philadelphia Declaration (1944).
5 The concept is inspired by the title of the well-known work by Ronald Dworkin. Ronald Dworkin *Taking Rights Seriously* (Harvard University Press, Cambridge, MA, 1978).
6 In this and following paragraphs, Alain Supiot summarises and synthesises the content of the book to which this chapter was an introduction (see note 1). In order to retain the flow of the argument, references to sections of the original publication have been retained here.
7 (Translator's note) There is no separate English translation of this term which is usually simply rendered by 'globalisation'. The difference as explained by the author is that *globalisation's* focus is 'the uniformisation of the world as a total market'. *Mondialisation* puts the emphasis on 'a world made liveable through the intelligence and diversity of civilisations and of their growing interdependence'. It is thus a much broader concept than globalisation, which is restricted to the economic sphere. In order to maintain the distinction in the translation, the term *mondialisation* will be used as in the original.
8 See note 6.
9 See note 6.
10 Milton Friedman "The Social Responsibility of Business is to Increase Its Profits" *New York Times Magazine* (13 September 1970).
11 (Translator's note). Cf. the common law concept of vicarious liability, which is employed *infra* in the translation.
12 Draft proposal to reform the law of obligations (Articles 1101 and 1386 of the French Code civil, 22 September 2005 (draft article 1360).
13 (Translator's note). The Rana Plaza was an eight-storey garment factory in Bangladesh which collapsed in 2013, killing over a thousand people.
14 Cour de Cassation, Première chambre civile, 9 June 1993 Arrêt no. 91–11.216.
15 Directive 85/374/CEE 25 July 1985.
16 Ibid.
17 Paul Valéry *Mauvaises pensées et autres* (Gallimard, Paris, 1942).

6 Responsibility and the transformative role of law

Neetu Sharma

Responsible behaviour has been an intrinsic and integral component of humanity and human relationships from time immemorial. A scrupulous sense of responsibility towards each other has nurtured not only these relationships but has also been at the very basis of civilised society. It may not be an exaggeration to say that the adherence or non-adherence to responsibility was the key determinant defining what theorists described as the social contract. Responsibility, at the core of the social contract between a socio-professional group, such as scientists, journalists and civil servants, and the rest of the society, mitigates corporatist or sectoral interests or loyalty to a limited grouping with the consciousness of being part of a larger community. Thus, the concept of co-responsibility expands the ideal of the social contract from the local to the global level.

Responsibility and the law: historical perspective

The wellbeing of society is directly associated with the phenomenon of a just and equitable social order. However, the coexistence of deprivation and affluence has been a key feature of modern democratic societies and while both welfare and rights approaches to development are in vogue, little has been done to aid their convergence. The prevalence of widespread vulnerabilities and apparent evidence of negligible progress towards their reduction help expose such dichotomies. A responsibility framework provides an alternative and organic approach towards ensuring human wellbeing.

The concept of responsibility seems to be implicit in the arguments of John Locke and Jean-Jacques Rousseau. Both believed that we gain civil rights in return for accepting the obligation to respect and defend the rights of others, giving up some freedoms to do so.

A close scrutiny of the theory of natural rights also seems to have been influenced by both responsibility and ethics. One of the proponents of the natural rights theory, Hugo Grotius, postulates that each individual has natural rights that enable self-preservation and he uses this idea as a basis for moral consensus in the face of religious diversity and the rise of natural science. He seeks to find a minimalist basis for a moral beginning for society, a kind of natural law that everyone could accept. He goes so far as to say in his *On the Law of War and Peace* that even if we were to concede what we cannot concede without the utmost wickedness, namely that there is no God, these laws would still hold.[1] People have inherent rights as human beings but a delineation can be made between those rights because of each person's moral compass; everyone has to accept that each person as an individual is entitled to try to protect himself. Each person should, therefore, avoid doing harm to, or interfering with, another. While this may seem like a minimalist aspect of responsibility, it also assumes importance in a highly fragmented and disparate society.

A similar but more constructive sentiment lies at the basis of Gandhian philosophy and is manifested in his remark that "a duty well performed creates a corresponding right" and the rights spring from the duties well done.[2] Thus, the very right to live accrues to us only when we assume the duty of citizenship of the world. The phenomenon of responsibility continues to be a moral basis for the modern day society, political economy and governance. Otherwise, society will be riven with conflict and contention.

The history of modern society is a reflection of the responses from the state, civil society and individuals to various situations and circumstances in all spheres of human activities. While society's ascribing to underlying principles of ethics and responsibility in all aspects of life may minimise the occurrence of conflict and contention, the reality is that ethics are personal ethos and values, so are not uniformly held. In the public sphere the holding of widely divergent ethical principles can lead to outright conflict. In such a situation there needs to be some commonality in the society's ethics to the survival of our only and fragile planet. These common ethics must have deep roots in our different cultures, philosophical or religious traditions and reflect the interconnectedness of our universe. Responsibility is at the core of this common ethic, as reciprocity, caring and management of the commons has always been the condition precedent to being part of a community. Therefore, even the poorest persons and communities claim not only their rights but also their responsibility, towards children, elders and the commons, as the expression of being a citizen of the world.

Evolution of contradictions between rights and responsibility

In modern times, the articulation of responsibility as the core value in the process of social transformation is relatively new. This newfound assertion has primarily been a result of the trivialisation, and at times complete privation, of the responsibility of individuals, families, communities, corporates and even states in philosophical and legal discourse. Against the backdrop of two world wars that witnessed widespread atrocities, collateral damage as well as blatant violation of human dignity, rights and lives, the rights discourse captured the imagination of the whole world, resulting in international declarations that followed the wars. The Universal Declaration on Human Rights (UDHR) and subsequent covenants dealing with civil and political rights, as well as on economic, social and cultural rights, were strongly rights-centric and the principle of responsibility was largely limited to states.

In the post-war period, and especially in newly independent nations, constitutions began reflecting a strong dislike of tyrannical regimes and hence fundamental rights became the nucleus for constitutional development. While fundamental duties found space in some constitutions in South Asia such as India and Nepal, these remained fundamental only in the sense of their essence and significance for humanity and human values and not from the application and enforcement point of view. However, that by itself is not the issue. It is natural for the people to cherish, and do all that it takes, to protect their liberties. While the principle of responsibility insinuated itself into some legal frameworks, such as the inclusion of reasonable restrictions on the exercise of fundamental freedoms and special protections from the state for marginalised and vulnerable people, the inclusion of positive and constructive responsibilities was generally minimal and largely tokenistic.

The rights-based approach was further fortified in legal discourses in the Global South during the second half of the last century; the state became the ultimate duty bearer and people, the rights holders. In the popular democracies, this rights-based approach manifested in the creation of special protections and entitlements for the marginalised.

Today, throughout the world most governments have policies, laws and programmes designed to protect and promote the wellbeing of marginalised and vulnerable people and those who have been traditionally discriminated against, such as tribals, and dalits in India. It is disappointing to note that despite all these measures, these vulnerabilities continue to exist in their classic form. Additionally, external factors, such as globalisation, corporatisation and technological advances, are either aggravating or rendering these vulnerabilities much more complex. While legislation has created legal entitlements, the lack of an environment conducive to the enjoyment of these entitlements renders the legislation impotent.

Achieving harmony between rights and responsibility and the role of law

There are also other areas of social interaction that require the creation of a conducive environment, the promotion of human wellbeing and evolution in the most sustainable and affirmative way. Collectively, the environment, public spaces and the public good make up the fulcrum of human existence. The nature of this interaction and the use that is made of the three elements define human life now and in the not-too-distant future. While regulatory mechanisms do help, the sense of responsibility for the planet, and for future generations, needs to guide the human actions in these spheres.

The responsibility principle propounds the existence of an inherent sense of responsibility of all human beings and upholds it as a virtue and a key factor in the transition towards sustainable societies. Each individual, group, family or community has responsibilities towards everyone else. Like human rights, human responsibilities are also universal, although there are varying views on their extent. Some commentators attach the principle of proportionality to responsibility, meaning that the level of responsibility owed is proportionate to the power exercised. In practical terms, although even the most marginalised has responsibilities, the amount of responsibility increases in proportion to the power, and the most powerful has the highest amount.

There is a complex relationship between the law and responsibility. In most legal frameworks, whether instruments at international level or in domestic domains, rights have superseded responsibilities. Even where responsibilities have been included, these have largely remained ambiguous, limited and devoid of any effective enforceable mechanisms. Adequate and lucid articulation of the content of responsibilities seems to be the missing link attributing to the lack of observance and importance being attached to responsibilities, especially in comparison with rights and entitlements. This is the rationale for the promotion of inclusion of clear, enforceable and, if possible, measurable responsibilities, in legal frameworks. The integration of specific responsibilities into law, especially into those laws creating entitlements and special protections, enables both their implementation and enforcement. The content of such responsibilities should be specified at various levels – individual, family, community and institutional. This would then create a legal environment which enables everyone to exercise his/her rights and which contributes towards universal wellbeing.

While the integration of the responsibility principle into law enhances its chances of being implemented, it also challenges the very nature of responsibility itself. Since responsibility, unlike law, is a virtue emanating from the inner human self, making responsibilities legally enforceable challenges the basic underpinning of the responsibility approach itself. The proponents of the responsibility approach themselves have been grappling with this dichotomy while trying to address the complicated dynamics between law and responsibility. Despite a near universal recognition of the importance of responsibility and responsible behaviour in all spheres of human life, applying the principle in the present day's sociocultural and economic environment has been mired by several challenges.

Advent of human rights approach

In the Global South, the scepticism about a responsibility framework emanates from the emphasis on universal responsibilities and the assumption that the vulnerable and deprived people also have responsibilities, in the same amount and extent as others. Human rights opponents and proponents have reservations about the implications of a responsibility approach. The human rights paradigm defines states and their agencies and institutions as duty bearers, and individuals and communities as rights holders, making a clear distinction between the two. However, the ubiquitous nature of the responsibility principle denotes everyone, individuals, communities, states and their agencies, the bearer of responsibility. Human rights proponents believe that the incorporation of responsibility into the human rights discourse will not only allow states to abdicate their responsibilities, but would also result in diminution of achievements in the area of protection and promotion of human rights. The inclusion of responsibilities for individuals and communities in the legal framework, or making the responsibilities enforceable by law, would result in a situation wherein individuals and communities will themselves be held responsible for their problems and finding solutions for the same. All this may potentially lead to transgressed state power and amplified state authority leaving individuals vulnerable to states' coercive power.[3]

The concept of proportionate responsibility can build a bridge between the human rights and responsibility approaches since it propounds that the state has the ultimate responsibility by virtue of having the ultimate authority. Although the concerns expressed by the human rights defenders and theorists are legitimate, the importance of the responsibility approach cannot be undermined; the principle of responsibility demands human observance because it is a virtue and a basic tenet guiding human behaviour and defining human relations. The dichotomy of the relationship between law and responsibility, however, becomes invisible when the role of law is contextualised for modern societies transitioning into sustainable societies. The transformative, positive and constructive role of law needs to be explored, not only for explaining and upholding the necessity for responsibility but also for the legal instruments to remain relevant.

Experience has shown that an irresponsive or inadequate environment around people fails to encourage and keep them motivated to act responsibly in interpersonal relations or in public life, and there seems to be a trend towards blatant self-interest; on the other hand, selfless endeavours for general wellbeing also are appreciated. A major reason that is attributable for irresponsible social behaviour is the inconvenience or discomfort or the possibility of it that may be caused to the individuals who acts responsibly. While inherent human nature does prompt people to conduct themselves responsibly and to contribute to the public good, most are wary of personal repercussions. What is the incentive to act responsibly if such behaviour causes inconvenience and does not provide any reward or positive outcome? A classic example of this is a situation where a victim of a road accident is left unaided because others are unwilling to go through the inconvenience of dealing with hospitals, police and probably courts. In this scenario, the law in its regulatory role indirectly routes people towards irresponsible behaviour.

The relationship between individual autonomy and regulated responsibility also requires closer examination. The general belief that autonomy or individualism limits responsibilities may not be always correct. Self-governing principles also endeavour to accommodate, instead of separate and perpetuate, singularity and society. This is very similar to the misunderstanding of Kant's expression "under the idea of freedom", where he defines freedom within the moral domain. He says that freedom is a universal idea and imperative basis of that are morality and responsibility.[4]

Responsibility as a virtue needs to be observed in private as well as public spaces. Although the debate on individual autonomy perpetuates the idea of legitimacy of individuals, morals can help codify responsibilities. One fundamental limitation which confronts the law is its inability to operate within and regulate private spheres. Responsibility complements the authority of law by filling this gap. However, the aspiration of having provisions in law to enforce responsibilities in private spaces is in itself contradictory. There is a need to strike a balance between inherent and legally imposed responsibility, especially in the private spaces; this is dependent on needs and circumstances. It is also relevant to mention here that while responsibility infuses soul into the law, law imparts tangibility and pragmatism to responsibility and brings it out from the realm of abstract idealism. Law also saves responsibility from convenient customisation and consequent dilution.

Climate change: a global challenge

Unbridled and irresponsible exploitation of natural resources has been the most melancholy aspect of the technological advancements and developments in various fields such as transportation, putting planet Earth and its inhabitants at risk, with temperatures increasing at an unprecedented pace, glaciers melting and waters and land negotiating violently for space. The number and extent of natural calamities in recent years has been unparalleled, as have human and animal lives lost due to such natural disasters. Many of these have been primarily caused by human interventions with nature. These environmental disasters, and many more crises, especially financial, have one thing in common and that is irresponsible behaviour by certain groups of people. Since much of this behaviour could not be held to be illegal, the irresponsible behaviour could not be sanctioned.

This challenge is compounded and deserves even more attention in the case of vulnerable groups towards whom everyone has a responsibility. These responsibilities encompass respecting, protecting and proactively promoting the well-being of these groups who are either traditionally discriminated against or have remained at the lowest rung of development because of age, gender, ability or other discrimination.

Notwithstanding these challenges, the need to intensify efforts and to augment responsibilities cannot be underestimated in the contemporary world. These challenges ensued from the advent of a highly individualistic society, which arose as a consequence of free and unregulated competition in the social, political and financial arenas. While it is true that healthy competition may encourage excellence and innovation, in modern times it has led to a creation of ever increasing disparities. Development in the economic and technological fields has not been an inclusive one, and a class of people has always remained at the periphery of these gains. Such disparities have also given birth to widespread vulnerabilities as well as discontent that have contributed to the unrest and violence in many parts of the world.

Of all potential solutions to the challenges facing humanity, the responsibility approach is the most viable option. Concomitant with the need to embed this into our foundational norms is this requirement to integrate responsibility with law, given the omnipresent nature of the latter. This will ensure that responsibility, as part of the legal framework, will consciously be brought into operation.

Transformative role of law

The origin of law is traditionally traced back to the need to have rules for settling disputes and ensuring order in the society. With the evolution of society the role of law has also undergone tremendous change. Law and legal instruments can be effective and remain relevant only when they reflect and respond to changes in the social milieu, new developments, vulnerabilities and challenges with which humanity is confronted. Law may be a double-edged sword; it may help reinforce prevailing social and economic relations, or it may be a powerful tool in the hands of those seeking to resist, challenge or transform those relations.[5]

Law in an interdependent world and need for propelling social harmony

In the contemporary interdependent world, the role of law has gone well beyond its regulatory functions. This view is upheld by minimalist and utilitarian perspectives on law and justice which have been the driving theoretical underpinnings of the laissez faire and free competition schools of thought. Such individualistic views have been challenged by the egalitarian approaches as well as the proponents of a just world order, such as Thomas Pogge. Pogge argues that the global rich have a duty to eradicate poverty because they have violated the principal of justice to not unduly harm others by their coercive global order. In *World Poverty and Human Rights: Cosmopolitan Responsibilities and Reforms* (2002), Pogge explains that the poorest 44 percent of humankind have 1.3 percent of global income, and their purchasing power per person per day is less than that of $2.15 in the US in 1993; 826 million of them do not have enough to eat. One-third of all human deaths are from poverty-related causes: 18 million annually, including 12 million children under five. At the other end of the spectrum, the 15 percent of humankind in the developed countries have 80 percent of global income.[6] Another recent study[7] states that more than 70 percent of the world's adults own under $10,000 in wealth. This 70.1 percent of the world holds only 3 percent of global wealth. The world's wealthiest individuals, those owning over $100,000 in assets, total only 8.6 percent of the global population but own 85.6 percent of global wealth. Pogge argues that shifting 1 or 2 percent of the wealthy states' share toward poverty eradication is morally compelling and cannot be ignored by affluent people. The same corollary also applies to the world order, where rich countries need to take moral responsibility for the countries that are poor and respond to this situation in a constructive manner rather than manipulating their situation.

While libertarianism emphasises freedom, individual liberty, voluntary association and respect of property rights, utilitarianism holds that the proper course of action is that the overall "happiness" is maximized; actions are right if they are useful or for the benefit of a majority. With the advent of egalitarianism that favours equality, of some sort, among living entities and advocates the removal of inequalities among people, the emphasis has transferred onto the transformative role of law. Law acts as a tool for social transformation and social engineering towards a more egalitarian society, and it is a *sine qua non* that the law be effective. It is expected that the law will play a positive, proactive, progressive and constructive role, given the need for social transformation towards an equitable society. This is not applicable to domestic regimes only but is equally important for creation and maintenance of an equitable and just global order.[8]

Enforcement and application of responsibility

For the law to be constructive and transformative, it is crucial that responsibility be incorporated and mechanisms provided to ensure that responsibilities are observed. Other aspects of transformative law, such as recognition of diverse needs, protection of vulnerable groups, promotion of sustainable practices, public participation, protection of public goods and advancement of humanitarian values, and the protection of the planet, also need to be articulated and clearly defined responsibilities, for each of these must be incorporated. The need for transformative law is linked to the need for ensuring justice and equity across all of society.

The real test of the legal provisions lies in their application and enforcement. One can find innumerable examples of legal frameworks that are just, positive and transformative towards sustainable society in their intent, but which fall short on operational mechanisms and hence fail. The responsibility approach to law emphasises the articulation and identification of clear responsibilities for functionaries in the system, other individuals, institutions and agencies involved in implementation, as well as those who are to benefit from such law. Going a step further, this approach also suggests the inclusion of accountability mechanisms for those who fail to act responsibly and redress provisions to compensate for damage incurred. Inadequate and insufficient articulation of responsibilities acts as a dampener on the creation of responsible and sustainable societies.

Need for organic relationship between law and responsibility

The relationship between law and responsibility needs to develop organically, rather than the two being superimposed on each other. It is important to work with a set of fundamental principles based on the ethos of responsibility while engaging with the law-making process especially when those laws will have implications for the environment, protection of the marginalised or the general wellbeing of humanity and planet Earth.

The first and most important principle is the universality of responsibility. Hence, the philosophy of co-responsibility must inform any understanding and interpretation of law. Further, participation is a fundamental part of citizenship; it is the process by which all groups can influence decision-making which affects their lives, so as to bring about positive change. Participation is not solely the act of expressing an opinion and having that opinion taken seriously, but of being able to construct that opinion freely through accessing information, meeting and debating with others. It is a responsibility of the lawmakers to ensure that participatory mechanisms are embedded in the legal framework. Decisions that affect the groups must be taken in consultation with them and the means for enabling this consultation must also be built into the legal framework. Any stumbling blocks to personal and collective participation should be identified and rectified.

Each individual, group and institution has responsibilities towards vulnerable groups. But even the vulnerable have responsibilities, including raising their voices against the injustice and exploitation and demanding an equitable share in the dividends of development. However, most importantly these responsibilities are proportionate to a person's or group's power, authority, capabilities and resources. While fixing and defining responsibilities, the respective abilities of various actors must be taken into account and the responsibilities must be articulated in proportion to these abilities. Logically then, the State bears the ultimate responsibility towards all.

Very often the protection of environment and marginalised or vulnerable groups are subjected to violation by third parties in pursuit of either market interests or profit making. This is particularly important in an increasingly globalised world, where even nation states are gradually losing control over their economies and means of production. Legal frameworks must ensure the protection of vulnerable groups' interests from any external and private party invasion. But, lack of protection mechanisms should not provide an excuse for state inaction. Such protection must also encompass the wellbeing and protection of individual interests vis-à-vis utilitarian objects.

The primary function of the transformative law is not just to reconcile conflicting interests between individuals and to bring societal harmony but rather to protect social interest through social justice. Since it is not easy to define these expressions in tangible terms, it is important to protect larger social interests and include relevant provisions in the legal instruments. Dealing with social issues, removing uncertainties in law, ensuring effective representation, encouraging public participation in governmental decision-making, implementing the general will, and so on all form part of collective responsibility in a democracy. This also includes ensuring fair and just laws, transparency and accountability of the authorities, and the means of dealing with corruption. All these need to be enabled by the legal framework.

Despite fundamental differences in the nature and disposition of law and responsibility, they complement each other. The absence and non-observance of the responsibility principle make law less effective and less able to be an agent of social change. Responsibility, on the other hand, remains a non-executable virtue based purely on personal motivations, in the absence of a legal regime capable of enforcing it. The integration of responsibility into law creates an enabling environment into which it becomes embedded. Further, legal backing of responsibility helps encourage people to believe in their own inner sense of responsibility and to act accordingly.

Incorporation of responsibility in legal frameworks

Legal frameworks must be based on the vision of the integration of all the vulnerable groups ensuring that their voices are heard and that they are able to influence decision-making, benefit from the development paradigm and are in a comparable situation to other groups. International conventions and treaties include many provisions aimed at protecting and promoting the wellbeing of humankind. Some countries have adapted many of these provisions into their respective domestic legal frameworks, lending them enforceability and justiciability; many others have signed and ratified a number of such provisions and some of these have also been translated into legally enforceable provisions. However, there are still many that require legal sanction. Responsibilities and obligations which form part of international agreements must be brought fully into domestic law. A similar perspective may also apply to corporate social responsibility. While in a libertarian society and liberal democracies, there is minimal regulation of private companies which justifies the making of profit by any fair means, the idea of giving back to society has gained currency in the wake of widening social and economic disparities as well as chronic exploitation of natural resources.

Acknowledging their responsibility towards society and the environment, businesses and corporates have been engaging in philanthropy for a long time. In order to streamline the philanthropic activities and ensure accountability and transparency, the government of India made it mandatory for companies to undertake corporate social responsibility (CSR) activities under the Companies Act 2013. The concept of CSR is defined in section 135 of the Act, and it is applicable to companies which have an annual turnover of INR 1,000 crore[9] or more, or a net worth of INR 500 crore[10] or more, or a net profit of INR 5 crore[11] or more. Under this section, these companies are supposed to set aside at least 2 percent of their average profit in the last three years for CSR activities.[12] The law has listed a wide spectrum of activities under CSR, which cover activities such as promotion of education, gender equity and women's empowerment; combating HIV/AIDS, malaria and other diseases; eradication of extreme poverty; contribution to the Prime Minister's National Relief Fund and other central funds; social business projects; reduction in child mortality; and improving maternal health, environmental sustainability and employment-enhancing vocational skills among others.[13]

There have been concerns that these CSR efforts are oversold, window-dressing from profit won at the expense of other rights' violations by poorly regulated companies. Such anxieties speak to the need for duties that go beyond insurance against the worst abuses; they must serve the pursuit of economic justice, not simply help businesses to advertise their ethical propriety.

Public trusteeship

The idea of public trusteeship has been the source of inspiration for many thinkers and philosophers for a very long time. In the context of India, Gandhian theory of trusteeship had spirituality in its undercurrents and was applied to advocate for an egalitarian society. He said, everything belonged to God and was from God. Therefore everything on the planet was for His people as a whole, not for a particular individual. When an individual had more than his proportionate share, he became a trustee of that portion for God's people. God who was all-powerful had no need to store. He created from day to day; hence men also should in theory live from day to day and not stockpile things. If this truth was accepted by people generally, it would become legalised and trusteeship would become part of the legal system. Gandhi wished this notion of trusteeship to be a gift from India to the world. Then, there would be no exploitation. He said that disparities in resources lay the seeds of a war more virulent than the last two world wars.[14] The Gandhian theory of trusteeship provides a means of transforming the capitalist order of society into a more egalitarian one.

Another manifestation of universal responsibility is the doctrine of public trust, which may operate as a fundamental basis in the creation of legal instruments in administrative and environmental laws. In the case of administrative law, it implies that the public officers are holders of public trust and that their authority flows from public good. Thus, all individuals who occupy public positions must act in public good. Similarly, the idea of a "collective trusteeship" for the integrity of the global environment and common areas such as the oceans, atmosphere and outer space has also inspired evolution of international environmental law, and national regulations for the environment.

There are instances of recognition of public trusteeship as a critical doctrine that has the potential to provide legal protection for the environment, freshwaters, air and oceans. A statute granted legal personhood to Whanganui River in New Zealand and a court in India recently also granted similar status to the rivers Ganges and Yamuna. The court in the city of Nainital in Northern India declared that the Ganges and Yamuna were "legal and living entities having the status of a legal person with all corresponding rights, duties and liabilities."[15] The court also appointed three officials as custodians of the rivers and ordered that a management board be created within three months to execute the order. The outcome and impact of these legislative and judicial decisions are yet to be seen. Several administrative issues of concern in the court orders are cited by the national/central government and these are being analysed by different wings of the government, but the order is of supreme importance in so far as it recognises the rights of natural bodies and environment. While this decision was later stayed by the Supreme Court of India in July 2017 and the final outcome remains uncertain, such legal and judicial developments do reaffirm the need for collective responsibility for the common good. Legal backing provides impetus to the public trusteeship approach to be used for common good. It is in this context that the association between law and responsibility needs to be developed and extended to trusteeship, without which, as in the case of other similar doctrines, it will remain a desirable theory. The social change and transition towards an egalitarian society is possible only when law plays a positive and constructive role and incorporates relevant responsibilities for carrying out the various functions.

Notes

1 Hugo Grotius *On the Law of War and Peace, 1625* (de Iure Belli AC Pacis: Libri Tres, in Quibus Ius Naturae Et Gentium, Item Juris Publici Praecipua Explicantur. Cum Annotatis Auctoris (1919) (Latin). A.W. Sijthoff, Leiden, 1919).

2 Mohandas Karamchand Gandhi*: Essential Writings* (J. Dear ed, Orbis Books, New York, 1970).
3 This view is based on the author's direct interactions with the human rights defenders, teachers of human rights and movement leaders, in India and the rest of South Asia.
4 Immanuel Kant *Groundwork of the Metaphysic of Morals* (Oxford University Press, Oxford, 1785/2002).
5 World Bank "World Development Report 2017: Governance and the Law" (January 2017).
6 Thomas Pogge (January 2005) 7(5) *Ethical Theory and Moral Practice* 537–550.
7 "Global Wealth Report: Where Are We Ten Years After the Crisis?" *Credit Suisse Research Institute*, 2017 <www.credit-suisse.com/corporate/en/articles/news-and-expertise/global-wealth-report-2017-201711.html>.
8 Astrid Paulsson "Thomas Pogge's Theory of a Minimally Just Global Institutional Order" (Dissertation, University of Skövde, 2011).
9 Approximately USD 153.8 million.
10 Approximately USD 77,020,000.
11 Approximately USD 750,000.
12 Section 135 of the Indian Companies Act, 2013.
13 Sangeeta Bansal and Shachi Rai "An Analysis of Corporate Social Responsibility Law in India" (2014) 49(50) *Economic and Political Weekly* <www.epw.in/>.
14 Mohandas Karamchand Gandhi "Harijan" in *Trusteeship* (J.T. Desai, Ahmedabad, India, 1960) ch 2.
15 *Mohd. Salim v. State of Uttarakhand* (March 20, 2017), Writ Petition (PIL) No. 126 of 2014.

7 The principle of responsibility in the global response to climate change

Origins and evolution

Adrian Macey

There can be no more challenging issue for the global community than climate change, well characterised as a "wicked problem" and high on both international and domestic policy agendas. The global response to climate change needs to reach deep into areas that are normally entirely within the responsibility of national governments. Its complexity and especially the variety of areas it affects – both directly and indirectly through what is required for the response – is unprecedented. Of the two dimensions of the response to climate change, adaptation and mitigation, adaptation (dealing with the effects of climate change) has a lesser international dimension than does mitigation (reducing the emissions that cause it). Adaptation is a national responsibility, albeit one which may be supplemented by finance and technology through international climate change instruments. But mitigation, being a quintessential global commons issue, is a collective responsibility.

Nations have wrestled with getting to a consensus on who should do what and how much to combat climate change – "burden-sharing" in the jargon of the international climate change negotiations. The concept of responsibility has always been present in these discussions but has proved highly contentious, and sometimes has been more of a hindrance than a help. This chapter considers how responsibility has evolved through the course of international climate change negotiations over the past quarter of a century, and the role it plays after the signing of the 2015 Paris Agreement. This evolution can be traced through formal documents, opinions expressed and the involvement of the various actors.

The first scientific research to demonstrate the problem of global warming, and its cause – the burning of fossil fuels – was that of Arrhenius and others in the late 19th century. There was a long gap before it passed from the science to the policy community. The transition was really only fully made in the last third of the 20th century. The 1979 World Climate Conference stimulated further work during the next decade. The establishment of the Intergovernmental Panel on Climate Change (IPCC) in 1988 created a bridge between science and policy; its work would inform the negotiations on a climate change treaty which began in 1990. After only 15 months of negotiation, the United Nations Framework Convention on Climate Change (UNFCCC) was opened for signature at the Rio Earth Summit in 1992; it came into force two years later.

Early expression of a responsibility principle

How was responsibility construed in this first global agreement on climate change? A core principle in the UNFCCC was "common but differentiated responsibilities and respective capabilities", usually referred to as CBDR. It should more properly be "CBDRRC"' for reasons that became apparent in the later stages of the negotiations.

What is to be understood by the principle? For a problem of such magnitude, the acceptance of "common" responsibilities was an important step. Some provisions of the UNFCCC are indeed expressed as universal obligations, which can be seen as flowing from this "common" element of responsibility. The core obligation under article 4.1 of the Convention, "commitments" applies to all parties and has a lengthy set of obligations. Article 4.1(b) is unequivocal in requiring all parties to undertake measures to mitigate climate change by addressing emissions of all greenhouse gases.

"But differentiated" introduces the notion of a distribution of responsibilities within the collective responsibility. How are responsibilities classed as "differentiated"? There are no criteria alongside the principle itself. The answer can be informed by the preamble of the Convention, which notes that the largest share of past and present emissions originated in developed countries, and that the developing countries' per capita emissions are low and their share of global emissions will grow. There is thus already a sense of a division between developed and developing countries. This is consistent with other United Nations treaties and international instruments.

A third element which was much less prevalent in negotiations and independent thinking about climate change until recently is "respective capabilities". This implies some conditionality between the degree of responsibility and the expectation of action. "Respective capabilities" acknowledges that is not solely the degree of responsibility for past emissions that determines what countries should be expected to contribute. Their capacity to do so must also be taken into account; how this is done may depend on many factors, but the major one would be wealth. Accordingly, the preamble to the Convention further recognises the need for developed countries to take "immediate action . . . as a first step towards comprehensive response strategies at the global, national . . . levels with due consideration of their relative contributions to the enhancement of the greenhouse effect". In the operational part of the Convention, article 3 states that developed countries should "take the lead".

However, in a decision that would have huge consequences for the evolution of the climate regime, a list of countries, Annex I, was included to cover the Organisation for Economic Co-operation and Development (OECD) members and the economies in transition of Eastern Europe. While not explicitly linked to CBDR, this list lent itself to a binary distinction of levels of responsibility and expectations of action. This is reflected in the non-binding goal of Annex I parties' emissions returning to 1990 levels by the year 2000 (article 4.2).

A further factor relevant to capacity is the nature of each economy and its mitigation potential, which will differ greatly according to its sectoral make-up. A country such as Uruguay, for example, with over 80 per cent of its emissions coming from the agriculture sector will have limited mitigation potential compared with a country with a large fossil fuel component in its energy system and a small agriculture sector. Capability is not, therefore, synonymous with responsibility.

CBDR differed from its nearest equivalent in the trade world, the longstanding special and differential treatment or "S&D" principle, as found in General Agreement on Tariffs and Trade (GATT) and World Trade Organisation (WTO) instruments. S&D recognises developing countries as a whole and within that, the additional category of least developed countries. The principle is applied to allow for some differential treatment of obligations, such as longer timetables for implementation of certain requirements. It is much less binary, though not without controversy. The question arises as to under what conditions should countries benefiting from S&D "graduate" to full obligations. But the concept of responsibility here does not have an explicit mention; the "capacity" element of CBDR is more applicable.

Responsibility in the Kyoto Protocol

For many in civil society, and especially the environmental non-governmental organisations, responsibility was, and is, simple: it lies with the "rich" countries. This view has been expressed in many ways, often very colourfully through demonstrations and street theatre during negotiating sessions. It has been encapsulated in slogans such as "rich countries pay your climate debt!" The second stage of international climate change negotiations, which produced the Kyoto Protocol in 1997, did nothing to advance the concept of responsibility, and instead cemented the binary division of countries into Annex I and non-Annex I, which was an oversimplification of CBDR. The civil society view referred to above was comforted by the Kyoto Protocol's specification of quantified emissions reduction limits (QELROs) for those same "rich" countries.

The first commitment period under Kyoto was duly negotiated with a binding five-year emissions budget for each Annex I party expressed as tonnes of carbon dioxide (CO_2) equivalent and listed in Annex B of the Protocol. During the negotiations, many Annex I parties made attempts to provide for the evolution of the protocol so as to accommodate, over time, commitments by non-Annex I countries – in other words, for the latter to begin taking on a greater share of the common responsibilities that were enshrined in the Convention. Provisions which would give effect to this (not immediately, but at least to provide a pathway towards it) were present through the negotiations but had to be dropped at the end as no consensus could be reached. This divide was starkly revealed in the final plenary which adopted the Kyoto Protocol. New Zealand stated that "Annex I Parties" constituencies needed assurances that developing countries would adopt binding emissions limitation commitments in a third commitment period. Opposing this view were nearly all developing countries other than the small island states. India objected to depriving developing countries of "equitable environmental room to grow".[1]

But as was soon to be seen, the Kyoto commitments were already inadequate because they covered a diminishing share of global emissions. The world's largest emitter, the United States, did not ratify the Protocol, and the fast-growing emerging economies were beginning to register a rapidly growing proportion of emissions.

Although Kyoto reinforced the binary division of the world and was clearly inadequate, the Kyoto *acquis* had much that could inform a universal agreement. While it did not advance the thinking on responsibility, "the Kyoto Protocol is seen as an important first step towards a truly global emission reduction regime", as the UNFCCC secretariat put it.[2] Kyoto accounting rules, in particular, to the extent that they do not reflect a binary division, are the most fully developed set of rules for the climate regime. Some of the Kyoto provisions on its flexibility mechanisms can inform the establishment of carbon markets under the Paris Agreement. In areas such as land use accounting, the Kyoto Protocol remains a point of reference.

Alternatives to responsibility – the "rights" approach

There has been much time, in and outside the negotiations, given to a rights approach to burden-sharing. Here, developing countries have invoked a right to sustainable development; a right, it is argued, that has already been exercised by industrialised countries. On fairness grounds this right should allow developing countries access to "atmospheric space" (a later version of India's "environmental room"), understood as the remaining window for using fossil fuels. This is deeply laden with ethical principles, and is certainly a possible window through which to view burden-sharing. The rights approach can be applied on a population basis to give one of the most commonly argued top-down burden-sharing methods, per capita emissions, which would simply allocate the same tonnage of emissions to every citizen on the planet. The "contraction and convergence" model would require countries to converge towards equality of per capita emissions. "Greenhouse development rights"[3] was another approach invoking rights.

A weakness of rights approaches is that the right to development, which is incontestable, has been too much subsumed by the right to emissions, whereas the whole emphasis, longer term, must be to decouple growth from emissions. There is another, more practical obstacle. Rights-based approaches as a basis for climate change treaties tend to fall at the first hurdle because they cannot get universal agreement. The per capita approach, for example, places the world's two most populous nations in opposition: India can accept it, China cannot. It does not take sufficient account of the differing make-up and dynamics of economies.

Some attempts have been made to build on such relatively simple notions, one example being the evolution of greenhouse development rights into an "equity reference framework" which takes more factors into account. The "Climate Action Tracker"[4] applies science and other factors to both intended nationally determined contributions (INDCs) and national greenhouse gas reduction policies, and it awards ratings. Such initiatives, while they may lack direct practical application to treaties, can be useful in public discourse. Whether one agrees or disagrees with them, they can stimulate and advance thinking. Most importantly, they provide independent scrutiny of country contributions untainted by the negotiations.

Historical responsibility

In a sense, historical responsibility was already implied in the Convention by the broad concept that Annex I countries should take the lead in greenhouse gas mitigation. It was undeniable that Annex I countries were responsible for most of past emissions and, in 1990, even most of current emissions. But it was not until later that it became a fully-fledged doctrine.

The concept of historical responsibility was strongly advocated by Brazil from the early days of the negotiations towards the Kyoto Protocol. Indeed, "the Brazilian proposal" became the generic description of the concept. This suggested that burden-sharing could be determined by what a country had emitted in the past. Its immediate effect would be to assign a much greater share of the burden to industrialised countries. There were many difficulties with this concept. For example, how legitimate was it to have to accept *responsibility* for past emissions when there was no knowledge of global warming at the time they took place, still less of the contribution to global warming that fossil fuels made? One way of reconciling the latter point with the principle would be to use 1990 as the reference point. It was incontrovertible that the problem was known in 1990, which was the base year for the calculation of emissions budgets under the Kyoto Protocol.

The term "historical responsibility" itself was controversial. It has remained without precise definition, but nonetheless has surfaced in various UNFCCC texts. Although it was not operational, it served as a reminder of a relevant dimension of responsibility, whatever the national positions taken on it. Brazil did point out that it could be used to create some evolution in burden-sharing away from developed countries alone by combining it with an income threshold, above which developing country parties would be expected to take on comparable commitments to developed countries.

Later, there were further elaborations on historical responsibility. As it became clear that what mattered to the climate was totality of emissions over time, the notion of "cumulative" was added. If applied to emissions before 1990 this would not make much difference to relative contributions, but it makes large and increasing difference if applied to emissions since then. It has scientific (leaving aside moral or other justifications) merit and accurately states a country's contribution to global warming. But with the emergence of China, Brazil, India and others as fast-growing economies, cumulative emissions would shift the burden heavily towards them, so the usefulness of it for advocacy in negotiations diminished. Even if Annex I emissions were to fall to zero, it would be impossible to reach a global target without reductions in non-Annex I countries.

The idea that burden-sharing must include an element of the past emissions continued. As recently as 2015, Bolivia's INDC[5] submission proposes a "climate justice framework" which combines historical responsibility with other factors. Its four criteria were described by Bolivia as follows:

a *Historical responsibility* for cumulative emissions since 1750.
b *Ecological footprint*. The amount of land, water and forest people of the countries need to satisfy all the goods consumed and to assimilate the waste they generate.
c *Capacity development*. The conditions of economic and social development of each country.
d *Technological capacity*. The ability of countries considering their technological development based on expenditure on research and development and industrial performance of each of them, and considering their capacity to produce and export goods with high technology.

The first two factors are about responsibility, the second two more about the capability aspect of CBDR. According to the Bolivian calculations of the resulting index, using an elaborate method applied to a global carbon budget derived from the IPCC's fifth assessment report, non-Annex I countries would have an 89 per cent share of the remaining carbon budget, with Annex I countries having only 11 per cent. It should be noted that the Bolivian analysis of the core problem sheets home the responsibility to the capitalist system, so it was not being argued that this method alone could solve the problem of global warming:[6]

> The structural cause that has triggered the climate crisis is the failed capitalist system. The capitalist system promotes consumerism, warmongering and commercialism, causing the destruction of Mother Earth and humanity . . . for a lasting solution to the climate crisis we must destroy capitalism.

Responsibility in phase three of the international climate negotiations

The lack of explicit built-in flexibility for passage from the non-Annex I to the Annex I list was to haunt the third phase of negotiations that began in 2005. The Kyoto Protocol had a trigger point for negotiation of further commitments for Annex I parties. But Annex I parties wanted a broader negotiation that would recognise the evolution of the world economy since 1990 and open the way for non-Annex I parties to contribute to emissions reductions – and for the United States to join in.

There was strong resistance to any suggestion of a negotiation that could lead to commitments from those parties which did not have them under Kyoto. Developing countries held firm to the binary Annex I/non-Annex I distinction and would not agree to the broader negotiation under the Convention that was being sought. The initial two years featured an imbalance in negotiations. The Kyoto track had a full negotiating mandate. The convention track was not a negotiation but a "dialogue", and could not lead to new commitments. Only two years later convention-negotiating mandate was adopted; it used the terminology "long term cooperative action" from the dialogue. At this time, most developing countries argued that developed countries should take on binding economy-wide commitments. They recognised that of necessity the United States would have to take these on under the convention track, but insisted that all Kyoto ratifiers should take their commitments under Kyoto. The risk of the perpetuation of these two tracks was that responsibility would remain more divided than common.

This insistence, which was the main obstacle to a single, coherent negotiation, was a core negotiating strategy of the developing countries as a bloc, even though divisions were starting to appear within the Group of 77 coalition (G77). The tracks finally converged and it became clearer that there was little future for Kyoto commitments after 2020, when there would be essentially one regime.[7]

Other approaches to quantification and assignment of responsibility

Many attempts have been made in academia and civil society to define responsibility from first principles. They have encountered many complications. The "polluter pays" principle, for example, might be seen as an obvious and already tested solution. But it proves far more difficult to apply to greenhouse gas emissions and climate change in general than to other types of pollution.[8]

The task has been made somewhat easier, however, with the clarification from science, especially regarding CO_2, that global cumulative carbon budgets can be determined to stay within a particular temperature range, and hence how much carbon remains that can be safely used.[9]

One approach, specific to climate change, is comparative mitigation potential, which is relevant to responsibility for reducing future emissions. Such an analysis was carried out for groups of countries by the UNFCCC secretariat during the Kyoto Protocol negotiations and was issued as "technical" papers. This approach could introduce a cost-based comparison. It is neutral as it is value-free. This work produced some interesting results, one of which showed that the choice of criteria did not make much difference for larger economies, but, by contrast, could greatly affect results for smaller countries. However, there has been no appetite for extending this work to non-Annex I parties and indeed strong resistance to such initiatives to assign responsibility to individual countries.

Responsibility evolves – towards Paris

Reference to the core responsibility principle of CBDR has been ever-present in the negotiations. It normally received a mention in the formal decisions of each conference of the parties. But during the third phase of negotiations there was movement. In parallel, the terms Annex I and non-Annex I were sometimes replaced by "developed" and "developing" countries. These two directions attenuated the binary division of responsibilities. The Copenhagen Accord used only developed and developing countries in its core sections, but elsewhere repeated

CBDR, and retained a distinction between Annex I and non-Annex I parties with the former expected to take on binding QELROs to 2020 under the Kyoto Protocol, and the latter "actions" under the Convention, understood to be non-binding. The United States was the outlier within Annex I as it was also under the "actions" category since it had difficulties with binding targets. Copenhagen was a pivot towards a more universal agreement. From then on, Annex I and non-Annex I were no longer used in the core decisions of the Conference of the Parties (COP).

There were two stages of evolution before the issue was settled enough to obtain the more robust consensus necessary for the final agreement. The United States stated that it did not object to CBDR per se, but argued that the way it was interpreted by developing countries, as a permanent binary fixed distinction, was unacceptable. In order to achieve the Durban mandate, which led the way towards the Paris Agreement, it was necessary to omit explicit mention of CBDR. Instead, there was a general reference to "strengthening of the multilateral, rules-based regime under the Convention". There was not even a reference that could have directly inferred CBDR from the "principles of the Convention", though the constructively ambiguous words agreed could have been taken implicitly not to exclude it.

This change was strongly resisted by developing countries, especially the newly formed "like-minded group", who were vigilant after Durban in trying to bring it back to the core decisions. In the following COPs at Doha (2012) and in Warsaw (2013), a reference to the "principles of the Convention" returned. But the explicit mention of CBDR was still absent from both texts. CBDR returned at the Lima COP (2014). This retained the mention "[work] shall be under the Convention and guided by its principles" and invoked CBDR but with an important addition, so that it now read:

> principle of common but differentiated responsibilities and respective capabilities, *in light of different national circumstances*.
>
> (emphasis added)

These new words originated in a joint declaration of the United States and China in Beijing a few days before the COP,[10] the conclusion of several months of discussions. This latest expression of the principle held for Paris, and can thus be said to have replaced the original formulation.

Responsibility in the Paris agreement – and beyond

Aside from this important change, which emerged through the negotiations, the external context had also changed. It was unequivocal that climate change required efforts by all states and all sectors.

The difference at Paris was that the 150 heads of state and government on the first day showed that they owned the problem, and that they wanted an agreement. Business and local government in two powerful shows of solidarity at the midpoint of the conference demonstrated that they, too, were fully cognisant of their responsibilities, and also wanted an agreement. Not only were they taking autonomous action (not solely or even principally for reasons of climate change regulations), but they needed their efforts to be facilitated by governments. In the case of the business sector, efforts had been made by COP presidencies to engage with them in and around the negotiations. Mexico and France were the most successful.

Another important point which highlighted the role of business was that it had been demonstrated through consistent economic analysis, that the massive energy transition needed would have to be financed very largely (over 80 per cent) by the private sector.[11] This had messages for both governments and the private sector. For the former, that the private sector had to be recognised and incentivised in the outcomes of the negotiations. For the latter, that they would bear much of the responsibility for making the changes happen. There is also a role for citizens in that their choices are part of the transition. The preamble to the Paris Agreement recognises the importance of the "engagement of all levels of government and various actors". The accompanying decisions are more explicit, with a whole section (Section V) on "non-party stakeholders" welcoming "the efforts of . . . civil society, the private sector, financial institutions, cities and other subnational authorities."

The Paris context also encouraged other sectors to demonstrate that they too accepted their share of responsibility. Previously, progress in the maritime and aviation sectors, not covered by UNFCCC or Kyoto Protocol disciplines, had been extremely slow or non-existent. At the time of adoption of the Paris Agreement, many commentators deplored the absence of these sectors from the text. But the Paris consensus provided a useful impetus, and after years of little progress, both the maritime and aviation sectors stepped up in the year following Paris with a more explicit acknowledgement of their responsibility, demonstrated by the action they were taking.

After the Paris Agreement, a maritime industry official commented, "the shipping industry remains committed to ambitious CO_2 emission reduction across the entire world merchant fleet, reducing CO_2 per tonne-km by at least 50 per cent before 2050 compared to 2007."[12] The International Maritime Organisation's Maritime Environment Protection Committee (MEPC), at its October 2016 meeting, agreed on further measures including a CO_2 monitoring system. At this meeting, frequent reference was made to the Paris Agreement and the need to front up to COP 22 with a positive story. Industry associations called for work to determine shipping's "'fair share contribution' towards reducing the world's total CO_2 emissions".[13]

It was a similar story for aviation. An air transport body, the Air Transport Action Group (ATAG), would have liked to see aviation included in the Paris Agreement, but nonetheless saw it as providing "positive momentum" for the sector. ATAG also reiterated the goal of carbon-neutral growth from 2020.[14] This momentum was real: less than a year later, in October 2016, the International Civil Aviation Organisation (ICAO) established a new global market-based measure (GMBM) to control CO_2 emissions from international aviation.[15]

One can still argue that the action by these sectors may not go far or fast enough, but the recognition of responsibility is a base that can be built on.

A further illustration of the new concept at work is the formation of the "2050 pathway platform." This is a multi-stakeholder initiative launched at COP 22, which groups state and non-state entities. The platform aims to support countries seeking to develop long-term decarbonisation strategies, including through the sharing of resources (including finance, capacity building), knowledge and experiences. It will also build a "broader constellation of cities, states, and companies engaged in long-term low-emissions planning of their own, and in support of the national strategies."[16] Essentially, it will be a space for collective problem solving. This is a new model of international multi-stakeholder engagement. Willingness to participate is a signal of responsibilities accepted.

The Paris Agreement is "applicable to all" and contains provision for convergence of levels of commitment that Kyoto lacked. The Agreement overcomes the rigidity of CBDR in another way, by retaining the reference to developed and developing countries but adding an expectation that the latter will move towards quantified economy-wide targets as they are able to. This nicely complements the reference to different national circumstances in article 2, and gives the flexibility that the Kyoto Protocol lacked. Developing countries are not expected to match the economy-wide emissions reduction contributions of developed countries in the first round of NDCs. However, a permanently enshrined binary distinction based on two fixed lists of countries would not be consistent with the Agreement. Only the least developed and small island developing states retain distinct recognition. Importantly, there are no separate lists of parties any more.

Responsibility of course needs to be assumed and acted upon. It is of little value if action does not accompany acknowledgement. The fact that responsibility is self-determined, rather than rigidly derived from a set of contestable assumptions, is a greater incentive to ambition.

There is still a role for the international climate regime in applying some of the methodologies referenced above as evidence of how well countries have assumed their responsibility in practice. They will complement the transparency and accountability provisions under the Paris Agreement, which replace the Kyoto Protocol's compliance and sanctions regime. Analysis by independent organisations will be an element that can be used both at home in lobbying governments and abroad, as peer pressure when discussing the adequacy of NDCs within the UNFCCC.

For the sake of completeness, it should be noted that the Paris Agreement contains other areas of responsibility, corresponding to the other elements of the climate regime that have been consolidated. There are traces of the binary distinction of earlier instruments, as the needs of developing countries for finance, capacity building and technology are recognised, but it is interesting that there is no assumption that this will be provided exclusively by developed countries, thus allowing for the reality of South–South cooperation, where developing countries such as China also provide aid.

Conclusion

The current concept of responsibility as it has evolved through the global climate change regime is somewhat diffused, but broader, more flexible and more aligned with what is needed to deal with climate change over a long period. Climate negotiations are characterised by rights and entitlement approaches in a "win-lose" context, where negotiators see their role as to maximise advantages or minimise commitments at the expense of other parties. Such approaches continue as the detailed rules needed under the Paris Agreement are finalised. But the Agreement embodies a powerful amended central principle applicable amongst states, and through its acknowledgement of the role of non-state actors, a more widely shared diffusion of responsibility through society. The binary distinction among states has largely gone, and where it is still present it is conditioned by "respective national circumstances". The focus of responsibility, too, has shifted from being entirely on states.

Acceptance of responsibility is thus a necessary part of efforts to combat climate change. As such it is capable of evolution, and of informing action taken, as well as the transparency and peer review processes under the Paris Agreement. In acknowledging the common responsibility which may be quantified, for example, to stay within a global carbon budget, the responsibility of the state and non-state actors can be invoked in order for them to undertake their best efforts – or highest ambition.

The principal shift has been to depict a willing assumption of responsibility at these different levels, without a rigid top-down definition or classification. Thus, common responsibility is expressed and implemented through a multi-actor effort where each actor has assumed its individual responsibility without being told what to do.[17] This contrasts with the rights and entitlement approach in a "win-lose" framing of negotiations that has made for low ambition. The role of central government is now to enable other actors to exercise their responsibility as well as to exercise its own. This fits with the current "hybrid" model where the state-level binding treaty provisions no longer purport to address the totality of the solution, but are a supporting and enabling framework for autonomous action.

With the momentum that has been achieved, it could be argued that explicit acceptance of responsibility is now less critical. That may be true at present, but it is very likely that when the UNFCCC undertakes the global stocktakes from 2023 – effectively exercising the *common* responsibility – (re-)acceptance of responsibility will again become critical to meet the expected shortfall. It is unlikely that the regime will have evolved far enough to have individual countries' future action quantified and assigned from above. So there will be reliance on states but also non-state actors to accept the consequences and act accordingly.

Over time, responsibility thus seems a more powerful, fair and effective organising principle. The essence of this conceptual shift towards responsibility, however, is that the existence of an international agreement and obligations is no longer the raison d'être of action. For the multi-decadal issue that is climate change, this is a much more robust basis that does not depend on the vagaries of international negotiations, and should be applicable to other global commons problems.

Notes

1 "Report of the Third Conference of the Parties to The United Nations Framework Convention on Climate Change: 1–11 December 1997" (1997) 12(76) *Earth Negotiations Bulletin* <http://enb.iisd.org/download/pdf/enb1276e.pdf>.
2 UNFCCC secretariat "What Is the Kyoto Protocol?" <https://unfccc.int/process/the-kyoto-protocol/what-is-the-kyoto-protocol>.
3 See Greenhouse Development Rights <gdrights.org>.
4 Climate Action Tracker <http://climateactiontracker.org/>.
5 Available at the UNFCCC NDC registry <www4.unfccc.int/ndcregistry/Pages/All.aspx>.
6 Ibid. at 1.
7 The evolution of the climate change negotiations towards a unified regime is described more fully in A. Macey "The Paris Agreement on Climate Change, Text and Contexts" (2016) 12 *Policy Quarterly* 77.
8 These difficulties are well canvassed in Simon Caney "Cosmopolitan Justice, Responsibility and Global Climate Change" (2005) 18 *Leiden Journal of International Law* 747.
9 For a global carbon budget calculator see <www.trillionthtonne.org>.
10 See "U.S.-China Joint Announcement on Climate Change" <https://obamawhitehouse.archives.gov/the-press-office/2014/11/11/us-china-joint-announcement-climate-change>.
11 The UNFCCC secretariat addressed this subject in 2007 and 2008 and used a figure of 86 per cent private sector investment and financial flows. See United Nations Framework Convention on Climate Change "Investment and Financial Flows to Address Climate Change" (2007) <http://unfccc.int/files/cooperation_and_support/financial_mechanism/application/pdf/background_paper.pdf>; "Investment and financial Flows to Address Climate Change: An Update FCCC/TP/2008/7" <http://unfccc.int/resource/docs/2008/tp/07.pdf>.
12 See other similar comments at <http://worldmaritimenews.com/archives/178732/cop21-paris-remains-silent-on-shiping-and-aviation>.
13 Baltic and International Maritime Council (BIMCO) press release October 2016 <www.bimco.org/News/Press-releases/20161019>.
14 Air Transport Action Group (ATAG) statement, December 2015 <http://aviationbenefits.org/newswire/2015/12/aviation-co2-emissions-to-be-dealt-with-next-year-at-icao>.
15 ICAO statement, 2016, <www.icao.int/Newsroom/Pages/Historic-agreement-reached-to-mitigate-international-aviation-emissions.aspx>.
16 For a description of the Pathway's aims and membership, see UNFCCC, 2017 "Why develop 2050 Pathways?" https://www.2050pathways.org/wp-content/uploads/2017/09/Whydevelop2050Pathways.pdf.
17 An illustration of the acceptance of responsibility at a political level is Indian Minister of State Piyush Goyal's comment that "Clean energy is not something that we are working on because somebody else wants us to do it. It's a matter of faith and the faith of the leadership in India. Nothing on Earth is going to stop us from doing that." *Times of India* (Mumbai, 28 January 2017) <https://timesofindia.indiatimes.com/business/india-business/india-committed-to-goals-on-renewable-energy-goyal/articleshow/56636317.cms>.

8 An ethic of responsibility in Samoan customary law[1]

His Highness Tui Atua Tupua Tamasese Ta'isi Efi

I dedicate this address to King Tuheitia. I am deeply honoured that despite your ill health you have come to join us today.

I wish to also acknowledge Sir Eddie Taihakurei Durie. Thank you for the scholarship that helped restore the self-respect and pride of our fanauga.

And lastly, I wish to say to our Pacific family, o le lave i tiga, o le ivi, le toto, ma le aano – he who rallies in my hour of need is my bone, my flesh and my blood.

Let me begin . . .

When Betsan invited me a few months ago to participate in this symposium, she explained that it was about "responsibility within law and custom", focusing particularly on the management and governance of water. In our discussions about the symposium's focus she mentioned the notions "climate change", "climate justice", "public good", "common good", "western law" and "indigenous custom". She suggested that the symposium would benefit from having perspectives on these from the wider Pacific fanauga, beyond Aotearoa New Zealand, and from cultural custodians such as myself.

I accepted Betsan's invitation because I am committed to the indigenous cause. I consider it my duty as a cultural custodian to share with the young what I believe is the best of my Samoan indigenous culture and customs. To do this I have had to probe and make visible uncomfortable areas of discussion within contemporary Samoan society and culture. This has been no easy task and I worry constantly about how best to do it. Much of the discomfort has largely been because the Samoan indigenous reference has been unfairly relegated to the sidelines of Samoan society, for it refers too much for many to what Samoans have described as a time of "darkness"; a time that many would prefer not to remember or have been colonised to believe is not worth remembering.[2]

Over the years I have made suggestions towards a methodology for probing these areas, both lovingly and critically; noting that such a methodology requires deliberate attention to, among other things, the question of how best to involve the young in this conversation. If we – meaning us elders – want the wisdom and values of our forebears to live beyond us, we have a duty, indeed a *responsibility*, to involve the young, to listen to them, to advise and guide them, and to learn from them.

Today I wish to share some of the wisdom that was imparted to me by the cultural custodians of my youth, so that their knowledge and my rendering of it can be exposed to the rigours of good critical intellectual debate in this time and space. So that it can live and grow and hopefully find meaning in the hearts and minds of present and future generations who have or will have the challenge of managing our public goods for the good of all.

Samoa has undergone significant changes since becoming an independent nation-state. As a nation-state, she has drastically changed the way she manages her environmental resources. She has relegated her belief in a sacred kinship between people and animals, plants, waterways, ocean, mountains and other parts of the biosphere to the background in favour of the modern twin technologies of domination, what Max Weber called the spirit of capitalism and the protestant ethic.[3] The familiarity that Samoans have shown with biblical concepts such as heaven, hell and original sin, and with the ethic of industry in Proverbs 10:4 which says: "Lazy hands make for poverty, but diligent hands bring wealth", far exceeds their familiarity with our own Samoan indigenous concepts and sayings, some of which I will explore further on.

By sidelining, sometimes even condemning, our Samoan indigenous reference in favour of modern industry and Christian prejudices, Samoa altered the sacred balance she once honoured between people and the environment, where the environment was believed to be kin. We have, as Cardinal Maradiaga describes, bought into the arrogance of the modern mind and "deified ourselves as owners of the planet" and "turned our backs on our role as God's stewards on Earth."[4] We have become a conceited race in need of what the cardinal describes as "creatural humility" – the kind of humility that brings us literally back to earth and finds balance and intimacy in our knowledge of and respect for the sacred kinship we share with the environment and with God. This was always a part of our indigenous theology.

As a result of turning our backs on the wisdom of our forebears, we can find redemption in owning up to the truth of Maradiaga's words:[5]

> Only through universal unitedness between men, animals, plants and things will we be able to push aside the conceit of our race – which has come to think of itself as the despotic ruler of Creation – and turn it into the elder brother of all of its fellow creatures.

It is my contention that in disregarding our indigenous reference we have made it easier for us to walk the path of environmental destruction. And, because of the dire impact that rising sea levels is having on our homes and livelihoods right now, the wisdom of our decision to sideline our indigenous knowledges must be relooked at and relooked at now. In light of the very real evidence presented by scientists on the causal connections between rising sea levels and other climate changes and industrial pollution, our Pacific countries must rally together to force those most accountable for the breakdown of nature's protective mechanisms to take responsibility for their abuses. We must work together as a united collective towards redressing our wrong. Real solutions can only be sustained by working together. This includes working together to revive the wisdoms of our indigenous past. As Pierre stated so eloquently on Sunday, the problem of climate change is not just about ensuring that we put up a good fight against the industrial abusers, but that we find the will as individuals, as respective nations and as a region to come together to work towards the protection of this place – the Pacific – that we call home.

Every country has its own challenges and must devise its strategies accordingly in order to rally its troops. Gaining buy-in is as much about changing mindsets and dealing first with issues in-house as it is about changing the mindsets and actions of corporate giants who live and manoeuvre from outside.

In Samoa, no longer are individuals, families or villages perceived by members to be responsible for managing their own waste. Rather it is perceived as the responsibility of the government or state. Moreover, no longer are individuals, families or villages believed responsible for sorting through their wrong-doing. Again this is perceived as the responsibility of the government or state. In resolving disputes, people are drawn to the courts – a state-run machine – as a first rather than last resort. The state has become judge, standard-bearer and arbiter of what is good, responsible and ethical. But who is the state? Who is the court? And, what dominates and influences their minds and actions? We are the state. We are the court. And we, as humans, dominate and influence our own minds and actions.

The centralisation of government in Samoa has meant that traditional or customary environmental management systems have changed to suit the new global order. Thinking through how best to develop a new paradigm of responsibility that can take seriously the values of our forebears requires bringing their values back to the forefront of our minds and hearts, re-energising them, even re-creating and re-casting them if need be, as Sister Vitolia Mo'a advocates in our recently launched book *Whispers and Vanities*.[6]

Engaging in forums such as this can help. These forums provide much needed opportunities to sharpen our understanding of the issues. They offer an opportunity to think more widely and deeply about central concepts sometimes taken for granted in this highly complex debate. And such forums offer the opportunity to converse about these concepts with others of similar convictions and purpose. Core concepts such as "the indigenous" and "indigenous customs", for example, deserve close attention in this conversation.

Like its use here in Aotearoa New Zealand, the term "indigenous" for me signals a reference to the native people of a land (i.e. tangata whenua in Māori; or *tama* or *tagata o le eleele* in Samoan) and to their customs, traditions and worldviews. Unlike Māori, however, the indigenous population of Samoa are the majority or dominant ethnic population and/or culture group.[7] Ninety-three per cent of Samoa's population today is Samoan. Furthermore, the traditional Samoan chiefly system – the *faamatai* – is still an integral part of modern Samoan systems of government, even if somewhat modified. The Samoan language is used right throughout the country, in all aspects of life, and is a formal and informal part of government and educational literature and service delivery. The indigenous – or what some might prefer to describe merely as Samoan – is, therefore, still very much a part of our everyday modern lives.

What complicates and further demarcates the use of the term "indigenous" in the Samoan context from the way it is used in Aotearoa New Zealand is, as implied earlier, the question of religion. The way Samoans think about and practice their introduced Christian religious culture influences how they think about and define their Samoanness and arguably their "indigeneity". For, as Toeolesulusulu Damon Salesa describes, "Samoans became Christian, and Christianity became Samoan, much like the confluence of rivers".[8] There is a merging of rivers here that finds the Christian and the Samoan to be one and the same. Many Samoans find that they are no longer able to separate their Christianity from their Samoanness or their Samoanness from their Christianity. By probing what this means, I am forcing my Samoan people to address the underlying issue of arrogance that also insidiously pervades the mindsets of those who resist taking proper responsibility for the unnatural changes we are experiencing with our climate. That is, the issue of a loss of grounded humility. In both cases we have to admit that in our haste to assert our technical superiority as a species we seemed to have lost our way. By revisiting our indigenous references, we may be pleasantly surprised to find a new pathway forward.

Reflecting on questions of indigeneity is important to the cause of developing the new paradigm of responsibility advocated by the organising committee of this symposium. The intention or aim for this symposium, they state, is "to open a new paradigm of responsibility and guardianship or stewardship of water, which is different from rights and ownership approaches to public goods". A "trusteeship system" is proposed as an alternative to owning public goods such as water. And, an emphasis is placed on moving away from an "owning" mentality or ethos to one of "responsibility" and/or "guardianship/stewardship". This latter ethos we can again find extant in our traditional or indigenous references.

Let me illustrate this by reference to seven core principles or concepts in Samoan customary law. These include the concepts of *tuā'oi* (boundaries or jurisdiction), *tulafono* (laws, custom laws, lore), *aganuu* (general cultural principles and custom laws), *agaifanua* (cultural principles and custom laws relating specifically to a village or district or family), *matāfaioi* (designated work and/or responsibility), *tofā sa'ili* (the perennial search for wisdom) and *va tapuia* (relationships that are sacred or spiritual).[9] There are many more but these are sufficient to make my point.

Breaking words down into component parts or tracing their etymological histories gives useful context to meaning and allows us to trace shifts in meaning over time and to evaluate the whys, hows and wherefores of such shifts. Doing this also provides vivid insight into why a language and its words are said to carry the soul of a people. Let me begin with tulafono, which is generally translated today to mean "laws", that is, state or custom laws.

The word tulafono brings together two concepts. The first is the concept of a chiefly head or heads (*tula*). The second is the concept of a meeting (*fono*). The tula as the head of a chief is considered *tapu*, for it is the site of wisdom and discernment. What is produced from the collaboration of tula within a fono are tulafono or sacred laws. The process of producing tulafono is sacred in that it seeks a dialogue with God. The process usually involves six steps. These are:

Step 1. *Tuvao Fono* (literally meaning, "to step into the forest"). This was the stage when a tula would "break new ground" or raise new issues. It is usually the start of the fono.

Step 2. *Lo'u Fono* (literally referring to the "bending of a branch" – *lo'u* refers to a branch). This was the stage in the fono where an issue is raised and explored and those who had the right to critique were given the space to do so.

Step 3. *Lauga Togia* (*lauga* meaning "a speech" or the act of "speaking" and *togia* meaning to designate according to tradition and custom a right or privilege). This stage gave those who had been given the right to make interventions in formal deliberations the space to do so.

Step 4. *Faai'u Fono* (*faai'u* meaning to conclude or end). This stage gave those who had the right to conclude the meeting or fono the space to do so, or alternatively if they wished to rule that the fono revisit an issue again through the same speaking order, they could also do that.

Step 5. *Faaola Fono* (*faaola* means literally "to give life"). This usually involved situations where the wisdom and intervention of a *tamaalii* or high chief (as opposed to orator chief or *tulafale*) was required. His was the wisdom of the long view, the perspective of someone concerned with the bigger picture.

Step 6. *Tulafono*. This is the last stage of the tulafono process and involved the finalisation of a rule or law (also called tulafono) to be used for the governing of behaviour and/or setting of standards for the family or village.

In each of the above steps, even when the tulafono is more or less set, there is recognition that the tulafono or law is always open for negotiation and reprocessing (using the tulafono process) if new circumstances arose. While there was certainty and meaning in this customary process, there was also flexibility. Within this process operates the principle of tuā'oi, which is loosely translated as boundaries.

Tuā'oi as a word is shorthand for the phrase, "*i tua atu o i e le au iai lau aia po o lau pule*", meaning "your rights (*aia*) and/or authority (*pule*) do not extend beyond this point." It is here that the image of a boundary, a line that cannot be crossed, is made vivid.

By Samoan custom, tuā'oi demarcates rights and responsibilities but in relation to agreed boundaries. These boundaries can be physical, social and sacred. They are both designated (from God) and negotiated (between men) and when there is general consensus, usually through a "fono of chiefly heads" process, then they are usually observed, respected and enforced. When taken through this kind of rigorous process, the need to change the fundamentals of a tulafono and tuā'oi rarely arises.

The highest and most sacred tuā'oi was considered that between man and God. In that relationship there is a boundary that man cannot cross. Man's relationship with God informed the basis of the boundaries within all his other relationships: his relationships with fellow men, with the cosmos, with animals and the environment. And such boundaries or tuā'oi guided human understandings of rights and responsibilities. Like tulafono, while tuā'oi once established may seem immovable, there was always room for renegotiating boundaries where it was apparent to all that continuing certain tuā'oi created more harm than good.

Both these concepts of tulafono and tuā'oi assume a particular way of understanding the relationship between man and God, man and the environment, man and the cosmos, man and fellow men. In the Samoan customary context, God is understood as God progenitor not God creator, as in the Hebrew version of creation. God was indeed perceived God the Father but as both ancestor and paternal protector. This was because my forebears wanted their God to be close, not distant. They saw and felt His presence in ways that represented for them both the mysteries and the bonds of kinship.

In this Samoan version of God, God was, like the Christian God, a God of love and respect. He had all-knowing power and knowledge. He created and knew all, but in his act of procreation, He was with us as close kin, not as distant Father. All his creations were kin. We were family with the cosmos, the environment, the animals, the plants, the trees, the water, and so on and so forth. We lived on this earth as family. We protected each other as family. We respected tulafono and tuā'oi as family.

Within such a model of God and family there is immense loving and respect. It is on this basis that I cannot bring myself to believe that my Christian God, a loving God, did not speak or connect with my people for all those 3000-odd years before Christianity came to Samoa. And as I have written elsewhere, it seems a gratuitous insult to both God and my forebears to assume that there was a disconnect between them for all that time. This theology informed the basis of their customs or custom laws, today embedded deep within both our aganuu and agaifanua. Let me now turn to these two concepts.

The significance of aganuu and agaifanua is that both speak to the two frameworks of customary law that operate within Samoa today. Aganuu is a body of rules or laws of general application. It is differentiated from agaifanua by its common reference and use across villages and districts. In other words, when one speaks about aganuu one is usually referring to common Samoan conventions and customs. When one speaks of agaifanua one is usually referring to those conventions and customs considered particular to a village, district or family. There is an often cited saying, "*E tofu le nuu ma le aga-i-fanua*", translated to mean "for each village its own conventions". As stated in conversation with Sailau, this saying:[10]

> underscores the idea that while Samoan customs as general principles derive from the village context, when carried out each village has rules or practices

> that are idiosyncratic or particular to them. The boundary between one village and the next is protected by custom by the principle of tuā'oi, which assumes a concept of rights whereby the rights and authorities of one village will not encroach on those of another.

Through the four concepts discussed thus far of tulafono, tuā'oi, aganuu and agaifanua, one already gains a clear sense that our forebears had a system of law and order that was both logical and orderly and founded on a deeply spiritual and enlightened sense of morality and justice, and on a oneness and kinship with nature.

Each of these four concepts can be found within the methodological and epistemological imperatives of the *tofa sa'ili* (the perennial search for wisdom) and the *va*, especially the va tapuia – that relational space (va) that is protected by tapu or sacred boundaries (tuā'oi) which demands humility and grace from all people to all of God's creatures. The significance of these two concepts – the tofa sa'ili and the va tapuia – lies for our purposes in the way they force us as thinkers to consider by their mere existence how deeply enlightened and aware our forebears were of the importance of maintaining the kind of humility Cardinal Maradiaga speaks of today.

My last concept for analysis is that of matāfaioi. I have left this to last because it speaks most directly to the concern of this symposium, that of developing a paradigm of responsibility. This is a concept that originates from the environment, and in particular from working the land. Like tulafono, matāfaioi is made up of two main parts: *matāfai* and *oi*.

Reverend George Pratt suggests that the term matāfai refers to the use of land mainly for planting and harvesting of food crops such as taro. When Samoans speak of harvesting they usually use the word *faamatāfai* (*faa* is the prefix meaning to do or to be of). This harvesting or matāfai, however, is not random. It is done in an orderly fashion and involves harvesting land already understood to be apportioned to the harvester. Oi, on the other hand, refers to a cry of pain. When these two parts are brought together to form the word matāfaioi, the word is meant to conjure images of hard work and allude to the wisdom of the idea implicit within that hard work, which is that rewards do not come without hard work and hard work is not without pain and struggle. This is the image and wisdom implicit in the concept of responsibility.

Today the word matāfaioi is used to describe responsibility. Responsibility is assumed here to be something that is apportioned or designated. Sometimes that designation or apportionment is considered divinely ordained, that is a *tofi* or designation from God. But it can also be imposed by secular appointment. Either way it assumes a work ethic that engenders a faithfulness of service and a respect for the benevolence of God.

A paradigm of responsibility that can incorporate the indigenous must take into account all of the different nuances raised in this discussion, not only for the concept matāfaioi, but also for all the other six concepts and/or frameworks discussed. These seven concepts illustrate the richness of our Samoan indigenous reference and serve as starting points for discussion on how we might rethink and re-language an ethic of responsibility for the Pacific and for humanity moving forward.

Let me end by making reference to three things. First, as people of the Pacific, the Pacific Ocean is a central part of who we are. We cannot have a conversation today about responsibility for water and the environment without addressing issues of climate change and the devastating effects of rising sea levels on our many small low-lying islands. Climate change is an urgent priority for the world, but its effects are most especially felt by us here in the Pacific. We owe it to ourselves and our children to find ways to rally together to keep our homes and their homes from sinking under.

Second, in our rallying we would do well to remember that we share a proud history as indigenous peoples. This history and heritage holds some of the keys needed to unlock and re-energise our spirits and regain our humility. It is easy to feel overwhelmed and despondent by the magnitude of the climate change problem and the uncaring attitudes of those who perpetuate it. But Pierre is right. As individuals we are small, insignificant and powerless. But as a collective we are a force to be reckoned with.

And third, the main objective of our cultural or indigenous wisdom inherent in the seven concepts I have explored is to seek and identify love, justice, goodness and decency and to locate them in our lives. Before we spurn the wisdom of thousands of years of vision and experience on the false premise that we are too small to make a difference, we should remember the proverb: If you think you're too small to make a difference, then you have not slept with a mosquito.

Soifua.

Notes

1 Text of the Keynote Address by the Head of State of Samoa at the Law, Ethics & Responsibility Symposium, Hopuhopu, Ngaaruawaahia, Waikato-Tainui College for Research and Development, 25 November 2014. There are personal references in the text which are retained in this publication.

2 See Tamasailau Suaalii-Sauni and others *Whispers and Vanities: Samoan Indigenous Knowledge and Religion* (Huia Publishers, Wellington 2014).

3 Max Weber *The Protestant Ethic and the Spirit of Capitalism* (translated ed: Talcott Parsons (translator), Allen & Unwin, London, 1976).

4 Oscar Andrés Maradiaga SBD "Sustainable Humanity, Sustainable Nature: Our Responsibility" (Opening address to "Sustainable Humanity, Sustainable Nature: Our Responsibility" Conference, Vatican, May 2014).

5 Ibid. at 24.

6 Vitolia Mo'a "Le Aso ma le Taeao – The Day and the Hour: Life or Demise for 'Whispers and Vanities'" in T.M. Suaalii-Sauni and others (eds) *Whispers and Vanities*, above n 2, at 45–57.

7 Total population for Samoa as of 2014 is recorded as 195,000 <http://worldpopulationreview.com/countries/samoa-population/>.

8 Damon Salesa "When the Waters Met: Some Shared Histories of Christianity and Ancestral Samoan Spirituality" in *Whispers and Vanities*, above n 2, at 143–158.

9 More discussion on these concepts can be found in my earlier work, some of which has been published in the following edited collection: T.M. Suaalii-Sauni and others

Su'esu'e Manogi: In Search of Fragrance: Tui Atua Tupua Tamasese Ta'isi and the Samoan Indigenous Reference (2009) (Centre for Samoan Studies, National University of Samoa, Le Papaigalagala, Samoa).

10 Tamasailau Suaalii-Sauni. "'It's in your bones!' Samoan Custom and Discourses of Certainty" (2011) 14 *Yearbook of New Zealand Jurisprudence* 70 at 76–77.

References

Vitolia Mo'a "Le Aso ma le Taeao – The Day and the Hour: Life or Demise for 'Whispers and Vanities'" in T. Suaalii-Sauni and others (eds) *Whispers and Vanities Samoan Indigenous Knowledge and Religion* (Huia Publishers, Wellington, 2014).

Damon Salesa "When the Waters Met: Some Shared Histories of Christianity and Ancestral Samoan Spirituality" in *Whispers and Vanities: Samoan Indigenous Knowledge and Religion* (Huia Publishers, Wellington, 2014).

Tamasailau Suaalii-Sauni "'It's in Your Bones!': Samoan Custom and Discourses of Certainty" (2011) 14 *Yearbook of New Zealand Jurisprudence* 70.

Tamasailau Suaalii-Sauni and others *Su'esu'e Manogi: In Search of Fragrance: Tui Atua Tupua Tamasese Ta'isi and the Samoan Indigenous Reference* (Centre for Samoan Studies, National University of Samoa, Le Papaigalagala, Samoa, 2009).

Tamasailau Suaalii-Sauni and others *Whispers and Vanities: Samoan Indigenous Knowledge and Religion* (Huia Publishers, Wellington, 2014).

Max Weber *The Protestant Ethic and the Spirit of Capitalism* (translated ed: Talcott Parsons (translator), Allen & Unwin, London, 1976).

9 Indigenous law and responsible water governance[1]

Hon Sir Edward Taihākurei Durie KNZM

Had I met the fourth Lord President, Tun Suffian, I would have been keen to know of the experience of a Malay boy brought up under colonial rule and who, at age 31, became the first Malay to be a Magistrate. I was brought up as a Māori under an English legal system and became the first Māori to be appointed a Judge of the Māori Land Court, at age 34. However, by about age 44, Tun Suffian was a High Court judge, Chief Justice at about 56, and Lord President by age 57. At 58 he was awarded the title of Tun.

That would be a stellar performance in New Zealand today. In New Zealand in the 1900s, it would have been unheard of.

Tun Suffian is on record as contributing to the drafting of the Malay Constitution and subsequently as one of its ardent supporters. The New Zealand constitution is distributed over several statutes and conventions. There is a strong argument for a single constitutional document in New Zealand. Nonetheless, notwithstanding our dispersed constitution, the New Zealand Courts have been effective in maintaining and advancing democratic principles and the rule of law. Since the 1980s, this has been done with increased sensitivity to cultural minorities, including the indigenous minority.

This month in New Zealand we celebrated Māori Language Week. I was reminded that Tun Suffian's recognition of the National Language of Malay in the Merdeka University case would have struck a welcome chord amongst the growing numbers of New Zealanders promoting the Māori language today. There is much I would like to know about the role a Malay boy might have played last century in bringing to the British common law a distinctly Malay intelligence.

Māori interest in Malaysia grew following the period from 1959 to 1963 when our most prominent, modern warrior, the highly respected Sir Charles Moihi Bennett, was New Zealand High Commissioner to the newly independent Federation. At age 29, Sir Charles was commander of the Māori Battalion in the Second World War. Sir Charles became a personal friend of the first Prime Minister, Tunku Abdul Rahman, and in 1963 he was awarded a Malayan title as Honorary Commander of the Order of the Defender of the Realm. Some 4000 New Zealand soldiers served here, in Malaysia, at about that time.

In comparison with the legal pluralism of Malaysia, New Zealand has the tradition of a single jural order, introduced by English settlers in 1840. By 1858, the British settlers outnumbered the indigenous Māori. Māori are now 15% of the population. Nonetheless, the common law recognises native custom as a source of law and English law applies only so long as it is applicable to the local circumstance.

That leads to this paper on indigenous law and responsible water governance. The paper is about how other cultures, and different worldviews, can help us to develop better policy. In this case, the focus is on how the Māori worldview helped to reshape New Zealand water policy.

The different worldviews

The contrast between the Māori and English worldviews is profound. The English, who settled in New Zealand in the 19th century, believed that man is master of the world and the world is for him to exploit. They cleared the forests, drained the wetlands and built an economy based on the maximum exploitation of the new, man-made pastures.

In Māori tradition, the people are an integral part of a finely tuned ecosystem. Their economy is based on preserving as they are the forests, wetlands, rivers, lakes and streams.

The wholesale destruction of the wetlands took away the Māori's primary access to food, and materials for clothing and shelter. Those on the flats became dependent on the settlers for basic supplies. Those who once were warriors became labourers.

That Māori survived more from the oceans and inland waters than from the land is obscured by New Zealand's large land mass. In fact, before the English came, Māori had no farmable animals and few crops. The primary diet was fish, waterfowl and water-based plants. It is also no longer obvious that the flats were mainly wetlands, and that lakes and streams abounded. Naturally, it is these that were the focus of Māori collective harvesting. The largest Māori structures for the capture of wildlife were in rivers, and while the settlers used fences and stakes to mark out the ground, the Māori had staked the coastal seas and inland waters to delineate the family food-gathering boundaries.

In this century, after the unbridled exploitation of the land and the draining of wetlands, the government looked at the ongoing exploitation of the rivers, lakes and streams and the need for a clear policy. Once more, the old thinking kicked in. In 2014 the then Prime Minister, having regard to an opinion on English law, declared that no one could own water. The consequence, in his view, was that subject to obtaining the necessary local authority consents, the local authorities and commercial interests could exploit the natural water bodies for free, on a first come, first served basis. Commercial use included the discharge of waste to water bodies and the use of water for power generation, as well as the abstraction of water.

On the other hand, the New Zealand Māori Council, a statutory body to represent Māori interests, argued that Māori tribes had a proprietary interest in water bodies, contended that all people were entitled to access to pure water for domestic consumption and to clean water for recreation, and sought a management framework by which Māori, general public and commercial interests could be balanced. This required, in the Council's view, a constraint on commercial use and a charge on commercial usage.

To counter the Prime Minister's reliance on English law, the Council pointed to the Māori law and practice in relation to water. Unsurprisingly, given the historic, Māori reliance on water bodies, Māori law has settled views on proper water use. However, the land is important too and the principles for each are the same. I will therefore explore the Māori law concepts generally, the application of the principles today, and the uptake of the Māori Council water policy by several political parties in the 2017 elections.

Māori law and water policy

Māori communities and their law

The Māori people call their law "tikanga", which means that which is proper, correct or right. It requires no State to enforce it, for it is enforced at the level of the tribe (hapū), or self-enforced by being internalised in the mind.

The tribe was comprised of a few hundred people. They will have taken the name of a famed forebear from whom most members trace descent.

As the tribes grew they divided to spread across the district, typically along the rivers or lakes, so that the tribes of a catchment were invariably related, and came together as required, under the original ancestral name. Today, the tribal groups are relatively settled since the land is no longer theirs to spread over. Instead, a core group tends to staff the customary villages (papakainga) while most of the tribe's members live in nearby towns.

While the tribes are part of an ancestral coalition, each is autonomous in managing their own affairs. The governance was typically a council of 10 or so family heads (koromatua) guided by a single chief (rangatira), who was recognised by popular acclaim.

The relationship with the natural world

Māori law is based on spiritual beliefs connecting tribal members to their past and future, to each other and to the natural world. Here are some pointers:

1. All people have a spirit (wairua). Good health is determined by reference to both the body and the spirit.
2. The world is occupied by the living and the spirits of the departed. Orators address both. The living and the dead share the land and waters and hold them for the generations to come.
3. The Māori, the wildlife, the land and the waters are all related by descent from primordial ancestors. They are part of the same family and are interdependent. Māori are as much concerned for the good health of the wildlife and their environs as they are for their own health.
4. The land, mountains, lakes, rivers and streams each have their own life force (mauri). They descend from ancestors (tupuna) and they are treated as living

beings. In introducing themselves to other groups, Māori identify themselves according to the ancestral mountains and rivers of their customary villages.

5 Māori determine their own status, their place in the world and their relationship to other Māori throughout the country by the length and breadth of their genealogies. For example, I usually recite my own genealogy back 25 generations to one of the captains of the last set of voyagers from the Pacific. Others trace their genealogies much further back and to much earlier vessels, and some go back to the gods to establish their connections to other lifeforms. The breadth of these genealogies allow Māori to link to each other, no matter where they are from.

6 The places Māori occupy, and the things they do, are either sacred or profane. For example, the speaking place (paepae) on the main courtyard (marae) is sacred (tapu). On the other hand, the cookhouse is profane (noa). Hunting and foraging, or digging the garden, are secular activities, but in undertaking a significant journey or attending a house of learning, the participants are in a sacred state.

The law imposes a sense of personal responsibility in the way Māori relate to each other and to the environment, so that the people are protected from spiritual contamination in moving between sacred and secular conditions. The law is not based on individual rights but on the corollary of a right, the individual duty or responsibility.

The ethic of respect

The essential requirement for Māori, to keep peace with others, the living, the dead, the generations to come and the gods of the natural world, is continually to honour them and show respect. I will look separately at honouring other persons and other beings.

The respect for other persons is played out in set protocols when tribal communities meet and greet. It involves careful acknowledgement of the respective leaders, and the recitation of the genealogies by which the affected groups or individuals are connected, thus rekindling the bonds of consanguinity. It involves acknowledging significant persons who have passed on from all the tribes, not just one's own.

Ideal conduct for Māori groups, in treating with one another, is to host each other generously and to extol each other's virtues. One should seek to enhance the standing (mana) of others through words and by demonstrative acts of love, generosity and care.

Turning to the natural world, the respect for landforms is first played out, as already mentioned, by acknowledging the mountains, lakes and rivers of those with whom we meet.

Then, respect is paid to the lands and waters themselves, in managing everyday activities. For example, propitiations are made to Tangaroa, the god of seas and water life, before the start of a fishing expedition, seeking permission to take of his bounty. To show that the expedition is not motivated by greed or mindless exploitation, the first fish caught is given away, no more is taken than is necessary and the first large catch is for the elderly and needy. To ensure the survival of each species, the breeding stock are preserved and the correct lifecycles are observed.

To maintain the environment from which the fish are taken, the fish are not gutted on the water but well inshore. Even the shells of shellfish must be taken inland for disposal and no form of waste is discharged to water. On landing, the baskets of catch are not dragged across the beach but are carried, so as not to disturb the shellfish in the sand. On lifting a rock in a river to take the freshwater crayfish (koura), or the abalone (paua) from the coastal rockpools, the rock is replaced in the position that it was, so the lifeforce (mauri) of the water body is not disturbed.

Similarly, on land, no great tree is felled without the permission of the forest god (Tane). Again, if it is a major tree, it should not be felled for personal gain but for the good of all. It should be used to make a large canoe or meeting house which is for the benefit of all. The good of the community is paramount and humility is a virtue which is especially desired of leaders. The grand house in the community is the meeting house for all. The people's homes are modest and that of the chief is indistinguishable from the others.

Turning again to the water bodies, the rivers, streams, springs, lakes, wetlands and groundwater, they too are ancestral entities and are addressed as living organisms. In Māori terminology, a water body has its own lifeforce (mauri), giving it a distinct character (ahua), personality (whakatangata) and authority (mana).

The water bodies supplied all that might be expected of water bodies for human survival. They supplied drinking water and a great range of fish, waterfowl and edible plants. Water bodies provided the materials for clothing and shelter and timber from the swamp forests (kahikatea). They provided medicines and the means for transport.

And the water too comes from the gods. The water protects people when undertaking sacred functions and releases them from a sacred state. It assists those who are sick through spiritual imbalance or contamination. Springwater is preferred for most rituals, flowing water for child baptism and the still water of a pool to assist the retention of knowledge. Washing and bathing is conducted in separate streams where practicable or otherwise in discrete parts of the river, or by carrying the water away from the river's edge.

Waste, including human waste, was discharged only to land at specified locations. The discharge of any form of waste to water, no matter how small, was forbidden. The contamination of water was not just a wrong (he), but a spiritual offence (hara) which would bring misfortune to the offenders and their tribe. When Māori first built homes in Western form, they built washhouses and toilets a distance from the house to prevent its contamination, and the waste was discharged to land pits. Boiled water used for cooking is seen as dead water, which also was not discharged to living water that supplies food. The kitchen sink where food is prepared could not be used for washing clothes or the body.

Water may also be contaminated in other ways. It becomes impure or unsanitary when its natural flow is disturbed or is modified by unnatural means, or when separate watercourses are fused so that the lifeforce of the waters unnaturally mix.

The strength or health of most water bodies may be measured by the abundance of wildlife and water demons which inhabit it. The waterfowl and demons (taniwha) are presented as guardians who protect both the waterbody and the associated tribe. Birds (manu) are well known to Māori as warning people of danger. Observations in nature were critical to survival and the birds were closely read. However, when the birds and demons abandon a water body, they portend of disaster. Their absence or reduction in numbers is a serious omen for the tribe.

The means of enforcement

While there are definite no go areas in Māori law, the main focus is actually on aspirational values. One should strive to be like famous forebears and be courageous, generous, caring of others, strong but humble and so on. Occasional lapses will be overlooked if, overall, the person is striving to do good for the people. The focus is not on punishing the bad in persons but on encouraging them to give of their best.

Compliance with the law is largely self-enforced, driven by shame (whakama) or the fear of spiritual retribution (mataku); while the driver for doing good was community recognition. Where a punishment was needed it took the form of a raiding party which took the goods of the family of the wrongdoer (muru). But the focus was on maintaining balance rather than punishment. For example, if something was stolen something had to be taken to replace it. Indeed, if a child drowned through no one else's fault, the family might still be raided to compensate the community's sense of loss.

Ownership of water bodies

When the Prime Minister declared that no one owned water, some Māori implicitly agreed, for in Māori law, land and water are not capable of being owned in the sense of the private ownership of a tradeable commodity. Māori were only caretakers of the land for future generations. But what the tribes had was exclusive authority (mana) over the land and waters, subject to regulation by no one, and with the power to exclude access and use by others. Mana covers both ownership (the right to use and possess against all others), and the over-riding political authority to control the use and management. What they effectively had was ownership plus. They had mana over the lakes and wetlands in their districts (takiwa) and over the rivers and the water in the rivers while it flowed through their district. Similarly, they owned the springs and the water flowing down from the spring to the point where it leaves the tribal area. The same applies to wild creatures, like fish. Only the tribe can hunt them while they are in the tribal district. That is the Māori law.

How the principles are applied today

In 2012, the Māori Council claimed that the government's authority over the country's waterbodies had not been properly determined in accordance with a founding treaty between Māori and the Crown. As mentioned, the Council sought a policy to resolve matters. The Council claimed that in Māori law, which government was bound to respect, the tribes owned the water bodies and that the tribal interests had not been extinguished in a treaty-compliant manner.

In 2014, the Council proposed a policy for consideration. The Council acknowledged that most New Zealanders today were not of Māori stock but all were entitled to free access to water for reasonable domestic needs and to swim in most of the country's rivers and lakes. The Council did not agree with the Prime Minister's view that commercial users should have free access on a first come, first served basis. The Council argued that commercial users should pay, and that Māori should have a share of the royalties on account of their customary, proprietary interests.

The Council particularly urged that the pollution of most of the water bodies was totally unacceptable to Māori interests and that reforms were required. The government had delegated pollution controls to local governments, but the local governments tended to be dominated by commercial interests, who became judges in their own interests. The Council therefore proposed that an independent, expert commission should set the standards and exercise controls.

The Council then opposed the prevalent English law approach, which sets bottom lines for human conduct and punishes transgressors. The Council pointed out how this had led to widespread and graphic pollution. The Council pointed to the aspirational top lines of Māori law, and the preference to recognise and benefit those who strived best to achieve them.

Since the Council's plan was disclosed, the country has seen a significant change in public opinion, with most of the political parties in contention for the 2018 election accepting the greater part of the Council's proposals. There is now an increased awareness of the need to change the policy, notwithstanding the impact on the economy as viewed in Western terms. People are now more conscious of the traditional Māori stance for the protection of the natural world, and while there are doubts about what is seen as superstition in the Māori legal system, there are increasingly fewer doubts about the need for such objectives as the Māori in fact achieved.

Conclusion

I end by repeating a couple of points. The first is that embedded in Māori law is a concept which I think sits above the right to use what we possess, and that is a concept of the responsible use of such as we should have.

The second is that different worldviews can enhance the development of a country's policies and laws, and question such longstanding views as that Man is master of the world and the world is for him to exploit.

I think back then to a Malay boy, who was born into the richness of Malaysian culture but rose to the highest position in a legal system largely inherited from abroad, what an extraordinary potential there would have been to develop the law from a wide-ranging set of autochthonous principles.

Note

1 This chapter is a revision of Edward Taihakurei Durie's Paper "Law, Responsibility and Maori Proprietary Interests in Water". It was further developed for the Tun Suffian Memorial Lecture in Kuala Lumpur September 2017, to which Hon. Sir Taikākurei Durie was the guest of honour. Tun Suffian was Lord President of the Federal Court from 1974 to 1982. The editors preferred to use this paper for this book because of the development on the thinking on indigenous law in this paper. The editors have retained the references to Malaysia as it gives the writing a wider frame of reference. Durie's earlier paper can be accessed at <www.response.org.nz>.

10 Governance of water based on responsible use – an elegant solution?

Linda Te Aho

Introduction

> The Earth is the elemental womb to which we must all return. For the future, despite the depletion and abuse of natural resources, we must find hope in the wisdom of the past.[1]

The inspiration for this chapter is a proposal said to represent "a paradigm shift" for the governance of freshwater, articulated by Sir Edward Taihakurei Durie in 2014.[2] Arising out of challenges to a government plan to sell its shares in power-generating companies,[3] the Durie proposal has at its heart a possibility for reconciling Māori rights and interests and wider general interests in freshwater. It is based on the assumption that Māori and the general public have a legitimate interest in the natural water regimes of the country. However, the source of the interest is not the same. The Māori interest is proprietary and is sourced in their status as the indigenous first peoples of the land who were guaranteed continuation of their tino rangatiratanga in respect of their lands and waters in Te Tiriti o Waitangi.[4] The public interest is sourced in the British laws that superimposed Māori laws through processes of colonisation. The heart of the Durie proposal is that those utilising water for commercial purposes should be charged and that an independent commission would be responsible for overseeing charging and revenue collection and disbursement. A proportion of the funds would be allocated to Māori authorities in recognition of the Māori interest. Whether in public or Māori hands, the funds should be applied to the maintenance or improvement of the natural water bodies of the area or the assurance of water supplies to all homes. In short, the proposal focuses upon responsibility.

The philosophy of responsibility refers to the respectful relationship human beings can have with their social and natural environment. In New Zealand, it is said, worldviews upon which the philosophy is based "find their expression in the culture, knowledge and lifeways of the Māori who see themselves as part of a familial web in which humans are junior siblings to other species, beings and forms of life."[5] Proponents of responsibility emphasise "responsiveness", an ability to respond to challenges and changes in the environment.[6] This chapter traces some of the history of Māori responsiveness to the historical and continued dispossession and destruction of their lands and waters. These violations are closely tied to global environmental challenges such as climate change, water scarcity and food security.[7] The framework of Māori responses to these challenges appears to have been one of rights. However, it is a theme of this chapter that a key driver in the assertion of Māori rights has been the desire to fulfil stated responsibilities to the natural world and to future generations.

This has led to a "curious situation"[8] in which there is a growing trend towards collaboration between the government and Māori in managing natural resources and a greater respect for ecosystems. At the same time, New Zealand faces a freshwater crisis aided and abetted by the government's reluctance to recognise Māori proprietary rights in water.

The wisdom behind the Durie proposal is that it promotes a change in jurisprudence away from focusing upon rights-based mechanisms and language of ownership, towards restoration and collaborative governance based on shared responsibility – a seemingly elegant solution.

This chapter draws upon domestic case studies to illustrate the strong similarities between indigenous laws and values and the principles of responsibility. It provides insights into how such "wisdom of the past" might be applied in contemporary contexts and help to shape the future of how well we live on this planet. It also contains a cautionary note about settling into a culture of compromise.

A changing legal landscape

New Zealand is a water-rich nation, and despite its reputation for being "clean and green",[9] it faces the challenges of climate change and environmental devastation as a result of the over-exploitation of ecosystems. New Zealand is very slowly coming to grips with "the impacts of raised water temperatures and wildly swinging weather extremes from drought to flood."[10] Climate change expert, Dr Adrian Macey,[11] has warned of the risks of New Zealand continuing to deforest and farm in ways that have led to erosion and to contaminants such as *E. coli*, nitrogen and phosphorus leaching into freshwater streams and rivers – many of which are no longer drinkable or swimmable, or even wadeable.[12] And, there is still no solution on the horizon for dealing with the unfair distribution and allocation of water.[13]

We have arrived at this point as a result of adhering to principles of British common law that reflect a Western worldview in relation to the environment, and in particular the anthropocentric notion that[14]

> Wonders are many on earth, and the greatest of these is man . . . He is master of ageless Earth, to his own will bending . . . He is lord of all things living; birds of the air, beasts of the field, all creatures of sea and land.

In this tradition, at common law there has never been ownership in naturally flowing water. Rights to water resources were derived from land ownership. For the purpose of determining the extent of such rights, and providing regulation for public interests such as for navigation and consents for the use of natural resources such as minerals, rivers were separated into beds, banks, and waters, and into tidal and non-tidal, navigable and non-navigable parts, and lakes were separated in similar ways. The common law presumed that owners and occupiers of adjacent land had rights to take and use water on or under that land subject to certain restrictions. They were also entitled to riparian rights to the beds and banks of rivers and lakes.[15]

Such precepts were foreign to Māori, who had their own conceptions of waterways and their own laws regulating use and control. From the 1840s, when these British laws were superimposed in New Zealand, water law and policy focused on allocating and protecting individual rights to water resources in response to the needs of colonial settlers.[16] Rivers and streams could be declared public drains.[17] Wetlands were drained for agricultural production.[18] Conservation did not become a priority in water management in New Zealand until 1967 when the Water and Soil Conservation Act (WSCA) was enacted.

The WSCA represented a profound change to the law in terms of incorporating conservation values into legislation. However, the Waitangi Tribunal highlighted the absence of Māori cultural values as a flaw and recommended that the legislation be amended.[19] A further shift occurred in 1987 as a result of a landmark High Court decision, the *Huakina* case,[20] which imported Māori spiritual and cultural values as criteria governing the Planning Tribunal's functions under the WSCA. The case was led by Nganeko Minhinnick (who later became Dame Nganeko) and the Huakina Development Trust, who opposed an application for consent to discharge treated dairy shed waste into a stream, relying upon the Treaty of Waitangi and the spiritual values and relationship of Māori to the waters of the region. Since the WSCA was silent as to the criteria governing applications, the court ruled that Waitangi Tribunal interpretations of the Treaty could assist to ascertain Māori spiritual values. The *Huakina* litigation was part of a comprehensive and deliberate strategy by Māori in the Waikato region of raising concerns about the impact of cooling water, of mixing freshwater with salt water, of discharging industrial waste into water, and other "sacrilegious" actions that impeded the ability of Māori to exercise kaitiakitanga, an environmental ethic fully discussed below.[21] The case and the wider strategy became part of a change in consciousness that ultimately led to the introduction of sections 6, 7 and 8 of the Resource Management Act 1991, to Treaty Settlements such as the Waikato River Settlement, and, more recently, the inclusion of Te Mana o te Wai[22] into decision-making frameworks relating to freshwater.

The Resource Management Act 1991 (RMA) is the principal statute for the management of natural resources, including water. The RMA has a single broad purpose of "sustainable management" of natural and physical resources.[23] The idea of sustainable management stems from the Brundtland Report, which defines "sustainable development" as "development that meets the needs of the present without compromising the ability of future generations to meet their own needs". Sustainable development provided a framework within which to promote economic and social advancement in ways that would avoid environmental degradation and over-exploitation.[24]

In aiming to achieve sustainable management, decision makers are bound to recognise and provide for various matters of national importance, including "the relationship of Maori and their culture and traditions with their ancestral lands, water, sites, waahi tapu [sacred places], and other taonga [treasures]."[25] Lands, waters, fisheries and reefs have all been identified as such treasures.[26] The principles of the Treaty of Waitangi are to be taken into account.[27] And, particular regard is to be had to a list of environmental factors, beginning with "kaitiakitanga", a term now embodied and defined in the Act as "guardianship of resources by the Maori people of the area".[28] From a Māori perspective, it means so much more, as explained below.

Kaitiakitanga as right and responsibility

> *Hūtia te rito o te harakeke, kei whea te kōmako e kō?*[29]

According to Māori laws and customs that existed prior to colonisation, the protection of natural resources was imperative. For instance, when harvesting flax for its medicinal properties or to craft clothing and baskets from its fibres, it is customary that the youngest, finest shoot of the flax plant that grows between two larger parent leaves remains untouched. Harvesters also respect the parent leaves, for they will keep the youngest warm, and ensure the life of the plant.[30]

This ethic of protecting the environment for its own sake, as well as for present and future generations to use and enjoy, is kaitiakitanga. The root word is "tiaki" which means to care for, to foster, to nourish, and the concept of kaitiakitanga is explained by the redoubtable scholar, the Rev Māori Marsden:[31]

> The ancient ones (tawhito), the spiritual sons and daughters of Rangi and Papa were the 'kaitiaki' or guardians. Tane was the kaitiaki of the forest; Tangaroa of the sea; Rongo of herbs and root crops; Hine Nui Te Po of the portals of death and so on. Different tawhito had oversight of the various departments of nature. And whilst man could harvest those resources they were duty bound to thank and propitiate the guardians of those resources.

The distinctions between this earth-centred worldview and the anthropocentric worldview outlined earlier in the chapter are obvious. A contemporary example that explains the fullness of kaitiakitanga[32] comes from the circumstances surrounding a recent environmental disaster that occurred when the container ship MV *Rena* ran aground on Ōtaiti (Astrolabe Reef) near the North Island city of Tauranga in October 2011. An estimated 350 tonnes of heavy fuel oil leaked from its ruptured hull into the bay. The indigenous groups most affected by the *Rena* disaster were clear as to their responsibility for the reef: "we inherited a pristine reef and we have an obligation to pass that same pristine reef on to our children and our children's children and beyond."[33]

The reef is a significant treasure to the peoples of the harbour. Traditionally, those who fished on the reef would offer incantations to acknowledge and preserve the life force of the reef so that it would continue to be a source of sustenance. The right to fish also creates a responsibility to ensure that resources are preserved for the future. This meant that there were seasons, such as breeding times, when a resource might not be taken or used. Or when the numbers of a particular resource were down and needed time to recover. There was also a management regime for the use of a resource. For example, taking of shellfish might be restricted to those of a particular size to preserve breeding stock.[34] Many Māori continue to exercise these rights and responsibilities to this day.

Kaitiakitanga then is based on both on rights and responsibility. The significance of the reef for less tangible reasons can be difficult for people from other cultures to understand. For the people of the area, the reef and other surface-breaking rocks and reefs are seen as stepping stones for the spirits of their deceased back across to the sea to their ancestral homeland.[35] The continued presence of the wreck on the reef and the damage that it caused is therefore a source of spiritual distress and has implications on their ability to carry out their kaitiaki obligations. For these reasons, they are of the view that the wreck must be removed in its entirety.

In a report on the Māori claims to the Waitangi Tribunal seeking the removal of the wreck, the Tribunal explained that the Treaty of Waitangi signed by the British Crown and the Indigenous Māori in 1840 requires that the Crown provide ways for Māori to fulfil their obligations as kaitiaki over the things they treasure.[36] The Crown has opted to allow parts of the wreck to remain, based on its evaluation of "the environmental, cultural and economic interests of New Zealand and the likely cost and feasibility of the complete removal of the wreck including international comparisons".[37]

The Waitangi Tribunal has confirmed that one of the continuing rights held by Māori under the Treaty is the right to exercise political authority or rangatiratanga in the management of their natural resources (whether they still own them or not) through their own forms of local or regional self-government or through joint-management regimes at a local or regional level.[38] As noted above, the framework set out in the RMA provides strong directions which are to be borne in mind at every stage of the planning process.[39] However, the way in which Māori interests have been evaluated against a host of other matters in the Act has drawn criticism on more than one occasion from the Waitangi Tribunal as being inconsistent with Treaty principles. The Tribunal has concluded that while the RMA originally promised considerable protection for Māori interests, "it has failed to deliver on that promise" and recommended a number of reforms for a Treaty-compliant environmental management regime.[40] These recommendations are not binding on the government, but some of the recommendations for more effective participation are reflected in recent reforms to the RMA that encourage greater participation by Māori in shaping policies and plans for resource management.[41]

A rights discourse

The sorts of advancements represented by including references to Māori laws and philosophies in resource management legislation follow a long history of strategies by Māori to gain recognition of their traditional rights and title to lands and resources, both domestically and internationally. These strategies have ranged from passive resistance to outright warfare, establishing political forums, bringing grievances to the attention of parliament, the domestic courts and more recently the Waitangi Tribunal as well as deputations to international assemblies such as the United Nations.[42] Whether framed as aboriginal rights, human rights or rights guaranteed and protected under the Treaty of Waitangi, the result has been that domestic law has become more inclusive of a Māori worldview. In a series of Court of Appeal cases in the 1980s and 1990s, the courts urged the Crown to engage with Māori to address the recognition and protection of rights that were affirmed in the Treaty of Waitangi and claimed in respect of lands, forests and other natural resources.[43] Ultimately, this led to the development of a process for directly negotiating Treaty settlements, which runs parallel to the Waitangi Tribunal process. With tribunal hearings often taking many years to complete, and the recommendations that follow not being binding on the Crown, some claimants prefer to engage in direct negotiations, bypassing the tribunal process. Where claimants have opted for the tribunal process, the ensuing report often forms the basis for negotiations. Settlements are intended to "heal the past and build a future" by the Crown acknowledging grievances that arise from breaching Treaty of Waitangi principles, and then providing fair, comprehensive, final and durable settlements; as well as establishing an ongoing relationship between the Crown and the claimant group based on the principles of the Treaty of Waitangi.[44]

As explained below, settlements reached in respect of rivers and lakes provide stronger tools than those that exist in the RMA regime to protect the environment, to protect Māori proprietary rights and interests, and to enable Māori to exercise kaitiakitanga. They also embody two of the key concepts that underpin the philosophy of responsibility: collaboration and sustainability.[45]

I have written elsewhere about an innovative power-sharing model for restoring a major river in New Zealand that attempts to integrate Western legal concepts with Māori legal concepts.[46] In addressing claims that focus on the degradation of the Waikato River, the settlement legislation recognises the river as an ancestor with its own life force, and has as its overarching purpose, the restoration and protection of the health and wellbeing of the river for present and future generations. The settlement has ushered in a new era of co-management that has led to changes in regulatory frameworks regarding land use and freshwater, as well as changes in community expectations.[47] In the wake of the river settlement, two seats on the regional council, which makes major decisions in respect of freshwater management, are now reserved for Māori, and the Council has shown leadership in exploring pathways to improve relationships with local Māori. Excellent platforms exist in planning documents for recognising Māori rights and interests. There are issues around implementation and enforcement, but there is no doubt that the landscape has changed. These co-management models are becoming increasingly common and include joint management regimes for reserves, mountains, national parks, islands, rivers and lakes. They restore Māori to governance roles and restore direct relationships with natural resources, with the overarching purpose being, more often than not, to restore and protect the health and wellbeing of the natural world for future generations.[48]

One settlement that has attracted global attention recently is the settlement for the Whanganui River:[49]

> [The river] is ingrained in our hearts and in our minds. I think that this piece of legislation, with its framework that has a human face for our [river], is charged with the responsibility of ensuring that the health and well-being of [the river] – is able to be maintained, not so much for us here today but for future generations.

The settlement deals primarily with the restoration and protection of the health and wellbeing of the river by providing funding for restoration projects and improving planning processes and relationships between local government and Māori. In granting legal personality to the river, this settlement gives emphasis to the profound relationships that the local iwi have with their ancestral river and is intended to provide an opportunity for more effective recognition of the rights and interests of the river itself. The settlement explicitly refers to the peoples' responsibilities in relation to the "mana and mouri" of their ancestral river.[50] It also provides for collaboration and co-management,[51] and it is telling that the name of the post-settlement governance entity is Ngā Tangata Tiaki, the people who will care for the river.

Though Treaty settlements and the court cases that led to the development of the settlement process were framed in terms of rights to lands and other resources guaranteed and protected under the Treaty of Waitangi, the freshwater settlements are prime examples of the battle to protect those rights being underpinned by principles of responsibility. Similar insights can be found in the articles of the United Nations Declaration on the Rights of Indigenous Peoples.

United Nations Declaration on the Rights of Indigenous Peoples

As a state, New Zealand participated from the early stages of drafting the United Nations Declaration on the Rights of Indigenous Peoples.[52] Nganeko Minhinnick and her family became involved in the shaping of the Declaration from the 1980s. They along with others, such as Moana Jackson and Aroha Mead, made a significant contribution, working alongside other indigenous representatives in advocating a model of indigenous rights, as human rights, based on indigenous peoples' similar experiences of colonisation and settlement.[53] The result is a Declaration that affirms a right to self-determination, historical redress, free prior and informed consent, and rights to property and culture.[54] Sir ET Durie celebrated state support of the Declaration:[55]

> Notwithstanding the progress made through all the tribunal reports and court cases from the 1980s, and the consequential changes in legislation and official policy, I would still rank the day that New Zealand gave support to the

> Declaration as the most significant day, in advancing Maori rights, since 6th February 1840.

In affirming rights to language, culture, traditions and philosophies, and the right to act freely in pursuing these, rights articulated in the Declaration are underpinned by notions of responsibility.[56]

Now that the dust has settled on the negotiations and endorsement phases in respect of the Declaration, focus has moved to overcoming challenges in implementing the Declaration amongst criticism regarding the degree of compromise reflected in the ultimate form of the Declaration. Some of this criticism will be considered below in the context of a theme of this chapter, that the history of Māori responsiveness demonstrates flexibility and pragmatism in strategies to reconcile grievances.

Conceptions of property and ownership

A significant part of that history relates to the dispossession and destruction of lands and waters. Concepts that continue to perplex Māori minds are those of property and ownership. According to oral tradition, land is a source of identity for Māori. Being direct descendants of the Earth Mother, Papatūānuku, Māori see themselves as not only "of the land", but "as the land".[57] Possession of land was custodianship,

> a caretaking for future generations, and an acknowledgement of the temporariness of individual human life . . . A vast number of Maori people, when questioned, will respond: 'The land is my Mother. I cannot sell her – for if I do, I sell part of myself.'[58]

Legislation converted and assimilated Māori customary land tenure into what would become the New Zealand land law system, constituting a basis of ownership previously quite unknown to Māori.[59] However, when bringing challenges before the courts, Māori framed their claims in the language that the colonisers understood, such as aboriginal title, or breaches of rights that had been guaranteed in the Treaty.[60] As a result, the common law of New Zealand recognises the pre-existing property rights and cultural rights of Māori as a qualification on the sovereign title of the Crown:[61]

> Aboriginal title is a compendious expression to cover the rights over land and water enjoyed by the indigenous or established inhabitants of a country up to the time of its colonisation. On the acquisition of the territory, whether by settlement, cession or annexation, the colonising power acquires a radical or underlying title, which goes with sovereignty. Where the colonising power has been the United Kingdom, that title vests in the Crown. But, at least in the absence of special circumstances displacing the principle, the radical title is subject to the existing native rights.

This position was reaffirmed in the *Ngati Apa* case where the Court of Appeal confirmed the jurisdiction of the specialist Māori Land Court to investigate the status and ownership of land as Māori customary land, in relation to the foreshore and seabed. It also found that rangatiratanga and kaitiakitanga status and obligations as affirmed in the Māori version of the Treaty of Waitangi encompass a wider application than simply possession, occupation and use rights as captured in the common law doctrine of aboriginal title. Aboriginal title rights range from hunting, fishing and other types of access and passage through to exclusive ownership.[62] The Crown has recognised prior rights to lands, fisheries and forests. Whilst the Crown maintains that there is no right to own water at common law, this position is the subject of ongoing debate.[63] In the absence of clear and plain legislative direction to extinguish such rights (as occurred in the case of minerals and the foreshore and seabed), it remains open to argue that Māori have ownership rights in freshwater.[64]

The Waitangi Tribunal has found that Māori rights in 1840 included rights of authority and control over taonga (treasures), and are rights that are akin to the English concept of ownership.[65] It has also said that a right to development of property or taonga is guaranteed under Te Tiriti o Waitangi.[66] The freshwater settlements do not provide for ownership in water, and they vary in respect of transferring title to the beds of lakes and rivers.

The Waikato River settlement did not incorporate the return of the riverbed, and the issue of ownership of water was explicitly deferred. To ensure that Waikato-Tainui's position as to their authority over the Waikato River is made clear, the preamble to the settlement Act records a statement from the time they first became concerned that the Crown might itself claim authority over the river. When the governor's intentions to put an iron steamer on the river became known late in 1862, Patara Te Tuhi, editor of the tribal newspaper, expressed the opposition of the chiefs warning that the gunboat might not enter the river without permission. He asserted tribal authority over the river in these words: "E hara a Waikato awa i a te kuini, engari no nga Māori anake". (The Waikato River does not belong to the Queen of England, it belongs only to Māori).[67] Other provisions were included in the Act to record the agreement to defer any engagement about water ownership should the Crown change its position.[68]

The Te Arawa Lakes Settlement Act 2006 vests the lakebeds in the relevant tribal confederation, but the Crown retains ownership of the "stratum", the fictional space occupied by water and the space occupied by air above each Te Arawa lakebed.[69] These mechanisms were created to avoid Māori owning water and the space above water, thus preventing any charging for use of either. There are some Māori groups who maintain that water is incapable of being owned.[70] For example, the Whanganui River settlement transfers title to Crown owned parts of the riverbeds, but contains explicit statements regarding ownership. The legislation makes it clear that vesting of the riverbed does not create or transfer a proprietary right in water.[71] Because of this, the Whanganui River settlement falls short of the Waitangi Tribunal's recommendations in its substantial Whanganui River Report of 1999. There the Tribunal recommended, among other things, that the Crown negotiate with Whanganui iwi with a view to vesting the river *in its entirety* in an iwi ancestor, and that resource consent applications in respect of the River would require the approval of the iwi governance entity.[72]

The legislative solution to the controversy around the potential for Māori to own foreshore and seabed was to clearly and plainly vest the foreshore and seabed in the Crown. That legislation was replaced by an Act that declares the foreshore and seabed incapable of ownership and recognises certain customary rights.[73] In light of the Waitangi Tribunal's report on Māori rights and interests in water, and political tension around Māori ownership of natural resources, the government has engaged in a process to explore ways of recognising Māori rights and interests whilst maintaining its position that water is incapable of being owned. In this context, Māori-generated research has found that stronger tools that are additional to, and that complement, Treaty settlements are needed to appropriately recognise Māori rights and interests in freshwater to enable the exercise of rangatiratanga and kaitiakitanga.

The Durie proposal is one such solution, and insofar as it references the philosophy of responsibility and draws upon Māori laws of kaitiakitanga, it seems like an elegant solution consistent with international trends.

A responsibility discourse

The philosophy of responsibility refers to the respectful relationship human beings can have with their social and natural environment. While a duty is something imposed by others, responsibility invokes an ability to respond, to make choices.[74] Initiatives such as the Earth Charter and the Charter for Human Responsibility, and indigenous initiatives such as the Rights of Mother Earth proposed by Bolivia, are global examples of "reaching towards responsibility for the viability of life on the planet."[75]

The Earth Charter

The 1992 United Nations Conference on Environment and Development (also known as the Rio de Janeiro Earth Summit) created a movement for sustainable development as a way to address climate change challenges. Following the conference, the Earth Charter was developed to focus attention on environmental devastation, depletion of resources and extinction of species occurring as a result of economic over-exploitation of ecosystems. The Earth Charter provides a shared vision based on basic values: respect and care for the community of life, ecological integrity, social and economic justice, democracy, nonviolence and peace. It urges action. Champions of the Earth Charter such as the Global Ecological Integrity Group[76] call for a radical change of ethical outlook, drawing upon the wisdom of Aldo Leopold, who wrote in 1948:[77]

> We abuse land because we regard it as a commodity belonging to us. When we see land as a community to which we belong, we may begin to use it

with love and respect. There is no other way for land to survive the impact of mechanized man.

The proposition of a Charter of Human Responsibilities builds on the groundwork of the Earth Charter. According to the preamble:[78]

> The burden of collectively caused damage must be morally acknowledged by the group concerned, and put right in practical terms as far as possible. Since we can only partially understand the consequences of our actions now and in the future, our responsibility demands that we must act with great humility and demonstrate caution.

This charter is a step towards developing a democratic global governance based on human responsibilities, and towards developing a legal framework within which these responsibilities may be exercised. It recognises that sometimes society faces hard choices, such as the need to encourage economic development while protecting the environment and respecting human rights. In such cases, human responsibility dictates that none of these imperatives should be sacrificed to the others.

Proponents of responsibility draw upon the work of philosophers such as Emmanuel Levinas and Karen Barad.[79] They emphasise "responsiveness", or "respons*ability*", rather than "a burdensome sense of guilt".[80] They also recognise that indigenous peoples have long articulated a discourse of "relational responsibility", an obligation to others and to natural environments, for "relationality is at the heart of indigenous consciousness."[81] As discussed in the Māori case studies above, there is a strong resemblance between the basic values of these charters and indigenous wisdom.[82]

Indigenous solutions – living well with the earth

In arguing that the existing sustainable development agenda has not delivered on its promise of improved environmental sustainability, Deborah McGregor postulates that many international undertakings, including those led by the United Nations, continue to marginalise the involvement and voice of indigenous peoples.[83] Perhaps this is the reason that the Earth Charter and the Charter for Human Responsibility have not attracted the same levels of attention in New Zealand as compared with the developments in South America and the United Nations Declaration on the Rights of Indigenous Peoples.[84]

Turning to South America first, Bolivia passed the Rights of Mother Earth Act 2010 recognising Mother Earth as a living dynamic system (article 3) and granting her comprehensive legal rights that are comparable to human rights. Under article 7, Mother Earth has a number of rights including the right to life – the right to maintain the integrity of living systems and natural processes that sustain them as well as the capacities and conditions for regeneration. Other rights include the right to diversity of life, to water, to clean air, to balance, to restoration, and to live free of pollution. The object of the Act is to recognise these rights, as well as the obligations and duties of the plurinational state and of the society to ensure respect for these rights (article 1). Despite concerns about the perceived idealism, and questions about how the laws will be realised on the ground, these laws recognise that the world community is pushing Mother Earth past sustainable limits. Article 5 recognises the earth as being of public interest. Often, public interest trumps environmental concerns, and the public interest in not often defined as the wellbeing of the earth community or the earth, but is determined by largely economic standards. At the very least, the Bolivian laws recognise in a substantive way that humans will not thrive if the earth as a whole cannot.

The 2008 Ecuador Constitution also provides for legally enforceable Rights of Nature. Under article 395, the State guarantees

> a sustainable model of development, one that is environmentally balanced and respectful of cultural diversity, conserves biodiversity and the natural regeneration capacity of ecosystems, and ensures meeting the needs of present and future generations.

The Constitution is supreme law, and provides that any international treaties entered into shall be subject to its provisions.

More recently, the Rio+20 Declaration: Indigenous Peoples International Declaration on Self-Determination and Sustainable Development offered an alternative paradigm for achieving sustainable development:[85]

> Indigenous peoples call upon the world to return to dialogue and harmony with Mother Earth, and to adopt a new paradigm of civilisation based on Buen Vivir – Living Well. In the spirit of humanity and our collective survival, dignity and well being, we respectfully offer our cultural world views as an important foundation to collectively renew our relationships with each other and Mother Earth and to ensure Buen Vivir/living well proceeds with integrity.

The Rio+20 Declaration rejects the "dominant neo-liberal concept and practice of development based on colonisation, commoditization, contamination and exploitation of the natural world and policies and projects based on this model"[86] and calls for the renewal of a more ancient concept of sustainability, as expressed through the notion of living well.[87]

There is a clear correlation between the aspirations of the Earth Charter and the Charter for Human Responsibilities and those of indigenous peoples in relation to the environment, all offering alternative frameworks for living on this earth and in our environment. However, Māori emphasise that their rights and responsibilities in respect of kaitiakitanga exist in a delicate balance with their proprietary and development rights.

Contemporary discourses

> We believe we have a right to be involved in the management of water, and we also believe that we have a right to an allocation of water . . . If you look at all iwi in

> the country we are staunch on kaitiakitanga, but we're also all actively involved in business, and yes we will be using [water] economically.[88]

The Iwi Chairs Forum is a platform for sharing knowledge and information across tribal groups. Iwi leaders are clear in their view that kaitiakitanga and cultural rights include rights of sustainable and commercial use. A recent example is that of Māori opposing the establishment of an ocean sanctuary as a breach of their rights affirmed in a national fisheries settlement, demonstrating that while conservation principles are high on their agenda, they also have to protect their commercial and economic rights.[89]

Iwi leaders have continued to champion improvements to water quality, seeking to expand some of the best practice models from the freshwater settlements.[90] They have worked with the Crown in ensuring that the national significance of freshwater is recognised in policy by incorporating the principle of "Te Mana o te Wai". This principle recognises the innate relationship between the health and wellbeing of water and the wider environment, and their ability to support each other, while sustaining the health and wellbeing of the people. At the same time, iwi leaders have commissioned research into how Māori proprietary rights in water might be reflected in the creation of a fairer process for distribution and allocation of water. The current process for allocation is based on a premise of "first in first served". Māori are advocating for a system that encourages efficiency and discourages water hoarding. Iwi leaders are proposing that limits on water takes are set and enforced, and then focus can shift to sustainable use of the remaining allocatable flow. This, too, is a way of giving effect to Treaty rights and interests and ensuring that Māori and new users who can demonstrate that they are good kaitiaki of the water have fair access to water for sustainable development options that enable and protect Te Mana o te Wai.[91]

Proposals being put forward by Māori groups such as the iwi leaders and the New Zealand Māori Council acknowledge that while the co-management regimes established under the freshwater Treaty settlements provide some recognition of Māori rights and interests, they do not go far enough. In light of the Crown's continuing policy that no one owns water and recognising that the dominant legal system in New Zealand prioritises proprietary rights, Māori have proposed pathways forward that avoid the ownership issue. Instead, they focus upon drawing out the strongest mechanisms from the freshwater settlements:

1 Vesting ownership of riverbeds and lakebeds in iwi without the need for individual Treaty settlement processes. Title could be declared to be inalienable title under iwi control.
2 Vesting ownership of the "water column" in iwi, providing them with strong leverage in their communities to ensure that their respective rights and interests are recognised in ways that align with their values and responsibilities and that also allow them to commercialise their property rights if they so desire. A precedent for this is the Lake Taupō model. Lake Taupō is an iconic lake in the central North Island. Key elements of the arrangements in respect

of the lake, relevant to the rights and interests discussion, include that iwi own the lakebed and the "water column" (the fictional area that surrounds the water in flow). This mechanism has provided strong leverage for the iwi to ensure their rights and interests are recognised in ways that align with their values and obligations as kaitiaki and that also allow them to once again commercialise their property rights. Historically, the iwi charged for transporting products such as milk across the lake and for fishing guide services. It is an excellent example of how the Crown has given over real rights to iwi that has made them "significant players" in their communities and have provided commercial opportunities.[92]

A discourse of compromise

Avoiding the controversial and complicated issue of ownership is a thread in a pattern of pragmatism and compromise. This pattern is demonstrated in the focus on enhancing a single justice system that better recognises indigenous laws "for the sake of national cohesion" rather than advocating for a plural legal order.[93] Ani Mikare has warned that Māori should not[94]

> settle for mere improvements in the Pākehā system as being the ultimate goal. It is all very well to be making Pākehā law and legal institutions as Māori friendly as possible, but only so long as we do not become comfortable that we forget to aim for something more . . . to remind ourselves constantly about what it is that tino rangatiratanga ultimately demands.

The result of making mere improvements to a single justice system has been the undermining of Māori rights and interests as the rights and interests of others are given more weight.[95] Consequently, the environment has suffered. Compromise is evident in the political compacts that are the freshwater settlements. It is evident, too, in the wording and description of the United Nations Declaration on the Rights of Indigenous Peoples (the Declaration). In relation to the Declaration, New Zealand objected to the notion of human rights as collective rights, arguing "human rights are universal and apply in equal measure to all individuals, meaning that one group cannot have human rights that are denied to other groups within the same nation-state."[96] Andrew Erueti discusses the refusal by successive governments to recognise Māori political and property rights on the basis that this would be discriminatory to non-Māori. Erueti concludes that this approach "reads down" the article 2 guarantee to Māori of tino rangatiratanga.[97] New Zealand's later support of the Declaration was based on the premise that the document is non-binding, "an expression of aspiration" which will "have no impact on New Zealand law and no impact on the constitutional framework."[98] Karen Engle has decried the significant compromises in the Declaration and the serious limitations to the very rights it is praised for containing. In Engle's view, indigenous advocates compromised too much by pursuing a strategy of emphasising cultural elements of their claims and downplaying claims to "strong forms of self-determination", for example, "right of secession or independence as a nation state."[99] The effect has been to "reify identity and indigenous rights and displace many of the economic and political issues that initially motivated much indigenous advocacy: issues of economic dependency, structural discrimination, and lack of indigenous autonomy."[100]

Conclusion

Conscious of the degradation and depletion of natural resources and the breakdown of natural systems, there is a growing number of global movements looking to better protect this planet. Examples from New Zealand illustrate how Māori have responded to climate and environmental challenges over generations by asserting their rights and responsibilities in respect of their lands and waters. As a result, among other things, state law is becoming more accommodating of Māori laws, values and worldviews. But the reality of progressing rights in an era of practical reconciliation is an ongoing series of compromises for Māori, given the state's reluctance to adapt British legal notions of property in relation to water, and the related mindset that the recognition of Māori property rights to water is undemocratic privilege. The proposal to move towards a governance framework for freshwater based on responsible use is worth further consideration as an elegant solution to encourage respect for difference, and to find agreement for direction moving forward.

Notes

1 Ngahuia Te Awekotuku "He Wāhine, He Whenua, Māori Women and the Environment" in *Mana Wāhine Māori* (New Women's Press, Auckland, 1991) 66 at 70.

2 E.T. Durie "Law, Responsibility and Maori Proprietary Interests in Water" (paper presented at Law, Governance and Responsibility, University of Waikato, Hamilton, November 2014), also Chapter 10 in this volume. Sir E.T. Durie is a former Chief Judge of the Māori Land Court and High Court Judge, and is the Chair of the New Zealand Māori Council and its spokesperson on freshwater issues. Since the publication of Durie's proposal, political parties have produced water policies that involve some form of water levy that will contribute to restoring water quality. Some also recognise a Māori proprietary right.

3 Waitangi Tribunal *The Stage 1 Report on the National Freshwater and Geothermal Resources Claim* (Wai 2358, 2012) at 14.

4 The Treaty of Waitangi, signed between the British Crown and Māori in 1840, guaranteed Māori the full exclusive and undisturbed possession of their lands and estates, forests, fisheries and other properties which they desired to retain. The Māori version guaranteed "*tino rangatiratanga*", full authority and rights to govern. Whichever version one accepts, there is a clear recognition of and protection for Māori rights to govern natural resources, which they desired to retain.

5 Te Ahukaramu Royal and Betsan Martin "Indigenous Ethics of Responsibility in Aotearoa New Zealand: Harmony With the Earth and Relational Ethics" in Edith Sizoo (ed) *Responsibility and Cultures of the World: Dialogue Around a Collective Challenge* (6th ed, Peter Lang, Brussels, 2010) 47 at 48. See also T.K. Hoskins "Māori and Levinas: Kanohi ki te Kanohi for an Ethical Politics (PhD thesis, University of Auckland, 2010) cited in T.K. Hoskins, B. Martin, M. Humphries "The Power of Relational Responsibility" (2011) *Electronic Journal of Business Ethics and Organizational Studies* 6.

6 Royal and Martin, above n 5.

7 Deborah McGregor "Living Well With the World" in Corinne Lennox and Damien Short (eds) *Handbook of Indigenous Peoples' Rights* (Routledge, Oxford, 2016) 167 at 169.

8 A term used by Tom Bennion "Impact on Resource Management Practice" (paper presented at the "*Huakina*: *'The Fabric of New Zealand Society'*: A 30 Year Retrospective and Way Forward" Conference, Waikato Tainui College of Research and Development, Hopuhopu, June 2017).

9 Ministry for the Environment "Our Clean Green Image, What's It Worth" (2001) <www.mfe.govt.nz>. Mike Joy "The Dying Myth of a Clean, Green Aotearoa" *The New Zealand Herald* (online ed, Auckland, 25 April 2011).

10 Tom Bennion, above n 8, citing the National Institute of Weather and Atmospheric Conditions: <www.niwa.co.nz/>.

11 Adrian Macey, Chapter 7, this volume.

12 These are aspirational standards in government policy: <www.mfe.govt.nz/> and <www.waikatoregion.govt.nz/ >. See Adrian Macey, Chapter 7.

13 Lara Burkhardt "A Freshwater Allocation to Iwi: Is it Possible Under the Resource Management Act 1991?" (2016) 24 *Waikato Law Review* 81–96.

14 Alexander Gillespie *International Environmental Law, Policy, and Ethics* (2nd ed, Oxford University Press, Oxford, 2014) at 4.

15 *Embrey v. Owen* (1851) 6 Exch 353 at 372–373, 155 ER 579; Linda Te Aho "Ngā Whakataunga Waimāori" in Janine Hayward and Nicola Wheen (eds) *Treaty Settlements* (Bridget Williams Books, Wellington, 2012) 102.

16 Nicola Wheen "A Natural Flow: A History of Water Law in New Zealand" (1997) 9 *Otago Law Review* 71 at 78.

17 Public Works Amendment Act 1889.

18 Land Drainage Act 1893.

19 The Tribunal is a permanent bicultural commission of inquiry that hears claims and makes recommendations about breaches of the Treaty of Waitangi: see www.waitangitribunal.govt.nz/. The Tribunal's report on the *Kaituna River Claim* (Wai 4, 1984) made recommendations upon an application to abandon a scheme to build a pipeline from a wastewater treatment plant to a culturally significant river.

20 *Huakina Development Trust v. Waikato Valley Authority* [1987] 2 NZLR 188 (HC) at 210 per Chilwell J.

21 For example: Decisions of the Planning Tribunal, A116/84 ; A661/84; A 119/84; A120/84; and Waitangi Tribunal *Report of the Waitangi Tribunal on the Manukau Harbour* (Wai 8, 1985).

22 The principle of "Te Mana o te Wai" recognises the innate relationship between the health and well-being of water and the wider environment, and their ability to support each other, while sustaining the health and well-being of the people. It is discussed more fully below.

23 Resource Management Act 1991, s 5.

24 Geoffrey Palmer QC "The Resource Management Act – How We Got It and What Changes Are Being Made to It" (paper presented to Resource Management Law Association, Devon Hotel, New Plymouth 27 September 2013).

25 Section 6(e).

26 Waitangi Tribunal *The Final Report on MV Rena and Motiti Isalnd Claims* (Wai 2391 and 2393, 2015) [*Rena Report*].

27 Resource Management Act 1991, s 8. The principles of the Treaty emerged from a series of Court of Appeal cases in the 1980s where Māori opposed the transfer of state-owned assets to separate legal entities, thereby putting them beyond the reach of Māori claims under the Treaty. For a criticism of the principles, see Jane Kelsey *A Question of Honour: Labour and the Treaty 1984–1989* (Allen & Unwin, Auckland, 1990) at 217.

28 Resource Management Act 1991, s 7(a).

29 Traditional saying "If you remove the young shoot, from where will the bellbird sing?"

30 Te Awekotuku, above n 1, at 66.

31 There is reference here to the children of Rangi, the sky father, and Papa, the earth mother in Māori creation stories. Te Ahukaramu Charles Royal (ed) *The Woven Universe: Selected Writings of Rev Maori Marsden* (Estate of Maori Marsden, Otaki, 2003) at 67 cited in R. Benton, A. Frame and P. Meredith *Te Matapunenga:* A Compendium of References to the Concepts and Institutions of Māori Customary Law (Victoria University Press, Wellington, 2013) at 112.

32 I have written extensively about *kaitiakitanga* and freshwater elsewhere. See, for example, L. Te Aho "Indigenous Challenges to Enhance Freshwater Governance and Management in Aotearoa New Zealand – The Waikato River Settlement" (2010) 20 *The Journal of Water Law* 285; L. Te Aho "Ngā Whakataunga Waimāori: Freshwater Settlements" in N.R. Wheen and J. Hayward (eds) *Treaty of Waitangi Settlements* (Bridget Williams Books Ltd, Wellington, 2012) ch 7.

33 *Rena Report*, above n 23, at 14.

34 Ibid. at 14.

35 Ibid.

36 Ibid. at 12.

37 Ibid. at 36.

38 Waitangi Tribunal *Ko Aotearoa Tenei Te Taumata Tuatahi* (Wai 262, 2011) at 112.

39 *McGuire v. Hastings District Council* [2001] NZRMA 557 at 566.

40 Waitangi Tribunal *Ko Aotearoa Tenei Te Taumata Tuarua* (Wai 262, 2011) ch 3.

41 Recently enacted Resource Management Act amendments provide for Mana Whakahono a Rohe arrangements (MWR). MWR are written agreements between local government and iwi authorities to record how the latter will participate in the preparation, change or review of a policy statement or plan, Resource Management Act 1991, ss 58O–58U.

42 These strategies have not been linear and are well documented. For a general discussion, see Ranginui Walker *Ka Whawhai Tonu Matou, Struggle Without End* (Penguin, Auckland 1990).

43 *New Zealand Māori Council v. Attorney General* [1987] 1 NZLR 641 (CA); *New Zealand Māori Council v. Attorney General* [1989] 2 NZLR 143 (CA) *New Zealand Māori Council v. Attorney General* [1994] 1 NZLR 513 (CA); *New Zealand Māori Council v. Attorney General* [1996] 3 NZLR 140 (CA).

44 Office of Treaty Settlements *Ka Tika a Muri, Ka Tika a Mua: Healing the Past and Building a Future* (2nd ed, Office of Treaty Settlements, Wellington, 2015) at 23.

45 Te Ahukaramu Royal and Betsan Martin, above n 5, at 62.

46 See Te Aho, above n 32.

47 Waikato Regional Council Healthy Rivers Plan Change project and process: <www.waikatoregion.govt.nz/healthyrivers/>.

48 Examples include Ngāi Tahu Claims Settlement Act 1998; Te Arawa Lakes Settlement Act 2006; Ngāti Pāhauwera Treaty Claims Settlement Act 2012; Tapuika Claims Settlement Act 2014.

49 Adrian Rurawhe, Member of Parliament for the area. First Reading of Te Awa Tupua (Whanganui River Claims Settlement) Bill (24 May 2016) 714 NZPD 11220.

50 See Te Awa Tupua (Whanganui River Claims Settlement) Act 2017, s 71(1)(b) and (2)(c).

51 Sections 27–34.

52 United Nations Declaration on the Rights of Indigenous Peoples GA Res 61/295, A/RES/47/1 (2007) [UNDRIP].

53 Aroha Mead "Keynote Presentation" (paper presented to the *He Manawa Whenua Conference*, Hamilton, March 2017).

54 Andrew Erueti "Implementation of the United Nations Declaration on the Rights of Indigenous Peoples in Aotearoa – Theory and Practice" <www.waikato.ac.nz/law/news-events/undrip-symposiun/context>.
55 Sir E.T. Durie quoted in Tracy Watkins, "Judge Hails Big Advance for Maori" <stuff.co.nz> (online ed, New Zealand, 22 April 2010).
56 See for example UNDRIP, above n 50, arts 3, 8, 9, 11–16, 26, 27, and 31.
57 Ministry of Justice "Whenua" in *He Hinatore ki te Ao Māori a Glimpse into the Māori World* (Ministry of Justice, Wellington, 2001) 43 at 44.
58 Te Awekotuku, above n 1, at 68–69.
59 *In re the Bed of the Whanganui River* [1962] NZLR 600 (CA) per Gresson P.
60 *R v. Symonds* (1847) NZPCC 387; *Wi Parata v. the Bishop of Wellington* (1877) 3 NZ Jur (NS) 72 (SC); *Nireaha Tamaki v. Baker* [1901] A C 561 (PC); *Tamihana Korokai v. Solicitor-General* (1912) 32 NZLR 321 (CA); *Te Weehi v. Regional Fisheries Office* (1986) 1 NZLR 682 (HC).
61 *Te Runanganui o Te Ika Whenua Inc Society v. Attorney-General* [1994] 2 NZLR 20 (CA). In this case, the Court found that there was no aboriginal right to generate electriciy. The common law principle regarding aboriginal title was affirmed in *Ngati Apa v. Attorney-General* [2003] 3 NZLR 643 (CA) [*Ngati Apa*].
62 *Ngati Apa*, above n 61, at [33] per Elias J.
63 *Embrey v. Owen*, above n 15. See also *Report to the Iwi Advisory Group from the Freshwater Iwi Regional Hui*, November 2014 at 10 <http://iwichairs.maori.nz/>.
64 Jacinta Ruru "Maori Legal Rights to Water: Ownership, Management, or Just Consultation?" (2011) *Resource Management Theory and Practice* 119 at 120–123. The Crown Minerals Act 1991, section 10, claims all petroleum, gold, silver and uranium existing in its natural condition in the land (whether or not the land has been alienated from the Crown) as the property of the Crown. The Marine and Coastal Area (Takutai Moana) Act 2011 creates a special status for the common marine and coastal area and says that it is incapable of ownership, although the Act recognises customary interests in the area and customary marine title in sections 11 and 58.
65 See Waitangi Tribunal *Te Ika Whenua Rivers Report* (Wai 212, 1998) at 126. See, generally, Waitangi Tribunal *The Whanganui River Report* (Wai 167, 1999), and more recently, Waitangi Tribunal *The Stage 1 Report on the National Freshwater and Geothermal Resources Claim*, above n 3, at 80.
66 Waitangi Tribunal *Te Ika Whenua Rivers Report* (Wai 212, 1998) at 120.
67 Ibid. at [4].
68 Waikato-Tainui Raupatu Claims (Waikato River) Settlement Act 2010, ss 64 and 90.
69 Te Arawa Lakes Settlement Act 2006, s 23.
70 Iwi Leaders Report on Freshwater, above n 63.
71 Te Awa Tupua (Whanganui River Claims Settlement) Act 2017, s 46.
72 The Waitangi Tribunal *Whanganui River Report* (Wai 167, 1999) at 343.
73 Marine and Coastal Area (Takutai Moana) Act 2011.
74 Pierre Calame and Edith Sizo "Towards a 2015–2025 Strategy to Promote a Global Culture of Responsibility and Responsibility-based Legislation" at 1.
75 Hoskins, Martin and Humphries, above n 5, at 24.
76 Laura Westra and Mirian Vilela (eds) *The Earth Charter, Ecological Integrity and Social Movements* (Routledge, New York, 2014).
77 Aldo Leopold, A Sand County Almanac and Sketches Here and There (Oxford: Oxford University Press, 1968, viii–ix; as quoted by Prue Taylor and David Grinlinton in *Property Rights and Sustainability* (Martinus Nijhoff, The Hague, 2011) at 1.
78 *The Earth Charter: A Declaration of Fundamental Principles for Building a Just, Sustainable, And Peaceful Global Society in the 21st Century* (Earth Charter Commission, The Hague, 2000), see <www.earthcharter.org>.
79 Betsan Martin "Reponsibility Matters: A Perspective for Public Good" at 1 <www.waikato.ac.nz/__data/assets/pdf_file/0020/227351/Martin-Responsibility-Matters-Public-Policy-Nov2014.pdf>.

80 Royal and Martin, above n 5, at 1.
81 Ibid. at 3.
82 See also Linda Te Aho "Indigenous Aspirations and Ecological Integrity: Restoring and Protecting the Health and Wellbeing of an Ancestral River for Future Generations in Aotearoa New Zealand" in L. Westra, K. Bosselmann and C. Soskolne (eds) *Globalisation and Ecological: Integrity in Science and International Law* (Cambridge Scholars Publishing, Newcastle upon Tyne, UK) at 346.
83 Deborah McGregor "Living Well With the Earth" in Corinne Lennox and Damien Short (eds), *Handbook of Indigenous Peoples' Rights* (Routledge, London, 2016) ch 12.
84 Discussed above in text to n 51 and 52.
85 Rio+20 International Conference of Indigenous Peoples on Self-Determination and Sustainable Development, 19 June, 2012, Rio De Janeiro. Adopted by networks, organizations, traditional leaders, spiritual leaders and indigenous peoples from the 7 regions of the world, participants of the Conference. Endorsed by Campamento Terr Livere-Culpa dos Provos. See <www.iitc.org/wp-content/uploads/2013/07/>, at [3].
86 Ibid. at [16].
87 McGregor, above n 78.
88 Sir Mark Solomon, on behalf of the Iwi Chairs Forum, Waitangi 2016.
89 Te Ohu Kaimoana <www.teohu.maori.nz/>.
90 Waikato Regional Council Healthy Rivers Plan Change project and process: <www.waikatoregion.govt.nz/healthyrivers/>; and see http://iwichairs.maori.nz/our-kaupapa/fresh-water/.
91 Burkhardt, above n 13.
92 "Te Hapori o Maungatautari" Case Study Report: <http://iwichairs.maori.nz/our-kaupapa/fresh-water/> at 4.
93 Moana Jackson "Māori and the Criminal Justice System: A New Perspective, He Whaipaanga Hou" (Department of Justice, Policy and Research Division, Wellington, 1997).
94 Ani Mikaere "Tikanga as the First Law of Aotearoa" (2007) 10 *Yearbook of New Zealand Jurisprudence* 24 at 26.
95 *Te Runanga o Ngai Te Rangi Iwi Trust v. Bay of Plenty Regional Council* [2011] NZ EnvC 402.
96 HE Ms Rosemary Banks "Statement on behalf of Australia, New Zealand and the United States" <www.australian.org/unny/Soc_161006.html> and cited by Karen Engle, "On Fragile Architecture: The UN Declaration on the Rights of Indigenous Peoples in the Context of Human Rights" (2011) 22 *EJIL* 141 at 146. See also the discussion in Andrew Erueti "Māori Rights to Freshwater: The Three Conceptual Models of Indigenous Rights (2016) *Waikato Law Review* 1.
97 Erueti, above n 97 at 6–7.
98 (20 April 2010) 662 NZPD 10238 (Prime Minister John Key).
99 Engle, above, n 97, at 145 and 147.
100 Erueti, above n 97, at 1.

11 Reflecting on landscapes of obligation, their making and tacit constitutionalisation

Freshwater claims, proprietorship and "stewardship"

Mark Hickford

Introduction

In recent powerful contributions, Dame Anne Salmond has spoken of "ontological collisions" and "quarrels" in discussing how different contested theories of existence or being might fare in imagining rights to natural resources, engaging both state and indigenous viewpoints.[1] In this chapter, and leveraging both my approaches to political constitutionalism in indigenous-state relations[2] and Salmond's core theme of ontologies, I examine how incrementalism in public policy and legislative design has contributed to creating a landscape of obligations. Contemporary New Zealand settings for the settlement of historical indigenous claims against the Crown are salutary. These human messy processes of negotiation against a background of *ontological* dissonances may yet yield landscapes of obligation[3] replete with new or different questions, imperfections and frailties. Specifically, in a number of instances where the ancestral force of a river or lake is recognised or given attributes as a legal person, we are seeing landscapes to which (or even to whom) obligations are owed. To put this point into philosophical terms, a novel or differently expressed *deontological* commitment or set of obligations emerges *vis-à-vis* a site or resource such as a lake, territory, waterway or catchment area comprising many watercourses. These commitments are imperfectly and incompletely theorised. That is, the rationale or understanding underlying the textual language resorted to in a negotiated deed of settlement or subsequently enacted statute may (and often does) conceal diverse, perhaps disjointed understandings.[4] These can reveal ontological dissonances; in other words, a non-alignment of, or lack of concord in, underlying views and values as to being or being-ness or existence. This is not a criticism. Rather it is an important observation in any given negotiation that the words ultimately settled upon to express or reflect agreement tend to mask a number of different ways of seeing the relationships and obligations regarding natural resources. They also speak to different audiences and constituencies of opinion. In two recent settlements concerning Te Urewera and the Whanganui River and catchment tributaries, the resources themselves are (or are to be) given legal personality with human representatives.[5] They are seen expressly as epistemic and ontological *subjects* as opposed to merely ontologically objective things or objective facts.[6]

Furthermore, these commitments are multifariously relational. They are not uniform. Various individuals and different values are engaged and entangled, perhaps conflicting, even internally to the individuals themselves. Participants in administering the legislation will have their own "stewardship" obligations arising from different sources, including the State Sector Act 1988, which defines "stewardship" broadly as "active planning and management of medium- and long-term interests, along with associated advice". The interests engaged in terms of *other-regarding* "responsibility" or stewardship can be many, expressing various logics as to what policies might require. These concerns may include a sense of managing the Crown's engagement in Crown-iwi-hapū relations generally, as evidenced particularly in settlement legislation and post-settlement relationships which its officers promote through the legislature, or ensuring the Crown's interests across time, not merely its inheritances handed down from diverse pasts – regulatory regimes or rights, for example – but also how these might be refined, amended or departed from. Legal texts are generated but ultimately the interpretative variations these texts portend or afford in practice, the operational behaviours that are shaped and incentivised (or not) through these legalistic regimes, require intense scrutiny. Within the limitations of this essay, the discussion cannot be comprehensive. What follows will explore these arguments from a self-consciously anglophone, legalistic and political perspective. Nonetheless, the observations made here are salient to a range of jurisdictions internationally in view of state-indigenous negotiated engagements contending with re-narrating relations of authority and obligation to space (including landscapes) and also being able to be presented as aligned with conceptions of "stewardship".

Claiming rights and interests

Claims relevant to these geographical places or sites, sometimes expressed through litigation in the ordinary courts or in specialist statutory jurisdictions such as the Māori Land Court (once named the Native Land Court), have occasionally been precursors to these settlements. A number of these have been recast as claims before the Waitangi Tribunal on the part of "any Māori", alleging, for example, any acts or omissions "at any time on or after 6 February 1840, or proposed to be done or omitted, by or on behalf of the Crown" within the meaning of section 6(1) of the Treaty of Waitangi Act 1975.[7] Under that provision, any claim would assert that "the act or omission, was or is inconsistent with the principles of the Treaty" and adumbrate the likely prejudicial effect of the specific acts or omissions at issue. The schedule to its legislation includes two texts of the Treaty of Waitangi, one in English and another in Māori, although, historically, the version in Māori was predominantly signed or marked at assorted sites from 6 February 1840 (except at Waikato heads). These texts have occasioned considerable debate but, simply put for the purposes of this chapter, the Treaty comprises three brief articles and involved an exchange of kāwanatanga or "governorship" to the incoming Crown in return for the guarantee of "te tino rangatiratanga [the full or complete chieftainship] o ratou w[h]enua o ratou kainga me o ratou taonga katoa [all their lands, settlements and other treasures]".[8] The interpretations of these terms have been debated, particularly as to what they signify in practice in and through time.[9]

Institutionally the Tribunal is a standing commission of inquiry. Its jurisdiction is largely recommendatory, except for statutorily specified provisions relating to lands or interests transferred to state-owned enterprises where it can make binding recommendations.[10] The Tribunal's own reasoning in a range of reports has supplied ways of presenting a different understanding of water bodies. These patterns of reasoning lie as a resource, potentially able to be gathered up, revisited and tested (or even re-tested) in the ordinary courts or in discussions with executive branch policy officials from time to time. It can, therefore, supply a conceptual repertoire or a narrative arc that can be resorted to in future litigation before the courts or, more extensively, in negotiations with officials in the executive branch of government and in localities. Processes of influence are gradual and somewhat erratic, to say the least. Each inquiry panel membership in a Tribunal hearing is specific to that inquiry, and earlier reports are not viewed as legally binding or as having precedential effect (although they may, of course, be cited or used, perhaps repeatedly). The reports may generate distinct forms of emphasis or analysis in reasoning on allied topics. In its *Te Ika Whenua Rivers Report* in 1998, for instance, the relevant Tribunal used the conception of "residual proprietary interest" to characterise the extant indigenous entitlements relating to riverine water, while refraining from specifying the metes and bounds of that residue. "This", it advised, "should be a matter for negotiation and settlement between the Crown and the claimants", although it was clear that it should be an interest of "reasonable substance".[11] As to a "right of development", that Tribunal inquiry concluded, "the residual interest of Te Ika Whenua in the rivers included full and unrestricted rights of use, including the right to development, except where those uses were detrimental to or incompatible with the rights of other users".[12] This notion of a "residual proprietary interest" or "entitlement" proved to be resilient, as it was reiterated in 2012 in the Tribunal's *Stage 1 Report on the National Freshwater and Geothermal Resources Claim*.[13] The Tribunal's most detailed recommendations on what "exclusive rights" and "possession" of a water resource might imply in practice relative to the existing Resource Management Act 1991 regime are to be found in *The Whanganui River Report*.[14] It suggested two options for considering in any negotiations, proposing in one of these that the river be vested in an ancestor or ancestral representative enabling a distinct ownership consent-power under real property law to be exercised through its legal representatives (as trustee),[15] whilst any resource consent application pertaining to the river would require approval of the Whanganui River Māori Trust Board.

Recently the Supreme Court, now the ultimate appellate court in New Zealand, has observed that the "Tribunal is the body to which claims that the Crown has failed to meet its political obligations under the Treaty must be addressed".[16] In that same decision, McGrath J commented:[17]

> In general, because the Tribunal process is a recommendatory one, whether and what redress ultimately will be provided to Maori claimants is a decision

for the government, with outcomes usually being the result of settlements between the Crown and Maori claimants.

Although, generally, the courts have assessed these Tribunal reports as having referential value or as being entitled to judicial respect, Tribunal findings and reasoning are not binding on the superior courts, and its jurisdiction is restricted to operating within its constitutive legislation – the Treaty of Waitangi Act 1975.[18] Given its inquisitorial, principally recommendatory aspects, it is certainly apt to describe its role as one of assisting "a political settlement of [grievances] through independent examination and informed advice."[19] "The crucial point", the Court of Appeal noted bluntly in *Te Runanga o Muriwhenua v. Attorney-General*, "is that the Waitangi Tribunal is not a Court and has no jurisdiction to determine issues of law or fact conclusively."[20]

Irrespective of how these natural resource-related claims have been expressed linguistically or conceptually, or their particularities of framing, they have become inheritances, part of the fabric of these islands – their pasts, presents and futures. With the Whanganui River, for instance, there were lengthy histories of claiming, including proceedings before the Native or Māori Land Court, the Supreme Court[21] and the Court of Appeal. These have been considered in a number of academic works and other fora.[22] In 1936, rivers such as the Whanganui were listed amongst "Māori claims" in a Solicitor-General's memorandum to the then Prime Minister, with other waterbodies named like Lakes Waikaremoana and Omāpere.[23]

The contemporary settlement process purports to wrap up and settle all claims defined as "historical", settlement by settlement, whether already registered as claims in the Waitangi Tribunal or not. They are negotiated political compacts given expression through legislative enactment. The process has exhibited a range of policy styles across more than two decades. Officials and political principals were aware from the outset that natural resource management required attention, although the assorted ways in which settlements have sought to provide non-financial or so-called cultural redress have occasioned some innovations, particularly in connection with water bodies like the Waikato.[24] As a number of scholars have identified, there are limitations to the processes underpinning these settlements and their published or officially promulgated outcomes.[25]

The term "historical Treaty claim" means

> a claim made under section 6(1) that arises from or relates to an enactment referred to in section 6(1)(a) or (b) enacted, or to a policy or practice adopted or an act done or omitted by or on behalf of the Crown, before 21 September 1992.

Treaty settlements permit a particularising of relations and behavioural expectations sensitive to place and histories. So, whilst larger scale national regulatory regimes like the Resource Management Act 1991 might be in place, customised Treaty settlements can allow for much more granular, regionally sensitive approaches. The design of these sorts of locally attuned perspectives can be up-front through providing more specific signals in the settlement legislation or associated deeds of settlement. Dealing with particular catchment areas or territories, they can avoid some of the challenges of large-scale or national-level jurisdiction regulatory reform – fewer political touchpoints. Conversely, the localised approaches they reflect may not be as well integrated from a central government perspective.

Avoiding the vocabulary of proprietorship? Legal personality, non-ownership and responsibility

Recalibrating relations of power in landscapes

J.R. Searle has explored the ontology of institutional and social facts like legal persons.[26] In discussing indigenous orders in the context of freshwater and energy resources, Salmond speaks of "ontological styles", as is fitting given that ontologies relevant to the discussion here are not immutable, fixed or bounded but rather dynamic, adaptive, entangled and flexible.[27] Statutes can harbour these diverse understandings as ontological dissonances. This is an issue writ large in the complexities of co-existence between indigenous negotiators and those representing the Crown in an archipelago such as New Zealand. Terms might be deployed in legislation that comprise implications as to meaning and being or existence not shared or fully understood by those engaged in the design of the regime. This is perhaps heightened as a possibility where the term or concept used *resonates* with (or proxies in part for) an indigenous understanding but is in itself an imported notion, experiment, innovation or adaptation. How these terms might be interpreted or construed awaits the implementation on the part of decision-makers and interactions with the courts. A concept of value might not be shared on the part of different interests or communities such that core aspects or features are not comprehended on the part of others not privy to that "value".[28] The ancestral force or energy of a place or waterbody may be one such example. Disagreement on underlying values might lurk despite agreement on legislative language. Under section 12 of Te Awa Tupua (Whanganui River Claims Settlement) Act 2017, "Te Awa Tupua is an indivisible and living whole, comprising the Whanganui River from the mountains to the sea, incorporating all its physical and metaphysical elements." Section 14 declares Te Awa Tupua to be "a legal person [with] all the rights, powers, duties, and liabilities of a legal person", represented by human guardians, Te Pou Tupua.

What to one ontological style (to use Salmond's expression) might be an inanimate object or geographical feature is accorded personhood at law. In *Mullick v. Mullick*, a case before the Judicial Committee of the Privy Council, a religious idol representing or instantiating a household deity was found to be a "juristic entity" with human custodians owing it certain duties.[29] Imperial legal orders were aware of these diverse approaches to phenomena in empire, a once global system. This case has been referred to in the Waitangi Tribunal report on the Whanganui

River and in New Zealand courts such as *Huakina Development Trust v. Waikato Regional Authority* in 1987.[30] Juxtaposing or interweaving different legal-political conceptions of landscapes or natural resources, including common pool resources like water, within a legal term or notion is not unheralded. Property itself can be treated in such a fashion, particularly if those exercising powers observe or comply with a sense of stewardship principles they share or agree on.[31] Evidently, these propositions or principles can also be enunciated and set out in legally binding criteria. Furthermore, an agreement to disagree is also possible. None of these messy complexities should be startling. Certain conceptions of claiming supervisory authority in the use of natural resources can be reserved in the negotiations and expressed transparently awaiting more propitious times for recognition by others, one example being indigenous rights of government.[32]

Notwithstanding attributing "legal personality" to the river, the characteristics or incidents of proprietorship remain relevant. This is because any settlement negotiations had to engage with concepts of proprietorship already a part of the *status quo ante*. For one thing, the Land Act 1948 applied to those parts of the riverbed that could be regarded as Crown land not administered as conservation land subject to the National Parks Act 1980 or the Reserves Act 1977; that is, areas that have been subject to the administration or jurisdiction of the Commissioner of Crown Lands.[33] Under section 24(1)(a) of the Land Act 1948, the Commissioner's powers and duties include that of preventing "unlawful trespassing or intrusion upon or occupation of Crown land" (those without appropriate consent). Section 40 of Te Awa Tupua (Whanganui River Claims Settlement) Act states that from settlement date any Crown-owned part of the bed of the Whanganui River ceases to have that status. The "bed" of the Whanganui River is defined as meaning "the space of land that the waters of the Whanganui River cover at its fullest flow without overtopping its banks" and "includes the subsoil, the plants attached to the bed, the space occupied by the water, and the airspace above the water".[34] Likewise, with Te Urewera (formerly Urewera National Park), the "legal personality" is invested with the fee simple estate, which is not simply the surface of the territory. These are useful reminders to those not familiar with the laws of real property that vesting proprietorship of land (including submerged lands such a lakebed or a riverbed), unless expressly said otherwise, limited or excluded, ordinarily implies the vesting of the superjacent space (that occupied by the water column and the airspace to a reasonable height) and subterranean space, subject to any relevant regulatory provisions.[35] Proprietorship contemplates three dimensional space as well as temporal qualities (or slices of time). Aspects of the Whanganui River were not owned in that the coastal marine area from the mouth of the Whanganui River to the Cobham Street bridge in Whanganui township itself was subject to the Marine and Coastal Area (Takutai Moana) Act 2011. That area was not owned because section 11(2) of that 2011 statute provides: "Neither the Crown nor any other person owns, or is capable of owning, the common marine and coastal area, as in existence from time to time after the commencement of this Act". Aspiring towards indivisibility, therefore, had to contend with endemic compartmentalisation of the river system by virtue of several statutory regimes.

Despite certain views suggesting the contrary, proprietorship as a concept is not as unidimensional or limiting as some have presented it. How its incidents might be exercised can depend very much on the predilections of those entitled to hold property in relation to a resource. Evidently, legal criteria around its exercise constrains and disciplines what decision-makers may relevantly consider at law. Proprietary rights are socially constructed and entail ordering and gradating power relations relative to a site, space or thing, in and through time.[36] Both time and spatiality remain relevant practical and conceptual dimensions. For a start, time is engaged, as a fee simple estate is not time-bound in the manner of, say, a leasehold interest. Contextually, it must be borne in mind that a reported proposal to vest the fee simple estate of Urewera National Park in Ngāi Tūhoe (thereby divesting the Crown) was rejected within the executive branch in May 2010 in a very public manner reported in the media.[37] This failed attempt preceded the ultimate use of "legal personality" as one technique to ameliorate any perceived anxieties as to a non-Crown actor excluding through proprietorship any third parties who might have enjoyed relatively unfettered access. Importantly though, the substantive incidents of any fee simple vesting were preserved or carried over into the ultimately agreed settlement, like, illustratively, the relevant concessions approving power.[38] To some, proprietorship implies attributes of partisan control, whereas a seemingly more abstract or neutral notion of non-ownership or of, say, legal personhood might be presented as less discomforting. Other techniques included preserving public access in addition to declaring a space or landscape as unowned or as having its own legal personality status to which duties are owed.

Now, indigenous legal scholar Carwyn Jones has cautioned, "Although a key aspect of the Māori worldview in relation to the natural environment is that landscape features such as rivers have their own *mauri* (life force) and their own mana, this is not the equivalent of a legal personality", which he identified as a Western legal concept.[39] *Mullick* perhaps, let alone the philosophical warnings of Kwame Anthony Appiah, suggests a measure of care must be observed in essentialising any given concept or term as "Western" in these particular circumstances.[40] Ideas as to cultural "authenticity" are also problematic in view of the dynamism of cultural relations with strangers.[41] But it is pertinent to note that, once settled on by way of agreement, a conception like legal personality might be able to converse with, or speak (make sense) to, different audiences or constituencies who need to be persuaded that the change or innovation wrought by a settlement is not overly discomforting or disrupting (to some) or goes some way to improving the conditionalities of Crown-iwi relations. Here, the salience of the messaging will depend on the specifics of the audience, their preferences, anxieties and perspectives. Te Awa Tupua, understood as a legal personality, is an innovation in terms of its application to a river system, one that is able to resonate with *aspects* of Whanganui River iwi constituencies and those governmental ministers and officials engaging with numerous other publics, such as non-governmental organisations with localised and trans-regional portfolios of interest that might also happen to include iwi members as well. It should be obvious, but citizens are able to share in many identities, occasionally in conflict or discord.[42] Thus, different aspects of the implications of "legal personality" and its contexts within the settlement might be emphasised, appealing to different communities of interest at a veritable multitude of places or times. For the Crown and a range of publics that might engage with the settlement directly or observe it from a distance, deploying "legal personality" skirts around the issue of non-Crown or non-state proprietorship of riverbeds or national parks, effectively neutralising it whilst also maintaining or grand-parenting general public entitlements such as existing navigation rights or general access. Herein lies the salience of the "commons" or even common pool resources, where a resource like a watercourse is shared, but uses or entitlements to use an allocated share[43] subtract from the enjoyment that others might have of resource as a whole.

Unpropertised common pool resources or commons, nonetheless, may be subject to regulatory regimes.[44] Indeed, whether a freshwater body or territorial sea is being considered, and as with proprietary rights, neither non-ownership nor legal personality precludes the ongoing relevance of regulatory overlays. Non-ownership of flowing water neither prevents nor inhibits regulatory regimes placing the Crown, local authorities or other nominated entities in a decision-making role as to how such a resource might be accessed by users. That is, proprietorship or non-proprietorship does not displace the possibilities of overlaying regulatory requirements that discipline or constrain how access to the resource can occur. Permissions to access the resource may be given with the regulator in a distributive mode subject to terms including length of tenure to access before seeking additional approval, the possibilities of access entitlements being varied adaptively or even suspended for periods of time.

Many years ago, Alex Frame saw the concept of "legal personality" residing in a landscape as something that could align with, or proxy for, indigenous notions.[45] In doing so, he acknowledged the work of Christopher Stone in the United States on suggesting that natural features of the environment be accorded legal standing but observed (correctly) that environmental outcomes were not his focus. As always, important tropes of statutory interpretation, with their own customary practices, will also come to the fore, including the Interpretation Act 1999 and the conventional approach in settlement legislation to insert a provision, stating, "It is the intention of Parliament that the provisions of this Act are interpreted in a manner that best furthers the agreements expressed in the deed of settlement" (section 6 of Te Urewera Act 2014, for example).

Also unaffected by the vesting in Te Awa Tupua are any "existing private property rights, including customary rights and title" to the extent that these have not been otherwise extinguished.[46] Here, then, is a useful reminder that there is potential for extant or remaining customary rights and title to be recognised still, and these are not regarded as settled in any treaty settlement process. This, then, incentivises the possibility of seeking legal recognition of such rights layering landscapes of obligation with other notions of proprietorship and responsibility (customary). With rivers, the situation is somewhat complicated. Under section 354(1) of the Resource Management Act 1991, the Crown asserts continuing proprietorship to so-called navigable riverbeds dating back to the vesting of such riverbeds in the Crown under the Coal-mines Act Amendment Act 1903,[47] whilst what is exactly "navigable" under that original vesting is an obscurely illustrated, rather open-textured, evidentially dependent term that has received recent judicial interpretation. The possibilities of unextinguished customary rights existing in relation to rivers has been recently reinforced before the Supreme Court in its interpretation of "navigability" deriving from the initial 1903 vesting.[48] Complexities continually look our way in Crown-indigenous relations, whether with settlement negotiations or in other policy-operational domains. It is fitting to embrace these tangles. The finitude of human individuals, the complicatedness of human co-existence, renders this observation a truism. Yet these vexed challenges of diversity, difference and disagreement, as well as concord and multiple allegiances within given communities, carry implications for those ventures involved in designing textual markers for relationships with landscapes and other human beings (those dwelling in the area or even visiting it for instance). Disappointments inexorably travel with these processes. Reconciling the complexities of co-existence must invariably deal with the legacies of assorted rights, interests and uses arising through colonial settlement even where the inherent legitimacy of some of those uses or the regulatory authorisations underpinning them is contested.[49]

Interactions can be caustic and unforgiving with clusters of opinion proving changeable and sometimes fragile, internally to the executive and negotiating teams or "out-of-doors". This is so whether one is endeavouring to address resource management, environmental concerns or revising or reframing a regulatory regime. "Political rule, even liberal rule, requires ruling over a group of people some of whom will disagree with you, your decisions, or even your right to rule in the first place".[50] To act politically is to engage in action or courses of direction with many others, navigating or traversing disparate viewpoints, orientations or understandings for, as Hannah Arendt observed, relational plurality – a diverse, complicated multitude of human lives – is the *sine qua non* of politics in operation.[51] Democratic settings multiply these touchpoints or footholds for dissent. Mutual reliance is involved, as political activity requires enlisting or garnering support or coalitions of opinion, if only for a moment in time – what Arendt characterised as the "interdependence of action". It is invariably exhausting, indeed remorselessly so. Disruptions to influential discourses occur incrementally with few observable sudden ruptures in thought. Relationally, as negotiations proceed, preferences are compromised in policy and practice. Unsurprisingly, parties cannot expect to obtain all that they might have desired on entering into negotiations.

A letting-go in discrete areas of narratives or ways of thinking and seeing is involved in any compromise or working through, even though the agreed outcomes might be seen as waypoints on a longer journey towards adjusting relations of influence or authority. What I have referred to elsewhere as an "interpretative risk" results, as strangers to the processes of negotiations end up interpreting what was agreed at earlier moments in time and constructing different ways of understanding those concepts captured in legislation and deeds of settlement.[52] Possibilities of mutual incomprehension persist but, as with any such interaction or "middle ground" weaving assorted tropes or practices in an area where different views might coalesce or co-exist,[53] this does not undermine workability in practice. There is no necessary dawning of understanding, however. The words speak different things to different audiences and constituencies, which is often a key part of how to get to success in any negotiated arrangements. Getting deeds of settlement or agreements in principle across the line incentivises these approaches to drafting. Such is the way of negotiated settlements of historical claims. Constraints operate on all parties but there is little doubt that the Crown is placed in a stronger bargaining position given its Treaty settlement negotiation parameters or policy settings.

Specific environmental outcomes, whether (say) sustainability or sophisticated forms of adaptive management as environmental circumstances change, are not guaranteed. It would be erroneous to suggest otherwise. For one thing, various footholds are created for contest and dispute in legislative instruments such as statutes and it is conceivable that certain decision-making processes will be contested through litigation (judicially reviewing decisions relative to statutory criteria) and political influences. In vesting thirteen defined lakebeds (such as Rotorua) in Te Arawa Lakes Trustees while leaving in place a so-called "Crown stratum" comprising "the space occupied by water and the space occupied by air above each Te Arawa lakebed", Te Arawa Lakes Settlement Act 2006 accorded certain Te Arawa voices decision-making authority and influence in conjunction with Crown representatives on whether to permit new commercial activities or structures in the lakes. Discipline and constraint is exerted through legislation in setting out criteria for decision-making processes, supplying points for critique of those decisions and constraints on the discretionary powers of those responsible for the landscape. A peculiarly accented politics is given rise to through these settlements. Yet an arena of action of certain plausible sort is encouraged through the legislative regime because certain questions are posed of the resource or landscape, such as (in the case of the Whanganui River as Te Awa Tupua) how decision-makers under other regulatory frameworks interact with the work of the strategy group Te Kōpuka. The purpose of Te Kōpuka is to "act collaboratively to advance the health and well-being of Te Awa Tupua". Moreover, persons exercising or performing a function, power, or duty under listed statutes in clause 1 of the second schedule like the Conservation Act 1987, the Biosecurity Act 1993 or the Fisheries Act 1996 "must recognise and provide for" both Te Awa Tupua status and Tupua Te Kawa. The concept of Tupua Te Kawa is explicated in section 13 as those intrinsic values that represent Te Awa Tupua, including "The iwi and hapū of the Whanganui River have an inalienable connection with, and responsibility to, Te Awa Tupua and its health and well-being."

Tacit constitutionalisation and the possible relevance of state sector stewardship

A form of tacit constitutionalisation in a legal and political sense is also involved with these landscapes of obligation arising from or being recast through settlements of historical Treaty claims. Behind the scenes, rich interactions occur at many levels and in a variety of public policy domains. These entanglements, to use an appropriate term, are reflective of political and constitutional orders, including indigenous-state relations of which the Treaty of Waitangi is an influential part but not an exhaustive representative of the variety and norms of those relationships. "Entanglement" here signifies what Nicholas Thomas once construed as the intersection of histories that might be linked, but not necessarily shared, in the sense that certain areas of indigenous and colonial socialities remain relatively untouched or reserved from the colonial effects of inter-cultural exchange or incomprehensible to them.[54] Where entanglement occurs and does effect change, then adaptations are wrought on the participants through the processes of interaction and exchange but not completely, as not all is shared or comprehended. Certain concepts, such as mana, cannot and should not be ensnared within the introduced legal system, and the complexities of entanglement do not touch all aspects of indigenous ontology. It is proper that a withholding from the introduced colonial legal system is retained.

Constitutionalisation is occurring because where state-indigenous concerns intersect or interweave in settlements and policy domains, the political relation of state-indigenous power and the conditionalities of the relationship between state and indigenous or first nations' communities are being incrementally revisited and reframed. State or Crown proprietorship is seen as a means for non-exclusive, public or nationalised entitlements being maintained. These settlements instantiate or reflect a recalibrating or revisiting of public power relations tied to particular geographical areas or features. Iwi groupings are recognised as being localised or regionally based interpreters of public interest, and a landscape of obligations in relation to watercourses, lakes or territorial areas is buttressed by statute in bespoke, discrete ways. As with the Te Arawa Lakes Settlement Act, then, new voices or hitherto long-neglected voices of legal and political relevance are inserted into a landscape. They have a legal and power presence that must be noticed and engaged with. Within the bounds of those statutory provisions, *how* decision-making authority or influence might be exercised remains to be determined by elements of each indigenous community.

The avenues for these tacitly constitutional negotiations are myriad. They include specific Treaty settlements concerning historical claims, as well as direct policy engagements between executive branch officials and iwi leaders, such as with the Freshwater Iwi Leaders group and the supporting iwi advisors' group, as well as interventions on the part of other entities, like the New Zealand Māori Council.[55] Among other things, under the Freshwater Iwi Leaders Group document entitled *Nga Matapono ki te Wai*:[56]

> Iwi want to re-establish and maintain an enduring relationship with their ancestral/traditional water-bodies – mana whakahaere – recognising both their inherent mana and associated kaitiaki responsibilities over these water bodies.

The ordinary courts form an episodic part of the overall universe or cosmos in which these Crown-indigenous discussions, entanglements and contests occur. As the Ngāi Tūhoe and Whanganui River settlements were being formulated, the question of rights and interests in freshwater and geothermal resources was receiving attention in the Waitangi Tribunal and the courts throughout 2012 and 2013. Ignited in the context of sell-down, where in certain state-owned enterprises the Crown shareholding was to be reduced to no less than 51 per cent of any class of issued shares or of voting securities as part of a mixed ownership model policy, this litigation before the ordinary courts led to what Matthew Palmer has characterised as an exercise in "judicial statecraft" on the part of the Supreme Court in February 2013.[57] In that decision, the judges noted that it "appears from the policy initiatives [in freshwater policy development and Treaty settlements] and from the assurances given in the litigation that the message that there is need for action on these claims has been accepted".[58] The language or grammar of rights in water placed indigenous claims in an intriguing position. Elsewhere Salmond has identified the "double bind" (multiple binds, I would suggest) afflicting the multi-dimensionalities of indigenous being-ness relative to water, as reflected in witness evidence before the Waitangi Tribunal in the freshwater and geothermal resources inquiry.[59] She noted how evidence spoke to the language of "ownership" whilst honouring understandings as to ancestral, metaphysical forces. These elements will continue as the second phase of the Tribunal's inquiry progresses. Indeed, the second stage of the inquiry poses the following central queries: first, "Is the current law in respect of fresh water and freshwater bodies consistent with the principles of the Treaty of Waitangi?" and, second, "Is the Crown's freshwater reform package, including completed reforms, proposed reforms, and reform options, consistent with the principles of the Treaty of Waitangi?"[60] The New Zealand Māori Council has presented its own substantial paper on *Ngā Wai o Te Māori* (the waters of the Māori) to the Tribunal as part of this phase, advancing a potent analysis of indigenous political authority and proprietary entitlements relative to water resources.[61]

As to the larger context, the question of indigenous rights and interest in freshwater resources is one of long standing. Jacinta Ruru, for one, has undertaken extensive work concerning indigenous rights and interests in freshwater resources, including a literature review.[62] The significance of customary relations is partly temporal in that they predate the arrival of the colonial legal system and need not rely upon any treaty relations. In the New Zealand context, all territorial space remained clothed by indigenous authority and proprietorship, although the courts have been explicit as to proprietorship alone thus far.[63] Broadly speaking, these rights are treated as continuing and capable of recognition in the introduced legal system provided that they have not been subject to any extinguishing events that have legally removed these rights completely through, for instance, purchase or confiscatory acts. Regardless, therefore, of whether a logic of proprietary rights or that of entitlements to govern is used, customary notions conventionally obtain priority in time relative to an incoming colonial polity.[64] Importantly, however, since the earliest period of official relations with indigenous communities such engagements were often seen through the lenses of proprietorship and legal-political jurisdiction (including indigenous entitlements to govern territorial space).[65] Such ways of speaking and seeing suffused official understandings of indigenous communities and interlocutors with whom they interacted. Even the reporting of indigenous accounts were woven through notions of "ownership" or contested rights to government, with hapū being presented in official dispatches as asserting "independence".[66]

"Stewardship" appears in the State Sector Act 1988 but not in any allied Māori form (kaitiakitanga). Under section 32 of that Act, it is a principal responsibility borne by public service departments and departmental agencies as defined under section 27A towards their relevant portfolio ministers. Other entities within the state services, such as the Commissioner of Police, are not covered. Regulatory agencies such as the Ministry for the Environment, which has charge of fresh-water policy development (along with the Ministry for Primary Industries), conceives of its state sector stewardship obligations as extending to Crown-iwi-Māori relations. "How to address iwi rights and interests in a post-settlement era" is understood as an issue confronting the Ministry for the Environment's regulatory frameworks.[67] Regarding its freshwater policy programme, it states:[68]

> We have also worked closely with the Iwi Leaders Group to develop proposals for addressing iwi and hapū rights and interests. The [Group] has undertaken nationwide hui to draw together iwi and hapū views on their rights and interests

Stewardship is not merely restricted to policy domains for which public service departments are currently responsible although they may be a convenient starting point for organising departmental focus. To deliver on stewardship effectively when performing departmental portfolios, agencies have to be mindful of systems across sectors of policy and operational concern, whether in social or natural resources policy areas, and including working with other departments and non-governmental actors or collaborators. The operational capabilities and behavioural shifts or continuities that might be required within any public service department to address "stewardship" expectations under the State Sector Act 1988 and their continuing evaluation will be an ongoing challenge. As a concept it is understood to require dynamic, adaptive behaviours, especially since it is defined as "active planning and management of medium- and long-term interests, along with associated advice" in section 2 of the State Sector Act 1988.

It must also be mindful of custodianship of those legal stances, norms or policy understandings inherited from various pasts – a sense of historicity – and crystallising advice as to whether such inheritances ought to be retained, refined or adjusted, or dismissed. The value of historicity should not be neglected, as I have contended elsewhere, but it is not to be regarded as a straitjacket in policy development or discussions. Having said that, it remains important to the Crown to comprehend why its assorted officials have formulated the legal-policy stances they have (bequeathed to successors in time) let alone what might be unwittingly or inadvertently marginalised or lost if insufficient attention is paid to these diverse strands. The orthodox English common law position as to flowing water is stated in *Embrey v. Owen*, where Baron Parke stated:[69]

> flowing water is *publici juris*, not in the sense that it is *bonum vacans*, to which the first occupant may acquire an exclusive right, but that it is public and common in this sense only, that all may reasonably use it who have a right of access to it.

Treaty settlements contribute to and challenge state sector stewardship performance themselves through requiring a focus on Crown-iwi-hapū relations, adjusting regulatory settings to accommodate (potentially) much more localised or regional, indigenous operational or practice expectations. Given the negotiabilities inherent in political compacts, let alone the fiscal and other policy constraints exerted by the Crown, the process is, at best, a work in progress. Kaitiaki or kaitiaki appears in historical texts, connoting caretaker, custodian or guardian and those responsibilities associated with such a concept.[70] These need not be seen as expressions of a Treaty of Waitangi-grounded interest or right in the sense that the treaty texts, instantiated in the reduced language committed to parchment, a much more complicated, enriched range of relations to peoples, inheritances and places.[71]

A challenge, however, is that common pool resources can attract other logics in policy thought, including the idea that these resources require an allocative mechanism in the form of proprietary rights determining access and transfer entitlements. Associated with market understandings of regulatory design, and also with certain official views and non-governmental approaches in the Land and Water Forum, market-based allocative mechanisms can encourage proprietary-like models coupled with pricing signals.[72] For some interlocutors, such logics better correspond with indigenous claims to "own" or "possess" the water resource rather than a notion of unowned public resources. They also assert that it would amount to a responsible legal-policy position (aligned with stewardship values) because they claim proprietorship would assist efficient allocation of water resources under high demand through pricing signals and less inhibited transfer entitlements. Security of tenure for a period of time would incentivise investment decisions across the longer term rather than short-term self-interested behaviours. A consultancy report of this sort was provided to the Iwi Advisors Group on the costs and benefits of an allocation to iwi of freshwater resources.[73] Locally held proprietary rights may permit such holders to exclude others.[74] If a non-ownership or other approach is to be used, then proxies for these values could be specified legislatively in non-proprietary language with a clearly expressed regime stressing the interests were simply privileges to access a community resource on specified terms for a time (vulnerable to adjustments like "haircuts" subject to altering contexts, such as sustaining catchment volumes or anticipating stresses).[75] These tensions in the appropriate stances to apply to "responsibility" persist and amply demonstrate the on-going "ontological" dissonances in play in reflecting on landscapes of obligation. Regardless of what particular frameworks might be adopted, implementation needs to be constantly evaluated in view of the inexorable risks of, say, transmission failures in understanding as to *why* certain norms or principles are used in a particular regime, particularly as personnel change and institutional knowledge is lost.[76] As with any human endeavours, some totalising utopian idyll predicated on unanimity or broad consensus around what "responsibility" entails in practice as an operational policy is not possible (or preferable) and should not be expected if we are to respect dissent and difference. Embracing the complexities of human co-existence implies a readiness to acknowledge frailties, incompleteness and disappointment.

Conclusion

My conclusion is brief. Incremental developments through negotiations have reflected and fostered the flexibility in contemporary state-indigenous relations in New Zealand. These relations are not a counsel of perfection for crafting a firmly theorised, generic "law of responsibility". Technocratically honed policy or legal preferences as to substantive outcomes do not win out. The political compacts formulated through practice and negotiations are invariably political-open-textured[77] or deliberately vague in aspects of their terminology and compromised, reconciling diverse viewpoints, while rubbing out the harder edges of disagreement. Managed case by case, these localised compacts can pose coordination and integration challenges to larger regulatory frameworks, but this is a human tension that persists regardless. "Responsibility" is a notion in which there may very well be disputes as to what it implies operationally and behaviourally, and how one might achieve outcomes across altering circumstances, even if one can agree on outcomes in a contested process. Different logics vie with one another in public policy domains as to how governance of water resources ought to be designed or play out. In the process of crafting or letting landscapes of obligation emerge, however, we are seeing an enlargement and diversifying of a New Zealand-accented *res publica* or the "public thing" through permitting additional, plural voices to have influence and weight in legal-political relations to water and other resources, lending a tacit constitutionalisation to these indigenous-state relations in the process. This enlargement is premised not on democratic majorities but on an underlying rangatiratanga, imperfectly and incompletely expressed or reflected, and plural indigenous communities predating the Crown's arrival from elsewhere.

Notes

1 Dame Anne Salmond "Ontological Quarrels: Indigeneity, Exclusion and Citizenship in a Relational World" (2012) 12 *Anthropological Theory* 115.

2 Mark Hickford "The Historical, Political Constitution – Some Reflections on Political Constitutionalism in New Zealand's History and Its Possible Normative Qualities" (2013) *New Zealand Law Review* 585; Mark Hickford "Looking Back in Anxiety: Reflecting on New Zealand's Historical-Political Constitution and Laws' Histories in

the Mid-Nineteenth Century" (2014) 48 *New Zealand Journal of History* 1 at 1–8. Law is a critical part of political constitutionalism such that they are not mutually exclusive.

3 Mark Hickford "Interpreting the Treaty: Questions of Native Title, Territorial Government and Searching for Constitutional Histories" in B. Patterson, Richard Hill and Kathryn Patterson (eds) *After the Treaty: The Settler State, Race Relations and Power in Colonial New Zealand* (Steele Roberts, Wellington, 2016) 92 at 114. "Geographically dispersed landscapes of claiming and obligation were identified. These were, of course, as much landscapes of the living and innovation in how to relate to others or strangers such as settlers as of recounted pasts and ancestors kept alive through memory and memorialisation (recited and acted out)."

4 Here, as I have done elsewhere (see, for example, Mark Hickford *Lords of the Land: Indigenous Property Rights and the Jurisprudence of Empire* (Oxford University Press, Oxford, 2011) at 23–24), I am deliberately using Cass Sunstein's useful conception of an "incompletely theorized agreement" in Cass Sunstein "Incompletely Theorized Agreements" (1995) 108 *Harvard Law Review* 1733 at 1735–1736.

5 At the time of writing, a Te Awa Tupua (Whanganui River Claims Settlement) Bill was before the New Zealand House of Representatives and a deed of settlement had been signed (5 August 2014). By the time of the copy-editing process, it had received the Royal assent (20 March 2017). Section 7 of this Act defined the Whanganui River as including "all tributaries, streams, and other natural watercourses" flowing intermittently or continuously into the stem of the river.

6 For ontological objectivity and ontological subjectivity, see J.R. Searle *Making the Social World: The Structure of Human Civilization* (Oxford University Press, New York, 2010) at 18.

7 There is a measure of complexity in the language of section 6 and the Treaty of Waitangi Act 1975 generally, which I cannot explicate in full here. For a convenient point to approach the Tribunal's jurisdiction, see G. Melvin "The Jurisdiction of the Waitangi Tribunal" in Janine Haywood and Nicola Wheen (eds) *The Waitangi Tribunal: Te Roopu Whakamana i te Tiriti o Waitangi* (Bridget Williams Books, Wellington, 2004) at 15–28.

8 "Treaty of Waitangi", C[olonial] O[ffice]209/9, fo.417, enclosed with Hobson to principal Secretary of State for Colonies, 26 May 1841, CO209/9, fo.416a (National Archives, Kew, London).

9 Claudia Orange *The Treaty of Waitangi* (Bridget Williams Books, Wellington, 2011).

10 Treaty of Waitangi Act 1975, ss 8A and 8B; State-Owned Enterprises Act 1986, ss 27B and 27C. For a discussion, refer to Melvin, above n 7, at 24–26.

11 Waitangi Tribunal *Te Ika Whenua Rivers Report* (Wai 212, 1998) at 127. It was also stated that, "Regardless of present-day circumstances, such as access and legal title to the banks and beds of the rivers, the interest must be of reasonable substance. However, the ability of Te Ika Whenua to control and deal with their interest because of their riparian land holdings may support a claim to a greater proprietary interest" [ibid].

12 Ibid. at 137.

13 Waitangi Tribunal *Stage 1 Report on the National Freshwater and Geothermal Resources Claim* (Wai 2358, 2012) at 235.

14 Waitangi Tribunal *The Whanganui River Report* (Wai 167, 1999).

15 Ibid. at 343. The Whanganui River Māori Trust Board, already constituted under section 4 of the Whanganui River Trust Board Act 1988.

16 *Paki v. Attorney-General (No 2)* [2014] NZSC 118, [2015] 1 NZLR 67, at [165] per Elias CJ.

17 Ibid. at [193].

18 Matthew Palmer *The Treaty of Waitangi in New Zealand's Law and Constitution* (Victoria University Press, Wellington, 2008) at 272–274.

19 Melvin, above n 7, at 16.

20 *Te Runanga o Muriwhenua v. Attorney-General* [1990] 2 NZLR 641 at 651. The Court also commented in the same passages, "Those observations are not directed to

mandatory resumptions of land or interests in land transferred to a State enterprise. That is a special field where the Waitangi Tribunal's recommendations impose an obligation on the Crown by virtue of sections inserted in the State-Owned Enterprises Act 1986 by the Treaty of Waitangi (State Enterprises) Act 1988, s.9."

21 Now the High Court and not to be confused with the Supreme Court of New Zealand established under the Supreme Court Act 2003 (the legislation that ended appeals to the Judicial Committee of the Privy Council).

22 Miranda Johnson *The Land Is Our History: Indigeneity, Law and the Settler State* (Oxford University Press, New York, 2016) at 132–160; *Whanganui River Report*, above n 14.

23 Letter from Cornish to Savage, 19 June 1936, T1 52/587 (Archives New Zealand, Wellington).

24 Linda Te Aho "Nga Whakataunga Waimaori: Freshwater Settlements" in Nicola Wheen and Janine Hayward (eds) *Treaty of Waitangi Settlements* (Bridget Williams Books, Wellington, 2012) at 102; Jacinta Ruru "Undefined and Unresolved: Exploring Indigenous Rights in Aotearoa New Zealand's Freshwater Legal Regime" (2009) 20 *Water Law* 236.

25 See, for instance, Maria Bargh "The Post-settlement World (so Far): Impacts for Maori" in Nicola Wheen and Janine Hayward, above n 24.

26 John Searle *Making the Social World: The Structure of Human Civilization* (Oxford University Press, New York, 2010).

27 Dame Anne Salmond "Ontological Quarrels", above n 1, at 125.

28 Kwame Anthony Appiah *The Ethics of Identity* (Princeton University Press, Princeton, 2005) at 47–67.

29 *Mullick v. Mullick* (1925) LR 52 Ind App 245. His Honour Justice Durie noted its relevance extra-judicially in E. Durie "Constitutionalising Māori" in Grant Huscroft and Paul Rishworth (eds) *Litigating Rights: Perspectives From Domestic and International Law* (Hart Publishing, Oxford, 2002) 241 at 244.

30 *Whanganui River Report*, above n 14, at 25 n 33. (Durie J was the presiding officer); *Huakina Development Trust v. Waikato Regional Authority* [1987] 2 NZLR 188 (PC) at 214 "That the Courts can cope with metaphysical considerations is illustrated by the 1925 Privy Council judgment in *Mullick v. Mullick* in which a Hindu idol was held to be a juristic entity capable of suing and being sued".

31 Kevin Gray "Property in Thin Air" (1991) 50 *CLJ* 252 at 297–299.

32 Mark Hickford "The Historical, Political Constitution – Some Reflections on Political Constitutionalism in New Zealand's History and Its Possible Normative Qualities", above n 2, at 619–620.

33 Note that different officials of the Crown are relevant to administering the Reserves Act 1977 or National Parks Act 1980. Both of those statutes are listed in the first schedule of the Conservation Act 1987. Accordingly, the land-owner function included the ability to approve concessions where these would have been attributes of proprietorship, such as a lease.

34 Te Awa Tupua (Whanganui River Claims Settlement) Act 2017, s 7.

35 See Gray, above n 31.

36 Gray, above n 31; Kevin Gray and Susan Gray *Elements of Land Law* (Oxford University Press, Oxford, 2005) at 102.

37 For instance, "Tuhoe Agrees $170 m Deal With Crown" *Radio New Zealand* (online ed, 11 September 2011) <www.radionz.co.nz/news/national/115593/tuhoe-agrees-$170m-deal-with-crown> which included the statement "Negotiations hit a roadblock in 2010 when Prime Minister John Key refused to support a proposal to cede ownership of the national park."

38 Section 62 of Te Urewera Act 2014, for example. See also above, n 30.

39 Carwyn Jones *New Treaty, New Tradition: Reconciling New Zealand and Maori Law* (University of British Columbia Press, Vancouver, 2016) at 98.

40 Appiah, above n 28, at 336–337 n 59 and Kwame Anthony Appiah "Mistaken Identities: Creed, Country Colour, Culture" (Reith Lecture, BBC, UK, 2016).
41 Appiah, above n 28, at 76–77.
42 Ibid. at 62–154; Dame Anne Salmond "Tears of Rangi: Water, Power and People in New Zealand" (2014) 4 *Hau: Journal of Ethnographic Theory* 285 at 301.
43 Even where adjustable relative to overall volume or flow.
44 Gray "Property in Thin Air", above n 31 at 268 and n 4.
45 Alex Frame "Property and the Treaty of Waitangi: A Tragedy of the Commodities?" in Janet McLean (ed) *Property and the Constitution* (Hart Publishing, Oxford, 1999) 224 at 236–238; Salmond "Tears of Rangi", above n 42.
46 Te Awa Tupua (Whanganui River Claims Settlement) Act 2014, s 46(2)(b).
47 Coal-mines Act Amendment Act 1903, 3 Edw VII 80.
48 *Paki v. Attorney-General (No 1)* [2012] NZSC 50, [2012] 3 NZLR 277.
49 There is insufficient space to address the ongoing questions of legitimacy here. There is already a well-developed scholarly literature, including Andrew Sharp *Justice and the Maori: The Philosophy and Practice of Maori Claims in New Zealand Since the 1970s* (2nd ed, Oxford University Press, Auckland, 1997) at 268–272. It should also be clear that the Tribunal in *Te Ika Whenua Rivers Report* and in the *Whanganui River Report* endeavoured to recommend ways in which these non-indigenous forms of interaction with the landscapes in question could be reconciled with indigenous understandings.
50 Matt Sleat *Liberal Realism: A Realist Theory of Liberal Politics* (Manchester University Press, Manchester, 2013) at 174.
51 Adapting Hannah Arendt *The Human Condition* (University of Chicago Press, Chicago, 1958) at 189.
52 Hickford *Lords of the Land*, above n 4, at 14, 28, 230–231, 260 and 461–462; Hickford above n 3, at 100–101.
53 A "middle ground" is a term of art, peculiar to certain historical contingencies, which Richard White developed and explicated in Richard White *The Middle Ground: Indians, Empires and Republics in the Great Lakes Region, 1650–1815: Twentieth Anniversary Edition* (Cambridge University Press, Cambridge, 2011) at xii–xiii.
54 Nicholas Thomas *In Oceania: Visions, Artifacts, Histories* (Duke University Press, Durham, NC, 1997) at 13.
55 On criticisms of the Iwi Chairs Forum as an influential elite, see Annette Sykes "2010 Bruce Jesson Memorial Lecture". For the New Zealand Māori Council see <www.maoricouncil.com/>.
56 *Nga Matapono ki te Wai* <http://iwichairs.maori.nz/wp-content/uploads/2015/06/Nga-Matapono-ki-te-wai-Framework.pdf>. The document addresses "objectives", "values", "governance", "limits", "allocation" and "transitional phase".
57 Palmer, above n 18, at 170.
58 *New Zealand Māori Council v. Attorney-General* [2013] NZSC 6, [2013] 3 NZLR 31 at [148].
59 Salmond "Tears of Rangi", above n 42, at 303.
60 Waitangi Tribunal, memorandum-directions of the Presiding Officer, 31 May 2016, Wai 2358, #2.5.62.
61 Edward Taihākurei Durie, and others, *Ngā Wai o Te Māori: Ngā Tikanga me Ngā Ture Roia* (a paper presented for the New Zealand Māori Council, 23 January 2017).
62 Jacinta Ruru *The Legal Voice of Maori in Freshwater Governance: A Literature Review* (Landcare Research, Lincoln, 2009).
63 *Paki v. Attorney-General (No 2)* [2014] NZSC 118, [2015] 1 NZLR 67, at [68]. (On indigenous authority, see, for example, Hickford *Lords of the Land*, above n 4, at 9–10, 13, 17–19, 398–399, 401–405, 426–429; Hickford "Interpreting the Treaty", above n 3.
64 Hickford "The Historical Political Constitution – Some Reflections on Political Constitutionalism in New Zealand's History and Its Possible Normative Qualities", above n 2, at 615–623.

65 Hickford *Lords of the Land*, above n 4, 9–10, 13, 17–19, 30–31, 213–214, 229–230, 398–399, 401–405, 426–429; Hickford "Interpreting the Treaty", above n 3, 99–102, 119–120.
66 Hickford "Interpreting the Treaty", above n 3, 100.
67 Ministry for the Environment *Our Regulatory Stewardship Strategy* (Ministry for the Environment, Wellington, 2016) at 13.
68 Ibid. at 27.
69 *Embrey v. Owen* (1851) 6 Ex 353 at 369, 154 ER 1047 (emphasis added). For an excellent discussion, see Joshua Getzler *A History of Water Rights at Common Law* (Oxford University Press, Oxford, 2006).
70 Richard Benton, Alex Frame and Paul Meredith *Te Matapunenga: A Compendium of References to the Concepts and Institutions of Maori Customary Law* (Victoria University Press, Wellington, 2013) at 105–111 especially.
71 Hickford "Interpreting the Treaty", above n 3, at 92–102, 122–123; Hickford, *Lords of the Land*, above n 4, 37–39.
72 See the discussions in *Third Report of the Land and Water Forum: Managing Water Quality and Allocating Water* (October 2012), recommendations 56–59.
73 Kieran Murray, Marcus Sin and Sally Wyatt Report prepared for the Iwi Advisors Group *The Costs and Benefits of an Allocation of Freshwater to Iwi* (Sapere Research Group, New Zealand, 2014) (available at <www.iwichairs.maori.nz/wp-content/uploads/2015/06/Commissioned Reports>) at 10. "For an economist, the quality of a property right is determined by the nature of the right (exclusivity, duration), ownership limits (minimum or maximum quantities) and limits over transfers (divisibility, restrictions on sale, leasing options". Assimilative capacity is also important, namely the quantity of contaminant that can be discharged into a waterbody.
74 Elinor Ostrom *Governing the Commons: The Evolution of Institutions for Collective Action* (Cambridge University Press, Cambridge, 1990) at 205.
75 Assimilative capacity would still need to be considered, however, as contaminants might need to be discharged from certain economic and urban uses.
76 Ostrom, above n 74, at 273–274.
77 Herbert Lionel Adolphus (H.L.A.) Hart *The Concept of Law* (2nd ed, Oxford University Press, Oxford, 1994) at 123 and 128.

References

Appiah, Kwame Anthony *Cosmopolitanism: Ethics in a World of Strangers* (Allen Lane, London, 2006).

Appiah, Kwame Anthony *The Ethics of Identity* (Princeton University Press, Princeton, 2008).

Appiah, Kwame Anthony "Mistaken Identities: Creed, Country, Colour, Culture" (Reith Lecture, BBC, London, 2016).

Arendt, Hannah *The Human Condition* (University of Chicago Press, Chicago, 1958).

Bargh, Maria "The Post-settlement World (So Far): Impacts for Māori" in Nicola Wheen and Janine Hayward (eds) *Treaty of Waitangi Settlements* (Bridget Williams Books, Wellington, 2012).

Benton, Richard, Frame, Alex and Meredith, Paul *Te Mātāpunenga: A Compendium of References to the Concepts and Institutions of Māori Customary Law* (Victoria University Press, Wellington, 2013).

Durie, Edward Taihākurei. "Constitutionalising Maori" in Grant Huscroft and Paul Rishworth (eds) *Litigating Rights: Perspectives From Domestic and International Law* (Hart Publishing, Oxford, 2002).

Frame, Alex "Property and the Treaty of Waitangi: A Tragedy of the Commodities?" in Janet McLean (ed) *Property and the Constitution* (Hart Publishing, Oxford, 1999).

Getzler, Joshua *A History of Water Rights at Common Law* (Oxford University Press, Oxford, 2006).
Gray, Kevin "Property in Thin Air" (1991) 50 *CLJ* 252.
Gray, Kevin and Gray, Susan *Elements of Land Law* (Oxford University Press, Oxford, 2005).
Hart, Herbert Lionel Adolphous (H.L.A.) *The Concept of Law* (2nd ed, Oxford University Press, Oxford, 1994).
Hickford, Mark *Lords of the Land: Indigenous Property Rights and the Jurisprudence of Empire* (Oxford University Press, Oxford, 2011).
Hickford, Mark "The Historical, Political Constitution – Some Reflections on Political Constitutionalism in New Zealand's History and Its Possible Normative Qualities" (2013) *NZ L Rev* 585.
Hickford, Mark "Looking Back in Anxiety: Reflecting on New Zealand's Historical-Polit ical Constitution and Laws' Histories in the Mid-Nineteenth Century" (2014) 48 *New Zealand Journal of History* 1.
Hickford, Mark "Interpreting the Treaty: Questions of Native Title, Territorial Government and Searching for Constitutional Histories" in B. Patterson, Richard Hill and Kathryn Patterson (eds) *After the Treaty: The Settler State, Race Relations and Power in Colonial New Zealand* (Steele Roberts, Wellington, 2016) 92.
Johnson, Miranda *The Land Is Our History: Indigeneity, Law, and the Settler State* (Oxford University Press, New York, 2016).
Jones, Carwyn *New Treaty, New Tradition: Reconciling New Zealand and Māori Law* (University of British Columbia Press, Vancouver, 2016).
Melvin, G "The Jurisdiction of the Waitangi Tribunal" in Janine Hayward and Nicola Wheen (eds) *The Waitangi Tribunal: Te Roopu Whakamana i te Tiriti o Waitangi* (Bridget Williams Books, Wellington, 2004) 15.
Ministry for the Environment *Our Regulatory Stewardship Strategy* (Ministry for the Environment, Wellington, 2016).
Murray, Kieran, Sin, Marcus and Wyatt, Sally *The Costs and Benefits of an Allocation of Freshwater to Iwi* (Sapere Research Group, New Zealand, 2014).
Orange, Claudia *The Treaty of Waitangi* (Bridget Williams Books, Wellington, 2011).
Ostrom, Elinor *Governing the Commons: The Evolution of Institutions for Collective Action* (Cambridge University Press, Cambridge, 1990).
Ostrom, Elinor *Understanding Institutional Diversity* (Princeton University Press, Princeton, 2005).
Palmer, Matthew *The Treaty of Waitangi in New Zealand's Law and Constitution* (Victoria University Press, Wellington, 2008).
Palmer, Matthew "Judicial Review" in Mary-Rose Russell and Matthew Barber (eds) *The Supreme Court of New Zealand 2004–2013* (Thomson Reuters, Wellington, 2015) 158.
Ruru, Jacinta *The Legal Voice of Māori in Freshwater Governance: A Literature Review* (Landcare Research, Lincoln, 2009).
Ruru, Jacinta "Undefined and Unresolved: Exploring Indigenous Rights in Aotearoa New Zealand's Freshwater Legal Regime" (2009) 20 *Water Law* 236.
Salmond, Anne "Ontological Quarrels: Indigeneity, Exclusion and Citizenship in a Relational World" (2012) 12 *Anthropological Theory* 115.
Salmond, Anne "Tears of Rangi: Water, Power, and People in New Zealand" (2014) 4 *Hau: Journal of Ethnographic Theory* 285.
Searle, John R. *Making the Social World: The Structure of Human Civilization* (Oxford University Press, New York, 2010).

Sharp, Andrew *Justice and the Māori: The Philosophy and Practice of Māori Claims in New Zealand Since the 1970s* (2nd ed, Oxford University Press, Auckland, 1997).

Sleat, Matt. *Liberal Realism: A Realist Theory of Liberal Politics* (Manchester University Press, Manchester, 2013).

Sunstein, Cass "Incompletely Theorized Agreements" (1995) 108 *Harvard Law Review* 1733.

Sykes, Annette "2010 Bruce Jesson Memorial Lecture" <www.brucejesson.com/annette-sykes-2010-bruce-jesson-memorial-lecture>.

Te Aho, Linda "Ngā Whakataunga Waimāori: Freshwater Settlements" in Nicola Wheen and Janine Hayward (eds) *Treaty of Waitangi Settlements* (Bridget Williams Books, Wellington, 2012) 102.

Thomas, Nicholas *In Oceania: Visions, Artifacts, Histories* (Duke University Press, Durham, NC, 1997).

Waitangi Tribunal *Te Ika Whenua Rivers Report* (Wai 212, 1998).

Waitangi Tribunal *The Whanganui River Report* (Wai 167, 1999).

Waitangi Tribunal *The Stage 1 Report on the National Freshwater and Geothermal Resources Claim* (Wai 2358, 2012).

White, Richard *The Middle Ground: Indians, Empires, and Republics in the Great Lakes Region, 1650–1815 – Twentieth Anniversary Edition* (Cambridge University Press, Cambridge, 2011).

12 Rivers as ancestors and other realities

Governance of waterways in Aotearoa/New Zealand

Dame Anne Salmond

Te Awa Tupua (Whanganui River Claims Settlement) Act 2017

In March 2017, the Te Awa Tupua (Whanganui River Claims Settlement) Act was passed by the New Zealand Parliament. For the first time in the world, a river was recognised as a living being with its own legal personality, rights and responsibilities. In the Act, the Whanganui River, the longest navigable river in New Zealand, is described as "an indivisible and living whole, comprising the Whanganui River from the mountains to the sea, incorporating all its physical and metaphysical elements."[1]

In this Act, the values that define the essence of the river are expressed in te reo Māori, the Māori language, as Tupua te Kawa. The Whanganui River is described as the source of ora (life, health and well-being), a living whole that runs from the mountains to the sea, made up of many tributaries and binding its people together. It is stated that the iwi and hapū (tribes and sub-tribes) of the Whanganui River have an inalienable connection with, and responsibility to, Te Awa Tupua and its health and well-being. This is expressed in a saying often used by Whanganui people, "*Ko au te Awa, ko te Awa ko au*" (I am the River, the River is me).[2]

In ancestral Māori understandings, the relationship between people and the earth is defined by whakapapa (roughly, genealogy) – an overarching, dynamic set of kin networks that encompass all forms of life, not just human beings. In Māori cosmological accounts, fresh water – lakes, rivers, streams and springs – are the tears of Ranginui, the sky father, mourning for his wife Papatuānuku, the earth mother, after their sons forced them apart to let light into the world. Although Tū, the ancestor of humankind, defeats his brothers in the great battle that follows, earning the right to take their offspring as food (birds, fish, berries and root crops), people remain fundamentally linked with all other life forms as kin, through their shared descent from earth and sky.[3]

In this relational schema, ancestors are literally planted in the earth (*take* or "root" ancestors whose bones or umbilical cords rest in the land). For this reason, they are known as tāngata whenua (land people). Like plants, their offspring might flourish and multiply, or wither and die. When an orator stands to speak on a marae (ceremonial centre), they recite the names of their ancestral mountain and river. When one person asks another in Māori to identify themselves, they ask, "Ko wai koe?" (literally, which water are you?).[4] The tears of Rangi flow across Papatuānuku, bringing fertility and abundance – the lifeblood of the land. In Māori, your birthplace is known as te ū kai pō, the place where you drank your mother's milk at night.

Sometimes, river currents are spoken of as whakapapa, lines of ancestry tied to a post representing a great rangatira or chief. In 1894, for instance, Kerehona, a Whanganui elder lamented, "Our land is nearly all gone, and we, too, are a vanishing people, and will soon be like the moa, extinct (*ka ngaro ā moa te iwi nei*)." Hailing his ancestor Tutairoa as "the stone pillar from whom descended all the chiefs of Whanganui, even to the Rangitāne tribe," he expressed a hope that this man's mana might save the people:[5]

> All the *taniwha* (great chiefs) of this river of Whanganui come from this chief – all the great chiefs who have been heard of in this island, commencing at the source, even to the mouth of the river . . . Hence the saying, 'A spliced rope, if broken, is made whole again.'

A century later, in their claim to the Waitangi Tribunal, Whanganui elders described their river as a "three stranded rope," binding together the upper, middle and lower river iwi (tribes) – a motif expressed in carvings in Whanganui meeting-houses,[6] helping the different kin groups to join forces in advancing their claims about the river. Standing before the Tribunal, Whanganui elders lamented the current state of their ancestral waterway, saying what it meant for Te Atiahaunui (the Whanganui people):[7]

> It was with huge sadness that we observed dead *tuna* [eels] and trout along the banks of our *awa tupua* [ancestral river]. The only thing that is in a state of growth is the algae and slime. Our river is stagnant and dying. The great river flows from the gathering of mountains to the sea. I am the river, the river is me. If I am the river and the river is me – then emphatically, I am dying.

Whakapapa and waterways

When Te Awa Tupua Act was passed by Parliament in March 2017, it seemed that this existential interlock between Whanganui people and their ancestral river had finally been recognised in law in New Zealand. Certainly, the Act was greeted with international acclaim. The *Huffington Post*,[8] the *New York Times*,[9] the *Washington Post*[10] and the *Guardian*[11] all reported its passage:

> In a world-first, a New Zealand river has been granted the same legal rights as a human being. On Wednesday, hundreds of tribal representatives wept with joy when their bid to have their kin awarded legal status as a living entity was passed into law. "The reason we have taken this approach is because we consider the river an ancestor and always have," said Gerrard Albert, the lead negotiator for the Whanganui iwi [tribe].

Although Te Awa Tupua Act declared the Whanganui River to be a legal person, however, this only roughly approximates ancestral realities. A tupua is precisely not a person but a being from Te Po, the ancestral realm; and an awa (river) is not an individual, but a living community of fish, plants, people, ancestors and water, linked by whakapapa. As indigenous lawyer Carwyn Jones has argued, making the Whanganui River a legal person with its own rights is still essentially a modernist device.[12] Except for the statements of value in Māori in the Act, an underlying cosmic model in which Man stands apart from and above Nature is unchallenged.[13]

In Te Awa Tupua Act, furthermore, while the Crown makes formal apologies to Whanganui iwi for its failure to uphold the promises made in the Treaty of Waitangi, it also makes clear that the Act does not create or transfer proprietary interests in water or life forms in the river. According to the Crown's lawyers, waterways in New Zealand cannot be owned as private property. In making this argument, they cite ancient precedents. In Roman law, for instance, according to the Code of Justinian, "By the law of nature these things are common to mankind – the air, running water, the sea."[14] In his *Commentaries on the Laws of England*, Sir William Blackstone followed the Roman precedent.[15] Although he quoted the Genesis creation story as the source of all property rights, when Adam and Eve were given "dominion over the fish of the sea, and over the fowl of the air, and over every living thing that moveth upon the earth,"[16] Blackstone specifically excluded waterways from this framework:

> A man can have no absolute permanent property in these, as he may in the earth and land; since they are of a vague and fugitive nature, and therefore can admit only of a precarious and qualified ownership, which lasts so long as they are in actual use and occupation, but no longer.

At the same time, these use rights were balanced by responsibilities. Under the common law, according to Blackstone, freshwater users must act with due consideration for the rights of others:[17]

> It is a nuisance to stop or divert water that used to run to another's meadow or mill; to corrupt or poison a water course, or in short to do any act therein, that in its consequences must necessarily tend to the prejudice of one's neighbour. So closely does the law of England enforce that excellent rule of gospel morality, of 'doing to others, as we would they shall do unto themselves.'

Indeed, such an expectation still underpins popular understandings of how fresh water should be managed in New Zealand, informing many contemporary critiques of freshwater management regimes that allow various parties such as farmers, corporates (including water bottling and forestry companies, and municipal authorities) to pollute, drain and divert rivers, lakes, streams, springs and aquifers with relative impunity. There is widespread indignation that the law has failed to protect other citizens by treating these practices as injuries against their entitlement to the "lawful enjoyment" (and care) of waterways across the country.

Somehow, it seems, when British common law was transplanted to New Zealand in the wake of the signing of the Treaty of Waitangi, while waterways were held in common, the requirement that water users should respect the interests of others was largely lost in translation, certainly in relation to Māori kin groups, but also in general. Over many generations, as successive reports to the Waitangi Tribunal have shown,[18] sheep dip, effluent and other farm waste, sewage, waste water, sediment and industrial pollutants have been allowed to flow into New Zealand waterways, and their large-scale drainage and diversion (including the practice of piping waterways underground) became commonplace. In a new country, old conventions about respecting the rights of others to enjoy fresh water and waterways were often set aside as a tiresome inconvenience.

As is clear from the evidence presented in claim after claim to the Waitangi Tribunal, Māori have struggled to uphold their relationship with ancestral waterways – through fighting, petitions, pleas to Royalty and other Crown authorities, and legal action.[19] In their 1990 claim to the Waitangi Tribunal, for instance, Whanganui people appealed to the Treaty of Waitangi, signed with the British Crown in 1840. In Article 2 of the English version of the Treaty, Queen Victoria guaranteed "to the Chiefs and Tribes of New Zealand the full exclusive and undisturbed possession of the Lands and Estates Forests Fisheries and other properties which they may collectively or individually possess." In terms of the Treaty of Waitangi, their counsel argued, the river was one of their properties, a fishery as well as a highway and an ancestral being.

In reply, Crown counsel (quoting William Blackstone) asserted that no-one could own fresh water. While the Crown did not claim to own the Whanganui river, under Article 1 of Te Tiriti (the Treaty in Māori), the rangatira had absolutely given (tuku rawa atu) to Queen Victoria the kāwanatanga (variously translated as sovereignty, government, governance, or the right to have a Governor) of their lands, and the Crown had the right to manage fresh water for the nation.[20]

In their report on the Whanganui River claim, issued in 1999, the Waitangi Tribunal focused almost entirely upon this matter of rights in waterways – of the Whanganui kin groups on the one hand, and the Crown on the other. From the evidence that they had heard, the Tribunal concluded:[21]

> Control, not ownership, is the key element in managing natural resources. Perhaps this points to a prospective merger of the two laws, for if we look to Māori history from the time of colonisation, as we do in the next chapter, it is not ownership but control that was central to their thinking, and respect for the mana of different peoples.

Nevertheless, they found that Māori kin groups could legally claim a property interest in ancestral rivers:

> The conceptual understanding of the river as a *tupuna* or ancestor emphasises the Māori thought that the river exists as a single and undivided entity or

> essence. It does not matter that Māori did not think in terms of ownership in the same way as Europeans. What they possessed is equated with ownership for the purposes of English or New Zealand law.

Unusually for the Tribunal, a dissenting view on this finding was included in its report. Written by John Kneebone, this upheld a view of waterways as "moveable, wandering" things that cannot be owned by people:[22]

> To suggest that a river as an entity should be alienated and legally transferred to a particular and specific descent group is not in my view a viable option. Such an action could not escape the interpretation that naturally occurring, free-flowing water, and access to it, will become subject to private control, which must then lead to the potential for private exploitation of an essential natural resource.

For these reasons, Kneebone dissented from the Tribunal's recommendation that Atihaunui should be granted proprietary rights in the river.

Although Whanganui people who spoke to the Tribunal often expressed their anger about the state of their ancestral river, the Tribunal report barely mentions the duty of the Crown to protect users of the river (including iwi) against the "fouling" and "diversion" that might deprive them of their "lawful enjoyment" of the waterway. In Article III of Te Tiriti, the Queen had promised to care for (tiaki) all the Māori (ordinary) people of New Zealand and give (tuku) them tikanga (customary rights and responsibilities) exactly equal to (rite tahi) those of her people of England; while in Article III of the English version of the Treaty, the Queen confirmed and guaranteed to the "Natives of New Zealand" her royal protection and "all the rights and duties of British subjects."

This presumably included the rights of Whanganui kin groups to be protected against common law injuries including the fouling and diversion of waterways, as well as a duty of care for their ancestral river – matters repeatedly raised before the Tribunal. The clause in Article III of Te Tiriti about the Queen giving Māori "ngā tikanga rite tahi" (rights and responsibilities, laws or customs exactly equal) to those of English people, however, also opens the way for a "prospective merger of the two laws" which was hinted at in the Tribunal's Report. In fact, in the subsequent negotiation of the Whanganui River claim between kin groups and the Crown, something like this seems to have happened.

At the same time, in the heated public debates that followed the release of the Whanganui River Report and other freshwater claims by iwi, the government has continued to assert that rivers and other waterways cannot be owned by people.[23] This explains why in Te Awa Tupua Act, it is made clear that the Act does not create or transfer any proprietary interests in water or life forms in the river; while existing public uses, private property rights and resource consents are specifically excluded. At the same time, the Iwi Leaders Forum has advanced a legal claim for proprietary rights to ancestral waterways across New Zealand.[24]

Property rights, trusteeship and fresh water

While the Waitangi Tribunal has discussed property rights as the only way of legally recognising Māori relationships with ancestral rivers, many of those who participated in the Whanganui claim found this difficult to deal with. As Whanganui elder Toni Waho exclaimed, "It's not an ownership issue . . . it's kaitiakitanga [guardianship], it's mana. My Māori heart says let it cease; but my Western mind says perhaps we can find a solution." He added, "But here's the problem. There is no place where things can be graded with proper legal form in our world [Te Ao Māori], here in our land [New Zealand], which is able to resolve the conflict of the two worlds [*Te Ao Māori, Te Ao Pākeha* – the Māori and Western "worlds"]."[25]

Although in New Zealand, ownership has been phrased as the only way for Māori kin groups to achieve legal recognition of relationships with ancestral waterways, it is interesting that in Hawai'i, another way has emerged of recognising the relationship between indigenous Hawaiians and their ancestral streams and rivers, in the face of those who would deplete or degrade them. In the United States, the right of all citizens to enjoy and take care of those "things [that] by the law of nature are common to all" (as framed by the Code of Justinian) has been recognised in a "public trust doctrine", based on a United States Supreme Court decision in 1892 which declared that each state holds certain natural resources (including water) in trust for its citizens and must protect these resources from the "obstruction or interference of private parties."[26]

In 1973, the Supreme Court of Hawai'i – which until then had consistently ruled that a party that owned land also owned the surplus water of any stream that ran over it – ruled that all freshwater in the State was "held in trust by the state for the common good of its citizens."[27] In the *Waiāhole Ditch* case in 2000, native Hawaiians and local farmers fought to restore water to streams diverted by powerful former sugar plantation companies, whose predecessors had participated in the 1893 overthrow of the Hawaiian monarchy.

In their judgment, the Hawaiian Supreme Court declared that the public trust doctrine is "a fundamental principle of constitutional law in Hawai'i that applies to all water resources without exception," and stated that it[28]

> demands adequate provision for traditional and customary Hawaiian rights, wildlife, maintenance of ecological balance and scenic beauty, and the preservation and enhancement of the waters for various uses in the public interest.

In 2012 in the *Four Great Waters* case, the Hawaiian Supreme Court further expanded the public trust doctrine. By granting water permits to two powerful companies that set instream flows insufficient to sustain four major waterways on Maui, the Supreme Court ruled that the Commission on Water Resource Management for the State of Hawai'i had failed to "display a level of openness, diligence, and foresight commensurate with the high priority these [public trust] rights command under the laws of our state," or to consider their impact on "traditional and customary native Hawaiian practices." The water permits were overturned, and the rights of ordinary citizens to defend their "public trust" interests in fresh water were strengthened.[29]

The public trust doctrine has been extended further still in other countries, including Ecuador and India.[30] In Ecuador, for instance, the rights of nature itself (*Pacha Mama*) are enshrined in the constitution.[31] In India, the Supreme Court derives the public trust doctrine from law "imposed on us by the natural world [that] must inform all of our social institutions,"[32] along with Indian "society's respect for plants, trees, earth, sky, air, water and every form of life."[33] Here, the courts have recently followed the New Zealand precedent by recognising the Ganges and Yamuna rivers as living entities with their own legal rights and responsibilities.

In New Zealand, while Te Awa Tupua Act has gone some way in recognising Māori notions of kinship, this could be taken much further. In the spirit of bringing "two laws" together, for instance, a local version of the public trust doctrine might recognise *both* the common law entitlement of all citizens to the "lawful enjoyment" of waterways and whakapapa relationships between particular Māori kin networks and ancestral springs and rivers. Rather than "rights", one might speak about relationships between people and springs, aquifers, rivers and lakes that aim to ensure the ongoing well-being (ora) of people and waterways alike, and draw on notions of reciprocal kaitiakitanga (guardianship).

While the idea of kinship with the Whanganui is already reflected in the Māori language sections of Te Awa Tupua Act, kin relations between people and waterways could be recognised for other ancestral water bodies in New Zealand. Injuries such as "fouling," "corrupting," "poisoning," "stopping" and "diverting" waterways might be recognised as injuries to the waterways themselves, as well as to their human users,[34] and damages might be paid to the water bodies themselves, and devoted to their care and restoration.

These possibilities are under active discussion in New Zealand at present, for instance in the "Te Mana o te Wai" section of the National Policy Statement on Freshwater, that requires regional councils in their decision-making about fresh water to consider "the innate relationship between *te hauora o te wai* (the health and *mauri* [roughly, life force] of water) and *te hauora o te taiao* (the health and *mauri* of the environment), and their ability to support each other, while sustaining *te hauora o te tāngata* (the health and *mauri* of the people)."[35]

It is quite possible that, over time, all waterways across New Zealand will be seen as living entities whose hau ora must be protected, so that they and their communities of plants, animals and people can prosper together. Such ideas are in keeping with Māori ideas about binding together different lines of people, opening up new kinds of futures. As my mentor Eruera Stirling used to chant:

Whakarongo! Whakarongo! Whakarongo!	*Listen! Listen! Listen!*
Ki te tangi a te manu e karanga nei	*To the cry of the bird calling*
Tui, tui, tuituiā!	*Bind, join, be one!*
Tuia i runga, tuia i raro,	*Bind above, bind below*

Tuia i roto, tuia i waho,	*Bind within, bind without*
Tuia i te here tangata	*Tie the knot of humankind*
Ka rongo te pō, ka rongo te pō	*The night hears, the night hears*
Tuia i te kāwai tangata i heke mai	*Bind the lines of people coming down*
I Hawaiki nui, i Hawaiki roa,	*From great Hawaiki, from long Hawaiki*
I Hawaiki pāmamao	*From Hawaiki far away*
I hono ki te wairua, ki te whai ao	*Bind to the spirit, to the day light*
Ki te Ao Mārama!	*To the World of Light!*

Notes

1 Te Awa Tupua (Whanganui River Claims Settlement) Act 2017, ss 12 and 13(b).
2 Ibid., s 13.
3 For a more detailed account of Māori understandings of fresh water and contemporary debates, see Dame Anne Salmond "Tears of Rangi: People, Water and Power in New Zealand" (2014) 4 *Hau: Journal of Ethnographic Theory* 285. For a wider discussion of freshwater issues in New Zealand, see D. A. Salmond, M. Tadaki and T. Gregory "Enacting New Freshwater Geographies: Te Awaroa and the Transformative Imagination" (2014) 70 *New Zealand Geographer* 47.
4 It's interesting to note that by analysing the isotopes in the teeth of a dead person, forensic scientists can trace the main sources of water they drank as a child.
5 Waitangi Tribunal *The Whanganui River Report* (Wai 167, 1999).
6 Ibid. at 32.
7 Turama Thomas Hawira "Brief of Evidence for the Whanganui District Inquiry" (do B28) at 11.
8 George Bowden "Whanganui River in New Zealand Awarded Human Rights" *The Huffington Post* (16 March 2017) <www.huffingtonpost.co.uk/entry/whanganui-river-new-zealand-human-rights_uk_58ca51afe4b0ec9d29d8c161>.
9 Bryant Rousseau "In New Zealand, Lands and Rivers Can Be People (Legally Speaking)" *The New York Times* (13 July 2016) <www.nytimes.com/2016/07/14/world/what-in-the-world/in-new-zealand-lands-and-rivers-can-be-people-legally-speaking.html?_r=0>.
10 Travis Andrews "This New Zealand River Now Has the Same Legal Rights as a Human Being" *The Washington Post* (16 March 2017). <www.washingtonpost.com/news/morning-mix/wp/2017/03/16/this-new-zealand-river-now-has-the-same-legal-rights-as-a-human-being/?utm_term=.6e4a9ea80e35>.
11 Eleanor Ainge Roy "New Zealand River Granted Same Legal Rights as Human Being" *The Guardian* (16 March 2017) <www.theguardian.com/world/2017/mar/16/new-zealand-river-granted-same-legal-rights-as-human-being>.
12 Carwyn Jones *New Treaty New Tradition: Reconciling New Zealand and Law* (Victoria University Press, Wellington, 2016) at 98.
13 This is also the case with many contemporary anthropological discussions of Polynesian realities, even those that address ontological issues – see for instance Marshall Sahlins, Marshall "Hierarchy and Humanity in Polynesia" in A. Hooper, and J. Huntsman (eds) *Transformations of Polynesian Culture* (The Polynesian Society, Auckland, 1985).
14 *Code of Justinian*, Book II 1.1.
15 For an authoritative account of how freshwater rights evolved in the English common law, with an extensive commentary on Blackstone's ideas, see Joshua Getzler

A History of Water Rights at Common Law (Oxford University Press, Oxford, 2006). Many thanks to Mark Hickford for alerting me to this source, and for invaluable feedback on an earlier draft of this chapter. Note that Blackstone, like John Locke, traced the origins of property back to the Genesis story: "In the beginning of the world, we are informed by holy writ, the all-bountiful creator gave to man 'dominion over all the earth.' This is the only true and solid foundation of man's dominion over external things" (William Blackstone *Commentaries on the Laws of England* [Clarendon Press, Oxford, 1825] Book II, ch 2 at 3). As Getzler notes, Blackstone also drew on "the conventional four-stage social theory of the Enlightenment evoked by Henry [Homes] and Adam Smith, whereby hunting societies were followed by pastoral, agricultural and finally commercial societies with organised States, governments and laws" Getzler at 162.

16 King James Bible, Genesis 1:28.

17 At Book III, ch 8:1.

18 See for instance Brad Coombes's excellent report on the environmental history of Turanga-nui/Gisborne, which documents successive planning and policy decisions and their impacts on local waterways in Brad Coombes "Ecological Impacts and Planning History: An Environmental History of the Turanganui Casebook Area" (Wai 814, 2000) at #A20.

19 As documented in various Waitangi Tribunal reports on particular waterways and fresh water (for example Waitangi Tribunal *Mohaka River Report* (Wai 119, 1992); Waitangi Tribunal *Ika Whenua Report* (Wai 212, 1998); Waitangi Tribunal *Whanganui River Report* (Wai 167, 1999); Waitangi Tribunal *The Stage I Report on the National Freshwater and Geothermal Resources Claim* (Wai 2358, 2012).

20 *The Whanganui River Report*, above n 5, at 20–21.

21 Ibid. at 102.

22 Ibid. at 346.

23 For articles that discuss these debates in some detail, see Jacinta Ruru "Indigenous Restitution in Settling Water Claims: The Developing Cultural and Commercial Redress Opportunities in Aotearoa, New Zealand" (2013) 22 *Pacific Rim Law & Policy Journal* 311; and Dame Anne Salmond "Tears of Rangi: Water, Power, and People in New Zealand", above n 3.

24 Taihakurei Durie "Law Responsibility and Māori Proprietary Interests in Water"; see also Taihakurei Durie and others "Ngā Wai o te Māori: Ngā Tikanga me Ngā Ture Roia. The Waters of the Māori: Māori Law and State Law" (Paper prepared for the New Zealand Māori Council, 2017).

25 Toni Waho, oral evidence, quoted by Crown counsel, closing submissions, Waitangi Tribunal 2012: 88.

26 *Illinois Central Railway Co v. Illinois* 146 US 387, see Marie Kyle, "The 'Four Great Waters' Case: An important expansion of Waiahole Ditch and the Public Trust Doctrine" (2013) 17 U *Denver Water Law Review* 1. Many thanks to Betsan Martin for alerting me to the significance of the "public trust doctrine" relating to waterways in the United States, and particularly in the state of Hawaii.

27 Ibid. at 4–5.

28 James T. Paul *The August 2000 Hawaii Supreme Court Waiahole Ditch Decision: Comments and Excerpts regarding the Public Trust Doctrine* (2nd ed, Hawaii's Thousand Friends, Honolulu, Hawaii, 2001) at 3. For a fine account of the *Waiahole Ditch* case and its background, see D. Kaupua'al Sproat and Isaac H. Moriwake "Ke Kalo Pa'a o Waiāhole: Use of the Public Trust as a Tool for Environmental Advocacy" in Clifford Rechtschaffen and Denise Antouni (eds) *Creative Common Law Strategies for Protecting the Environment* (Environmental Law Institute, Washington, DC, 2007) at 247–284.

29 Kyle, above n 26.

30 Michael Blum and Rachel Guthrie "Internationalizing the Public Trust Doctrine: Natural Law and Constitutional and Statutory Approaches to Fulfilling the Saxion Vision" (2012) 45 *UC Davis Law Review* 741. Many thanks to Mathew Smith and Mike Joy for locating and sharing this source.
31 Ibid. at 791–801.
32 Ibid. at 761.
33 Ibid. at 762.
34 In 2009, for instance, the Idaho Supreme Court stated that the "public interest doctrine" in relation to waterways included a declaration that "the streams [of Idaho] and their environments be protected against loss of water supply to preserve the minimum stream flows required for the protection of fish and wildlife habitat, aquatic life, recreation, aesthetic beauty, transportation and navigation values, and water quality." Centre for Progressive Reform *Restoring the Trust: Water Resources and the Public Trust Doctrine, a Manual for Advocates* (Centre for Progressive Reform, Washington DC, 2009).
35 National Policy Statement for Freshwater Management, <www.mfe.govt.nz/sites/default/files/media/Fresh%20water/nps-freshwater-ameneded-2017.pdf> at 11.

13 The power and potential of the public trust

Insight from Hawai‘i's water battles and triumphs

Kapua Sproat and Mahina Tuteur

Introduction

For Native Hawaiians, *he ali‘i ka ‘āina; he kauwā ke kanaka* – the land is the chief and people are the stewards.[1] Similar to other indigenous societies, our relationship to our natural and cultural resources is familial: land is an ancestor; fresh water is deified as a physical embodiment of one of our principal gods; and we as younger siblings have a *kuleana* – a unique cultural duty – to care for these resources as a public trust for present and future generations. For us, kuleana infuses responsibility that must be shouldered before any "right" may be claimed.

In Hawai‘i, epic battles over our freshwater resources have illuminated the power and potential of the public trust as a legal tool. This idea that water is a resource belonging to all and owned by none, but managed by the sovereign for the benefit of generations yet unborn, is an inherently Native Hawaiian concept. A foundation of Hawai‘i's laws since the earliest days of the sovereign Kingdom and enshrined in the State Constitution since 1978, this directive is a unique hybrid of Native Hawaiian custom and Western law. Its indigenous origin informs the public trust's manifestation and interpretation and outlines the kuleana (responsibility and privilege) for resource managers and beneficiaries alike. This chapter explores Hawai‘i's experience with the power and potential of the public trust as a legal tool and highlights lessons from water battles and triumphs relevant to all communities seeking sustainability in the age of global climate change.

Water's role and significance in ancient Hawai‘i[2]

Water as a public resource in native Hawaiian society

Ola i ka wai: Water is life. Since time immemorial, fresh water has been the lifeblood of Hawai‘i's indigenous people, culture, and resources. Internalizing the innate spiritual connection that Kānaka Maoli[3] share with natural resources is key to understanding how the public trust has evolved in Hawai‘i as a legal concept. One creation story is in the Kumulipo, the great chant of the cosmos that traces the birth of Kānaka Maoli to the beginning of time in Hawai‘i.[4] The Kumulipo explains that Maoli descend from *akua* (ancestors or gods) and are physically related to all living things in the Hawaiian archipelago.[5] As younger siblings, Native Hawaiians are bound to our extended family and have a kuleana to care for Hawai'i's natural and cultural resources.[6] Given the familial relationship between Maoli and our native environment, elder siblings support younger ones by providing the resources necessary to sustain human and other life.[7] In return, Kānaka Maoli care for our elder siblings by managing those resources as a trust for present and future generations.[8]

As island people who rely on fresh water to survive, Kānaka Maoli developed an intimate and complex relationship with our resources. Fresh, free-flowing water was necessary for distributing flow sufficient to cultivate the staple crop *kalo* (*Colocasia esculenta* or taro). Water was also revered as a *kinolau* (physical manifestation) of Kāne, one of the Hawaiian pantheon's four principal akua (gods, ancestors). Kāne was the "embodiment of male procreative energy in fresh water, flowing on or under the earth in springs, in streams and rivers, and falling as rain (and also as sunshine), which gives life to plants."[9] Given the physical and spiritual nature of our relationship to these sacred and life-giving waters, Kānaka Maoli held these resources in trust.

Laws and customs preceding Western contact and continuing through Hawai'i's independent Kingdom reflected these important principles, recognizing that water could not be owned in any sense, but instead must be proactively managed as a resource for generations to come.[10] For instance, the Kingdom of Hawai'i's first Western-style constitution in 1840 included strong public trust provisions, declaring that the land along with its resources "was not [the king's] private property. It belonged to the chiefs and the people in common, of whom [the king] was the head, and had the management of the landed property."[11] These ancient values were embedded in Hawaiian society long before any written constitution and were strictly enforced by *kahuwai* (water stewards) who managed the flow of water within and between *ahupua'a* (loosely defined as watersheds) to ensure, for example, that if water was taken from a stream for kalo cultivation, it was returned to the same stream so that downstream users had enough water to satisfy agricultural or other needs. These management practices respected the environment while also taking into account the competing needs of the larger community.

Water as "private property" in plantation society

The institution of private property via the Māhele,[12] subsequent consolidation of land ownership by foreign (largely United States') interests, and growing recognition that Hawai'i's climate and year-round growing season made plantation agriculture, and especially sugar cane, a lucrative business, drove the foreign takeover of Maoli ancestral land. Water resources seemed destined to follow this history of dispossession.

To establish and expand plantations, massive irrigation systems were constructed to transport and use water in ways that nature never intended. To satisfy thirsty crops, sugar planters constructed ditches that diverted streams from wet, windward (or *Ko'olau*), predominantly Maoli communities, to the drier central and leeward plains where sugar was cultivated, and also drilled wells to siphon groundwater. All of this was done with no consideration of or consultation with affected Maoli communities. This rapid change altered the natural environment while also inflicting significant physical and cultural harm on Kānaka Maoli, much of which remains unaddressed to this day. Plantations and their irrigation systems took root on each of the major Hawaiian islands, fundamentally changing how and where water was used. Sugar's rise to dominance rewrote the social contract. Despite Kingdom laws (such as the 1840 constitution) that formalized Native Hawaiian custom and tradition in writing, large agricultural plantations increased their influence and soon controlled a large portion of Hawai'i's resources. The law was no exception, and cases during Hawai'i's Kingdom and territorial periods also began to reflect increasingly Western approaches to water use and management.

Soon, conflicts over water ensued – first, between plantation interests and Kānaka Maoli, and later, between competing sugar plantations. The case of *McBryde Sugar Company v. Robinson* (1973) brought the tensions over water as public resource or private property to a head.[13] Two sugar companies litigated their respective rights to take water from the Hanapēpē River on Kaua'i. The Hawai'i Supreme Court, led by the late, great Chief Justice William S. Richardson (who was a Kanaka Maoli), addressed the larger issue of water managment in Hawai'i and clarified that although the parties in that case may have had rights to use water, they had no ownership interest in the water itself.[14] Those rights were never included when a hybridized form of private property was instituted in Hawai'i via the Māhele. Instead, the court ruled that the State holds all water in trust for the benefit of the larger community.[15]

Other cases followed, including *Robinson v. Ariyoshi* and *Reppun v. Board of Water Supply* (both decided in 1982), which respectively considered the public nature of Hawai'i's water resources and the rights of downstream kalo growers to maintain Maoli agricultural practices.[16] Despite the Hawai'i Supreme Court's consistent rulings upholding the public trust over Hawai'i's water resources, opposition by entrenched powers persisted. The black letter of the law carried moral and legal authority, which collided with the political power wielded by plantation and other aligned interests. Thus, more needed to be done to bring legal protections to life on the ground in our communities.

Legal regime for water resource management in Hawai'i[17]

Around the time that the *McBryde* litigation was unfolding, sugar plantations began to lose their economic dominance to tourism and the military. Concerned communities took this opportunity to reexamine the legal regime and manage Hawai'i's water resources more proactively for the benefit of the larger community. The 1978 Constitutional Convention ("ConCon") proved critical in this regard. Thanks to the efforts of young Maoli and environmentally conscious delegates and staff, the ConCon crafted amendments that were later ratified by

Hawai'i's voters to enshrine resource protection and Native Hawaiian rights as constitutional mandates.

Article 11, section 1 of the Hawai'i Constitution now declares:

> For the benefit of present and future generations, the State and its political subdivisions shall conserve and protect Hawaii's natural beauty and all natural resources, including land, water, air, minerals and energy sources, and shall promote the development and utilization of these resources in a manner consistent with their conservation and in furtherance of the self-sufficiency of the State.[18]

Article 11, section 7 affirms that the State "has an obligation to protect, control and regulate the use of Hawaii's water resources for the benefit of its people."[19] Hawai'i's highest court has confirmed that these two provisions, "article XI, section 1 and article XI, section 7 adopt the public trust doctrine as a fundamental principle of constitutional law in Hawai'i."[20]

In addition, delegates independently safeguarded traditional and customary Maoli rights and practices. Article 12, section 7, "reaffirms and shall protect all rights, customarily and traditionally exercised for subsistence, cultural and religious purposes and possessed by ahupuaa tenants who are descendants of native Hawaiians who inhabited the Hawaiian Islands prior to 1778."[21]

In 1987, the State Legislature enacted Hawai'i's Water Code (Hawai'i Revised Statutes chapter 174C), establishing a comprehensive water resource management regime that sought to balance resource protection with "reasonable and beneficial use," with specific provisions protecting Maoli rights and practices.[22] The legislature gave the Commission on Water Resource Management ("Commission") primary authority over water use and management, although the constitutional nature of the public trust doctrine in Hawai'i reserved an important role for the Hawai'i Supreme Court.[23]

Today, under Hawai'i's Constitution, Water Code, and common law, the "water resources trust" applies to "all water resources without exception or distinction."[24] The public trust establishes "a dual mandate of (1) protection and (2) maximum reasonable and beneficial use."[25] The Water Commission, therefore, has an "affirmative duty to take the public trust into account in the planning and allocation of water resources, and to protect public trust uses whenever feasible."[26]

Organizers and Maoli communities wasted no time utilizing these new legal tools to seek justice and redress the more than century-long theft of these life-giving waters. The first major case seeking stream restoration under the new legal regime arose in Waiāhole, O'ahu.

The law of Waiāhole

Ke Kalo Pa'a o Waiāhole: the hard taro of Waiāhole

Waiāhole Valley is nestled along the windward side of the soaring Ko'olau mountain range on the island of O'ahu. The largest streams on the island flowed through

Waiāhole and its neighboring valleys, enabling cultivation of the most extensive *lo'i kalo* (wetland taro terraces) on the entire island and sustaining a thriving Maoli community and culture. At the turn of the 20th century, plantation owners sought water for their fields on O'ahu's dry central plain. In 1916, a 25-mile tunnel and ditch system was completed that drained the majority of surface and groundwater from the windward valleys to subsidize O'ahu Sugar Company's operations on the other side of the island. Massive diversions of windward water began without any thought to the communities or resources that depended on it. These diversions, which continued unchecked for almost 100 years, devastated streams and destroyed fishponds and estuaries, forcing many to abandon their subsistence lifestyles.

In the early 1990s, a small but dedicated coalition of Kānaka Maoli, family farmers, and community activists (collectively, the "Windward Parties") took on some of the most powerful economic and political forces in the State in a protracted legal battle over windward stream flows, which resulted in the first distillation of what the constitutional public trust actually means in Hawai'i. The case secured the first-ever restoration of streams in Hawai'i's history, fundamentally changing the course of water law across our archipelago. Traditional *mo'olelo* (stories or history) about this area speak of Ke Kalo Pa'a o Waiāhole, the hard taro of the region, which also alludes to the character of its people, who are steadfast in the face of adversity.

In 1992, in response to a community petition, the Commission designated windward O'ahu a groundwater management area under the Water Code, bringing water in the area under the Commission's regulatory control and requiring water users to apply for permits. Soon after, O'ahu Sugar announced that it would be closing. This set the stage for the pitched battle over the future allocation of this life-giving resource. The Windward Parties sought the return of water to their streams and communities via the establishment of "instream flow standards," as mandated by the Code. At the same time, a dozen users (the "Leeward Parties"), which included some of the largest landowners and powerful political interests in Hawai'i, coveted that water for large-scale agribusiness, private golf course development, and landscaping, among other things. Several county, state, and federal agencies also joined the fray, and were all in favor of maximizing stream diversions. In fact, the collective water demands of the Leeward Parties exceeded the entire flow of the Waiāhole Ditch System.

Years of proceedings followed, including a 10-month administrative trial, which involved hundreds of exhibits, dozens of witnesses, and a dizzying number of motions and other filings. In 1994, a mediated agreement between the parties partially restored stream flows on an interim basis, and then a 1997 Commission decision split the water between the windward streams and leeward users, from which three separate appeals were filed over the course of more than a decade. Ultimately, the Hawai'i Supreme Court played a crucial role in rising above the political wrangling that had tainted the Commission's decisions, and the plantation mentality that had subverted the public trust for more than a century.

Key lessons from the Waiāhole litigation

In August 2000, the Hawai'i Supreme Court issued its opinion, which was recognized globally for its pronouncements on the public trust doctrine and also returned to windward streams and communities roughly half of the diverted flows that had been appropriated for nearly a century.[27] This landmark decision affirmed the public nature of Hawai'i's water resources, clarified the burden of proof for those seeking stream restoration and diversions, and explicitly recognized the value of free-flowing streams and the perpetuation of indigenous culture. Both legally and metaphorically, *Waiāhole* created significant opportunities for Maoli and other communities throughout Hawai'i to seek justice through law, and illuminated both the promise and potential of the public trust doctrine in particular.

The Hawai'i Supreme Court's distillation of the public trust in *Waiāhole* grounds the doctrine in Hawai'i law (including indigenous custom and tradition) while incorporating elements of seminal cases from other jurisdictions, weaving them into a comprehensive declaration of law and policy. After reviewing the history of the public trust, the court first addressed the diverters' argument that the Hawai'i Water Code superseded the public trust doctrine, holding that the public trust was "an inherent attribute of sovereign authority" and ultimately a constitutional doctrine.[28] Because these constitutional trust provisions are "self-executing," parties could invoke the constitutional public trust on its own, apart from the Water Code or other statutory law. The court clarified that the Code "does not evince any legislative intent to abolish the common law public trust doctrine. To the contrary, . . . the legislature appears to have engrafted the doctrine wholesale in the Code."[29] The constitutional foundation "inform[s] the Code's interpretation, define[s] its permissible 'outer limits,' and justif[ies] its existence."[30] Thus, the public trust operated like other constitutional doctrines by establishing foundational principles that guided the courts' interpretation and sometimes limited the Code's more detailed regulatory provisions.

The court then turned to the "state water resources trust," interpreting Native Hawaiian law to conclude that this public trust extends to "all water resources without exception or distinction."[31] In rejecting the Leeward Parties' argument that the public trust excluded groundwater because Native Hawaiians did not use such water, the court highlighted the ancient use of springs, and emphasized the critical interconnection between surface and groundwater, maintaining that "the public trust, by its very nature, does not remain fixed for all time, but must conform to changing needs and circumstances."[32]

Having defined the trust's "scope," the Hawai'i Supreme Court then considered its "substance," including the "purposes or uses it upholds and the powers and duties it confers on the State."[33] To fulfill this duty, the Hawai'i Supreme Court identified a handful of "public trust purposes," including environmental protection, traditional and customary Maoli practices, appurtenant rights, domestic water uses,[34] and reservations for the Department of Hawaiian Home Lands,[35] all of which have priority over private commercial uses, which do not enjoy the same protection.[36]

The court then examined decisionmakers' powers and duties under the public trust.[37] Critically, the State maintains a kuleana "to ensure the continued availability and existence of water resources for present and future generations."[38] The court described the public trust as establishing "a dual mandate of (1) protection and (2) maximum reasonable and beneficial use."[39] The former involves a "duty to ensure the continued availability and existence of [state] water resources for present and future generations."[40] The latter requires "the most equitable, reasonable, and beneficial allocation of state water resources, with full recognition that resource protection also constitutes use."[41] In view of "legal and practical requirements and its historical and present circumstances," and drawing from the seminal California case *National Audubon Society v. Superior Court of Alpine County*, also known as the *Mono Lake* case, and other sources, the court framed the "fundamental principles" of Hawai'i's public trust doctrine.[42]

Starting with the public trust's "dual concept of sovereign right and responsibility," the court declared that "[u]nder the public trust, the state has both the authority and duty to preserve the rights of present and future generations in the waters of the state."[43] Regarding the state's trust authority, the court affirmed the public nature of Hawai'i's water resources:

> The continuing authority of the state over its water resources precludes any grant or assertion of vested rights to use water to the detriment of public trust purposes. This authority empowers the state to revisit prior diversions and allocations, even those made with due consideration of their effect on the public trust.[44]

As to the state's trust duties, the court adopted *National Audubon*'s famous ruling that decisionmakers have an "affirmative duty to take the public trust into account in the planning and allocation of water resources, and to protect public trust uses whenever feasible."[45] The court acknowledged the doctrine's limitations, noting that "this duty may not readily translate into substantive results,"[46] and also recognized that "reason and necessity dictate that the public trust may have to accommodate offstream diversions . . . to the unavoidable impairment of public instream uses and values."[47]

Having recognized the necessity of a balancing process, the court determined that "any balancing between public and private purposes [must] begin with a presumption in favor of public use, access, and enjoyment" and "use consistent with trust purposes [i]s the norm or 'default' condition."[48] Thus, offstream diverters who seek water for their private commercial gain bear the burden of justifying proposed uses in light of protected rights in the resources, including traditional and customary Maoli practices.[49]

Elaborating on the duties of the trustee under the public trust, the court focused on process – less on "what" decisionmakers do, and more on "how" they do it. The Hawai'i Supreme Court declared that the State must not relegate itself to a "mere umpire passively calling balls and strikes for adversaries appearing before it but instead must take the initiative in considering, protecting, and advancing public rights in the resource at every stage of the planning and decisionmaking process."[50] The State must take a global, long-term perspective and must always act with "openness, diligence, and foresight" in its decision-making.[51]

The court concluded its public trust discussion by clarifying that courts must apply a heightened standard of review in cases involving the public trust. While recognizing the general rule of deference to agency decisions, it maintained that courts, as with other constitutional guarantees, had the "ultimate authority to interpret and defend the public trust."[52] The court would not substitute its judgment for that of the agency or legislature, but must take a "hard look" at agency or legislative action to assess whether it complied with the public trust.[53] This protection of judicial review has proved to be essential in high-stakes water battles where political expediency threatens the Commission's decision-making. In fact, the Hawai'i Supreme Court has overturned all but one of the Commission's decisions to date.

In addition to its pronouncements on the public trust, the Hawai'i Supreme Court also took the pioneering step of upholding the precautionary principle as an applied legal doctrine, adopting it as a corollary to the public trust, and was the first published decision to explicitly do so.[54] The court, focused on process, ruled that "the lack of full scientific certainty should not be a basis for postponing effective measures to prevent environmental degradation" and that "where [scientific] uncertainty exists, a trustee's duty to protect the resource mitigates in favor of choosing presumptions that also protect the resource."[55] The court recognized that the principle will change over time, but nevertheless agreed with what it considered the principle's "quintessential form: at minimum, the absence of firm scientific proof should not tie the Commission's hands in adopting reasonable measures designed to further the public interest."[56] *Waiāhole* demonstrated the contours of these process-based protections. The Hawai'i Supreme Court overturned much of the Commission's decision as lacking the level of rigor and clarity demanded by the trust, and also condemned the Commission's lack of initiative in the face of scientific uncertainty.[57]

The *Waiāhole* saga, and the larger political, cultural, and social struggle within which it unfolded, impart valuable lessons for community leaders and resource managers alike. Through its historic decision, the Hawai'i Supreme Court began to redress some of the cultural harms imposed on Kānaka Maoli, and offered a pathway to reclaim the natural resources necessary to improve social conditions and more fully exercise cultural sovereignty. In strongly affirming the public trust, the court elucidated its scope, substance, and role in managing freshwater resources and more. In the almost 20 years since the Hawai'i Supreme Court's initial decision in *Waiāhole*, however, the Water Commission and other decisionmakers have neglected to respect the public trust's edicts or utilize its procedural protections.

Public trust principles in practice

Though *Waiāhole* was a resounding victory, the fight to restore Hawai'i's streams and communities is far from over. On paper, much of the legal language appears favorable to both Hawai'i's indigenous people and the community at large.[58] But on the ground in communities, the law in general and the Water Code in particular have largely failed to achieve the stated purpose of protecting and restoring Hawai'i's freshwater resources and the cultural practices dependent upon them. There have been successes, most often achieved through protracted litigation, but also too many failures. As detailed below, communities have sought and continue to seek justice through law, and in doing so have both glimpsed the promise and potential of the public trust and grappled with the shortcomings inherent in its legal process.

The public trust as paradigm

The importance of the Hawai'i Supreme Court's affirmation and articulation of the scope and substance of the public trust cannot be overstated. Neither can the way in which this legal doctrine reached beyond agency boardrooms and judicial courtrooms to touch the hearts and minds of community members across the archipelago, igniting a fire in Native Hawaiian communities from Kaua'i to Hawai'i Island. Put simply: the public trust transcended the law. More than a set of rules, this doctrine embodied an entire worldview that is inherently Native Hawaiian. Its conceptual premise – that government officials hold natural resources in trust for the benefit of present and future generations – was less a legal holding and more a pure statement of societal vision. This "public trust paradigm" was critical to the *Waiāhole* victory and also galvanized community members to take action to protect their freshwater resources, spawning a series of cases on Moloka'i, Maui, Hawai'i Island, Kaua'i, and beyond.

Nā Wai 'Ehā: paradigm or political reality check?

Kaulana Nā Wai 'Ehā, famous are the four great waters of Waihe'e, Waiehu, Wailuku (also known as 'Īao) and Waikapū Streams in the heart of central Maui. Since time immemorial, Native Hawaiian songs and stories have lauded abundant freshwater resources and the natural and cultural resources that they enable. Historically, Nā Wai 'Ehā sustained the largest contiguous area of wetland kalo cultivation in all of the Hawaiian Islands, with lo'i kalo blanketing the land from Waihe'e to Waikapū.[59] These resources played a prominent role in the development of Maoli history in general as the site where *Haumea* (Earth Mother) planted a foundation of Maoli society in the Waihe'e River.[60] A proliferation of *heiau* (places of worship), sizable populations, and residences of *ali'i* (leaders) also identified Nā Wai 'Ehā as a region of considerable political power and religious significance, much of which flowed from its profusion of fresh water.[61]

These abundant resources did not go unnoticed, and by 1862 a predecessor to what is now Wailuku Water Company LLC ("WWC") was draining area streams for sugar cane.[62] Native Hawaiians documented the devastating impact of these diversions on their resources, culture, and communities in Hawaiian language newspapers and more. Despite these and other negative impacts, ditch systems and diversions were built and expanded until they completely bled Nā Wai ʻEhā streams of their fresh water and spiritual *mana* (power). On average, industrial agricultural interests took between 60–70 million gallons per day ("mgd") for roughly 150 years, obliterating native communities and resources.[63] In 2010, Hawaiʻi's Water Commission acknowledged that

> cultural experts and community witnesses provided uncontroverted testimony regarding limitations on Native Hawaiians' ability to exercise traditional and customary Native Hawaiian rights and practices in the greater Nā Wai ʻEhā area due to the lack of freshwater flowing in Nā Wai ʻEhā's streams and into the nearshore marine waters.[64]

Rose Marie Hoʻoululāhui Lindsey Duey, a *kupa ʻāina* (native to a particular place) of ʻĪao Valley, described how these impacts fueled her desire for justice: "For me, this struggle goes to the very essence of what it means to be Kanaka Maoli. When they take our fresh water, they are taking away a life force that feeds our culture and who we are as a people. This is genocide, plain and simple."[65]

Once communities such as Nā Wai ʻEhā learned of Waiāhole's legal and practical triumphs, they too sought to wield the public trust as a sword to protect and restore their resources. In many ways, the public trust was an inspiration for individuals and Native Hawaiians in particular to engage in legal and political processes. This idea of a "trust" cultivated notions of kuleana – the cultural responsibility and privilege Kānaka Maoli have to care for extended family, including freshwater resources. Again, these are inherently indigenous management principles and the public trust in Hawaiʻi is a hybrid of native custom and Western legal precepts. Although it is now enshrined in Hawaiʻi's State Constitution, its origin informs its manifestation and interpretation and – most importantly – impacts Kānaka Maoli at a gut level. The public trust resonated and continues to embody core cultural tenants; people understood that and answered the call to action.

In 2004, Earthjustice on behalf of Hui o Nā Wai ʻEhā and Maui Tomorrow Foundation filed a petition with the Water Commission to restore Nā Wai ʻEhā's streams and communities. This coalition was hungry to bring the public trust paradigm to life in its community. Before legal action was initiated, key organizers spent years researching the issues and strategically building a base of support. In doing so, the public trust also played a significant role. Litigation and public relations impacting natural and cultural resources are science-heavy, and thus laden with technical terms and legalese. While your average Kimo or Lani on the street may not be up on the importance of an interim instream flow standard, base flow, or continuous flow to amphidromous stream animals, they can more easily appreciate a "public trust," their individual kuleana as beneficiaries, and the importance of protecting and restoring resources for generations yet unborn. In this way, the public trust both inspired action and provided the language to communicate its core message while conjuring an indigenous vision of society that these terms so eloquently invoke.

And boy was this necessary. The public trust was vital to both inspire the public to engage in the legal process and help to shield community members from the politics at play. Emboldened by the Hawai'i Supreme Court's admonitions, Nā Wai 'Ehā community members expected that the Commission would utilize its process mandate, apply preferential burden shifting, and otherwise comply with the basic requirements articulated in *Waiāhole*. After all, the high court's decision made clear that the Commission must be more than a "mere umpire passively calling balls and strikes for adversaries appearing before it."[66] A global, long-term perspective is critical for agency officials who must act with "openness, diligence, and foresight" in decisionmaking.[67] Moreover, "any balancing between public and private purposes [must] begin with a presumption in favor of public use, access, and enjoyment" and "use consistent with trust purposes [i]s the norm or 'default' condition."[68] The administrative trial in Nā Wai 'Ehā and subsequent actions by the Water Commission dispensed an important reality check.

The Commission's initial efforts to investigate the issues and obtain information from the diverters WWC and Hawaiian Commercial and Sugar Company ("HC&S" and collectively with WWC, "the Companies") proved futile. After all, because the Companies controlled the water in the interim, they had no incentive to cooperate. After failed mediation and a prolonged trial that stretched on for 11 months, with testimony from nearly 80 witnesses and hundreds of exhibits, the Hearings Officer in the case issued a draft decision in 2009 that would have restored 34.5 million gallons per day or about half of the water diverted from Nā Wai 'Ehā's streams and communities each day.[69] That draft determined that water must be returned to each of the four streams, with a minimum flow below all diversions of 14 mgd in Waihe'e, 2.2 mgd in North Waiehu, 1.3 mgd in South Waiehu, 13 mgd in Wailuku, and a provisional release of 4 mgd in Waikapū.[70]

HC&S responded by playing its economic card. As the largest employer in Maui County with roughly 800 workers, it repeatedly threatened to shut down its plantation if it did not receive the bulk of the water it was taking.[71] During the final oral argument in the case, HC&S dispensed with its attorney and instead had its newly appointed manager essentially present the Commission with an ultimatum: "We do not believe that there was any intent to shut down HC&S through the proposed decision. Nonetheless, that will be the end result if you adopt the recommended decision."[72] The Commission responded by rejecting the Hearings Officer's draft and its June 2010 decision returned only 12.5 mgd to Waihe'e and Waiehu, leaving Wailuku and Waikapū – Nā Wai 'Ehā's other two streams – with no restoration whatsoever and essentially dry below plantation diversions.

The Hearings Officer sharply dissented and the case was appealed to the Hawai'i Supreme Court. In 2012, the high court invalidated the Commission's decision and sent the case back for more hearings. Ultimately, a settlement was brokered and in 2014 an additional 10 mgd was returned to the Wailuku River and 2.9 mgd to Waikapū Stream.[73] Since then, HC&S has closed down completely, and additional permitting proceedings will ultimately determine the fate of the water not already restored to Nā Wai 'Ehā streams.[74]

Ultimately, the doctrine's constitutional foundation and heightened standard of review proved critical as the Hawai'i Supreme Court – yet again – was a vital backstop, refusing to deny Native Hawaiians access to justice when the Commission bowed to political pressure.[75] In doing so, the court held that it had jurisdiction because, among other reasons, "the ramifications of an erroneous [instream flow standard] could offend the public trust, and is simply too important to deprive parties of due process and judicial review."[76] In doing so, it reiterated that due to the constitutional foundation, "the ultimate authority to interpret and defend the public trust in Hawai'i rests with the courts of this state."[77] *Nā Wai 'Ehā*, like *Waiāhole*, illustrated that the law is not set in stone – it is a constantly shifting battleground of competing interests – and disputes over water, society's most basic necessity and precious resource, are especially controversial and contentious. Despite a carefully crafted and seemingly sympathetic legal regime, the Commission proved unwilling to uphold the public trust when politics came into play. Despite the significant potential of a public trust paradigm, beneficiaries cannot blindly rely on the legal system to mete out justice; they must take an active role in ensuring that the public trust receives the regard the law and justice require.

Kaua'i Springs: how the public trust paradigm prevailed

In addition to *Nā Wai 'Ehā*, other cases on Moloka'i, Kaua'i, Hawai'i Island, and in East Maui have chronicled the Water Commission's persistent failures to respect the public trust's basic precepts (such as its process mandate, preferential burden shifting, and the precautionary principle) as well as the importance of the constitutional foundation and heightened standard of review.[78] Despite those disappointments, this paradigm is not purely aspirational. Government officials on Kaua'i, for example, have begun to apply the public trust in their own contexts – precisely as article 11, section 1 of the Constitution contemplates. This case – *Kaua'i Springs* – demonstrates how some decisionmakers have embraced the public trust paradigm and are proactively protecting freshwater resources.[79]

Kaua'i Springs operates a private water bottling business in Kōloa, Kaua'i where it distributes five-gallon containers to island residents and businesses.[80] The Company's processing facility is on land zoned for agriculture where water from a spring is purchased after being supplied through a former plantation ditch system.[81] For some, Kaua'i Springs' basic business model raised concerns – could a commercial operation bottle and sell public trust resources for private profit? – and challenged the very notion of water as a public trust. It was also emblematic of a global movement to commodify and privatize water resources.[82] The company operated for several years before being informed that it could not continue its industrial processing on agricultural land without securing permits from the County of Kaua'i.[83]

In 2007, the County Planning Commission denied Kaua'i Springs' applications for a use permit, class IV zoning permit, and special permit.[84] The Planning

Commission concluded that the company had failed to demonstrate that it was entitled to extract and sell water on a commercial basis.[85] Kaua'i Springs appealed to the circuit court, claiming that the Planning Commission improperly placed the burden on the company to establish the legality of its water use and the case made its way through both Hawai'i's circuit court and intermediate court of appeals. Ultimately, in 2014, the Hawai'i Supreme Court upheld the Planning Commission's decision and sent the case back to the county for more hearings.

With respect to the public trust, the high court strongly reaffirmed the doctrine as a fundamental principle of constitutional law in Hawai'i.[86] The court emphasized that applicants bear the burden of justifying proposed water uses in light of the protected trust purposes and that the public trust provides independent authority to guide decisionmakers in fulfilling their mandates.[87]

The court distilled six principles that agency officials and other decisionmakers must apply to fulfill the public trust and appropriately consider that paradigm in rendering determinations:

(1) "The agency's duty and authority is to maintain the purity and flow of our waters for future generations and to assure that the waters of our land are put to reasonable and beneficial use";
(2) Officials "must determine whether the proposed use is consistent with the trust purposes";
(3) Decisionmakers need to "apply a presumption in favor of public use, access, enjoyment, and resource protection";
(4) Authorities must "evaluate each proposal for use on a case-by-case basis, recognizing that there can be no vested rights in the use of public water";
(5) "If the requested use is private or commercial, the agency should apply a high level of scrutiny"; and
(6) Administrators must apply "a 'reasonable and beneficial use' standard, which requires examination of the proposed use in relation to other public and private uses."[88]

These principles establish "duties under the public trust independent of [any] permit requirements"[89] and provide more specific direction about what the heightened standard of review actually requires under a public trust paradigm. Moreover, these requirements apply to all state and county officials making determinations that affect the trust res.[90] Hopefully, this further elucidation will guide and inspire decisionmakers such as the Water Commission who have struggled in the nearly 20 years since the initial *Waiāhole* decision.

The court also underscored four affirmative showings that permit and other applicants must make to fulfill their responsibilities under the trust:

(1) "[T]heir actual needs and the propriety of draining water from public streams to satisfy those needs";
(2) The absence of practicable alternatives, including alternate sources of water or making the proposed use more efficient;

(3) "[N]o harm in fact" to public trust purposes "or that the requested use is nevertheless reasonable and beneficial"; and
(4) "If the impact is found to be reasonable and beneficial, the applicant must implement reasonable measures to mitigate the cumulative impact of existing and proposed diversions on trust purposes, if the proposed use is to be approved."[91]

Absent these requirements, "a lack of information from the applicant is exactly the reason an agency is empowered to deny a proposed use of a public trust resource."[92] The Hawai'i Supreme Court's articulation of these four showings provides more specific direction to Kaua'i Springs and others seeking public trust resources for their private profit under the preferential burden shifting and heightened standard of review already formulated in *Waiāhole.*

Kaua'i Springs is also one of the few examples where the precautionary principle appears to have been utilized. Although the Planning Commission did not identify it as a basis for its decision, this is precisely the kind of situation where agencies should employ the principle, e.g., where they are uncertain about the impacts of a proposed action. The precautionary principle is an important corollary of the public trust, which, at bottom, mandates that "where [scientific] uncertainty exists, a trustee's duty to protect the resource mitigates in favor of choosing presumptions that also protect the resource."[93] In too many other cases, such as groundwater disputes on the island of Moloka'i, the Water Commission has been unwilling to hold permit applicants to their burdens of proof, despite the preferential burden shifting under the public trust.[94] Here, where the applicant was unable to demonstrate a negative – the absence of an impact to public trust purposes – and the Planning Commission's independent inquiries to other government agencies proved inconclusive,[95] the trustee (Planning Commission) correctly erred on the side of protecting the resource and denied the permit applications consistent with public trust principles.[96]

Additional insight from Nā Wai 'Ehā, Kaua'i Springs, and beyond

Waiāhole and *Nā Wai 'Ehā* highlighted the public trust's ability to protect underrepresented communities from government and economic powers-that-be. In hotly contested cases, enduring public rights in our resources can help to counterbalance political forces, especially for groups who would otherwise be outgunned politically and/or financially. This was particularly true in *Nā Wai 'Ehā,* where the Companies used their economic influence in what most assumed should be a purely legal decision, highlighting the fact that there is no such thing as a "purely legal" decision. Although the Hawai'i Supreme Court ultimately upheld the public trust and vindicated the community group's position, this process was protracted and expensive, and the outcome was by no means guaranteed. It also harkened back to *Waiāhole* where "improper considerations [likely] tipped the scales in this difficult and hotly contested case," which "did nothing to improve public confidence in government and the administration of justice in this state."[97]

There, the court's concerns about undue political pressure resonated with public trust overtones and echoed the principle that the enduring trust sets higher standards beyond what the "present majority," or most powerful, happen to favor at any given moment.[98]

By contrast, *Kaua'i Springs* is one example where local agencies, faced with scientific uncertainty, remained committed to holding permit applicants to their burdens, even if it took multiple appeals for such a decision to be upheld.[99] In that way, *Kaua'i Springs* is a beacon of hope that some agencies (or at least one) embrace their kuleana under the public trust and this affirmation of the rule of law – that water is a trust resource, not a commodity – in such a politically charged atmosphere, is proving perhaps as important as the legal rules themselves.

This hope – that the public trust doctrine will be applied as the framers of the State Constitution intended, and that it will serve as a true expression of *aloha 'āina* (a deep love and respect for the land), a way of life passed down through the generations – remains, despite the uphill battle ahead. Thus far, Hawai'i's legal development of the public trust has evolved in the context of water, but the Hawai'i Supreme Court will soon have the opportunity to consider the plain language of article 11, section 1 of Hawai'i's Constitution and whether public trust protections extend to *'āina* (land or that which feeds), and Mauna Kea in particular. The proposed construction of the massive Thirty Meter Telescope ("TMT") in the conservation district atop Hawai'i's tallest mountain and a place considered sacred to Kānaka Maoli[100] became a rallying cry for a new generation of activists, and galvanized support for indigenous movements for the protection of land and water both within and beyond our shores. The legal battle enveloping Mauna Kea has been immensely complex, with civil and criminal proceedings spanning many years.[101] Most recently, in September 2017, the State Board of Land and Natural Resources ("BLNR") issued a permit allowing construction to proceed, ignoring the plain language of article 11, section 1, and claiming that the public trust is limited to water only.[102] This determination stands in stark contrast to the characterization of the public trust's scope found in the concurring opinion to the 2015 Hawai'i Supreme Court decision vacating a similar permit, in which two justices proclaimed that the public trust applies to the Mauna Kea summit and that this "conclusion is supported by the plain language of article 11, section 1, the historical context under which this provision was ratified, and this court's precedents."[103] An appeal from BLNR's decision has since been filed with Hawai'i Supreme Court, which will be tasked, once again, with defining the contours of the public trust. Inevitably, this will impact the doctrine's ability to continue to protect underrepresented communities from government and economic powers-that-be.

The power and potential of the public trust for other indigenous communities

Roughly two hundred years ago, *kahuna* (high priests) stood atop the walls of Pāku'i heiau on the island of Moloka'i and chanted a *wānana* (prophecy).[104] These kahuna foresaw the "burning death" and "heavy downpour" of rain that would overcome their island and people.[105] They prognosticated the onslaught of tremendous devastation, including the annihilation of traditional Hawaiian society.[106] But they were also confident that from this destruction the people of the land, deeply rooted in the *lepo pōpolo* (the earth's dark soil), would eventually rise up like a great wave and branch out into the heavens to take control.[107] That time has come.[108]

As prophesied by the wānana, communities in Hawai'i and around island earth are grappling with the deleterious impacts of climate change. As indigenous peoples struggle to protect, restore, and reclaim the resources that are both part of our extended family and define who we are as people, we must more closely integrate our traditional knowledge into legal and political processes. Grounded in Kānaka Maoli precepts, Hawai'i's public trust doctrine's current manifestation and continued evolution hold tremendous power and potential for those within and beyond our shores.

Legally, the public trust provides significant tools to facilitate both government accountability and more sustainable societies. In Hawai'i, it features a process mandate, preferential burden shifting, a constitutional foundation, heightened standard of review, and more. As both *Waiāhole* and *Nā Wai 'Ehā* demonstrate, this legal regime has the potential to produce real results, such as Hawai'i's first-ever government-ordered restoration of streams diverted for plantation agriculture. The process mandate and preferential burden shifting are designed to level playing fields, which is critical for indigenous and other under-resourced groups taking on entrenched interests with financial and political leverage. The constitutional foundation and heightened standard of review are also imperative, as advocates have had to repeatedly rely on an independent judiciary to overrule government agencies and officials who bowed to political pressure. *Kaua'i Springs* highlighted the fact that the public trust is also a prism through which decisionmakers must carefully examine their kuleana under the specific law(s) each agency is charged with enforcing and provides independent authority to guide decisionmakers in discharging their duties. Its inherent flexibility, along with decisionmakers' affirmative obligations to take the initiative and proactively protect resources (precautionary principle), provides opportunities for direct action and adaptive management.[109] Indeed, in *Waiāhole*, the Hawai'i Supreme Court declared that "the public trust, by its very nature, does not remain fixed for all time, but must conform to changing needs and circumstances."[110] In this way, the public trust in Hawai'i is particularly well situated to respond to the perils of climate change.[111]

But beyond legal rules, the public trust is also a paradigm that has and can continue to help in ways that transcend the law. More than a set of rules, it embodies an indigenous worldview and approach to resource stewardship that holds a key to the future success of other communities. In *Nā Wai 'Ehā*, the public trust cultivated notions of kuleana and inspired community members to engage in legal and political processes. At the same time, it provided the language to communicate its core message while also broadening the base of supporters who recognized the importance of protecting and restoring resources for generations yet unborn.

As the *Waiāhole* coalition first illustrated, and as Maoli communities from Maui to Kaua'i continue to realize, the public trust can be utilized to reclaim resources and power in pursuit of restorative justice. It is both a unique expression of our shared history and a vision for our future. It evinces a deep-rooted responsibility for generations to come, especially in light of colonialism's calamitous legacy for our culture, communities, and resources. From Mauna Kea to Standing Rock, indigenous peoples around the globe are rising up against the privatization and degradation of vital natural and cultural resources.[112] And courts around the world have reaffirmed that the public trust doctrine requires governments to protect natural resources for present and future generations.[113] In that spirit:

Hā'ule ka lālā lewa i ka lani
The suspended branches of the heavens shall fall
Hā'ule ka lā
The day shall fall
Hā'ule ka pō
The night shall fall
Hā'ule ka lani
The chiefs shall fall
Hā'ule ka nī'au
The highborn shall fall
Hā'ule'ule ka lewa i ka lālā
The high genealogies shall fall
Hā'ule'ule ka noho ā lani ka lālā lewa
All the high branches resting in the heavens shall fall
Hō'ale ka lepo pōpolo
The dirt-stained commoner shall rise
Hō'ale ka lepo pōpolo
The dirt-stained commoner shall rise
Hō'ale'ale ka lepo i ka lani i noho lā
The low born shall rise and rest in the heavens
Hō'ale'ale ke kua ha'a ka lepo ka lani i noho lā
The crooked-backs shall rise and rest in the heavens
Huli a Moloka'i
Moloka'i shall be overturned
Moloka'i nui a Hina
Great Moloka'i of Hina[114]

Notes

1 Mary Kawena Pukui *'Ōlelo No'eau: Hawaiian Proverbs & Poetical Sayings* (Bishop Museum Press, Honolulu, 1983) at 531.
2 Some text from this chapter previously appeared in D. Kapua'ala Sproat "A Question of Wai: Seeking Justice Through Law for Hawai'i's Streams and Communities" in Noelani Goodyear-Ka'ōpua, Ikaika Hussey and Erin Kahunawaika'ala Wright (eds) *Nation Rising: Hawaiian Movements for Life, Land, and Sovereignty* (Duke

University Press, Durham, NC, 2014) at 207 and D. Kapua'ala Sproat and Isaac H. Moriwake "Ke Kalo Pa'a o Waiāhole: Use of the Public Trust as a Tool for Environmental Advocacy" in Clifford Rechtschaffen and Denise Antolini (eds.) *Creative Common Law Strategies for Protecting the Environment* (Environmental Law Institute, Washington, DC, 2007) at 254.

3 Native Hawaiian, native Hawaiian, Hawaiian, Kānaka Maoli, and Maoli are used interchangeably and without reference to blood quantum. Kānaka Maoli or Maoli is the indigenous Hawaiian name for the population inhabiting Hawai'i at the time of the first Western contact. Mary Kawena Pukui and Samuel H. Elbert *Hawaiian Dictionary* (University of Hawai'i Press, Honolulu, 1986) at 127 (noting that Kānaka Maoli historically referred to a full-blooded "Hawaiian person").

4 See, e.g., Martha Warren Beckwith *The Kumulipo: A Hawaiian Creation Chant* (University of Hawai'i Press, Honolulu, 1972). The Kumulipo is detailed and complex with sixteen *wā* (intervals) and over 2,000 lines. Ibid. at 37. The Kumulipo explains that in the beginning there was *pō* or darkness, and from this darkness, came life. Ibid. at 42–49. Pō gave birth to two children: a son named Kumulipo and a daughter named Pō'ele. Ibid. at 50–93. Through their union, Kumulipo and Pō'ele created the natural world. Ibid. The first child born to them was the coral polyp, which created the foundation for all life in the sea. Ibid. at 55–56. Born in continuing sequential order were all of the plants and animals in Hawai'i nei, which became 'aumakua or guardians that continue to watch over Kānaka Maoli. Ibid. at 50–93. Pō had many children that comprised all aspects of Hawai'i's natural world. Ibid. at 37. After all of the Hawaiian Islands were born, Wākea (Skyfather) had a child with Ho'ohōkūkalani, which was stillborn. Ibid. at 117. They buried it outside of their home, and a kalo plant grew from its grave. Ibid. Wākea and Ho'ohōkūkalani had a second child, named Hāloa in honor of its elder sibling, which was the first Kānaka Maoli – the first human child born in Hawai'i. Ibid.

5 See Beckwith, note 4, at 117.

6 See Melody Kapilialoha MacKenzie et al. "Environmental Justice for Indigenous Hawaiians: Reclaiming Land and Resources" (2007) 21 *Natural Resources & Environment* 37.

> The land, like a cherished relative, cared for the Native Hawaiian people and, in return, the people cared for the land. The principle of *mālama 'āina* (to take care of the land) is therefore directly linked to conserving and protecting not only the land and its resources but also humankind and the spiritual world as well.
>
> Ibid.

7 See Ibid.

8 Ibid.

9 E.S. Craighill Handy and Elizabeth Green Handy with the Collaboration of Mary Kawena Pukui *Native Planters in Old Hawai'i: Their Life, Lore & Environment* (Bishop Museum Press, Honolulu, 1995) at 64.

10 *McBryde Sugar Co. v. Robinson*, 54 Haw. 174, 185–187, 504 P. 2d 1330, 1338–39 (1973).

11 *Translation of the Constitution and Laws of the Hawaiian Islands, Established in the Reign of Kamehameha II* (1842): 11–12, in Hawai'i State Archives, <http://punawaiola.org/saxon/SaxonServlet?source=http://Punawaiola.org/fedora/get/Punawaiola:771031842001/XMLText&style=http://Punawaiola.org:8080/KDA/Transforms/KDAGetTransform.xsl>. See also Hawai'i Kingdom Laws of 1839, reprinted and translated in *Translation of the Constitution and Laws of the Hawaiian Islands, Established in the Reign of Kamehameha III* (1842): 33, <http://punawaiola.org/> (reprinting an 1839 law respecting water for irrigation, which sought to manage water resources for the common good); see also D. Kapua'ala Sproat "Where

Justice Flows Like Water: The Moon Court's Role in Illuminating Hawai'i Water Law" (2011) 33 *University of Hawai'i Law Review* 537.

12 In brief, the Māhele refers to the process of instituting a hybridized private property regime in Hawai'i over the course of many years but beginning in about 1845; it resulted in stripping most Maoli of ancestral land and resources. For a detailed explanation of this process, see Lilikalā Kame'eleihiwa *Native Land and Foreign Desires: Pehea Lā E Pono Ai?* (Honolulu: Bishop Museum Press, 1992) and Kamanamaikalani Beamer *No Mākou ka Mana: Liberating the Nation* (Honolulu: Kamehameha Publishing, 2014).

13 *McBryde Sugar Co. v. Robinson*, 54 Haw. 174, 504 P. 2d 1330 (1973).

14 Ibid. at 186–187, 504 P. 2d at 1338–1339.

15 Ibid. at 186, 504 P. 2d at 1338.

16 *Robinson v. Ariyoshi*, 65 Haw. 641, 658 P. 2d 287 (1982); *Reppun v. Bd. of Water Supply*, 65 Haw. 531, 656 P. 2d 57 (1982).

17 Some text from this section previously appeared in Sproat "A Question of Wai: Seeking Justice Through Law for Hawai'i's Streams and Communities" note 2, at 207.

18 Hawai'i Constitution article 11, section 1.

19 Hawai'i Constitution article 11, section 7.

20 *In re Waiāhole Combined Contested Case* (*"Waiāhole I"*), 94 Hawai'i 97, 132, 9 P. 3d 409, 444 (2000). In addition, article 11, section 9 proclaims: "Each person has the right to a clean and healthful environment, as defined by laws relating to environmental quality, including control of pollution and conservation, protection and enhancement of natural resources. Any person may enforce this right against any party, public or private, through appropriate legal proceedings, subject to reasonable limitations and regulation as provided by law."

21 Hawai'i Constitution article 12, section 7.

22 The Code declares that the "traditional and customary rights of ahupua'a tenants who are descendants of native Hawaiians who inhabited the Hawaiian Islands prior to 1778 shall not be abridged or denied by this chapter." Hawai'i Revised Statutes (HRS) § 174C–101(c). The Code makes clear that such rights include but are not limited to the cultivation of *kalo* on one's own *kuleana*, as well as the ability to gather various resources for subsistence, cultural, and religious purposes, including: *hīhīwai* (or *wī*), *'ōpae*, *'o'opu*, *limu*, thatch, *kī*, *aho* cord, and medicinal plants.

23 Hawai'i Constitution article 11, section 7 (The Commission shall set overall water conservation, quality and use policies; define beneficial and reasonable uses; protect ground and surface water resources, watershed and natural stream environments; establish criteria for water use priorities while assuring appurtenant rights and existing correlative and riparian uses and establish procedures for regulating all uses of Hawai'i's water resources.).

24 *Waiāhole I*, 94 Hawai'i at 133, 9 P. 3d at 445.

25 Ibid. at 139, 9 P. 3d at 451.

26 Ibid. at 141, 9 P. 3d at 453 (emphasis removed) (quoting *Nat'l Audubon Soc'y v. Superior Court of Alpine Cnty.* (*"Mono Lake"*), 658 P. 2d 709, 728 (Cal. 1983)).

27 Sproat "A Question of Wai: Seeking Justice Through Law for Hawai'i's Streams and Communities" note 2, at 207.

28 *Waiāhole I*, 94 Hawai'i at 131, 9 P. 3d at 443.

29 Ibid. at 130, 9 P. 3d at 442 (citations omitted).

30 Ibid. at 133, 9 P. 3d at 445.

31 Ibid.

32 Ibid. at 135, 9 P. 3d at 447.

33 Ibid.

34 Domestic water uses include individual household needs, not the aggregate household uses of the general public, which are considered municipal. HRS § 174C–3.

35 *Waiāhole I*, 94 Hawai'i at 136–138, 9 P. 3d at 448–450. Appurtenant rights appertain or attach to parcels of land that were cultivated, usually with the traditional staple *kalo*, at the time of the Māhele. See *Reppun v. Bd. of Water Supply*, 65 Haw. 531, 563, 656 P. 2d 57, 78 (1982). The Department of Hawaiian Home Lands was established by the Hawaiian Homes Commission Act (1921).
36 *Waiāhole I*, 94 Hawai'i at 142, 9 P. 3d at 454.
37 Ibid. at 138, 9 P. 3d at 450.
38 Ibid. at 139, 9 P. 3d at 451.
39 Ibid.
40 Ibid.
41 Ibid.at 140, 9 P. 3d at 452.
42 Ibid. at 141, 9 P. 3d at 453; *see Mono Lake*, 658 P. 2d 709 (Cal. 1983).
43 Ibid. at 141, 9 P. 3d at 453 (citation omitted).
44 Ibid.
45 Ibid. (emphasis removed) (quoting *Mono Lake*, 658 P. 2d at 728).
46 Ibid.
47 Ibid.
48 Ibid. at 142, 9 P. 3d at 454.
49 Ibid.
50 Ibid. at 143, 9 P. 3d at 455 (citation omitted).
51 Ibid.
52 Ibid.
53 Ibid. at 144, 9 P. 3d at 456.
54 Ibid. at 154, 9 P. 3d at 466 (citation omitted).
55 Ibid. (quoting the Commission's decision).
56 Ibid. at 155, 9 P. 3d at 467.
57 See, e.g., Ibid. at 154–158, 9 P. 3d at 466–470 (vacating the Commission's stream flow allocations); Ibid. at 163–164, 9 P. 3d at 475–476 (vacating the Commission's water use permit allocations); Ibid. at 154–155, 9 P. 3d at 466–467; Ibid. at 158–160, 9 P. 3d at 470–472 (criticizing the Commission for its "permissive view towards stream diversions" in the face of scientific uncertainty).
58 *In re Wai'ola O Moloka'i, Inc.*, 103 Hawai'i 401, 417, 83 P. 3d 664, 680 (2004) ("The Code mandates consideration of the large variety of public interests. The definition of 'public interest' in the Code broadly encompasses the protection of the environment, traditional and customary practices of native Hawaiians, scenic beauty, protection of fish and wildlife, and protection and enhancement of the waters of the State.").
59 Handy, Handy and Pukui, note 9, at 496–497.
60 Ty P. Kāwika Tengan *Report on the Archival, Historical and Archaeological Resources of Nā Wai 'Ehā, Wailuku District, Island of Maui* (Prepared for the Office of Hawaiian Affairs, Honolulu, 2007) at 1–7.
61 Ibid. at 7–13.
62 Commission on Water Resource Management, *Findings of Fact, Conclusions of Law, and Decision and Order* (June 10, 2010), Contested Case Hearing, No. CCH-MA06–01 ("*Final D&O*"): 10.
63 Ibid. at 26, 32.
64 Ibid. at 10, 26–27.
65 Rose Marie Ho'oululāhui Lindsey Duey, Hui o Nā Wai 'Ehā, interview by D. Kapua'ala Sproat, February 19, 2012.
66 *Waiāhole I*, 94 Hawai'i at 143, 9 P. 3d at 455 (citation omitted).
67 Ibid.
68 Ibid. at 142, 9 P. 3d at 454.
69 Sproat "A Question of Wai: Seeking Justice Through Law for Hawai'i's Streams and Communities" note 2, at 211.

70 *Hearings Officer's Proposed Findings of Fact, Conclusions of Law, and Decision and Order* (April 9, 2009), Contested Case Hearing, No. CCH-MA06-01: 187–189.
71 *Final D&O*, note 62, at 136–137.
72 *Transcript of Closing Argument* (Oct. 15, 2009), Contested Case Hearing, No. CCH-MA06-01.
73 'Four Streams Will be Flowing in Settlement of Na Wai Eha', *The Maui News* (April 22, 2014), www.mauinews.com/news/local-news/2014/04/four-streams-will-be-flowing-in-settlement-of-na-wai-eha/.
74 Stephen McLaren "Hawaii's Last Sugar Harvest Paves the Way for a Fight Over the Land's Future" *The Guardian* (April 28, 2016) <www.theguardian.com/us-news/2016/apr/28/maui-hawaii-sugar-cane-crops-agriculture-hcs-monsanto>.
75 In *Nā Wai 'Ehā*, the Companies and the Water Commission itself argued that the Hawai'i Supreme Court did not have jurisdiction because the Community Groups and the Office of Hawaiian Affairs had no right to appeal. *In re 'Īao Ground Water Mgmt. Area High-Level Source Water Use Permit Applications & Petition* (*"Nā Wai 'Ehā"*), 128 Hawai'i 228, 238, 287 P. 3d 129, 139 (2014).
76 Ibid. at 244, 287 P. 3d at 145.
77 Ibid.
78 See, e.g., *In re Wai'ola 'O Moloka'i, Inc.*, 103 Hawai'i 401, 83 P. 3d 664 (2004); *In re Kukui (Moloka'i), Inc.*, 116 Hawai'i 481, 174 P. 3d 320 (2007); "East Maui Stream Flow Case Reopens; Parties Debate Evidentiary Standards" *Env't Hawai'i* (February 2017) <www.environment-hawaii.org/?p=9466>; "Water Commission Denies NPS Petition To Designate Keauhou Aquifer System" *Env't Hawai'i* (April 2017) <www.environment-hawaii.org/?p=9601>; Jessica Else "Water Diverted From Waimea River to Be Returned" *The Garden Island* (April 19, 2017) <http://thegardenisland.com/news/local/water-diverted-from-waimea-river-to-be-returned/article_b16eaa0b-2b8b-5f1b-b549–1834e68aefa2.html>.
79 *Kauai Springs, Inc. v. Planning Comm'n of the Cnty. of Kaua'i* (*"Kaua'i Springs"*), 133 Hawai'i 141, 324 P. 3d 951 (2014).
80 Ibid. at 146–147, 324 P. 3d at 956–957.
81 Ibid. at 146, 324 P. 3d at 956. The Eric A. Knudsen Trust owns the land underlying the spring and sells water to the company via a private ditch owned by Grove Farm Company. Ibid.
82 See Vandana Shiva *Water Wars: Privatization, Pollution, and Profit* (North Atlantic Books, Berkeley, CA, 2016).
83 Ibid. at 147, 324 P. 3d at 957.
84 Ibid. A use permit and special permit were required because the proposed use was not generally permitted in the agricultural district, and a class IV permit is a procedural requirement of a use permit in the agricultural district. Ibid.; Planning Commission of the County of Kaua'i, Findings of Fact, Conclusions of Law, Decision and Order re: Use Permit U-2007-1, Special Permit SP 2007-1, and Class IV Zoning Permit Z-IV-2007-1 (Jan. 23, 2007).
85 *Kaua'i Springs*, 133 Hawai'i at 152–153, 324 P. 3d at 962–963.
86 Ibid. at 171–175, 324 P. 3d at 981–985.
87 Ibid. In examining the interplay between the constitutional public trust and an agency's enabling statute, the Hawai'i Supreme Court in *Waiāhole* explained: "The Code and its implementing agency, the Commission, do not override the public trust doctrine or render it superfluous. Even with the enactment and any future development of the Code, the doctrine continues to inform the Code's interpretation, define its permissible 'outer limits,' and justify its existence. To this end, although we regard the public trust and Code as sharing similar core principles, we hold that the Code does not supplant the protections of the public trust doctrine." *Waiāhole I*, 94 Hawai'i at 133, 9 P. 3d at 445.

88 *Kaua'i Springs*, 133 Hawai'i at 174, 324 P. 3d at 984 (citations omitted).
89 Ibid. at 177, 324 P. 3d at 987.
90 Hawai'i Constitution, article 11, section 1; *Kelly v. 1250 Oceanside Partners*, 111 Hawai'i 205, 140 P. 3d 985 (2006) (holding that counties are political subdivisions of the State and therefore are subject to the public trust).
91 *Kaua'i Springs*, 133 Hawai'i at 174–175, 324 P. 3d at 984–985 (citations omitted).
92 Ibid. at 174, 324 P. 3d at 984.
93 *Waiāhole I*, 94 Hawai'i at 154, 9 P. 3d at 466.
94 See, e.g., *Wai'ola 'O Moloka'i, Inc.*, 103 Hawai'i 401, 83 P. 3d 664 (2004); *In re Kukui (Moloka'i), Inc.*, 116 Hawai'i 481, 174 P. 3d 320 (2007).
95 The Kaua'i Planning Department consulted with several state and county agencies, and was particularly concerned with the lack of input that it received from the Water Commission and the Public Utilities Commission, which regulates all public utility companies operating in the state. *Kaua'i Springs*, 133 Hawai'i at 147–153, 324 P. 3d at 957–963.
96 Ibid. at 179–180, 324 P. 3d at 989–990.
97 *Waiāhole I*, 94 Hawai'i at 127, 9 P. 3d at 439.
98 *See* Ibid. at 190 n.108, 9 P. 3d at 502 n.108 (responding to the dissenting opinion).
99 The Kaua'i Springs controversy continues as this chapter goes to press. In October 2017, upon remand from the Hawai'i Supreme Court, the Kaua'i Planning Commission's hearing officer recommended approval of the permits, provided that certain conditions are met. *Hearing Officer's Report and Recommendation of Contested Case Hearing* (Oct. 20, 2017), No. CC-2015-20. The hearing officer concluded that the water bottling operation met the high level of scrutiny required of commercial activities and that the application met "most" of the requirements of the public trust doctrine. Ibid. at 45–47. The Planning Commission has not yet decided whether to adopt this recommendation.
100 Mauna a Wākea is born of the gods Wākea and Papa, the progenitors of Kānaka Maoli, and is known as *wao akua*, the realm of the gods where water, snow, and mist are found. The summit is considered a *piko* (center; navel), the point where the sky and earth meet.
101 Various lawsuits have challenged the lease of the land itself, the management plan, and "emergency rules" promulgated by BLNR to restrict public access to the mountain. In 2013, the State granted a conservation district use permit to allow construction of the $1.4 billion TMT project in 2013, setting off a firestorm of controversy. In 2015, hundreds of Mauna Kea protectors blocked access roads to the proposed TMT site, and at least 31 demonstrators were arrested.

In November 2017, the Office of Hawaiian Affairs filed a separate lawsuit against the state, BLNR, and the University of Hawai'i alleging mismanagement of Mauna Kea.
102 Board of Land and Natural Resources (Sept. 28, 2017), *Findings of Fact, Conclusions of Law and Decision and Order*, Contested Case Hearing, No. BLNR-CC-16-002. While recognizing that article 11, section 1, has a much broader scope than the public trust doctrine as applied to date in Hawai'i case law, and that it expressly includes *all* natural resources, not simply fresh water, tidelands, and the shore, BLNR nevertheless concluded that the lands and resources at issue are not covered by the public trust doctrine. Ibid. at 238–239.
103 *Mauna Kea Anaina Hou v. Board of Land and Natural Resources*, 136 Hawai'i 376, 407, 363 P. 3d 224, 255 (2015) (Pollack, J., concurring). The concurrence noted that "[t]his court has never precisely demarcated the dimensions of the public trust doctrine as incorporated in Article XI, Section 1." Ibid. at 405, 363 P. 3d at 253.
104 Pāku'i, translation by Kumu Hula John Kaimikaua (unpublished oli, 1819) ("Wānana").
105 Wānana, note 104 ("*Puni i ka mauli a Moloka'i, Puni i ka make 'ā'ā Moloka'i, Lana uli a 'ōpaepae i ka Uhilawekūloku, Kūlokuloku ā loku ā puni.*" Overcome is the

spirit of Moloka'i, Overcome by burning death is Moloka'i, Drifting in layers are the clouds of Uhilawekūloku, Heavy downpour of rain upon the whole land.").

106 Ibid.

107 Ibid.

108 Ā Mau Ā Mau: To Continue Forever, produced by Nālani Minton (2000) (explaining that half of the prophecy has been fulfilled, and the second half – when *hō'ale ka lepo pōpolo*, the people of the earth, rise up like a wave – is taking place now as Kānaka Maoli reclaim their cultural heritage and resources).

109 Robin Kundis Craig "Climate Change and the Public Trust Doctrine: Are Changes to Water Law Coming?" 11(2) (February 2009) *ABA Water Resources Committee Newsletter* 2 (predicting that the public trust doctrine will become the first focal point of legal pressure to evolve water law in response to climate change).

110 *Waiāhole I,* 94 Hawai'i at 135, 9 P. 3d at 447.

111 See Robin Kundis Craig "Adapting to Climate Change: The Potential Role of State Common-Law Public Trust Doctrines" (2010) 34 *Vermont Law Review* 853.

To the extent that climate change impacts water supplies and thus public trust purposes, including navigation, recreation, and most importantly in Hawai'i, Native Hawaiian traditional and customary practices, communities may deploy the doctrine to protect those uses to the extent possible. The Commission may decide to reduce certain water uses in response to reduced flows caused by climate change to protect streams for the larger public benefit. Or perhaps climate change will inspire the Commission and state courts to reexamine the scope of the public trust doctrine, and employ the precautionary principle more vigorously.

112 See Ikaika Hussey "The Rise of a New, Global, Indigenous Left" *Summit Magazine* (May 10, 2017) <www.summitzine.com/posts/the-rise-of-a-new-global-indigenous-left/> (detailing struggles over water around the world, and depicting developing alliances between indigenous activists). By October 2016, Standing Rock had become the largest and most high-profile indigenous protest in the U.S. in the last four decades. Robinson Meyer "The Standing Rock Sioux Claim 'Victory and Vindication' in Court" *The Atlantic* (June 14, 2017) <www.theatlantic.com/science/archive/2017/06/dakota-access-standing-rock-sioux-victory-court/530427/?utm_source=atlfb>.

113 See, e.g., *Oposa v. Factoran*, GR No 101083 (Sup. Ct. Phil. 1993) (pathbreaking decision in which the Philippines Supreme Court declared an inherent right to ecological balance "exist[ing] from the inception of humankind"); *M.C. Mehta v. Kamal Nath*, 1 S.C.C. 388 (India 1997) (concluding that the public trust doctrine includes all natural resources and is enforceable by public beneficiaries). Courts in Uganda, Kenya, Indonesia, South Africa, Pakistan, Canada and the Netherlands have also upheld public trust claims.

114 Wānana, note 104. Only the final verses of the wānana are reproduced here. Ibid.

14 From rights to responsibilities using legal personhood and guardianship for rivers

*Catherine Iorns Magallanes**

Introduction

Legal responsibility for freshwater bodies is emerging worldwide. It is particularly evident in relation to rivers. While rivers comprise only a small amount of total fresh water worldwide, they provide water for a much larger percentage of people.[1] Rivers are thus conspicuous, particularly when they are degraded in quality or quantity.[2] New mechanisms are being sought for better implementing human responsibility for the condition and life of these rivers. A tool that seems to have sparked imagination and interest worldwide is legal personality. This involves making the river a person in law, much as legal systems do worldwide for companies and other such entities; this imbues it with certain legal abilities that it does not otherwise have: "the rights and liabilities of a legal person".[3] Such personality has been recognised in different legal systems, including civil and common law systems, on different continents. Yet each occurrence has been achieved in a slightly different way – each being a product of historical circumstance and practical realities more than of legal principle.

Interestingly, commentators have labelled these examples as adopting a 'Rights of Nature' approach.[4] Legal personality may well become part of a rights of nature toolbox, but it is not synonymous with rights of nature. Indeed, where legal personality has been adopted, it has occasionally been framed not as a matter of rights but of responsibility. This chapter surveys a range of examples whereby rivers have been given legal personality or similar rights, seemingly in an effort to uphold human responsibility better to protect them from degradation.

The examples are first drawn from the United States of America, where nature has been given a range of rights, in order to illustrate key rights of nature arguments. Then four examples of rivers in different countries are addressed: the Vilcabamba River in Ecuador, the Whanganui River in Aotearoa New Zealand, the Ganges River in India, and the Atrato River in Columbia. Two of these examples emphasise the rights of the rivers and two emphasise duties and responsibilities, while three of them create a separate legal personality for the river. The tools used to protect each of these rivers are slightly different from each other and they illustrate interesting comparisons and likely lessons, even though they are so very new.

A key lesson from this difference is that rights – including rights for nature – are useful tools, but also, that collective responsibility may be even more useful. All of the examples in this paper can help our societies and their legal systems evolve to protect nature more effectively and engender a greater appreciation of its importance. But explicit frameworks and tools of collective responsibility may provide a clearer path to the paradigm shift that is necessary to better respect humans' role within nature and ecosystems within which we live. Any framework or tool chosen needs to support a paradigm of collective responsibility and should be carefully designed and worded so as not to obscure or distract from that.

United States of America: rights of nature

The modern idea of legal personality and rights for nature most famously arose from Christopher Stone's work in 1972.[5] Stone's proposal was that legal personality should be awarded to all natural objects for better protection of them. Legal personality would enable nature to have rights that could be enforced. Such a legal person would not be considered property of another person, even while other persons would be necessary in order to uphold the rights of the natural object/person. Stone noted that nature would need a guardian, which could be appointed by a court – this could be provided for by legislation and/or enable individuals to apply to court to become guardians, whether on an enduring basis or for any single instance. This would be similar to the way a trustee or guardian is appointed for other purposes in law, such as for a child or other incompetent, a trust, bankruptcy or an estate.[6] This would enable the guardian to speak on behalf of the natural object, particularly before a court but also before administrative decision-makers.

Rights to prevent damage to nature itself could be enforced, as opposed to the current situation where largely only damage to other persons' property interests can be claimed.[7] Thus the natural object can become a beneficiary in its own right,[8] with "rights in substance" requiring procedural safeguards to be enacted to protect these rights.[9] The focus is on rights because that is the way interests were seen as being protected. Notably, Stone's idea arose from a particular resource proposal that was being challenged before a Californian court, and was aimed at persuading the judges in the case.[10] It was thus clearly situated within the United States legal framework and concept of rights and legal standing. Yet it drew on, for example, historical developments of legal persons and the rights, including in Roman times.[11] His ideas are thus more widely applicable than just to the United States legal system.

Some modern examples of declarations of rights of nature in the United States are the result of the work of the Community Environmental Legal Defence Fund (CELDF). CELDF explicitly set out in the 1990s to try to enable communities to exercise more democratic control over their local environmental decision-making. In response to existing problems, they first focused on drafting ordinances to enable communities to ban particular activities of (typically large) corporations in a municipality.[12] They next drafted ordinances that refused to acknowledge any constitutional personhood rights of corporations in the municipality in question.[13]

The third aspect and stage was the drafting of ordinances that included rights for nature, so that citizens could exercise these rights on behalf of the nature in question. This was in line with Christopher Stone's idea of legal standing, to enable humans to step in on behalf of the river or other body of nature to sue for its protection.

For an example, the City of Pittsburgh passed such an ordinance aimed at preventing natural gas fracking within the city's boundaries. It banned such fracking, removed certain rights of corporations and included rights for nature, including rights for the river through the city:[14]

> (b) Rights of Natural Communities. Natural communities and ecosystems, including, but not limited to, wetlands, streams, rivers, aquifers, and other water systems, possess inalienable and fundamental rights to exist and flourish within the City of Pittsburgh. Residents of the City shall possess legal standing to enforce those rights on behalf of those natural communities and ecosystems.

This model has spread widely across the United States.[15] For another example, Santa Monica in California passed an ordinance with similar rights for nature within the city:[16]

> Natural communities and ecosystems possess fundamental and inalienable rights to exist and flourish in the City of Santa Monica. To effectuate those rights on behalf of the environment, residents of the City may bring actions to protect these natural communities and ecosystems, defined as: groundwater aquifers, atmospheric systems, marine waters, and native species within the boundaries of the City.

While these examples focus on enumerating rights of nature, they do not establish a separate legal personality for nature. Instead, the assumption is that, by enumerating the relevant rights, those rights can thereby be protected by humans on nature's behalf. This assumes that someone will step in to protect them, in the face of any threat; so this establishment of rights is a mechanism to *enable* responsibility to be exercised rather than mandating that responsibility or protection *actually* be exercised. It can thus arguably be said to contain a strong statement of responsibility, even though it only assumes that responsibility will be exercised and even though it is predicated on the assumption that people will want to exercise it, now and in the future (which may or may not eventuate). The strength of protection is thus only as strong as the system for protecting these rights. Without other aspects of access to justice (including reasonable cost and representation, for example), a right of standing is not necessarily useful in achieving action. Thus, while these models are predicated on responsibility, this responsibility is implied at least as much if not more than it is expressed, and does not involve legal personality.

Ecuador: rights of the Vilcabamba River

In 2008 Ecuador adopted a new constitution which included a similar concept of rights for nature. Despite being drawn from the United States examples,[17] Ecuador's provisions establishing rights for nature are not the same as the United States ones and go further to explicitly identify duties of human responsibility. Notably, the Ecuadorian provisions are intended to give expression to local and indigenous concepts. In addition, they are a product of the New Latin American Constitutionalism,[18] which has the features of being adopted through a highly participatory process, including that of indigenous and other marginalised peoples, and the inclusion of "very strong statements in favour of nature and ecological diversity".[19]

The Ecuadorian Constitution is explicitly stated to be underpinned by the indigenous concept of *sumak kawsay*:[20]

> We women and men, the sovereign people of Ecuador . . . Hereby decide to build a new form of civil society, and diversity and harmony with nature, to achieve the good way of living (buen vivir), the Sumak Kawsay.

Sumak kawsayis most often translated as living in harmony with nature. It involves more than sustainability, with it also seeing nature as "an inherent part of the social being" and thereby not merely as a product for human use.[21] It is translated into Spanish as *buen vivir*.[22] The Ecuador Constitution provides that buen vivir must be the foundation of a new development model "that is environmentally balanced and respectful of cultural diversity, conserves biodiversity and the natural regeneration capacity of ecosystems."[23] It also upholds "the right of the population to live in a healthy and ecologically balanced environment that guarantees sustainability and good living (*sumak kawsay*)."[24] It is within this context that we find the provisions according rights to nature in the Constitution.

Chapter Seven of Title II of the Ecuador Constitution is titled 'Rights of Nature',[25] where nature is labelled as *Pacha Mama*, which is the Andean indigenous term, similar to 'Mother Earth'. Article 71 provides:[26]

> Nature, or Pacha Mama, where life is reproduced and occurs, has the right to integral respect for its existence and for the maintenance and regeneration of its life cycles, structure, functions and evolutionary processes. All persons, communities, peoples and nations can call upon public authorities to enforce the rights of nature.

In addition to statements of rights, the Ecuadorian Constitution also includes statements of duties to uphold the rights. Article 72 recognises nature's "right to be restored", and that this "restoration shall be independent from the obligation of the State and natural persons or legal entities to compensate individuals and communities that depend on affected natural systems." Article 396 states, "In case of doubt about the environmental impact stemming from a deed or omission, even if there is no scientific evidence of the damage, the State shall adopt effective and timely measures of protection."[27] Giving additional force to article 71, article 83(6) establishes a duty on all Ecuadorian citizens to "respect the rights of nature, preserve a healthy environment and use natural resources rationally, sustainably, and durably".

The Ecuador Constitutional Court has held that rights of nature and buen vivir are central to the Constitution[28] and stated that this reflects[29]

> a biocentric vision that prioritizes Nature in contrast to the classic anthropocentric conception in which the human being is the center and measure of all things, and where Nature was considered a mere provider of resources.

By 2016 there had already been 13 cases involving the application of the constitutional rights of nature provisions.[30] The most famous is that relating to a river: the Vilcabamba River.

In 2008, the Loja Provincial Government dumped rocks and excavation materials from road widening into the Vilcabamba River. This changed the river flow, including causing significant flooding in 2009 and 2010. Two resident United States citizens filed a "protective action" against the Provincial Government "in favour of nature, particularly in favour of the Vilcabamba River".[31] In 2011 the Provincial Court of Loja decided in favour of the plaintiffs for the river.[32]

The Court began by referring to a "democracy of the earth", where Nature has more rights than previously accorded; but also identified the fundamental premises as rights, rather than responsibilities. The Court stated:[33]

> [T]here are some premises that are fundamental to advance what can be identified as the 'democracy of the earth'; [this requires recognising that]: a) individual and collective human rights must be in a relation of harmony with the *rights* of other natural communities in the Earth; b) ecosystems have a *right* to exist and to carry on their vital processes; c) the diversity of life, as expressed in nature, has a value of its own; d) ecosystems have a value independent of their utility to human beings; and e) a legal framework in which ecosystems and natural communities have an *inalienable right* to exist and flourish would situate Nature at the highest level of value and importance.

The Court concluded that the dumping of materials from the road widening violated Nature's rights under article 71. The Court ordered the Provincial Government to prevent any future such dumping and to submit a plan to remedy and rehabilitate the existing damage.[34]

Given the influence of United States rights of nature advocates on the early concepts and drafting of these Ecuadorian rights of nature provisions, it is perhaps not surprising that they have taken a United States approach to emphasising rights more than responsibilities, and emphasising standing before a court as a method to uphold them. It is fitting that the Vilcabamba River case was brought by United

States citizens, given the American familiarity with the use of courts and with standing to enforce and uphold rights.

Yet the Constitution goes further than simple statements of rights, with its statements of duties on the State to adopt measures of protection. It merely does not go so far as to establish any structures or authorities for exercising these duties or adopting such measures, or ensuring that this occurs (apart from the ability for people to go to Court to enforce them).

One aspect that was left to the Court was the balancing of all the rights and needs concerned. The Court in this case balanced the rights of the river with the human needs for the road widening, but no explicit mention was made of the rights of other aspects of nature that might be affected; this was solely about the river and the road widening. Thus, for example, the Provincial Government was allowed to remove (and thereby kill) trees for widening the road, but not dump them in the river. This illustrates how a court may not be the best forum to decide on the balancing of the various rights and needs concerned. If a plaintiff only pleads one set of rights – such as those of a river – other relevant rights may or may not be represented by other plaintiffs or friends of the court; without arguments on any other rights, a court may not be able to properly consider them. This suggests that the role of the court and the rules and practices of the legal system within which it sits will likely determine how effective a court can be when undertaking such assessments of rights.

Aotearoa New Zealand: the Whanganui River as an ancestor

In March 2017 the New Zealand Parliament made a river a legal person and gave it a name, Te Awa Tupua: "Te Awa Tupua is a legal person and has all the rights, powers, duties, and liabilities of a legal person."[35] There are various aspects that are particularly notable about this New Zealand legal entity. One key difference from other examples of legal personality and rights of nature is the vesting of ownership of the riverbed in Te Awa Tupua itself. Another is the creation of statutory guardians to uphold the interests of the river. A third is the recognition of the river's own intrinsic value. Overall, it is an attempt to uphold indigenous rights and an indigenous concept of kinship with and responsibility for the river; yet the focus is responsibility rather than rights.

The Whanganui River – background

The Whanganui River is the longest navigable river in New Zealand, with a length of 290 kilometres, and passes through the traditional territory of a number of Whanganui tribes or iwi.[36] The river is said to be central to the tribes' existence, providing "both physical and spiritual sustenance to Whanganui Iwi from time immemorial."[37] Whanganui iwi regard the river as their tupuna (ancestor), and a belief that the people are inseparable from the river "underpins the responsibilities of the iwi [tribes] and hapū [subtribes] of Whanganui in relation to the care, protection, management and use of the Whanganui River."[38] It is this belief that has given rise to the Whanganui proverb, "Ko au te awa, ko te awa ko au" (I am the river and the river is me).[39]

In February 1840, fourteen indigenous Māori chiefs from various Whanganui iwi signed the Treaty of Waitangi, which included agreement for governance by the Crown in exchange for retaining the possession and control of their lands, estates, forests and fisheries.[40] In the years that followed, despite having never willingly or knowingly relinquished their rights and interests in the Whanganui River, Whanganui iwi, in effect, had both legal and actual control of the river removed from them by the Crown.[41] The Crown assumed ownership and undertook riverbed works, gravel extraction and water diversions for a hydroelectric power scheme.[42] These activities met with strong and persistent opposition from Whanganui iwi, but such objections were largely ignored. Grievances over the river were the subject of petitions to parliament, Royal Commission reports, Waitangi Tribunal claims and numerous court cases between 1938 until 2010.[43] In each case, the Whanganui iwi claimed that they were still the rightful kaitiaki (guardians) of the river and of its mauri (life force), and that the right to control its management should be returned to them. They also argued that the Crown's actions were both in breach of their property rights and in conflict with their cosmology.[44] The mixing and diversion of waters violated the various spirits of the river and undermined the tribes' duties as guardians.[45]

The New Zealand government has been undertaking a programme of settlement of Māori historical grievances since the late 1980s, each of which is given effect by legislation. An agreement in resolution of these grievances between the Whanganui iwi (tribes) and the government was reached in 2012, finalised in 2014 and enacted in 2017.[46] Significantly, this agreement incorporated the legal personification of the river and upheld the spiritual relationship of Whanganui iwi with it.[47]

The river as a legal person: Te Awa Tupua

The Te Awa Tupua Act 2017 created a new legal entity for the river in and of itself, *Te Awa Tupua*.[48] The Act recognises the indivisible connection between the Whanganui iwi and the Whanganui River, as well as the river's metaphysical status as a living being. In section 13, it provides (first in Te Reo Māori and then in English) that[49]

> Te Awa Tupua is an indivisible and living whole, comprising the Whanganui River from the mountains to the sea, incorporating all its physical and metaphysical elements . . . The iwi and hapū of the Whanganui River have an inalienable connection with, and responsibility to, Te Awa Tupua and its health and well-being.

In an effort to implement the Māori perception of the river as a living whole, connected to the Whanganui iwi but incapable of being 'owned' in an absolute sense, the Act grants Te Awa Tupua independent legal personhood. As stated in section 12, "Te Awa Tupua is a legal person and has all the rights, powers, duties, and liabilities of a legal person."[50] This endowment of legal rights and responsibilities enables the river to have legal standing in its own right.

A key feature of the river's legal personhood is the vesting of title to the riverbed in the name of the river itself, Te Awa Tupua.[51] This vesting does not quite fit the traditional Māori cultural conception of the river. First, the riverbed has been separated from the water, and ownership of the water is not included as part of the settlement; the river is thus not legally the indivisible whole that the Whanganui iwi would have liked.[52] In contrast and in its favour, the whole catchment including water is addressed in the definition of Te Awa Tupua and included for management purposes, even if title to it is not vested.

Second, the vesting of fee simple title to a river does not in itself represent traditional Māori concepts of responsibility and control, as they see themselves as "users of something controlled and possessed by gods and forebears".[53] However, such ownership title is said to be as close a fit as can be attained within the concepts of the current legal system.[54] Ownership of the river was "the heart, the core, and the pith of this [Whanganui iwi] claim", and vesting title to the riverbed in the river itself gives practical effect to the perception of the river as being "beyond possession."[55]

Te Awa Tupua Act 2017 embraces the Māori principle of kaitiakitanga (guardianship) in that legal guardians must be appointed to uphold and protect the interests of the Whanganui River. Two persons "of high standing," one appointed by the Crown and one appointed collectively by all tribes with interests in the river are to be the river's kaitiaki (guardians) and must act in the name of Te Awa Tupua.[56] This office of guardianship, called Te Pou Tupua, must "promote and protect the health and wellbeing of Te Awa Tupua," "act and speak on behalf of Te Awa Tupua," and act "in its interests and consistently with Tupua te Kawa [intrinsic values]."[57] While the office of Te Pou Tupua embodies a co-governance arrangement, with both Māori and non-Māori members, its powers enable stronger legal respect for the environment in line with Māori cosmology.

In order to implement responsibility and guardianship, the Act provides for the development of Te Heke Ngahuru, a 'Whole of River Strategy' that addresses and advances the health and well-being of the Whanganui River.[58] It also establishes Te Korotete o Te Awa Tupua, a 'River Fund' of NZD $30 million to support the health and well-being of the river.[59] At earlier stages of the negotiation, this was described as a clean-up fund for the river and the Te Awa Tupua Act allows it to be allocated "on a contestable basis."[60]

Notably, this Act did not make all rivers in Aotearoa New Zealand legal persons, solely this river. As a means of settling indigenous grievances, it is an attempt to uphold justice through upholding indigenous human and community rights. The creation of legal personality, owning title to its own riverbed, with guardians to protect its interests and an emphasis on intrinsic value all represent a significant step for environmental protection.[61] By ensuring that Te Awa Tupua is sufficiently robust, the Crown and iwi have created a powerful and ground-breaking vehicle for the exercise of indigenous responsibility.

India: legal personality and the state as parent

Also in March 2017, the Ganges River and the linked Yamuna River were declared by an Indian court to be legal persons.[62] Ten days after this decision, another decision declared related glaciers and other natural features to be legal persons, in need of protection.[63] While the initial decision is subject to appeal and may not last, both decisions are worthy of discussion for comparison with how the court envisaged responsibility was best implemented, and why and how the concept of legal personality for the rivers contributed to that.

The Ganges River

The Ganges River is the longest river in India and, in terms of water volume, the third largest in the world. The river is critical to the livelihoods of 400 million people who live along it. It provides the main source of drinking water, is used for navigation, bathing and cleaning, harbours fish stocks that play a large part in the local diet, and is also used for electricity generation and irrigation. In addition to its economic uses, the Ganges is considered sacred to Hindus along every fragment of its length. It is the embodiment of all sacred waters in Hindu mythology and is invoked whenever water is used in a Hindu ritual. According to traditional teachings, a dip in the river is thought to cleanse sins, particularly if taken at one of the famous fjords at Gangotri, Haridwar, Prayag or Varanasi.

Unfortunately, the Ganges is also the fifth most polluted river in the world.[64] Pollution in the Ganges threatens more than 140 fish species, 90 amphibious species, the endangered Ganges river dolphin and the stability of the innumerable human settlements along its banks. Today, bathing rituals are still common, especially at the famous fjords; however, in the towns of Varanasi and Prayag (Allahabad), which are further along the river's course, bathing is done at severe risk to human health. The levels of fecal coliform from human waste near Varanasi are more than 100 times the Indian government's official limit and in Allahabad the levels are even worse. With millions of litres of sewerage contaminating the waterways every single day, the water is unfit for bathing. In addition to pollution woes, the Ganges River carries the weight of an extensive network of dams, irrigation projects and tube wells. It is one of the most engineered rivers in the world and roughly 60 per cent of its flow is diverted to large-scale irrigation projects. The Haridwar Dam and others have exacerbated the decay of the Ganges, causing an increase in salinity, a reduction in nutrients, a loss of marshlands and a reduction in estuarine productivity.

Between 1985 and 2000, approximately US$226 million was spent on the Ganga Action Plan, an environmental initiative that was "the largest single attempt to clean up a polluted river anywhere in the world."[65] Despite this ambition, the Ganga Action Plan has since been almost unanimously described as a failure, and even as a major failure. Raw sewage and industrial waste was still flowing into the river years later, even if the amount had been reduced; and the custom of throwing dead bodies into the river still continued. The result was that water taken from the river for drinking and irrigation continued to be contaminated (and still is today).[66]

In December 2009, the World Bank agreed to loan India US$1 billion over the next five years to help clean up the river. In July 2014, the Government of India announced an integrated Ganges development project titled *Namami Ganga*; this would involve the formation of a National Ganga River Basin Authority that would have greater powers than before to plan, implement and monitor measures aimed at cleaning up and protecting the river.[67]

Ganges and Yamuna Rivers in the high court

In 2014, Mohammed Salim, a local resident of Nainital, a small alpine town of 41,377 people, petitioned the High Court, asking it to direct the government of the Himalayan state of Uttarakhand to remove illegal construction along the banks of the Ganges River. He further alleged that the state governments of Uttarakhand and neighbouring Uttar Pradesh were not cooperating with federal government efforts to set up a panel to protect the Ganges. He also sought a direction that the central government better manage land and water resources in the area. He did not petition the Court to grant the river legal status; rather, he was concerned with the issues of federalism, and whether a state, through its judiciary, could order the central government to take steps protect the Ganges River. Interestingly, the case was brought by an individual who lived more than 200 kilometres from the river and was heard by judges in the same location.

The judges decided that constitutional law enabled the state court to make such an order and were very concerned about the destruction and neglect of the rivers.[68] The Court directed that not only should mining of the beds of the Ganga and the Yamuna Rivers be banned immediately and respondents evicted, but also that the central government set up a Ganga management board to better manage the river, as requested. The most significant step taken was a decision that the Ganga and Yamuna Rivers were to become legal entities in their own right:[69]

> The rivers Ganga and Yamuna, all their tributaries, streams, every natural water flowing with flow continuously or intermittently of these rivers, are to be considered as juristic/legal persons/living entities having the status of a legal person with all corresponding rights, duties and liabilities of a living person.

The Court directed that the Director of Namami Gange, the Chief Secretary of the State of Uttarakhand and the Advocate General of the State of Uttarakhand be persons *in loco parentis* as the human face to protect, conserve and preserve the rivers and their tributaries. These officers are bound to uphold the status of rivers Ganges and Yamuna, and also to promote the health and well-being of these rivers. The Court also directed the Advocate General to represent at all legal proceedings to protect the interests of rivers Ganges and Yamuna.

While the petitioner did not argue for legal personhood, the Court gave three reasons in justification for it, as an extraordinary measure. The first was the negligence of the State in not following the previous orders:[70]

> 9. The Court shows its serious displeasure about the manner in which the State of U.P and State of Uttarakhand have acted in this matter. It is a sign of non-governance. We need not remind the State Governments that they are bound to obey the orders passed by the Central Government failing which the consequences may ensue under Article 365 of the Constitution of India. . . .
>
> 10. The . . . Rivers . . . are loosing [sic] their very existence. This situation requires extraordinary measures to be taken to preserve and conserve Rivers Ganga and Yamuna.

The second argument, and clearly more central to the Court's decision, was the constitutional argument that it was necessary to grant the river legal status in order to give effect to the Constitution. Article 48A of the Indian Constitution states that "The State shall endeavour to protect and improve the environment and to safeguard the forests and wild life of the country." Article 51A states that "It shall be the duty of every citizen of India to protect and improve the natural environment including forests, lakes, rivers and wild life, and to have compassion for living creatures." In effect, the judges held that the track record of environmental well-being for the Ganges was so poor that it could be said with some certainty that, unless legal personhood was granted, there was no realistic means by which article 48A can be satisfied and article 51A given effect. They do not comment on why they believe that legal personhood will be better for the health of the Ganges or why it might be the best tool available; rather, it is couched simply as a necessary part of an attempt to resolve such an environmental crisis.

The third reason for legal personhood came from Indian religious law. Indian law accepts that a deity embodied in a stone carving is a juristic person.[71] The Court found that it was consistent with Hindu teaching that the river be a legal person and was prepared to incorporate that into interpretations of Indian common law more generally. As the Court noted:[72]

> All the Hindus have deep Astha (spiritual connection) in rivers Ganga and Yamuna and they collectively connect with these rivers. Rivers Ganga and Yamuna are central to the existence of half of Indian population and their health and well being. The rivers have provided both physical and spiritual sustenance to all of us from time immemorial. Rivers Ganga and Yamuna have spiritual and physical sustenance. They support and assist both the life and natural resources and health and well-being of the entire community. Rivers Ganga and Yamuna are breathing, living and sustaining the communities from mountains to sea.

Thus, "to protect the recognition and the faith of society, Rivers Ganga and Yamuna are required to be declared as the legal persons/living persons."[73]

Himalayas glaciers case[74]

As a result of the Ganges and Yamuna Rivers case, a group of citizens immediately petitioned the same court asking that the "Himalayas, Glaciers, Streams, Water Bodies etc. [be declared] as legal entities as juristic persons at par with pious rivers Ganga and Yamuna." Perhaps unsurprisingly by now, the Court granted such a declaration, with the rights necessary to preserve the entities themselves. It stated,[75]

> We, by invoking our parens patriae jurisdiction, declare the Glaciers including Gangotri & Yamunotri, rivers, streams, rivulets, lakes, air, meadows, dales, jungles, forests wetlands, grasslands, springs and waterfalls, legal entity/legal person/juristic person/juridicial person/moral person/artificial person having the status of a legal person, with all corresponding rights, duties and liabilities of a living person, in order to preserve and conserve them. They are also accorded the rights akin to fundamental rights/legal rights.

Guardians were similarly appointed to the role of upholding the status of these legal persons and to promote their health and well-being.[76] The Court went further, explicitly noting that "the rights of these legal entities shall be equivalent to the rights of human beings and the injury/harm caused to these bodies shall be treated as harms/injury caused to the human beings."[77]

There were three key reasons given for this decision, two legal and one moral. The first legal basis was said to be "the fundamental duty of all the citizens to preserve and conserve" nature, and that "Courts are duty bound to protect the environmental ecology under the 'New Environment Justice Jurisprudence'."[78] These duties were deduced from the importance of the environment, both under Indian mythology as well as more generally.[79] Surveyed were international environmental law[80] and forest rights in Indian culture.[81] Even the New Zealand Te Urewera Act 2014 was mentioned.[82] The Court noted the "grave threat to the very existence of Glaciers, Air, Rivers, rivulets, streams, Water Bodies including Meadows and Dales".[83]

The second legal basis was said to be under the common law doctrine of *parens patriae*. Parens patriae refers to the inherent jurisdiction of the court to enable the state to act as the parent of any child who needs protection. Thus it can be used to require state intervention to intervene against an abusive or negligent parent, for example. While it has been extended beyond children to enable state intervention on behalf of other individuals who need it, it has not before been extended to apply to environmental legal persons. Yet the High Court held that states, within a federal structure, ought to assert parens patriae when their rivers have been polluted or diverted, or their environment has otherwise been harmed.[84]

The moral reason given for granting the declaration was simply the "duty to protect the environment and ecology".[85] The result was the need to "recognise and bestow the Constitutional legal rights to the 'Mother Earth'."[86] These duties and rights were interlinked, with the Court recognising that "Rivers and Lakes have intrinsic right [sic] not to be polluted" and all water bodies "have a right to exist, persist, maintain, sustain and regenerate their own vital ecology system."[87] Indeed, "[t]he rivers are not just water bodies. These are scientifically and biologically living"; they "are unified and are indivisible whole" and their integrity "is required to be maintained from Glaciers to Ocean".[88] The establishment of legal personhood was thought to best enable the rights of and obligations to these elements of nature to be upheld.[89]

These two decisions received a lot of attention, within India and worldwide. There was a lot of positive enthusiasm for the attempt at protection, but there was also concern about the lack of legal precedent for the decisions.[90] The first decision was very quickly appealed to the Supreme Court by the state of Uttarakhand, on the basis that the legal status to the venerated rivers was "unsustainable in the law". In its plea, the state raised a number of concerns about the decision.

One concern was that the High Court ruling did not consider other states where the river flows, and hence it was outside the judicial limits of the state court. The river passes through the states of Uttar Pradesh, Bihar, Jharkhand and West Bengal, as well as through Bangladesh. "Since the matter of cleaning the Ganga is not just restricted to Uttarakhand, as it also flows through West Bengal, how could the Chief Secretary and the Advocate General tackle all the issues related to the river".[91]

A second concern was that it is not enough to say that the rivers must be declared legal persons "to protect the faith of society"; more legal justification is required. A third concern was about unclear implications of legal personality and guardianship, such as whether the custodians or the state government was liable to pay damages to those who drown during floods, in case they file damage suits. Further, it was also likely that the High Court went beyond its jurisdiction in passing the verdict, as no plea was made for declaring the rivers as a living entity; the petitioner had only asked the High Court to remove encroachments.

The Supreme Court put a stay on the High Court decision, apparently agreeing with the concerns raised.[92] However, the first and third concerns could be overcome. For example, even if the river flows through other states, the Uttarakhand authorities could still be directed to clean up the river and activities occurring on it within their jurisdiction. And other implications of rights and liabilities do not all have to be decided in this one case; the common law typically only makes rules for one case and one issue at a time.

The final concern about the lack of a precedent and petition for the legal personality would be the most difficult to overcome. However, even this is not insurmountable, with a request for extra argument on personality and its implications, for example.

Ignoring the possible lack of legal basis or precedent for these Indian decisions, they are extremely helpful for illustrating a method or tool for ensuring human responsibility for nature. They establish legal personality but do not stop there; they also establish a set of legal guardians tasked with ensuring that the interests of the legal persons are upheld. In that sense, despite it being achieved by a court on its own, without the assistance of Parliament, it appears closer to the

New Zealand examples in approach than it does to the Ecuadorian. Even if these examples have been overturned by the Supreme Court, they illustrate a different way of thinking about how we could legally treat nature and organise or structure decision-making bodies to manage human activities to better uphold guardianship and an overarching human responsibility to protect nature.

Colombia: using rights to protect the Atrato River

On the 10th of November 2016, the Colombian Constitutional Court heard an action by the Center of Studies for Social Justice on behalf of community groups living on the Atrato River. Their claim centred on the health of the river and the considerable number of illegal mines in operation along its banks, and argued that the State had an obligation to remove these mining operations. In a novel decision, the Constitutional Court made the orders requested and also went further, recognising the river itself as a legal person with its own rights that needed protecting.

The Atrato River

The Atrato River ecosystem is one of the most biodiverse in the world.[93] It is also home to Afro and indigenous groups, as well as other minorities, and happens to be one of Colombia's poorest and most forgotten areas.[94] Perhaps unsurprisingly, the Atrato River is rife with drug trafficking. It has also been decimated by gold mining since Spanish colonial times.

For several years, alerts by the Afro-Colombian and indigenous communities and their representatives concerning the urgency of the problems in the Atrato region have largely been met with indifference by the Colombian government.[95] The problems have culminated in a significant environmental and humanitarian crisis due to the contamination of the river with toxic substances, erosion, accumulation of waste, deforestation and loss of biodiversity.[96] One of the biggest concerns is the extremely high mercury and cyanide contamination of the Atrato River, which has poisoned the communities living along it.[97]

Against this background, the non-governmental organisation Tierra Digna (Earth Dignity) submitted evidence to the courts that informal mining activities had contributed to an exponential increase of the problems in the region, causing massive and systematic violations of the fundamental rights of the communities. For instance, at least 37 children have died after drinking poisoned water, and at least 64 children have suffered other health consequences of poisoning (short of death).[98] Moreover, diseases such as diarrhoea, dengue and malaria have spread, especially among Afro-descendent communities.[99]

In the absence of an adequate government response to the dire humanitarian situation, Tierra Digna sought a legal decision stopping the use of heavy machinery and toxic chemicals for mining in the Atrato River, arguing that the informal mining activities not only caused irreversible damage to the environment, but also to the human rights of the communities. The government denied responsibility for the human rights violations.

The decision

The Colombian Constitutional Court found that the state authorities had failed to comply with their constitutional obligations to uphold these rights by failing to take concrete and effective measures to stop the illegal mining activities, thereby causing a serious humanitarian and environmental crisis in the river basin of the Atrato River, its tributaries and the surrounding territories. The Court thus decided that the authorities were "responsible for violating the fundamental rights to life, health, water, food security, the environment, the culture and territory of the [claimant] ethnic communities."[100] There are three key types of rights focused on in the decision: individual rights, community rights and "bio cultural" rights. These culminated in the Court recognising the river as a legal entity in its own right, with its own environmental rights. Elaborating on these three types of right in turn:

a The Right of Local Communities to Life, Water and Food

The Court was satisfied that informal mining activities around the river had gravely contaminated and threatened water sources and forests. Whereas water is not explicitly listed as a right in the Constitution, the Court determined that it was a fundamental right[101] and "a sine qua non for the exercise of other rights".[102] Water is essential to a life of dignity, as well as to the existence and preservation of ecosystems, upon which life depends.[103]

Regarding the right to food, the Court determined that the contamination of the river had threatened ethnic communities' access to food and forced them to give up their traditional ways of producing food. The Court concluded that the government was liable for the violation of the rights of the communities.[104] The Court also criticised that government authorities had not coordinated their actions to address the problems.[105]

b Cultural and Territorial Rights

The Court acknowledged that mining activities have had a strong impact on ethnic communities and their territories, generating displacement, elevated school drop-out rates, high levels of violence and prostitution and an erosion of traditional forms of subsistence, including artisanal mining.[106] This has affected communities' rights to physical, cultural and spiritual survival.[107] The mining activities had also imposed a model of development on the communities which is incompatible with their ancestral practices, thereby eroding traditional social structures and traditions.[108]

c Biocultural Rights and Legal Personhood

The Court inferred the concept of biocultural rights into Colombian constitutional law, recognising the direct interdependency between nature, natural resources and the cultures of ethnic communities and indigenous peoples. The Court emphasised that an eco-centric approach to human rights acknowledges that preserving biodiversity is intrinsically linked with the preservation and protection of different forms of human life and cultures.[109]

They held that biocultural rights are the precondition for the rights of ethnic and indigenous communities to exercise territorial autonomy in accordance with their own laws and customs. This includes the right of communities to administer the natural resources in the territories in which they have developed their culture, traditions and their special relationship with the environment and biodiversity.

The judges acknowledged the inherent interdependency between the environment and communities in the Atrato region. The Court accordingly recognised Colombia's Atrato River as a legal entity with environmental rights that need to be protected alongside the communities' biocultural rights. Legal personhood for the river was not at the centre of their decision; rather it was a way of reiterating the duties owed to the indigenous communities of the region including to protect their rights.

Thus rights were entwined with responsibilities; the "central premise" of biocultural rights:[110]

> is the relationship of profound unity and interdependence between nature and human species, and which has as a consequence a new socio-legal understanding in which nature and its environment must be taken seriously and with full rights. That is, as subjects of rights.

From this flow the sources of obligations on the state of protection of the environment.

Court orders

The Court made an order pronouncing the Atrato River itself as a legal subject with specific rights regarding its protection, conservation, maintenance and rehabilitation.[111] It ordered the government to establish a commission of guardians to safeguard the River Atrato; there would be two designated guardians, one from the local communities and one from the government, plus an "advisory team".[112] The role of the commission is to follow up on the protection and restoration that the State must provide for the river.[113] There will be a separate panel of experts for ensuring that the court orders are complied with, who may also "advise the work of the Atrato river guardians".[114]

The Court also ordered the government to take measures to protect the Atrato River and combat illegal mining in the region while taking account of environmental and social realities. The measures to protect the river include developing a clean-up plan, regulating all mining[115] and doing more to tackle illegal mining, including confiscating heavy machinery and prohibiting the use of toxic substances in the river. Perhaps the most unexpected order was one to regulate the gold trade in order to end impunity for corporate actors that have been funding illegal armed groups, drug trafficking or illegal gold mining.[116]

Comment

The Court interpreted the Colombian Constitution widely to strengthen the case for environmental action, but it made no specific orders outlining what that personhood would look like. It also did not specify how the rights of the river would be different from the indirect rights the river already enjoyed as the home of indigenous peoples. The Court acknowledged that its health was already a precondition of the well-being of those peoples. The imbuing of legal status could be said to be a symbolic gesture; a way to give effect to an eco-centric worldview.

Yet it was also arguably more than symbolism. The use of legal personality in this case was considered to be an element of recognising the river's rights, alongside those of the indigenous and other communities that lived along it. The establishment of the commission was seen as a way to ensure that the river and its environment was protected and restored. While it is a clearly labelled focus on rights, it can also be seen as a tool for implementing responsibility to ensure that these rights are respected and the clean-up measures adopted and implemented.

Especially in a country that has a large number and wide range of urgent issues to attend to, yet very limited institutional capacity and few resources to spare, it is essential that the means of upholding such protections is directly addressed and provided for. Given the situation on the ground, including that the Atrato River is located in a jungle where the minimum living standards such as food security, fresh water, energy, health and education are not available, there is still no guarantee that the court orders will be implemented sufficiently. There are enough difficulties in upholding regular laws in cities and municipalities where there is already a strong state institutional presence.[117] The difficulties in achieving this in the Atrato region will be greater, and practical matters such as replacing the livelihoods of the thousands of people that depend on illegal mining around the Atrato River will no doubt feature prominently. Yet, these practical difficulties detract from *any* measure that is proposed to stop the pollution of the river; they are not peculiar to awarding personality for the river. Being based on the recognition of existing rights, this method could well be one that better justifies and enables actions that were not able to be taken under different conceptualisations of the issues and remedies. Whatever the practical realities of upholding rights in the Atrato region, the framing of the state of the river as a matter of human responsibility and guardianship, particularly with appointing people to act as legal guardians, is a big shift in perspective as well as law. With the accompanying focus on biocultural rights, together they lay the foundation for a shift in mind-set and practice.

Conclusion

This chapter has illustrated the wide range of ways responsibility for rivers has been implemented using novel methods such as legal personhood and/or recognising rights of the river. These two techniques have not been seen as contradictory but mostly as genuine flip sides of the same coin, with both being necessary for the river's protection. What this survey and discussion has shown is that the biggest difference between the different examples is in the legal basis and justification for according personality and/or rights, with the second key difference being in the method for ensuring that responsibility is upheld.

In terms of rights, the legal bases include upholding human rights, but the human rights concerned have ranged from being separately recognised rights such as indigenous justice and reparations in New Zealand, to newer rights to a healthy environment, as in Colombia. In addition to human rights, an alternative basis found in some examples is inherent rights of the river, such as "to exist, thrive and evolve" (in the United States and Ecuador).

In contrast, the Indian decisions are not based on upholding human rights but on the constitutional duties to protect the environment. The closest human rights came into the decision was the spiritual connection argument for awarding personality to a deity.

Spiritual reverence for the (respective) river was recognised in Ecuador, New Zealand and India. This is particularly new in terms of being recognised in law, and is perhaps the biggest aspect of a shift in consciousness about a new relationship with the natural world. Regarding the river as an ancestor or a deity entails a completely different relationship and mind-set from considering it purely as a source of ecosystem services. It is this difference which particularly illustrates the difference between focusing on rights or on responsibilities. An ancestral relationship emphasises that we are duty-bound to care for nature as we would our grandparents. We do not talk about grandparents having rights to be cared for by their offspring as much as we talk about our familial responsibilities toward grandparents to care for them.

It is certainly true that, in rights-based legal systems, respect and responsibility are acknowledged through human rights. It is also true that one method for reordering the priority between humans and the environment is to recognise in law inherent rights of nature to exist and function. But at least the New Zealand and Indian examples were designed to better implement our *responsibilities* to protect and care for them. Parens patriae is the doctrine of responsibility of the State more than it is the right of the child.

The next key aspect of difference between the examples is the method of ensuring that responsibility is upheld. Ecuador and the United States have left it to the courts to enforce rights of nature, even while there are stated duties to uphold them, as in the Ecuador Constitution. In contrast, the New Zealand, Indian and Colombian examples all required the creation of a guardian in order to look after the interests of the river, including overseeing any necessary clean-up. Such guardianship is designed to ensure that all activities affecting the river are monitored, and at all stages the interests of the river are upheld by a body appointed to do just that. It doesn't leave the protection of these interests to the chance that a person might want to take a role as guardian on behalf of the river, such as by asserting standing in court. It requires the exercise of this role at all times and allows it to be exercised in other fora, not solely courts. Admittedly, operationalising and implementing eco-centric conceptions of legal personhood present a challenge for developing countries such as India, Ecuador and Colombia. However, mandating the establishment of a body to undertake guardianship over the longer term is likely to be more effective than ad hoc orders to ensure compliance with court orders, even if such orders are essential in their own right.

Another key difference between the examples in this chapter is the method of creating legal personality for nature. The enactment in a statute or an ordinance, or even a constitution, can establish the parameters of legal personality, or define its relevant rights more comprehensively, than can a court hearing a set of arguments on one particular pleading. Admittedly, the court decisions discussed in this chapter have been very wide-ranging, with the possibility of comprehensive definitions of rights; but the wider they range, the more they open themselves up to challenge. One advantage the statutory enactment for Te Awa Tupua has over the court decisions is that Parliament was able to vest Te Awa Tupua with title to its own riverbed, transferring that from the state-owned title. I imagine that not many countries' courts would be able to do that on their own.

An additional factor in favour of statutory recognition is the democratic mandate that it can give. This admittedly varies between countries, as does the longevity of a statute compared with a court decision. But it should be considered as a factor to use to compare the merits or otherwise of each approach in any particular country. For example, while the aim of enforcing responsibility for protection of the river is to be lauded, the Indian High Court decisions possibly illustrate the difficulty in going too far outside accepted norms of a judge's role.

Overall, I suggest that these embodiments in law of responsibility and care reflect an approach that could usefully be expanded throughout our law. What will be best for any particular country is the method that will best fit the domestic legal and political system. But even with that in mind, there are certain aspects and features of the examples discussed in this chapter that appear to better engender responsibility and care for our natural world.

The Ecuadorian and Colombian examples show that rights are a powerful tool, to be exercised within a system that understands the language and power of rights. But we need to ensure that the rights are accorded appropriate weight and are upheld in fact, not just on paper. For that, I suggest that we need the mind-set that comes with guardianship and responsibility, such that guardians are appointed more generally, not just to oversee individual judgments, for example.

The Aotearoa New Zealand examples show that such guardianship and responsibility can be articulated in legislation and standing guardian bodies can be established to uphold duties of care for nature on an ongoing basis, not just ad hoc as issues arise. The Indian examples show that courts might be able to do this themselves, if done to uphold constitutional protections, whether on the basis of the protection of a religious deity and/or also as part of the inherent common law jurisdiction of parens patriae.

Being so new and different, these examples appear revolutionary. They are arguably not revolutionary in their own right. Legal personhood is not new to law, nor is state guardianship. They are evolutionary in the way that they have arisen: all have been built on existing examples, such as of the grievance settlement history in New Zealand, and the existing common law in India, or the human rights in Colombia. They are also evolutionary in the way that they will be inserted into the mainstream legal and political systems. They suggest ways in which future law could evolve, such as ways in which structures of responsibility could be implemented.

Yet, what is revolutionary is that these examples arise from a different worldview or paradigm, one that adopts a relationship of respect for the earth and its natural systems. Adopting even individual elements of personhood and guardianship in law can help shift mind-sets and practices towards such a different paradigm. This can help the legal framework evolve accordingly, whereby societies better recognise the central role of nature and a respectful place of humans within it. Implementing responsibility in such ways currently involves pushing past the boundaries of our own existing cultural limitations and legal systems. This should in turn move these boundaries towards new paradigms of reordered relationships between humans and nature, which could be truly revolutionary.

Notes

* Many thanks are due to my research assistant Thomas Stuart for his help, especially when it involved translation.

1 See, for example, United States Geological Survey Water Science School "The World's Water" <https://water.usgs.gov/edu/earthwherewater.html>. Rivers are also essential for the health of the ecosystems that they serve. For comprehensive information on water worldwide, see, for example, United Nations Water: <www.unwater.org/>.

2 See, for example, United Nations Water "Water Quality" <www.un.org/waterforlifedecade/quality.shtml>. For information on the state of animal life within fresh water bodies worldwide, see, for example, the WWF Living Planet Report 2016, available at <http://wwf.panda.org/about_our_earth/all_publications/lpr_2016/>.

3 One example is Te Awa Tupua Act 2017, s 12 (New Zealand) <www.legislation.govt.nz>.

4 See, for example, Mari Margil "The Standing of Trees: Why nature needs legal rights," (2017) 34(2) *World Policy Journal* 8 at 9–10.

5 Christopher Stone "Should Trees Have Standing? Toward Legal Rights for Natural Objects" (1972) 45 *Southern California Law Review* 450.

6 Ibid. at 464.

7 Ibid. at 475–476.

8 Ibid. at 480–481.

9 Ibid. at 483–484.

10 See Stone's book about, and update of, his 1972 article: Christopher Stone *Should Trees Have Standing? Law, Morality, and the Environment* (3rd ed, Oxford University Press, New York, 2010) at xiii–xiv. The case in question was *Sierra Club v. Morton* 405 US 727 (1972).

11 Stone, "Should Trees Have Standing", above n 5, at 451.

12 Thomas Linzey "Of Corporations, Law, and Democracy: Claiming the Rights of Communities and Nature" (25th Annual EF Schumacher Lectures, Stockbridge, MA, October 2005).

13 Ibid. at 10.

14 City of Pittsburgh, The Pittsburgh Code, Title Six, Art. 1, Ch. 618.3(b) <www.harmonywithnatureun.org/content/documents/203Ordinance-Pittsburgh—.pdf>. This was

passed by the Pittsburgh City Council in November 2010, as part of a ban on fracking within the city.

15 See, for example, the list of United States Environmental Provisions at <www.harmonywithnatureun.org >.

16 City of Santa Monica, Santa Monica Municipal Code, Ch 4.75 ('Sustainability Rights Ordinance'), 4.75.040(b) <www.harmonywithnatureun.org >.

17 See, for example, Mari Margil "Stories from the Environmental Frontier" in Peter Burdon (ed) *Exploring Wild Law: The Philosophy of Earth Jurisprudence* (Wakefield Press, Adelaide, 2011) at 249, noting that CELDF was invited to Ecuador by the then president, on the basis of their rights for nature work in the United States. They assisted in drafting some provisions which eventually became adopted by Constituent Assembly. See also Linzey, above n 12.

18 As described by Joel Colón-Ríos: "The NLAC is usually identified, and in a way defined, by the new wave of constitution-making that took place in Latin America at the end of the 20th century and at the beginning of the 21st. More specifically, it is exemplified by the constitutions of Venezuela, Ecuador and Bolivia, adopted in 1999, 2008 and 2009 respectively" and "the Colombian Constitution of 1991". Joel Colón-Ríos, "The Rights of Nature and the New Latin American Constitutionalism" (2015) 13 *NZJPIL* 107 at 108–109.

19 Ibid. at 109.

20 Preamble, Constitution of Ecuador 2008.

21 Mónica Chuji, Amazonian Kichwa leader and spokesperson for CONAIE (Ecuador's indigenous peoples' alliance), as cited in Craig Kauffman *Grassroots Global Governance* (Oxford University Press, New York, 2017) at 188.

22 *Buen vivir* literally translated refers to the good life, or good living; but it means more than that in the Ecuador constitutional and legal context and instead includes these indigenous concepts of living in harmony with nature. The Constitution provides that buen vivir "requires that individuals, communities, peoples and nations . . . exercise their responsibilities in the context of interculturalism, respect for diversity and of harmonious coexistence with nature". Republic of Ecuador Constitution 2008, Art. 275.

23 Ecuador Constitution – Title VII.

24 Ecuador Constitution – Title II, Art. 14.

25 Ecuador Constitution – Title II, Ch7, Arts. 71–73.

26 The official (Spanish) version of Art. 71 reads: "La naturaleza o Pacha Mama, donde se reproduce y realiza la vida, tiene derecho a que se respete integralmente su existencia y el mantenimiento y regeneración de sus ciclos vitales, estructura, funciones y procesos evolutivos. Toda persona, comunidad, pueblo o nacionalidad podrá exigir a la autoridad pública el cumplimiento de los derechos de la naturaleza. Para aplicar e interpretar estos derechos se observaran los principios establecidos en la Constitución, en lo que proceda. El Estado incentivará a las personas naturales y jurídicas, y a los colectivos, para que protejan la naturaleza, y promoverá el respeto a todos los elementos que forman un ecosistema."

27 For more information, see, e.g., Joel Colón-Ríos "Notes on the Theory and Practice of the Rights of Nature: The Case of the Vilcabamba River" in Martin and others (eds) *In Search of Environmental Justice* (Edward Elgar, Cheltenham, 2015) at 120.

28 Corte Constitucional del Ecuador, May 20 2015, as cited in Colón-Ríos, ibid.

29 Ibid.

30 Craig M. Kauffman and Pamela L. Martin "Testing Ecuador's Rights of Nature: Why Some Lawsuits Succeed and Others Fail" (Paper presented at the International Studies Association Annual Convention Atlanta, GA, March 18, 2016) (copy on file with author).

31 The *acción de protección* is provided in the Constitution of Ecuador in order to remedy a violation of rights that has already occurred. Article 88 provides that it is "aimed at ensuring the direct and efficient safeguard of the rights enshrined in the Constitution".

32 Juicio No: 11121–2011–0010.

33 These statements, originally published in the website of the National Constituent Assembly of Ecuador (29 February 2008) were then reproduced in *Peripecias* No 87 (5 March 2008). As cited in Joel Colón-Ríos "The Rights of Nature and the New Latin American Constitutionalism" (2015) 13 *NZJPIL* 107 at 111 (emphasis added).

34 At the time of writing this chapter, it is unclear whether the Court's orders have been fully complied with, even five years later. Colon-Rios noted in 2015 that they had not been:

> For example, although it initially presented a Remediation and Rehabilitation Plan, this document was determined to be insufficient by the Ministry of the Environment. This has caused several non-governmental organisations to rightly request the full implementation of the judgment. (citation omitted) Colon-Rios, above n 27 (re Vilcabamba River).

35 Te Awa Tupua (Whanganui River Claims Settlement) Act 2017, s14. <www.legislation.govt.nz>. Note that this is the second time that the New Zealand Parliament has made a legal person out of nature, having done so for Te Urewera in 2014, which had been a listed National Park for the previous 60 years: "Te Urewera is a legal entity, and has all the rights, powers, duties, and liabilities of a legal person". Te Urewera Act 2014, s 11 <www. legislation.govt.nz>.

36 David Young "Whanganui Tribes" *Te Ara: The Encyclopedia of New Zealand* <https://teara.govt.nz/>.

37 Waitangi Tribunal *Ko Aotearoa Tēnei: A Report into Claims Concerning New Zealand law and Policy Affecting Māori Culture and Identity* (Wai 262, 2011) at 269.

38 Te Awa Tupua (Whanganui River Claims Settlement) Act 2017, s 69(1)–(2).

39 Section 69(3).

40 Treaty of Waitangi 1840.

41 Te Awa Tupua (Whanganui River Claims Settlement) Act 2017, ss 69(5) and (7).

42 Section 96(9).

43 Section 69(5).

44 Section 70(d).

45 *Ngati Rangi Trust v. Manawatu Wanganui Regional Council* NZEnvC Auckland A 67/04, 18 May 2004 at [318].

46 Office of Treaty Settlements *Whanganui Iwi (Whanganui River) Deed of Settlement* (2014); Te Awa Tupua (Whanganui River Claims Settlement) Act 2017.

47 Te Awa Tupua Act 2017, s 69(2).

48 Ibid., section 14.

49 Ibid., section 13.

50 Ibid., section 12.

51 Ibid., section 41.

52 For political reasons, the government would not allow the water itself to be the subject of ownership under the settlement agreement.

53 Waitangi Tribunal, *The Whanganui River Report* (Wai 167, 1999) at 35.

54 Ibid. at 35.

55 Ibid. at 332.

56 Te Awa Tupua Act 2017, s 18.

57 Ibid., section 19.

58 Ibid., section 36.

59 Ibid., section 57.

60 Ibid., section 59.

61 Ibid., section 13.

62 *Mohammed Salim v. State of Uttarakhand* (March 20, 2017), Writ Petition (PIL) No. 126 of 2014, High Court of Uttarakhand <http://lobis.nic.in/ddir/uhc/RS/orders/22-03-2017/RS20032017WPPIL1262014.pdf>.

63 *Miglani v. State of Uttarakhand* (March 30, 2017), Writ Petition PIL No. 140 of 2015, High Court of Uttarakhand at Nainital <www.livelaw.in>.
64 See, for example, "Pollution of the Ganges", *Wikipedia* <https://en.wikipedia.org/wiki/Pollution_of_the_Ganges>.
65 "Journey of River Ganga, From Purest to the Dirtiest River of the World", *India TV News Desk*, 19 October 2014 <www.indiatvnews.com/news/india/river-ganga-purest-river-dirtiest-river-37927.html?page=7>.
66 See, for example, George Black "What It Takes to Clean the Ganges" *The New Yorker* (online ed, 25 July 2016) <www.newyorker.com/magazine/2016/07/25/what-it-takes-to-clean-the-ganges>.
67 See, for example, "Pollution of the Ganges", above n 64; see also Black, above n 66.
68 *Salim* above n 62, at 4 [9]. On certain subjects within the federal structure of the Indian Constitution, the states are supreme in their field, and water is one of the most important such areas.
69 Ibid. at 11 [19].
70 Ibid. at 4.
71 Under that law, anybody who knowingly defaces a temple or the idols within can face up to two years in prison. See, for example, the 1999 case of *Ram Jankijee Deities v. State of Bihar* at 14, 16 and 19.
72 *Salim*, above n 62, at 11.
73 Ibid.
74 *Miglani v. State of Uttarakhand* (March 30, 2017), PIL No. 140 of 2015, High Court of Uttarakhand at Nainital <www.livelaw.in>.
75 *Miglani*, Direction 2, at 64.
76 *Miglani*, Direction 3, at 64–65.
77 *Miglani*, Direction 5, at 65.
78 Ibid. at 42.
79 Ibid. at 9–11.
80 Ibid. at 17–36.
81 Ibid. at 36–41.
82 Ibid. at 42.
83 Ibid.
84 Ibid. at 42–59.
85 Ibid. at 59.
86 Ibid. at 61.
87 Ibid.
88 Ibid.
89 Ibid. at 62.
90 It must be noted that the primary judge in question, Hon Rajiv Sharma, has a reputation throughout northern India for controversially liberal judgments, and has delivered many landmark judgments in his decade on the bench. These have included a complete ban on animal sacrifice in religious places and the granting of ancestral property rights to tribal girls, allowing them to inherit property in accordance with the Hindu Succession Act. Justice Sharma prescribes to the Dworkin school of thought, whereby the law is branch of morality, rather than more traditional approaches which envisage judges as mere interpreters, such as of rules created by parliament. The relationship between morality and law is mentioned in *Miglani*, above n 74, at 59–60.
91 Uttarakhand state government spokesperson Madan Kaushik. It is noted that the Ganges is a trans-boundary river; it winds through a number of Indian states, has tributaries coming in from Nepal, and is one of Bangladesh's major rivers (where it is called the Padma).
92 Bench of Chief Justice J.S. Khehar and Justice D.Y. Chandrachud, 7 July 2017. See, for example, <http://timesofindia.indiatimes.com/india/sc-stays-uttrakhand-hc-order-declaring-ganga-yamuna-as-living-entities/articleshow/59494002.cms>. A written judgment was not available at the time of writing this chapter.

93 *Tierra Digna v. Republic of Colombia* (10 November 2016), Constitutional Court, T-622 of 2016, at 2.
94 Ibid. at 4.
95 Ibid. at 6–7.
96 The decision details the evidence of effects of the mining and other activities on pp 107–122, with pictures at 126–130. For a popular summary in English, with pictures, see for example, Bram Ebus "Colombia's constitutional court grants rights to the Atrato River and orders the government to clean up its waters" 22 May 2017, Mongabay.com: <https://news.mongabay.com/2017/05/colombias-constitutional-court-grants-rights-to-the-atrato-river-and-orders-the-government-to-clean-up-its-waters/>.
97 *Tierra Digna*, above n 93, at 5. Evidence was that Colombia has the highest amount of mercury used in gold mining in Latin America. Ibid. at 96–97.
98 Ibid. at 6.
99 Ibid.
100 Ibid. at 131 [own translation]. Original text: "Conclusión. Las autoridades estatales demandadas son responsables de la vulneración de los derechos fundamentales a la vida, a la salud, al agua, a la seguridad alimentaria, al medio ambiente sano, a la cultura y al territorio de las comunidades étnicas demandantes por su conducta omisiva al no realizar acciones efectivas para detener el desarrollo de actividades mineras ilegales, que han generado la configuración de grave crisis humanitaria y ambiental en la cuenca del río Atrato (Chocó), sus afluentes y territorios aledaños."
101 Ibid. at 64.
102 Ibid. at 135–136.
103 Ibid. at 135–136.
104 Ibid. at 141.
105 Ibid.
106 Ibid. at 142.
107 Ibid. at 142–143.
108 Ibid.
109 Ibid. at 133.
110 Ibid. at 137. The original text at [9.28] reads: "derechos bioculturales, cuya premisa central es la relación de profunda unidad e interdependencia entre naturaleza y especie humana, y que tiene como consecuencia un nuevo entendimiento socio-jurídico en el que la naturaleza y su entorno deben ser tomados en serio y con plenitud de derechos. Esto es, como sujetos de derechos."
111 Ibid. at 158. Original text: "CUARTO.- RECONOCER al río Atrato, su cuenca y afluentes como una entidad sujeto de derechos a la protección, conservación, mantenimiento y restauración a cargo del Estado y las comunidades étnicas".
112 Ibid. at 158–159: "los dos guardianes designados y un equipo asesor".
113 Ibid. at 154.
114 Ibid. at 159: "Sin perjuicio de lo anterior, el panel de expertos que se encargará de verificar el cumplimiento de las órdenes de la presente providencia (orden décima) también podrá supervisar, acompañar y asesorar las labores de los guardianes del río Atrato."
115 This regulation includes a requirement to make sure that all legal mining projects strictly comply with the obligation of consulting with communities potentially affected by a planned activity.
116 *Tierra Digna*, above n 93, at 160.
117 For example, despite the fact that the constitution and other Colombian laws aim to protect human rights and individual freedom, indigenous leaders and journalists are still often the targets of killings and death threats in Colombia. Colombia also continues to appear in the top of International Amnesty and Human Rights Watch indexes for corruption and lawlessness.

15 Making law

Gerald Torres

Because I am a lawyer there can be little doubt that the lens through which I view most things is distorted by that training. Training in law requires (I suspect like most disciplines) the capacity to hold multiple mutually exclusive ideas in your head at the same time. For example, every law student knows that a house can be legally haunted despite the non-existence of ghosts.[1] Similarly, every first-year student learns to plead in the alternative: (1) I do not have a dog; (2) he did not bite you; (3) you kicked him first. In describing the "legal mind", famous legal scholar and lawyer Thurman Arnold once said, quoting Thomas Reed Powell, "If you think that you can think about a thing inextricably attached to something else without thinking of the thing which it is attached to, then you have a legal mind."[2] We must commonly do that and it produces not only a kind of psychological unease at first, but, and perhaps this is worse, the dissipation of that unease.

As the training takes hold, a strange thing happens. You forget what you know and you start to believe that imagined things are real and that things are the way they are because they *had* to be that way. Instead of recognizing the inherent contingency of life and of the institutions that structure social life, that contingency is boiled away even as this abstract mindset permits the expression of new forms of creativity that are prized.[3] The comedy of regulating lived life based on the make believe is lost on most people, but perhaps especially on people who give their lives over to legal training.

The deleterious effect of this process of abstraction is that the social and historical contingency that makes change possible remains hidden behind a screen of false necessity. Of course, most people believe that the world is as it is because it could be no other way (or for the religious, that it is the expression of some unknowable grand plan). Yet the belief in the necessity of certain social states of being is especially debilitating for the idea of democratic agency that lies at the core of the legitimacy of the modern democratic state.[4]

One of the problems for democratic society is that if institutions are abstracted from the people both who created and who run them, responsibility for the consequences of institutional action seems to exist nowhere. It is as if the institutions operated according to the laws of nature, like gravity, rather than according to human social convention or rules. Of course, constitutional institutions are the substrate on which all other institutions of governance rest. The meaning of constitutional powers and limitations (I will discuss those more later) is where the most serious political contestation occurs. Social contestation, what my colleague Sid Tarrow calls *contentious politics*, is where we make and remake our social life and write or rewrite our political commitments. This process affects all our social and political institutions, including courts and other formal venues for law making. One consequence of recognizing this is it requires legal theory to accommodate legal change that is made outside of the formal mechanisms that typically govern legal changes. There is great resistance to this idea because there is no generally agreed upon moment when it can be said with assurance that this or that activity outside of the formal processes has made law. Retrospect can provide the evidence and the guidance, but not the predictability.

Among legal scholars and those who attend to the ways in which legal institutions channel the popular understanding of the relationship between law and politics, the idea that "the people" can produce real legal changes outside of the normal institutional pathways is often considered deeply troubling. One of the problems, of course, is that for many commentators "the people" works well as a metaphor but not as description. "The people" as an empirical reality are difficult to categorize, their passions are messy, their ideological commitments fractious, their respect for authority is often both too strong and too weak. Yet, "the people" cannot just be metaphor in a political system predicated on consent. The solution to this problem has always been to rely on elites to channel the passions of the mob through the structures of institutionalized decision-making in order to make their desires politically intelligible. Structurally, this is the constitutional method for domesticating politics, for keeping the distinction between law and politics clear.

When conversations begin over the relationship between law and politics, there is always the tacit understanding that there is "law" and then there is "politics". No one really believes that there is a hermetic seal separating one discourse from the other, only that law should not *just* be politics. Of course, discourse is not just a way of talking – a discourse is the whole ensemble of activities that constitutes a subject and which derives its power by what it can exclude. Thus, the rhetorical move to logically separate law from politics serves a specific end. The domain of law can be insulated from politics understood as partisan claims as well as the rhetorical moves associated with ordinary politics. Within this discourse, law is the precipitate of politics and the conventional story is that only those passions that survive the formal institutional gauntlet to enactment are worthy of being called law. That story, as everyone knows, is radically incomplete. Yet it continues to exert some power both in the realm of ordinary law and in the realm of constitutional law. After all, the constitution is not only the operating system through which we constitute ourselves as a people, it is also the backstop that prevents popular passions of the majority from running roughshod over the minority.

Constitutional democracy as we have understood it is premised in this context on a liberal constitution and a liberal democracy. The thin version of that idea is that both the constitution and the democracy that it constitutes grants priority to the right over the good as well as recognizing the formal equality of all members of the polity. Democracy is supposed to protect the plurality of the good and politics is the forum where that struggle over the good is supposed to take place.

Surely, the role of mobilization and engagement through contentious politics cannot merely be to tee things up for the formal actors. Instead, correctly understood, contentious politics are a means through which the actions of the formal players are constrained. To this extent, the discourse constructed through the process of social movements creates the conditions within which laws can be made and, to the extent that they reframe the justifications for formal action, social movements can themselves create law. I recognize that is a complex and contestable claim, but without wanting to rehearse the varieties of ways that law can be made it seems indisputable that if social movements limit or expand the range of acceptable interpretations available to formal legal actors they have, in fact, made law. It may not have the crisp edges of a rule, but that is not a dispositive inquiry.

Nonetheless, the possibility of the people making law unmediated by democratic institutions is terrifying to democratic theorists even if popular sovereignty is the bedrock of legitimacy. The constitution modulates this possibility and quiets the fear. Whether it should is one of the questions that popular social movements ask. If the people themselves can make ordinary law, can they make constitutional changes as well? The framers of the constitution purposely made it hard to amend. Nevertheless, as Bruce Ackerman has demonstrated, the people themselves can amend the constitution in ways other than the formal processes contained in the operating system. Yet, this untethered power revives that fear. Constitutional scholar Reva Siegel puts the fear this way:

> There is reticence to analyze these pathways of responsiveness as providing goods we expect formal constitutional lawmaking to provide, because we see no ground to distinguish licit from illicit forms of constitutional change, in the absence of any procedure or metric for measuring democratic will. Without such criteria, it is easier to conceive of such pressures as threats to the Constitution's democratic legitimacy than as sources of it. Thus, even as Americans regularly mobilize to shape the ways that officials enforce the Constitution's commitments, Americans are deeply ambivalent about acknowledging the influence of movements on constitutional meaning.[5]

The contradictions in that characterization are troubling, because it is precisely constitutional meaning that is at stake in the most important moments of social contestation. We are always constituting and reconstituting ourselves as a people. American history in particular, but perhaps most of modern world history, is replete with popular efforts to shape a nation's constitutional commitments. We are in one of those moments now. It is a particularly fraught moment because it arises when questions of nationhood have supplanted questions of the state and its role. It is an old story, usually told at ceremonial gatherings, that the United States arose from a commitment to capacious liberal ideas of political community rather than being an expression of a particular ethnic idea. Perhaps that is why Walt Whitman's *Song of Myself* may come closest to an America epic poem. We have no *Iliad*, *Aeneid*, *Beowulf*, *Gilgamesh*, or *Song of Roland*.

We know what Whitman means when he says, "For every atom belonging to me as good belongs to you. . . . I am large, I contain multitudes." He is speaking the voice of Americans, as he understood it. It a capacious vision, muscular and spiritual at once. Published just before the war that would rend the country, the poem was already looking towards the essence of our reconstitution, which would be found not in some preexisting ethno-nationalist identity, but in an amalgam of selves that would confirm the motto *e pluribus unum* and which would be reconstituted in Lincoln's Gettysburg Address.

These moments and sentiments lead us to consider what binds us together. The law laces us together. It provides a way through the partial visions that hobble us all. Constitutional law, however, is not the only law that matters. The people can change the law at all levels and, as I will argue, it is through the contentious politics of social movements that this law making occurs. My argument will proceed in the following way. First, I will propose a version of what Professors Siegel and Post call *constitutional culture*. Constitutional culture has a thick version, a thin version, and perhaps a liberal version and an illiberal version. We have seen one expression of a thin version of the illiberal concept in the attempted implementation of an immigrant ban and perhaps a thick liberal version in the judicial repudiation of that ban. More importantly, we have seen a thick illiberal version in the administration's construction of the idea of a unitary executive with extensive plenary power and a liberal version of constitutional culture in resistance to that idea by ascribing constitutional meaning to presidential speech.

Second, I will describe what I mean by law. My version is in opposition to many of the brute positivist ideas of law and takes seriously the notion that law is the expression of bounded social consensus that is both fixed and fluid. Thus, contingency of social institutions as well as the felt fixity of institutional systems make law both real and indeterminate. It is a version of law that does not need a sovereign and thus despite the coercive power of existing institutions we should not mistake their power for legitimacy. Nonetheless, as Professor Rosaldo once said to me in conversation, the fact that witches do not exist is meaningless to the witch who is being burned at the stake.

Third, I want to describe social movements and suggest the ways in which such movements create law. Social movement theory is vast and conflicting. While I base my accounts on the literature, I also base them on experience with movements and my experience as an activist. Out of this experience, my frequent co-author Lani Guinier and I have developed the concept of demosprudence, which we define as the study of law making by the people. This kind of law making entails both formal and informal methods reflecting the various interpretive methodologies that govern our legal system and which account for the fundamental indeterminacy that is at the heart of law.

Professor Bruce Ackerman has written a magisterial account of constitutional amendment by concerted social movement activism validated through statute and elections. As we wrote of Professor Ackerman's work, We The People:

> Our essay largely agrees with this aspect of Professor Ackerman's book: it is the people in combination with the legal elite who change the fundamental normative understandings of our Constitution. We argue that social movements are critical not only to the changes Professor Ackerman chronicles, but

> also to the cultural shifts that make durable legal change possible. We believe that the role played by social movement activism is as much a source of law as are statutes and judicial decisions. Our goal, therefore, is to create analytic space to enable a greater understanding of lawmaking as the work of mobilized citizens in conjunction with, not separate from, legal professionals.[6]

If this account of law making is accurate, we are in an especially critical time. Resistance is thus not just opposition, but certification of an existing constitutional understanding that is under assault. Resistance is also the repudiation of an ethno-nationalist construction of the state and its various illiberal tendencies.

Constitutional culture

According to Professor Siegel, "[c]onstitutional culture mediates the relation of law and politics."[7] The nature of the mediation is crucial. In a recent lecture, Professor Siegel proposed two different visions of constitutional culture. The first views law as a mere reflection of the norms of the polity. The second entails a view of the law that reflects an understanding that is shared by professionals as well as non-professionals. In many ways, this distinction is captured in an historic dispute over the meaning of *Brown v. Board of Education*. One of, or perhaps the, leading constitutional lawyer of the time declared the decision lawless. Yet the response of another, in my view one of the most profound constitutional scholars, reflects the second view of constitutional culture. In defending Brown against the charge of lawlessness, Professor Charles Black said simply:

> If the cases outlawing segregation were wrongly decided, then they ought to be overruled. One can go further: if dominant professional opinion ever forms and settles on the belief that they were wrongly decided, then they will be overruled, slowly or all at once, openly or silently. The insignificant error, however palpable, can stand, because the convenience of settlement outweighs the discomfort of error. But the hugely consequential error cannot stand and does not stand.[8]

It is in the confluence of a popular view of the meaning of the constitution (popular, though highly contentious) and the dominant professional view that social dispute is viewed as capable of being integrated into the meaning of the constitution. We see this phenomenon happening right now.

Of course, the anti-immigrant, anti-birthright citizenship movement is not new; it is, however, part of the nativist tradition that was engrafted onto the original constitution. That is what gives it the weight of historical and professional pedigree. Yet, it has been, at least since the end of the Second World War and certainly by the middle of the Great Society, the minority professional opinion even as it has garnered wide popular support. The question of constitutional culture in this moment is which view of constitutional culture will prevail. The decisions enjoining enforcement of the immigrant bans promulgated through executive order have channeled the nativist anti-immigrant bias of the current administration through a broader understanding of acceptable constitutional argument. That is why the president's speech (through tweets and otherwise) are held to have a legal rather than merely a political dimension. It is not just that words matter, but that specific kinds of words matter in particular ways. Just as *Brown v. Board of Education* was not about "freedom of association," the ban on immigrants from specific countries is not about "keeping America safe." It implicates norms of religious liberty that nativists themselves are constrained to recognize or to mount a campaign against. We are seeing elements of both activities in the rhetoric surrounding the effort to exclude a subset of immigrants and refugees.

The campaign against Mexicans has a different constitutional valence. It is tied up both with naked nativist and white supremacist rhetoric but also with norms of trade, crime, family values, and economic nationalism. The constitutionality of this ideological stew really does implicate notions of constitutional culture. Which arguments are deemed to have valid legal and not just political weight? Which political arguments are most likely to be convertible to legal arguments? The arguments over the plenary authority of the president loom large because the constitution is mute and the exercise of what have come to be recognized as constitutional presidential power is what is at stake. Remember, in passing NAFTA the Congress gave away its trade regulatory powers that are granted to it in Article I of the constitution. Yet, in a similar, but exactly reverse move in 1871 the Congress prohibited the president from exercising one of his express constitutional powers. Both of those changes now are part of what we understand the constitution to permit. Considered professional and lay opinion agree. What are the terms of engagement that will show one side or the other in the immigration struggle to be speaking through the constitution rather than against it? How will the people instruct the formal political actors what they may do rather than what they can do? As Professor Siegel puts it:

> Constitutional culture preserves and perpetually destabilizes the distinction between politics and law by providing citizens and officials the resources to question and to defend the legitimacy of government, institutions of civil society, and the Constitution itself. Constitutional culture both licenses and limits change.[9]

It is within these conflicting versions of constitutional culture that social antagonists engage. It is an old field of battle, but it is consistently fresh. If not, then the statues honoring the confederate dead that line the capital grounds in Texas would not carry the legend: "Erected in honor of those brave soldiers who gave their lives in defense of the Constitution."

What is law?

The most common idea of law in circulation is one that is now largely discredited among legal professionals, although it has such staying power that it is often trotted out to deny the legitimacy of international law even by those who should know better. The idea is that law is a command of the sovereign that is backed by a sanction. The sovereign is the one whose will need be followed. The sovereign is the lawgiver. Of course, not all laws are commands and it is often unclear from where a law emerged. E.P. Thompson dedicates an entire book to detailing the ways in which the law (understood as a formal rule) emerged from customs and practices of communities such that any effort to command a different result would precipitate revolt or some other crisis of legitimacy.[10]

A better understanding of law is to see it as "a construction of social rules, which are themselves constructed from practice."[11] From this angle, law is seen as a congeries of social rules that are sorted out by practice and by the interactions of formal institutional actors (judges, legislators, administrative agencies, court clerks, etc.) and the people. Of course, the hazard, as discussed in the consideration of constitutional culture, is that there needs to be some criteria of validity to claim that this or that rule is a law.

So, law is the collection of rules that are derived from practice. But they are special kinds of rules. They are the rules that can be said to create obligations rather than merely oblige conformity. If someone can be said to have a right then someone else necessarily has a duty, for example. It is practice that creates this network of claims. There is an additional requirement to satisfy the criteria of validity; there must be a rule that says, in effect, these other rules are law. But of course, that rule itself is a function of practice. Take for example the idea that our system for deciding cases is predicated on prior decided cases (even in the case of statutory or constitutional construction). That is a practice that has become a rule of decision and is thus one marker of validity. So, every first-year law student learns that you never know what a case means until a subsequent court uses it to decide a case. (The decisions always have meaning for the litigants, but that is a function of the rule that created jurisdiction and finality.) But it is precisely this process that permits meaning to change over time.

The fluidity of meaning rather than any static meaning is what gives law its legitimacy. Thus the idiocy of so-called originalism or textualism. The better way to understand those interpretive gambits is to see them as methods for keeping the people out of the way of "experts" in the process of saying what the law is.

Social movements and making law

Social movement are engaged in saying "what the law is". Social movement must be distinguished from interest groups because where interest groups work within established institutional structures, social movements challenge those structures. As Sid Tarrow teaches us, social movements also are characterized by the centrality of "contentious politics" practiced by actors whose "core 'indigenous population' . . . tends to be 'the nonpowerful, the nonwealthy and the nonfamous.'" They are also typically animated by a moral vision of a better society and frequently reflect that vision in their own practices. There is no inherent ideological valence to social movements. They can be, to use the conventional typology, movements of the right or the left.

By challenging the existing set of social practices and the rules that those practices reflect, social movements almost by definition are engaged in a form of law making. They urge a normative vision that claims its legitimacy by reference to the actions of its members whose advocacy establishes a normative guide to conduct. Through their resistance, these social actors are always in conversation with elites. The mobilization of popular resistance requires the elites to justify the rules they are applying. Viewed from the perspective of judges, what effective social movement advocacy does is to make certain interpretations of existing law either more or less persuasive. One way to test this hypothesis is to see how the meaning of the legal canon has changed over time in response to social movement activism.

To take two recent examples, Black Lives Matter and Say Her Name have put the conduct of police in the spotlight such that what would have passed muster for a "reasonable" stop or "reasonable force" are now fit subjects of political debate. Occupy, which most people like to write off as a failure, in fact put the issue of economic inequality on the national agenda. Standing Rock has not only revealed law enforcement as a source of lawlessness, but has given environmental justice a profound and historical rhetorical footing. Black Lives Matter is also now understood as part of the environmental justice movement and it gives us, with Occupy, a way to understand Flint. The resistance on behalf of the undocumented is as much about the power to include as it is about the power to exclude. Resistance to the executive order banning immigration from certain countries has raised the issue of religious liberty in a way that reveals the racialist and nativist content of previous iterations of the claims.

Whether social movement resistance can transform social practices sufficiently to create real and durable legal change is an open question. What is not an open question is that even when resistance feels futile, it is not. The riddle of constitutional change is capable of being solved by the people themselves and the validating rule is found in the collection of formal decisions, large and small, that ratify the vision of resistance even as the formal institutions seek to domesticate social movements. Resisting domestication is what real democracy is about.

Notes

1 See, e.g., *Stambovsky v. Ackley*, 169 A.D.2d 254 (N.Y. App. Div. 1991).
2 Thurman Arnold *The Symbols of Government* (Yale University Press, New Haven, CT, 1935) at 101.
3 See for example the invention of credit-default swaps or the various financing devices used to promote the internal slave trade as documented in Professor Edward Baptiste's *The Half That Has Never Been Told* (Basic Books, New York, 2014).
4 "The effective practice of the programmatic imagination requires us to retain the idea of structural change while affirming the basic contingency of institutional histories, the divisibility and part-by-part replaceability of institutional systems, and the legal indeterminacy – the multiple possible forms – of abstract institutional conceptions like the market economy and representative democracy. . . . These enabling ideas come under the heading **false necessity.**" Roberto Mangabeira Unger, *Democracy Realized: The Progressive Alternative* (Verso, New York, 1998) at 23–24 (emphasis original).

5 Reva Siegel "Constitutional Culture, Social Movement Conflict and Constitutional Change: The Case of the de facto ERA" (2006) 94 *California Law Review* 1323, 1326 (footnotes omitted).

6 Lani Guinier and Gerald Torres "Changing the Wind: Towards a Demosprudence of Law and Social Movements" (2014) 123 *Yale Law Journal* 2740, 2743.

7 Reva Siegel, "Constitutional Culture, Social Movement Conflict and Constitutional Change: The Case of the de facto ERA" (2006) 94 *California Law Review* 1323, 1327.

8 Charles L. Black, "The Lawfulness of the Segregation Decisions" (1960) 69 *Yale Law Journal* 421.

9 Reva Siegel "Constitutional Culture, Social Movement Conflict and Constitutional Change: The Case of the de facto ERA" (2006) 94 *California Law Review* 1323, 1327.

10 See, e.g., E.P. Thompson *Customs in Common: Studies in Traditional Popular Culture* (The New Press, 1993); See also E.P. Thompson and Douglas Hay, *Albion's Fatal Tree: Crime and Society in Eighteenth Century England* (Pantheon Books, 1975).

11 Herbert Lionel Adolphous (H.L.A.) Hart *The Concept of Law* (3rd ed, Oxford University Press, Oxford, 2012) at xxvii, Introduction by Leslie Green.

Index